THE
STAINED
GLASS
WINDOW

◆ ◆ ◆

A Family History as
the American Story,
1790–1958

DAVID LEVERING LEWIS

PENGUIN PRESS   NEW YORK   2025

PENGUIN PRESS
An imprint of Penguin Random House LLC
1745 Broadway, New York, NY 10019
penguinrandomhouse.com

Photo credits: page 8 courtesy of the author; pages 16 and 17 courtesy of Elaine DeNiro;
page 49 courtesy of Ellie Loudermilk/Perry Area Historical Museum; page 64 courtesy of
Library of Congress, Geography and Map Division, Sanborn Maps Collection; pages 101, 126,
156, 163 courtesy of the author; page 198 courtesy of la Bibliothèque nationale de France;
pages 208, 221 courtesy of the author; page 244 courtesy of Pamela Lewis; page 247 courtesy
of the author; page 255 courtesy of National Park Service/Brian Schwieger; pages 259, 270,
289, 295 courtesy of the author; page 306 Atlanta University Bulletin, December 1953,
Atlanta University Printed & Published Materials, Atlanta University Center Robert
W. Woodruff Library; page 307 courtesy of the author.

Map illustrations by Jeffrey L. Ward

Book design and family tree illustration by Daniel Lagin

LIBRARY OF CONGRESS CATALOGING-IN-PUBLICATION DATA
Names: Lewis, David Levering, 1936– author.
Title: The stained glass window: a family history as
the American story, 1790–1958 / David Levering Lewis.
Other titles: Family history as the American story, 1790–1958
Description: New York: Penguin Press, 2025. | Includes bibliographical references and index.
Identifiers: LCCN 2024019978 (print) | LCCN 2024019979 (ebook) |
ISBN 9781984879905 (hardcover) | ISBN 9781984879912 (ebook)
Subjects: LCSH: Lewis, David Levering, 1936–Family. | Lewis family. | Bell family. |
Belvin family. | King family. | African American families–Southern States–Biography. |
African Americans–Southern States–Genealogy. | Multiracial families–Southern States–
Genealogy. | Enslaved persons–Southern States–Genealogy. | United States–History.
Classification: LCC E185.92 .L49 2025 (print) | LCC E185.92 (ebook)
LC record available at https://lccn.loc.gov/2024019978
LC ebook record available at https://lccn.loc.gov/2024019979

The authorized representative in the EU for product safety and compliance is
Penguin Random House Ireland, Morrison Chambers, 32 Nassau Street,
Dublin D02 YH68, Ireland, https://eu-contact.penguin.ie.

To my parents, John and Alice,
& my partner Dolores

CONTENTS

◆ ◆ ◆

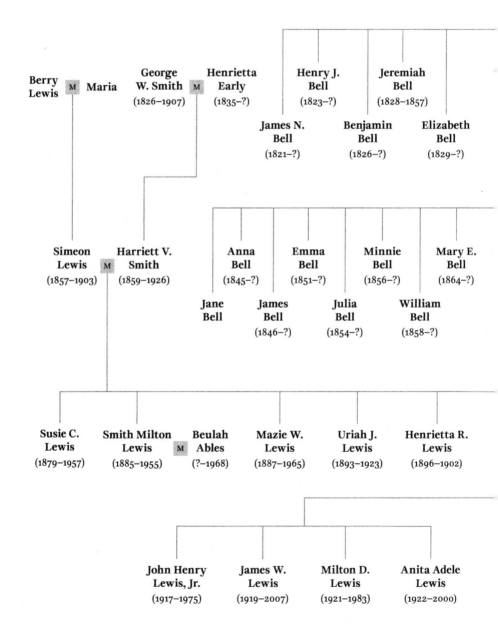

DAVID LEVERING LEWIS
Family Tree

Mary Ann
Fauling
Bradwell
(1786–1850)

Berry
Lewis — M — Maria

George
W. Smith — M
(1826–1907)

Henrietta
Early
(1835–?)

Henry J.
Bell
(1823–?)

Jeremiah
Bell
(1828–1857)

James N.
Bell
(1821–?)

Benjamin
Bell
(1826–?)

Elizabeth
Bell
(1829–?)

Simeon
Lewis — M
(1857–1903)

Harriett V.
Smith
(1859–1926)

Anna
Bell
(1845–?)

Emma
Bell
(1851–?)

Minnie
Bell
(1856–?)

Mary E.
Bell
(1864–?)

Jane
Bell

James
Bell
(1846–?)

Julia
Bell
(1854–?)

William
Bell
(1858–?)

Susie C.
Lewis
(1879–1957)

Smith Milton
Lewis — M
(1885–1955)

Beulah
Ables
(?–1968)

Mazie W.
Lewis
(1887–1965)

Uriah J.
Lewis
(1893–1923)

Henrietta R.
Lewis
(1896–1902)

John Henry
Lewis, Jr.
(1917–1975)

James W.
Lewis
(1919–2007)

Milton D.
Lewis
(1921–1983)

Anita Adele
Lewis
(1922–2000)

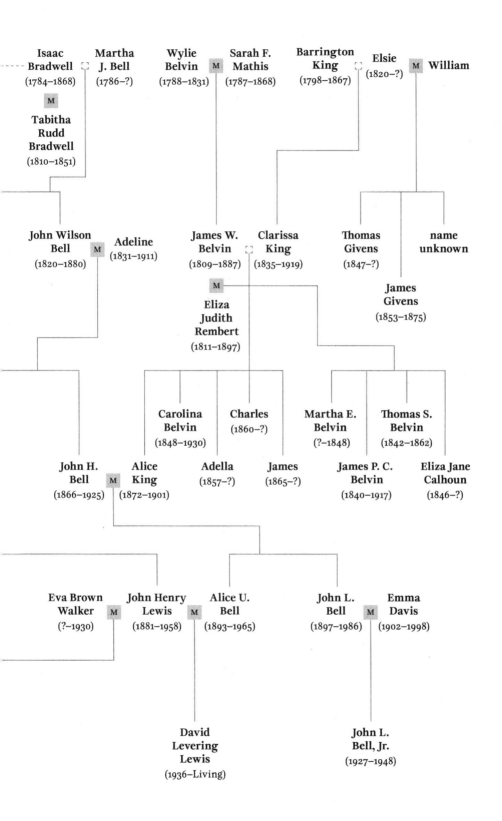

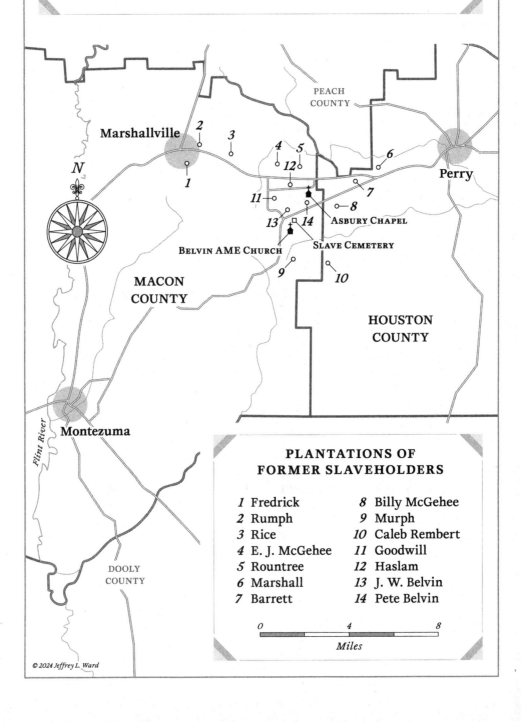

HOUSTON-MACON COUNTY GEORGIA PLANTATION COUNTRY 1860-1870

PEACH COUNTY

Marshallville

N

PERRY

ASBURY CHAPEL

BELVIN AME CHURCH

SLAVE CEMETERY

MACON COUNTY

HOUSTON COUNTY

Montezuma

Flint River

DOOLY COUNTY

PLANTATIONS OF FORMER SLAVEHOLDERS

1 Fredrick
2 Rumph
3 Rice
4 E. J. McGehee
5 Rountree
6 Marshall
7 Barrett
8 Billy McGehee
9 Murph
10 Caleb Rembert
11 Goodwill
12 Haslam
13 J. W. Belvin
14 Pete Belvin

0   4   8
Miles

© 2024 Jeffrey L. Ward

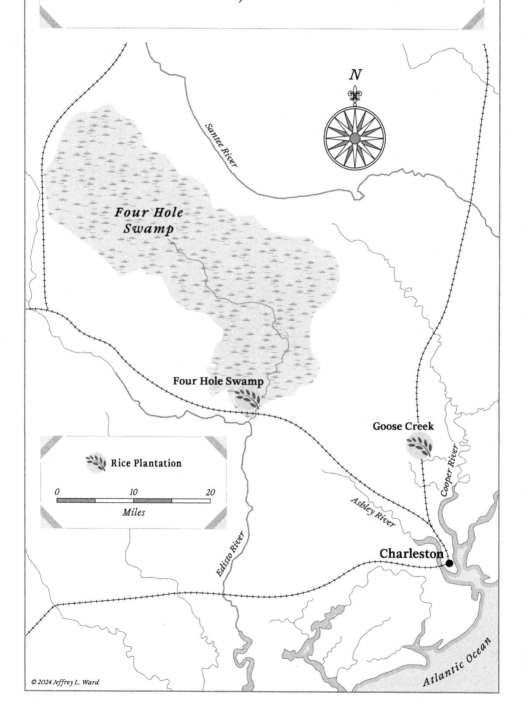

FOUR HOLE SWAMP AND GOOSE CREEK, SOUTH CAROLINA

N

Santee River

Four Hole Swamp

Four Hole Swamp

Goose Creek

Cooper River

Rice Plantation

0   10   20
Miles

Ashley River

Edisto River

Charleston

Atlantic Ocean

© 2024 Jeffrey L. Ward

THE

STAINED

GLASS

WINDOW

PROLOGUE

◆ ◆ ◆

A tlanta's tony First Congregational Church is a proud old black
church whose distinguished history half a pew of congregants
hardly remembers today. Its downtown location imperils its
landmarked survival, a sesquicentennial god box in a southern city famous for boasting of being "too busy to hate." More accurately it is a city
too fast for its past. Although church attendance was a long-ago-lost practice, I sat bemused that warm Sunday morning with my favorite cousin,
Bettye ("kissin' cousin," as they used to say), in her prominent pew. My
presence was remarked as unusual by the parishioners. Yet I was oddly
grateful to be there, in that faux Romanesque tabernacle where fifty
years ago compassionate Cousin Bettye had squeezed my hand as the
minister sermonized a moving farewell over my mother's closed coffin.

Eight months earlier I had endured my spouse's memorial service in
New York's Riverside Church. Ruth was my anchor of thirty years. Her
ovarian cancer prognosis resolved us to engage, to produce, to travel, to
explore together, as if we had a lifetime remaining. In that fateful time
frame, we saw Europe and Africa again, served our professional associations, produced papers and each a book; finally, I relinquished an endowed professorship at a great research university.[1]

And now I found myself somewhat unanchored in a church on an April Sunday morning in 2015. My Atlanta visit came as a delayed subconscious reaction. Often enough, even when dismissed in the moment, the fleeting presumptuousness of white people can register deeply. Just such an unprovoked annoyance had festered with me ever since a 2014 midwestern research trip to digitally record a round of interviews for a book. A talkative limousine chauffeur fetched me from the Indianapolis airport, volunteered a chamber of commerce inventory of local assets, commenced a genial interrogation inviting reciprocated inquiries—then, apropos nothing at all, abruptly declared that his immigrant ancestors were innocent of all discrimination against black people. Temporarily disconcerted, I found myself unable to formulate a worthwhile thought. The chauffeur, barreling on heedless of a response, told of his people coming from Poland with no English and no relatives, poor and unskilled. Simple folk like the chauffeur's hardworking grandfather, whose tannery and good credit had enabled the chauffeur's parents to own real estate, and the chauffeur, himself a retired supermarket manager, who was helping with his smart grandson's law school tuition. Whatever had happened to black people, not a one of his people had ever done anything against them, and he begged my acceptance of that truth. I refused the driver the satisfaction of a departing handshake, yet I strode into the hotel lobby suppressing a good deal of dissatisfaction with myself.

I, a prizewinning historian, had allowed myself that midwestern morning to be run over, in a manner of speaking, by yet another unremarkable white citizen smugly piloting his color-blind American Dream across a century of self-improvement and hard-earned success. Nor had my Hoosier chauffeur's protestations of racial innocence amounted to mere self-serving parochialism. They mirrored the prevailing judgment not only of the American mainstream but within much of the academy, ideas persuasively articulated in print and television by leading social scientists, historians, public intellectuals, and policymakers. The belated truth, until well into my seventies, was that I myself had been intellectually intimidated by scholarship that privileged the solace of liberal reform, the pragmatism of triage, or the stoicism of dysfunction—scholarship that found empirically compelling reasons why the so-called truly disadvantaged were inescapably black and brown people, why the intelligence bell curve diminished their progress, and why the nation was losing ground pursuing failed social experimentations.[2] Hadn't it become gospel that postal codes predetermining the life chances of the truly disadvantaged resulted from forces whose staggering costs of redress surpassed the available resources of the nation? That gospel, therefore, must surely excuse Caucasian chauffeurs of complicity and absolve the majority of Americans from the tragic judgment of their own history.

What I might have said to my well-meaning driver finally came to me a few weeks after my fateful decision to go to Atlanta. The old firebomb term suddenly made current in popular discourse by the truly gifted journalist Ta-Nehisi Coates—*reparations*—provoked a timely upheaval not so much in what I knew about what had happened in history as in my understanding of why so much that had not happened in history should have.[3]

A perfect chance to crystallize my thoughts about historical obligations in the building of the land of opportunity—about addressing what I occasionally told former students was the ethnic testosterone problem in American exceptionalism—had come my way earlier that year. Caught surprised on an early spring morning in 2015 when an admired colleague, David Nasaw, then president of the Society of American Historians, phoned to tell me of the society's bestowal of its Arthur M. Schlesinger Jr. Award for distinguished writing in American history, I sensed an unexpressed anxiety about an acceptance speech befitting the honor. For better or worse, I decided that by the evening of the award I would have composed something in the spirit of W. E. B. Du Bois, the great contrarian who identified the twenty-first century's contested meanings of the color line as fundamental to the failure of our great national experiment. In the meantime, however, had come the rendezvous with my Atlanta past.

ALTHOUGH BORN IN ARKANSAS AND RAISED IN THE NORTH, I HAD ALways felt the family roots were in Atlanta, where my striving Methodist father achieved early success and my independent Congregationalist mother circumspectly optimized an advantaged birthright. I had long ago resolved the inherited tensions of my parents' contrasting backgrounds, an amalgam of Black Belt peasants mixed with free colored persons — my father's up-from-slavery pride versus my mother's color-spectrum privilege. John Henry and Alice Urnestine were admired innovators in the segregated corridors of high school and college administration before *Brown v. Board of Education.* Yet, in a profound sense, even though their professional highs and lows remained salient, too much about their personal aspirations and struggles, as well as their forebears' provenances, I had either never known or had gradually forgotten over the years since my mother's death. As the last of John Henry's five children and only son of his second wife, Alice Urnestine, I grew up virtually as an only child who gradually outlived my several geographically scattered half siblings.

When I came to Atlanta with thoughts of the Schlesinger presentation gestating, John and Urnestine Lewis had lain in the city's old South-View Cemetery for more than a half century.[4] Nostalgia, a historian's intuition, and Cousin Bettye's encouraging sense that I was onto something important, somehow ratified that Sunday morning attendance at First Congregational, the church of my mother's people. My mother's church had risen from Atlanta's ashes in the winter of 1866 as a makeshift school in a converted Confederate commissary building on Jenkins Street in the heart of the city. I still remembered the story of First Congregational's ascension from her telling, a vivid fable footnoted, as it were, from my own recent reading. As soon as it had been safe after Sherman's departure, Yankee pastors and wives of the American Missionary Association (AMA) sped south to organize and uplift the newly freed black people. Historian Clarence Bacote's rich history of the church and the college they built in Atlanta's ashes profiled these New England men and women as missionaries, just like their twentieth-century Peace Corps spiritual descendants.[5] I recalled my mother's frequent invocation of their motto: "To Find a Way or Make One."

Mostly Yale men with *Uncle Tom's Cabin* in their knapsacks, Wendell Phillips as their model, and strategic funding from the Freedmen's Bureau, these Yankee missionaries followed a master plan conceived during the Confederacy's final months by the redoubtable Erastus Milo Cravath, the AMA's education superintendent and future founder of my undergraduate college, Fisk University. Records tell of their traveling "the length and breadth of Georgia," visiting the larger plantations and planning with the proprietors and the emancipated an educational center in Atlanta. School sites were identified, teachers recruited, buildings bought and built, and pastors assigned with such resourcefulness that within two years the AMA men and women sowed a remarkable confessional and educational experiment in Atlanta and across the Deep South. Their labor yielded more than a half dozen HBCUs and a large crop of tabernacles variously imbued with the New England ideals of learning, citizenship, and culture.[6]

The church's battered commissary, enlarged and named for its Congregational benefactor, became the Storrs School, regional magnet to hundreds of learning-hungry pupils, "some sent by their families, others to come unattached," wrote an AMA historian. "It was a strange thing to us," recalled an everlastingly impressed student of Yale's Edmund Asa Ware, future founder of Atlanta University, "to see a white man carrying wood and making fires for us, who had been taught . . . it was our duty to do the like for his kind." The dedication of its Yankee "schoolmarms" and precocity of its charges merited a famous 1868 Storrs School inspection by the Freedmen's Bureau chief, General Oliver Otis Howard. Indeed, my father had relished telling the story of Howard's question to the students, "What shall I tell the children in the North about you?" A boy of twelve years replied: "Massa, tell 'em we're rising!" That teenage boy whose remarks poet John Greenleaf Whittier made famous was Richard R. Wright, future valedictorian of Atlanta University's 1876 first graduation.[7]

Storrs School was the school of choice of advantaged freed people. My mother's mother learned her letters there. Storrs cradled the future Atlanta University and First Congregational Church, Mother's elite undergraduate college and church. And now that her church was central to my quest, I recalled the feelings of group accomplishment I felt on those infrequent Sundays when asked by my father to escort her there. First

Church had become self-supporting a year after Mother was born in 1893. Henry Hugh Proctor, Fisk classmate of W. E. B. Du Bois and a Yale Divinity School graduate, assumed the pulpit as its first African American pastor. Thirteen years later, in 1907, when Reverend Proctor broke ground for the present structure, built by the leading colored contractor Robert Pharrow, it was Booker T. Washington, honored guest of the church and the city, who shoveled the first spade of dirt.[8] I thought the church's extensive makeover some fifteen years ago had dialed back the sanctuary's solemnity, muting somewhat its grand history. Even so, I easily visualized the old interior's chiaroscuro, the unupholstered pews, the winged pulpit, but most especially those oak panels adjacent to the choir on which were inscribed the names of last century's distinguished invitees: Booker T. Washington, Theodore Roosevelt, Presidents Taft and Coolidge, Roland Hayes, and Walter White. To be sure, parishioners assured me after the service that the processional of notables continued, as with Senator Kamala Harris's presentation at the church's 150th anniversary or the occasional sermons of the Honorable Andrew Young, Atlanta's former mayor and a fellow Congregationalist.[9]

AS THE MORNING'S WORSHIPPERS DEPARTED, SOME NODDING WELCOMES, my cousin and I waited for Reverend Dwight Andrews, Yale Divinity School's latest gift, to walk with us to the stained glass windows in the rear of the sanctuary. When was it, some dozen years past, that I came expecting to see these windows—and one in particular, above all? They were leaded stained glass panes that prosperous church members, together with my maternal grandfather, had hired black master craftsmen to make so as to symbolize Christianity's four Gospels. They were twinned with illustrations of the Negro's emancipation and rise. The windows had been installed within two years after the new building's 1909 dedication. The last window in the "Motherhood Triptych," I recalled clearly, was an incandescent window depicting a Madonna and child, "dedicated to Alice K. Bell by her family." My grandmother had been placed in the

window frame next to the resplendent family homage to the Isaac Westmoreland matriarch, and that one next to the one dedicated to the
mother of Reverend Henry Hugh Proctor.[10] But my ancestor, along with
the others, was not to be seen when I had stopped in transit to Hartsfield-
Jackson Atlanta International Airport after an honorary doctorate award
ceremony at Emory University that afternoon in May 2003. Ruth and
I, accompanied by Emory University's ebullient Richard Long, Atticus
Haygood Professor of Interdisciplinary Studies, were flabbergasted to
find the sanctuary windows boarded up due to long-stalled renovations
whose completion the sanguine Reverend Andrews had assured us was
imminent.[11] Now, twelve years later, I finally gazed upon them admiringly
in the presence of Bettye and the beaming pastor.

Alice King Bell, my maternal grandmother, was the Madonna, deceased in childbirth at age twenty-nine in 1901. Her radiant representation in the Motherhood Triptych spoke of both premature bereavement
and wistful immortality—of a prosperous colored family's advertised devotion. Yet, despite all that meaningfulness, I realized how much the
sanctuary's Madonna and child remained unrevealed to me. All the people who could have known her were gone. Her children, my own beloved
mother and empathic uncle, had died in their early seventies just as I
turned thirty. John Henry Bell, Alice's handsome husband, survived
Alice by a score of years only to die tragically long before their children.

True enough, there was much that I recalled: memory echoes of the
Bells' Charleston, South Carolina, origins; of the place some miles outside Atlanta where the King dynasty reigned; of old studio photographs
of my presentable grandparents and of other hazel-eyed Bells, along with
their friends the Westmorelands and Whites, Ruckers and Yateses. But
I thought a good deal about what I should have asked my parents, and
about what they could have been pushed to reveal about their own parents'
survival as Reconstruction receded before Redemption and the one-drop
rule of second-class citizenship was codified. I recalled, too, the jolting
interview response about Mother's family given by a wizened church
lady speaking of long-ago Atlanta in Du Bois's time there: "no-nation

people," she cackled sympathetically. "They lived between the races," she had explained to the then future Du Bois biographer.[12] I had never heard such a term before, and certainly not to be applied to my own race-proud, middle-class family. Color gradations and their undeserved, fast-fading advantages within the African American population I had written about, perceptively, I believed, in a history of early Harlem. Even so, the dichotomous finality of the interviewee's description of my Bell line had been deeply unsettling. Its decreed deracination signaled a murkiness I had been unready to acknowledge until recently. Now I saw that I was being propelled by ancestral unknowns to find answers. I suspected that the woman whose born name was King, and whose dedicated sanctuary window had fascinated me from my teens, was a mystery wrapped in an antebellum conundrum of possibly outsize historical significance.

Woman in the Stained Glass Window, 1909

ROSWELL, GEORGIA, IS TWENTY-SIX MILES NORTH OF DOWNTOWN AT-
lanta, an affluent town of some ninety thousand mostly white souls fixed
in the aspic of the Lost Cause. A few weeks earlier, I had spent a profitable
day early in this journey reading about the village named for Roswell
King Sr. (1765–1844). I found that it was the old American success story
of work, luck, and theft. The senior King was a legendary entrepreneur
who parlayed his Windsor, Connecticut, origins into one of the South's
grandest slaveholding dynasties, an outsize life that was the bonus of im-
peccable timing. Cotton as North America's future economic engine was
still a gamble in the pivotal first decade of the nineteenth century. Yet he
established a profitable lumber, rice, and cotton business in 1780 in tiny
Darien at the mouth of Georgia's Altamaha River. It was a fortuitous
place for King's slave management talents to be discovered by one of the
country's largest slaveholders, Major Pierce Butler. In 1820, after eighteen handsomely rewarded years as Butler's overseer, Roswell King Sr.
arranged to be succeeded by his son Roswell Jr. (1796–1854) and resigned
to become an officer in the growing Bank of Darien.[13] His timing again
paid major dividends in 1829 when, as the bank's roaming gold prospec-
tor, he saw the Cherokee Nation's Edenic realm of hardwood forests,
rushing streams, and fertile valleys—all of it awaiting Andrew Jackson's
removal order.

Three years later, after Georgia issued its first lottery of Cherokee
lands, Roswell King Sr. purchased a large tract near the Chattahoochee
River and bided his time until the U.S. Army herded the tribe into en-
campments prior to the brutal confiscation of its lands and the western
expulsion of the Cherokees in 1838. Roswell then persuaded five Georgia
coastal dwellers to join him on the now confiscated up-country lands. He
incorporated the Roswell Manufacturing Company the following year,
its towering brick cotton mill powered by Vickery Creek, a Chattahoochee tributary. Seven years later, the mill factory added 3,500 spindles
and 400 looms manned by 150 white laborers, its cotton, yarn, cloth, and
rope products sold in Baltimore, Philadelphia, and Newark. More than

100 enslaved craftsmen had finished building the still-standing grand colonnaded mansions for Roswell's chums the Bullochs, the Dunwodys, the Pratts, and the Smiths.[14] Son Barrington King had carried on without a beat missed after his father's demise. A second cotton mill and a third dam over Vickery Creek at a cost of $220,000 achieved what the South's other cotton magnates mostly failed to undertake due to myopia, business ethic, or capital: the on-site milling of their own cotton and wool products. On the eve of the Civil War, the six buildings, two warehouses, and three dams of the Roswell Manufacturing Company were exporting high-quality textiles above the Mason-Dixon line as well as across the South. After Fort Sumter, its special cotton and wool blend—"Roswell Grey"—made the cloth worn by Confederate officers.[15]

I kept my Thursday morning appointment at the Roswell Historical Society and Research Library, driving there from Bettye Lovejoy Scott's large home four days after the Sunday spent together at First Congregational. An introductory telephone conversation a month earlier from New York with the chief archivist had gone, I thought, exceedingly well.[16] I had told the chief archivist of my curiosity about my maternal grandmother's patronymic, and I shared a once-buried memory of my mother's confidence that Alice King was a Roswell native. Roswell's chief archivist was a white woman I guessed to be in her late fifties, with an engaging professional manner. She informed me that her son, a recent NYU graduate and now law firm associate, had spoken of the high regard in which I was held by many students. That her son was a hire at the firm once headed by Wendell Willkie, subject of my forthcoming biography, quite delighted both of us.

Archivist Elaine DeNiro lent a sympathetic ear to my hypothesis, from an old studio family photo as well as my mother's belief, that Alice King Bell may have descended from an ancestor fathered by a Roswell King heir. Ms. DeNiro conceded that even though the hypothesis might be plausible, she doubted that Roswell's archives would prove corroborative. Thus far, there was no trace of an Alice King born in Roswell. To be sure, she added, more as a balm to my quest, I suspected, the Roswell Historical Society, together with other southern repositories, had learned to become aware of such possibilities since the Jefferson DNA revelations and Dr. Annette Gordon-Reed's scholarship. She especially commended two titles then unknown to me. The first was Erskine Clarke's luminous *Dwelling Place: A Plantation Epic*, which would soon prove a major learning-curve assist to my new journey into the South's Lost Cause bibliography. The second, Robert Manson Myers's *The Children of Pride*, a three-volume edition of Confederate family letters, proved to be professional catnip.[17] DeNiro also offered introductions to a local black historian, a Reverend Charles Grogan, whose voluminous multigenerational inventory of Roswell's black deceased might well, she thought, yield information about Kings.

I continued my search on Barrington Drive. I thought I had instantly recognized Barrington Hall as Margaret Mitchell's model for Tara in *Gone With the Wind*. The mansion house of Barrington King, the founder's son, epitomized in its gleaming whiteness, classic proportions, and Doric columns all the architectural arrogance of the antebellum South's master class. But Ms. DeNiro corrected my presumptions. Most probably it had been Bulloch Hall, she believed, birthplace of Theodore Roosevelt's mother, equally imposing though somewhat bulkier. At Bulloch Hall's gift shop, I exited in the spirit of the tour with *Cobb's Legion Cavalry: A History and Roster of the Ninth Georgia Volunteers in the Civil War*. We paused together at the old Presbyterian church, a small structure built by the enslaved and whose architectural chasteness almost seemed to protest the lordly mansions of the slave masters. (I discovered later that it mimicked Midway Church, Liberty County's historic eighteenth-century Congregational church, midway between Darien and Savannah and once beloved by local slave masters.)[18]

Eleven years after its municipal incorporation by the Georgia General Assembly, Union brigadier general Kenner Garrard's cavalry blazed through Roswell in early July 1864, demolishing the Roswell Manufacturing Company's cotton and wool mills but sparing the mansions of the mostly absentee elite. The tannery and warehouses were razed, the milling machinery thrown into Vickery Creek. Barrington King and his wife had repaired to Savannah, leaving a son, Captain James Roswell King, in command of the Confederate cavalry to blunt the march-to-the-sea destruction inflicted by Sherman's invaders. An eleventh-hour lease of the original Ivy Mill to a French businessman failed to preserve it when General Garrard's command to see the Stars and Stripes unfurled next to the Confederate tricolor went unanswered. Barrington's eldest son, Barrington Simeral, the family's valiant standard-bearer, fell nine months later leading his regiment near Charlotte, North Carolina. We surveyed from Vickery's Overlook what little survived of the unique Roswell Manufacturing Company. The machine shop was still standing, and I wondered if the lone brick mill might have produced the Roswell Grey cloth that Colonel Barrington Simeral King wore as he bled out near Charlotte. Ms. DeNiro said it had been built in the 1880s, however.[19]

I took leave of the gracious Ms. DeNiro and drove from Roswell straight to Hartsfield-Jackson Atlanta International Airport. It seemed to me that the morning had yielded little of personal genealogical relevance. An indication of how mistaken I was would come by registered mail four weeks later, and with it my remembering her enigmatic parting words. Almost whimsically, I thought at the time, Ms. DeNiro volunteered as we parted that her visitor's family history was far more significant than he realized.

THE SCHLESINGER SOCIETY'S ANNUAL DINNER, ALWAYS WELL CATERED and lubricated in one of Stanford White's grand Manhattan monuments, was held three weeks later on May 11. The evening's challenge for one of its past presidents was evident. My lighthearted obligatory tribute to Arthur Schlesinger's felicitous prose, versatile range of subjects, and combative advocacy seemed well received. I went on to remark that Arthur's critics, "of whom there were a good number," reproached the alloy of hubris and humor that made him such a formidable, yet generally agreeable, adversary. "It would be far worse if no one gave a damn what we said or did," Arthur used to say. It was typical late-career insouciance from a prolific, interpretive virtuoso who'd described entire ages of American history (Jackson, FDR, the Kennedys), located America's vital center, identified the cycles of American history, and profiled the imperial presidency while accumulating two Pulitzers and cultivating the best and brightest personalities from Harvard to Hollywood and Georgetown.[20] I began my address lauding the legacy of an illustrious historian, and I then segued to a lament of a historical fallacy. I said that I now agonized over the cruel mischief long wrought by our paradigm of exceptionalism; that I asked myself why we shouldn't conclude that what was exceptional about the exceptionalist national narrative were the historical exceptions to it—notably, people of color.

As I hardly needed to remind this audience, Africans in America had been both unique victims and unimpeachable critics of a nation corrupted at its inception by a political economy anchored to slavery. Yet it was also true that if ever an era belonged to a single people, the racial, abortion, gender, immigration, gay, and disabled rights won in the sixties and seventies were, I said, black people's gifts to the nation. Even so, yet another great American deception for people of color had come to pass after the ideology and economics of Reaganism nullified what survived of Great Society progressivism. Fast-forward to the recession of 2008, dominated by wealth outrageously maldistributed, health care and education unaffordable, paying jobs a memory, and middle-class impoverishment in a great recession. Against that bleak backdrop, the electorate wagered that it could deny race by affirming its nonimportance and thereby reinvigorate the vaunted exceptionalist narrative.

With Barack Obama's presidency nearing its term, I had felt compelled to write off its historic postracial reset. Surely, I postulated, when this decade ended, would it not have confirmed the relevancy of W. E. B. Du Bois's grim prophecy about America's everlasting racism?

Could historians help, and if so, then what was the Chernyshevskyan question? I wondered. Moderately good news was the definite signs of a historical revisionism that upended the hoary master narrative of Jeffersonian laissez-faire matched with Hamiltonian finance and unrivaled industrial takeoff gloriously replenished by hardworking immigrants. For too long, I believed, we had looked in the wrong place and race for the a priori genesis of the American story, Mr. Jefferson's soi-disant "empire of liberty." Sven Beckert's Bancroft Prize–winning monograph, *Empire of Cotton*, was bringing things into sharper focus because cotton, as he rightly says, "is the story of the making and remaking of global capitalism and with it of the modern world." Similarly, with Edward Baptist's *The Half Has Never Been Told: Slavery and the Making of the Modern Capitalism* we may have arrived by way of Eric Williams, David Brion Davis, Robin Blackburn, James Oakes, Robin Kelley, and others of the profession's vanguard at the frontier of a new metanarrative that stands on its head the color-blind paradigm of American exceptionalism.

I was convinced that it would become obvious how the institution of American slavery functioned as a vast concentration camp from which flowed the enormous wealth that made the industrial North possible and the surplus capital upon which the commercial and industrial paramountcy of New York and Philadelphia was built. How European immigrant labor was minted as the other side of the coin of America's first labor force — compulsory labor from Africa. I believed that this was the dreadful reality of a national success story that is inconceivable without the enforced indispensability of four million black lives that mattered. The evening's applause with Schlesinger's widow and son present was gratifying. I was especially pleased later when David Nasaw's complimentary mention elicited an invitation to publish the address in *The Nation*.

The speech was well received and it left me with an urgent need to conceive a way to tell the story through my ancestors in North America. My challenge, then, was simply to begin to find myself in a past I barely knew.

1

♦ ♦ ♦

SETTING UP SLAVERY

St. Simons Island to Roswell

T he Roswell Historical Society email arrived not quite two weeks after the Schlesinger presentation: "Dr. Lewis, I am cautiously optimistic that I have made a complete line to Alice King with documentation to back up the findings."[1] Not only had reading Malcolm Bell's admirable biography, *Major Butler's Legacy: Five Generations of a Slaveholding Family*, reinforced my suspicions about the Butlers' two King overseers, but Bell's candid February 1968 book talk at the Roswell Historical Society corroborated a genealogical fact: "The practice of miscegenation by the two Kings [Roswell and Barrington] is well documented." Reverend Grogan, author of the remarkably detailed inventory of Cobb County black families, found nothing to say about an Alice King, but, as he confided, "the Kings were noted for miscegenation."[2]

DeNiro's much-anticipated packet arrived with the photographed copy of Barrington King's bill of sale, dated January 3, 1822, which recorded the purchase of "all those negro and mulatto slaves named Nancy March Yorick Hester Elsie Candis and William" for the sum of $3,800. I was an old hand with historical documents: the Archives Nationales de France for the Dreyfus affair; Yale's Beinecke for the Harlem Renaissance; FOIA Justice Department files for the Du Bois biography. But reading an actual bill of sale for seven human beings was a nauseating novelty, or, as I expressed much more diplomatically to archivist DeNiro, an experience causing "a fair amount of astonishment."[3] By his ownership rights in the seven human beings sold by Maxwell and Waters, Savannah's leading slave traffickers, Barrington King, Roswell Sr.'s twenty-four-year-old heir, stood to profit as a matter of course "from the future increase of said female slaves."

What relevance this had to this family quest of mine became clear after construing the bill of sale's companion document. It was a long parchment page dated 1849 and photocopied from Barrington King's slave ledgers for the years 1835–1864. Two of the seven purchased in 1822—the enslaved William, age one, and enslaved Elsie, age two—had produced

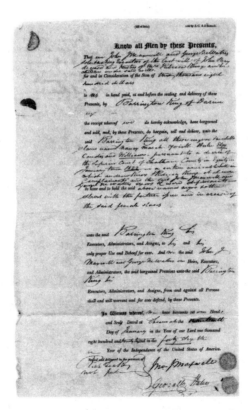

Barrington King's purchase
of Elsie and William, 1822

Barrington King's sale of Clarissa, Kitty, and child, 1835

three daughters and two sons by 1849; their oldest was Clarissa, born in 1835; Thomas, the youngest, was born in 1849. A line slicing through Clarissa's name channeled my eyes to the faded penciled notation in her master's hand: "Sold, September 1852." I realized that this young woman Barrington sold away from Roswell must be the mother of Alice.[4]

Barrington King, I remembered, had left Darien to join his father in Roswell in 1838, taking his human property along. Clarissa's mother, Elsie, must have been a tender thirteen when Clarissa was born. Her future husband, William, was just twelve at the time of Clarissa's conception, a procreative feat I thought Reverend Grogan might find interesting. My check of the U.S. Census for 1850 disclosed that of Barrington's seventy-odd slaves, half were under the age of ten and worked as domestics. Many of them must have been females who, like Clarissa, represented future revenue sources. Clarissa should have been seventeen in 1852. She would have lived all but three of her seventeen years in Roswell, and conceivably had enjoyed the dubious advantage of service as a domestic. Moreover, as I learned many years later, Clarissa's mother, Elsie, served as nurse and servant for Barrington King's first daughter. In any case, Clarissa and another enslaved young woman and her infant ("Kitty and child") had fetched $1,420 for Barrington.

My anxious inquiry as to Clarissa's buyer was answered as unknown. Archivist DeNiro added that she thought the sale was unusual for Barrington and that she found his ledger's silence on the matter of Clarissa's new master even more unusual. Nearly a decade of Clarissa's existence had gone missing. Neither her whereabouts nor her situation could be found in Barrington King's ledgers.[5] After a bit more digging, however, DeNiro discovered either Clarissa or a doppelgänger Clarissa ("Claricey") living in Georgia's Houston County as a servant, single, in the household of a James Wiley Belvin and spouse Eliza Judith after 1860. She is still there, free, in the 1870 census: Clarissa King, still single, but now with her children, Adela, Charles, and James.

My just-discovered great-grandmother was an altogether mysterious apparition. Still, I felt I knew enough about her world's racial and sexual etiquette to hazard a historically plausible story of Clarissa's Roswell creation and exit. Moreover, reflecting upon what I seemed to glimpse as the larger implications of her genealogy—the metanarrative of Clarissa King—I found myself exhilarated by its explanatory possibilities.[6] Could I not follow this as-yet-to-be-realized maternal great-grandmother's genealogical and circumstantial lineages, and her life lived in slavery and freedom, as emblematic of a national failure?

SLAVES HAD NO SURNAMES, BUT MY NEW GREAT-GRANDMOTHER APpears to have been the rare exception. She would insist on claiming the King patronymic until she could bear it legally after the Civil War. Roswell had been her crucible. Not all the decades elsewhere altered her superior certitude of being a King. No physical description of Clarissa existed. Her name, undoubtedly bestowed by Barrington King, evokes Samuel Richardson's *Clarissa*, Georgian England's sprawling bestseller about unconquered virtue. She was surely not fathered by Elsie's William, and given the sexual liberties of Roswell King's male line or, indeed, the plantation South's general interracial profligacy evidenced by "all the mulatto children in everybody's household," as sniffed candid Mary Boykin Chesnut, Clarissa's paternity was evident.[7] Since beginning this family history, recent revelations by two writers about racially mixed members among the Washington and Madison families have further complicated the founders' bloodlines.[8]

That Clarissa was sold when she reached the nubile age of seventeen raises unanswerable questions that her great-grandson needed, nonetheless, to ask. I wondered if she had become a distraction, à la Thomas Jefferson's "dashing Sally," to one of the King scions? James Roswell King, twenty-five, married comely Fanny Hillhouse Prince in Roswell that same year. Thomas Edward King, twenty-three years old, departed bachelorhood two years later. To be sure, I could not draw conclusions from intriguing coincidences. Still, I thought the timing of my great-grandmother's exile by sale from the sole place she had ever known beckoned more research. Whether Clarissa was a King "born," in the parlance of her time, "on the wrong side of the blanket" or merely one by virtue of her culture and psychology, her complicated lineage aroused my deepest professional and personal fascination.[9]

As much as Clarissa's fate was determined by her King slave masters, the Kings' own dynastic ascension after the Federalist Era (1789–1801) had come by way of two generations of subservient labor on behalf of American Founding Father and slave master *sans pareille*, Pierce Butler (1744–1822), and his grandson Pierce Mease Butler (1810–1867). The Founding Father whom Roswell King Sr. served just shy of twenty years as plantation overseer set foot on colonial American soil as a British officer in 1767. Like thousands of Anglo-Irishmen of his class, primogeniture dictated Major Pierce Butler's chosen career. The third son of Irish baronet Sir Richard and Lady Henrietta Percy of Garryhundon, he had served valiantly in the king's army as a teenager against the French in

Canada. Twenty-two years later, a veteran Major Butler and fellow officers of George III's Twenty-ninth Regiment of Foot disembarked in Philadelphia from Nova Scotia. From the outset, as it was plain to see, Pierce
Butler was on the hunt for a rich woman and had heard enough about the
well-dowered belles of South Carolina to make an expedition to the colony that year. In Charleston, Butler cut a swaggeringly appealing presence at the theater and among the St. Patrick's Hibernians, affected a
proper solemnity at St. Michael's Church, and boasted military accomplishments to impress the aristocratic Laurenses, Izards, and Pinckneys.
A string of dalliances over a couple of years eventually succeeded in winning the fabulously rich Mary Middleton's hand in 1771, along with several
huge properties and hundreds of slaves from her grandmother Mary
Bull's estate.[10]

The major's loyalty to his sovereign was still to be tested. The previous year, it seems he may well have watched from a distance what his superiors called the "incident on King Street." The record is silent, however,
as to what if any long-term significance Butler accorded the Boston Massacre at the time. Yet the detonations ignited throughout the colonies by
the "odious" Stamp Act—Boston Tea Party, Townsend Acts, First Continental Congress—inclined a pragmatic Pierce Butler to begin reassessing
his professional options. He busied himself mastering the art and science
of governing thousands of enslaved Africans toiling in rice fields or beside indigo vats along the Newport and Medway rivers of the Georgia
Low Country. His wife's Middleton kin, along with new associates like
future Revolutionary War patriots Henry Laurens and Miles Brewton,
had gained their great wealth in the triangle slave trade from Africa to
the Caribbean and North America, then across to Great Britain. Their
example and advice finally were more than enough to induce the major
to sell his officer's commission in the fall of 1773 for a tidy sum, matched
by family monies, and purchase with six thousand pounds a 1,700-acre
plantation on Georgia's St. Simons Island between the Altamaha River
and the Atlantic Ocean.

His regiment sailed without him that year.[11] From Hampton Point,
his St. Simons Island manor house, he commenced life as a Georgia and

Carolina planter and master of bonded men and women. Two years later, Butler took service in the American cause and served as justice of the peace in South Carolina. "No man on earth," he wrote to a Middleton relative, "has the Cause more at heart or wishes more ardently to serve it than I do." He proffered military advice to the Continental Congress about defense of the southern theater. Albeit he managed not to expose himself to the possibility of capture and hanging by his former redcoat brethren. He found it advisable to seek refuge in North Carolina when the Royal Navy occupied Charleston in 1780, during which period his properties were burned and more than two hundred of his slaves took refuge with the British. With military victory the following year at Yorktown, decisively enabled by the French fleet and infantry contingents, came the sausage making in peacetime after the Treaty of Paris in 1783. Admired for his service as South Carolina's wartime adjutant general, an outspoken advocate of reconciliation of defeated loyalists and winning patriots, a model man of wealth and defender of the interests of the Lower South, Butler was honored as one of South Carolina's three delegates to the Constitutional Convention of 1787.

"No slave state delegate had more to do with fitting those held in bondage into the United States Constitution than he did," judges Malcolm Bell, Butler's superb biographer. The pettifogging Charles Cotesworth Pinckney probably outshone Butler in parliamentary defense of their "peculiar institution" at the Philadelphia proceedings. Pinckney would boast in Charleston's lower house after the Constitutional Convention adjourned that the battle had been won "against restricting the importation of negroes . . . [and] that without them South Carolina would soon be a desert waste."[12] Butler, described as "of noble birth and inordinately vain of it," had spoken less. But when he did so, alarmed Quaker delegates linked forensic arms with humanitarian allies in order to buffer this lordly South Carolinian's fulminations around the "slavery question." To be sure, all had not gone his way in Philadelphia: Butler conceded the prohibition on the importation of African slaves after twenty years. He and his colleagues also failed to have their slaves counted as full persons for the purposes of representation, but he clung successfully

to retaining the fatal three-fifths compromise of the Articles of Confederation.

Butler's real contribution, however, was to embed a fugitive slave
clause at the center of the framers' equivocal new document. The fourth
article of the obsolescent Articles of Confederation had imposed the duty
of reciprocity on all states to deliver all fugitive persons "charged with
treason, felony, or other crime" to the states where the crime was committed. But after an adamant Pierce Butler had found "no good reason for
confining it to those crimes," the republic's new Constitution incorporated his crucially amended article decreeing that states had the right to
repossess a fugitive from justice, "let his crime be what it may." Article
IV, Section 2, Clause 3 therefore reads: "No Person held to Service or Labour in one State . . . , escaping into another, shall . . . be discharged from
such Service or Labour, but shall be delivered . . . to whom such Service
or Labour may be due." The reclamation of absconded slaves was a capital cause for Major Butler, more than two hundred of his bondspersons,
along with twenty-five thousand others, having sailed from Charleston
Harbor with the British fleet near the end of the Revolutionary War. Sixty-
one years later, Kentucky's Henry Clay, "the Great Compromiser," would
prescribe an ultimately calamitous refinement of the major's original solution to what had continued to be the unsolvable political problem for
the nation of slave labor.[13]

WHEN ROSWELL KING SR. HIRED ON AS BUTLER'S OVERSEER FOR SEVEN
hundred dollars per annum plus a house in 1802, he assumed his new role
as American history stood at a fateful crossroads—at a moment when the
direction taken was not inevitable. True enough, New England's active
involvement in the Atlantic triangle had persisted until the revolution,
forming, as African American scholar and Lewis family acquaintance
Lorenzo Greene revealed years ago, the very basis of its economic life.
"About it revolved, and on it, depended, most of her industries," Greene
established. "The vast sugar, molasses and rum trade, shipbuilding, dis-
tilleries, a great many of the fisheries, the employment of artisans and

seamen . . ."[14] From such profits great New England mercantile families had risen: Browns of Providence; Cabots and Faneuils of Boston; Crowninshields of Salem; Champlins of Newport. Even so, Enlightenment ideals enshrined in the Declaration of Independence, the high-mindedness of Quakers, and those egalitarian values annealed in war had inspired and embarrassed revolutionary elites to deplore slavery's domestic continuity and, perhaps honestly, predict its extinction as inevitable.

After all, the stinging reproach of England's Dr. Samuel Johnson was hard to ignore: "How is it that we hear the loudest yelps for liberty among the drivers of negroes?" Yelps from slave masters at least were excluded from the new territories of the Northwest Ordinance. Calculating New England businessmen had already begun transferring their capital from sea to land to make spermaceti candles and pig iron. The Browns swerved into banking and insurance. A similar swerve occurred in the Upper South, where declining tobacco revenues and soil depletion induced Virginia and Maryland to cap further importation of domestic slaves and side with advocates at the Constitutional Convention to end Atlantic importation of slaves by 1808. Historian Leon Litwack's *North of Slavery* encouraged faith in a bending arc of justice. He counted several thousand slaves remaining in 1800, "but almost every northern state had either abolished slavery outright or had provided for its gradual extinction."[15]

As the first U.S. Congress convened in November 1789, Thomas Jefferson returned home after his five-year ambassadorial mission to France having solemnly pledged to Lafayette, Condorcet, Chastellux, the duc de La Rochefoucauld-Liancourt, and other titled *Amercanistes* who had funded and fought for victory at Yorktown that chattel slavery would soon disappear from his republic. Concerned Americans were as unaware as were French aristocrats of the telling fact that the Declaration's author had not seen fit to accept the twenty-thousand-dollar legacy of friend and Polish Revolutionary War hero Thaddeus Kosciuszko to buy the freedom of as many slaves as possible. Less than three years later, Jefferson was to reify his master plan for the reinvention of iconic Monticello. To do so, however, as his least charitable biographer reveals, Thomas Jefferson of Albermarle in Virginia negotiated a line of credit with his Dutch bankers that "granted and conveyed . . . all his right and equity of redemption in the said hundred and fifty negro slaves in full and absolute right of dominion."[16]

DURING HIS TWENTY YEARS OF SERVICE, ROSWELL KING SR. WOULD SEE Pierce Butler no more than twice when the major visited St. Simons Island and Butler Island on Georgia's Altamaha River, and at Coosaw Plantation on South Carolina's Port Royal. These holdings amounted to thousands of coastal and estuary acres of long-staple cotton and rice production that yielded their owner, who lived in a grand Philadelphia town house, a possibly unequaled American fortune. Such was his mastery of enslaved people and record of increased staple yields that the tall, scrawny Roswell would leapfrog peers in a few years to stand at the pinnacle of his overseer profession. His experimentation with sugarcane native to Barbados would surprise: one hundred acres cultivated to bring his employer a "promised $30,000 a year."[17] His military discipline and deployment of the enslaved even caused an occasional reproach from Major Butler. Roswell King Sr. represented par excellence the tribe of slavery modernizers waiting offstage for starring roles in a kingdom created by cotton.

To be fair, though, Roswell himself would have relinquished his overseer role and turned his profit-making talents to consolidating the manufacturing operation near Atlanta before cotton and the Missouri Compromise unalterably changed the United States. Nonetheless, I saw two significant events occurring during 1803, Roswell's second year in Pierce Butler's service: one quickly forgotten by white people at the time for its bizarreness, the other uniquely epochal. Roswell's eyewitness report to the major described a cargo of seventy-five chained Ibo warriors fresh from West Africa on their way up the Altamaha to other St. Simons Island plantations. From what he could see, wrote Roswell King to Butler, "they landed very cheerful and happy." He added jokingly that even though Butler Island's slaves couldn't speak their language, "your young wenches are speculating very high for husbands."[18] What actually hap-

pened that May, however—a scene of which Roswell saw only a part—
would be soldered to Gullah people's memories.

Erupting from belowdecks, the Ibos tossed the frightened white crew
overboard and tillered the coastal vessel *York* into a creek at the rear of
St. Simons. Some twenty Ibos and their headman supposedly descended
into Dunbar Creek, where they marched, singing, until the waters rose,
drowning out their defiant voices. Thirteen of the drowned were said to
have been salvaged for insurance. Ruth and I had spent the Christmas holi-
days in 2013 on Georgia's Jekyll Island with a side trip to St. Simons Island, where we heard the story of the "Igbo Landing Mass Suicide." A
colleague of mine, Harvard's Orlando Patterson, defined slavery as *social
death* in his admirable opus of the same title. It seemed to me that these
"saltwater" Ibos had anticipated Orlando Patterson and thus chosen a
symbolically superior exit.[19]

The loss of a number of Ibos in Dunbar Creek must have soon
dropped from Roswell's mind. The national firestorm set off weeks later
by the wholly unexpected Louisiana Purchase, however, promised a fabulous expansion of his business in slave labor management. An extraordinary fire sale offer by First Consul Napoleon Bonaparte to President
Jefferson's representatives, the purchase—unanticipated, unauthorized,
unconstitutional—had been closed on the spot in Paris for fifteen million
dollars, eighteen dollars per square mile, doubling the size of the new
United States. As few men of affairs grasped at the time, other than Alexander Hamilton, Jefferson's real estate bargain would create American
history's greatest ontological paradox. I recalled that it was Du Bois's *The
Suppression of the African Slave-Trade* that first linked Jefferson's acquisition of Louisiana to Haiti's bloody insurrection and her defeat of the
large expeditionary force sent by Napoleon to reconquer the island.[20]

Speaking for his Federalist Northeast, its seaports threatened by
much loss of trade down the Mississippi, its congressional representation
overwhelmed by multiple thousands of additional three-fifths bonds-
men, Creole Founding Father Hamilton scoffed, "To the deadly climate of
St. Domingo and to the . . . obstinate resistance made by its black inhabi-
tants are we indebted." Following Du Bois, historian Edward Baptist

reported that Napoleon's gigantic Haitian invasion fleet of fifty thousand
was to be followed by a Louisiana occupation army of twenty thousand
"to plant the French flag." From General Leclerc's vanquishing of Tous-
saint Louverture on the island of Santo Domingo would have come a
powerfully reenergized Louisiana Territory, retroceded to Napoleonic
France from senescent Spain and run with Gallic efficiency from New
Orleans. Truly, the nation's debt to Haiti was existential.[21]

Their country spared probable dismemberment by revolution in Haiti,
Jeffersonian Americans proceeded to make a new world reserved for
slaveholders. The array of fierce objections from the Federalist Northeast
(including a threat of regional secession) and congeries of reservations
from the middle states were parried by quick and easy-term loans from
England's great Baring Brothers bank and by a never-honored commitment
to prohibit "any slaves brought from Africa since 1789." Beguilingly, it
was claimed that this great land purchase promised diminishment wherever excess slaves existed through an ameliorating "diffusion" scheme (a
Jeffersonian construct) across thousands of new square miles. Indeed,
was not slavery most everywhere but South Carolina said to be in decline? Above all, the Jeffersonian sales pitch of Louisiana as an "Empire
of Liberty" for the posterity of the yeomanry—his "chosen people of
God"—proved narcotic.[22]

I had no doubt that Roswell King would have smiled slyly had the
Mississippi Valley been described to him as a great realm wherein "migrants from the East would naturally be transformed into freeholding,
republican yeomanry. Spread out across the landscape, white farmers
would have to provide for themselves; they would be too removed from
cities to be reliant upon them for their basic needs . . . too distant from
credit networks to find themselves ensnared." Little of which would
come to pass. Not only did Mr. Jefferson's Mississippi Valley not become
an Arcadia for his white, freedom-loving yeomanry, but a large number
of people living there long before the European age of exploration—
Choctaw, Osage, Creek, Chickasaw—were given eviction notices, to be
delivered later by Andrew Jackson in person. Land that had been promised to white yeoman farmers was to be worked by black slaves.[23]

From the 1790s to the Civil War 1860s, the number of enslaved people sold downriver from the Upper South into the Mississippi Valley's
maw of cotton and sugar cultivation was probably more than one million. Jefferson spoke for his Virginia class when he called tobacco "a culture of infinite wretchedness" as he switched to wheat at Monticello.
Chesapeake planters "diffused" their surplus enslaved at a steady profit.
South Carolina's indigo production had already petered out after the
British market vanished during the Revolutionary War. Princely rice
crop revenues from South Carolina and Georgia coastal plantations
shrank in perspective as cotton production rapidly increased after 1810.
Whitney's 1793 cotton gin deserved its mechanical renown. The supple,
long-staple cotton of the Butlers, Balls, and Hammonds grew only near
water. By 1820, though, planters everywhere were feeding their gins
short-staple cotton crossbred with Mexican varieties whose large bolls
virtually picked themselves. Thomas Jefferson's Empire of Liberty became
Frederick Law Olmsted's Cotton Kingdom in less than a generation.[24]

In 1790, the United States had produced 1.5 million pounds of cotton.
By 1800, when biographers Ellis, Malone, Wiencek, and others noticed
Jefferson's silence on the subject of slavery (Gabriel Prosser's organized
plot to capture Richmond that year ended talk of manumission), the
amount produced had risen to 35 million pounds. "A remarkable increase of 2,200 per cent," tabulates economic historian Ronald Bailey.
Fast-forward twenty years for a remarkable count of 160 million pounds
raised before Jefferson's demise six years later. Seventeen years later (in-
terrupted by a temporary market collapse), the American South would
produce two thirds of all the nation's exports. Add another twenty years
in which President Polk swallowed up Mexico's Texas and the slavocracy
grabbed Kansas, and the acreage under cotton seemed to defy computa-
tion. As South Carolina's Beauregard prepared to fire on Fort Sumter,
cotton production peaked at 2.3 billion pounds. Some small farmers had
participated in the cotton surge, but in the aggregate, as Beckert's comprehensive history of the crop that propelled the industrial maturation
of Great Britain and the American North confirms, "they produced only
a small share of the total crop. Indeed, 85 percent of all cotton picked in

the South in 1860 was grown on units larger than a hundred acres; the planters who owned those farms owned 91.2 percent of all the slaves."[25]

Abolitionists crowed that slavery was in decline throughout the world. If so, then the Mississippi Valley, where the institution found its Eden, must have been on another planet. "By 1860, there were more millionaires per capita in the Mississippi Valley than anywhere else in the United States," notes economic historian Walter Johnson. Edward Baptist found only a single millionaire in New York in 1860, whereas South Carolina numbered eleven. The 1860 U.S. Census counted a total national population of 31,443,000, of which 3,953,000 were enslaved like Clarissa King, their Deep South numbers never less than a third of state totals. Two thirds of the exported wealth of the United States that year came from the unpaid labor of black southerners subjected to corporal discipline, denied the vote, barred from literacy, their family members sexually abused and arbitrarily sold, their appeals at law minimal when allowed, and who by that time were engulfed in the slaveholding South's dehumanizing capitalist agrarian project. In the sunset years of the colonial era, the average daily load of cotton picked per capita by the enslaved ran from thirty to fifty pounds. By 1850, the daily amount had ballooned 400 percent, "owing," editors Sven Beckert and Seth Rockman determined in their indispensable *Slavery's Capitalism*, "to the advances of the disciplinary technologies brought to bear on plantation management."

Clarissa's great-grandson translated antiseptic "disciplinary technologies" to mean bullwhips extracting 350 cotton pounds in a dawn-to-dusk day from field hands marching in lockstep row by row as redneck guards pushed them forward. Differences existed. Paternalism was said to mitigate inhuman bondage in the Upper South and along the Atlantic coast. But the aggregate production rhythm in the new cotton lands reached a tempo by the 1830s that also transformed the speeds at which New England laborers toiled to keep up with it. A mind-boggling figure stipulated the exponential output of bonded black labor: "The total gain in productivity per picker from 1800 to 1860 was almost 400 percent."[26] From 1819 to 1860, the efficiency of workers who tended the spinning machines in the cotton mills of Manchester, England, and Lowell,

Massachusetts—like that of the enslaved pickers—also surged a mind-boggling 400 percent. By 1860, cotton manufacturing was America's leading industry, as measured by capital and labor employed and "net value of the product." The South's slave labor camps disgorged inexhaustible quantities of the fiber that was both the industrial North's lifeblood but also increasingly the nemesis of its sociopolitical system.[27]

Charles Sumner, the plantocracy's great senatorial scourge, memorably deplored what he saw as the republic's fatal compact: "the unhallowed alliance between the lords of the lash and the lords of the loom." The hard figures offered by leading contemporary economic historians confirmed my once impressionistic assumptions about the Cotton Kingdom's launch of the national industrial takeoff—a takeoff to be found along the Mississippi rather than in the mills of Massachusetts. To Du Bois goes the last word: "The slave barons looked behind them and saw to their dismay that there could be no backward step. The slavery of the new Cotton Kingdom in the nineteenth century must either die or conquer a nation—it could not hesitate or pause."[28] Nor could I, taking leave of this first chapter, hesitate or pause in finding as much as I could about my own family's enslaved and free experiences in the story of American slavery and American freedom.

2

* * *

CLARISSA'S BARGAIN

The Belvins of Houston County

A work-in-progress biography of a liberal Republican presidential candidate, *The Improbable Wendell Willkie*, delayed my getting to know the life that Clarissa King had lived. Wendell Willkie absorbed me, but it was clear that Clarissa wanted her story told as more than a historical trope—a shadowy figure devoid of agency. I knew Barrington King had sold her in service to another planter named Belvin on the Georgia frontier, but there was much more to learn about her life. Truthfully, I was yet to assimilate her reality as Alice King's mother. I had no recall of my ancestrally proud mother ever having mentioned her as a forebear.

At archivist DeNiro's request, the president of Georgia's Perry Area Historical Society, Ellie Loudermilk, had forwarded a small xeroxed portion of an extraordinary document—some half dozen pages of dark typescript—to me: "The Story of James Wiley Belvin, His Ancestors and Descendants." As these several pages made clear, the document was a descendant's private labor of love written in the hope that atonement of guilt and negation of apology could be achieved by a full, unvarnished, opinionated story of his slaveholding ancestors' rise and decline. On first reading his few pages, it occurred to me that full access to "Pete" Belvin's family history might be like reading the diary of some unembarrassed servant of the Third Reich–Albert Speer's Spandau diaries, say.

Elaine DeNiro's enclosed note revealed not only that Major James Wiley Belvin's wife's maid was called Claricey but also the inscrutable fact that the major bequeathed Atlanta property to this Claricey—family clues that ought to have sent me to Houston County at the earliest possible opportunity. When told about these leads from Roswell Historical Society, two well-read friends almost matched my astonishment: one a retired bank officer and avocational local historian, Clarence White, born and bred in rural Georgia; the other a Georgetown University Latin American scholar and ancestry sleuth, Carol Preece, whose exploration of family lines had become a secondary pursuit in retirement.

A decade earlier and out of the blue, the retired banker had emailed me his remarkably complete typescript biography of my father, John Henry Lewis Sr., Clarence White's Georgia high school idol. Learning of a Belvin property bequest, the irrepressible Clarence White, now a retired resident of Atlanta, located a barely readable 1881 handwritten indenture in the files of the clerk of Fulton County Superior Court. My ancestry sleuth friend Carol, in turn, claimed she found "Belvin cousins all over the place—especially a JW now living in Australia."

To complicate further my origin story came a city map from Roswell that actually located the Atlanta property described in the document found by Clarence White.[1] Indeed, pondering this Auburn Avenue discovery evoked personal, parental, professional, and other long-dormant memories: "Big Bethel," the huge African Methodist Episcopal (AME) Church where my father was buried; the Odd Fellows Building where my uncle's medical practice was located; Atlanta Life Insurance; Citizens Trust Bank; *Atlanta Daily World* (the country's only African American daily newspaper); Ebenezer Baptist Church, across from the Martin Luther King family home.[2] I remembered that at the top of the last century the street was called "Sweet Auburn." It now seemed my mother's family lived in a house given by a former slave owner to his wife's female servant.

SOME FIFTY YEARS BEFORE ROSWELL KING SR. CAME FROM CONNECTI-
cut to seek his fortune on the Georgia coast, Scottish Highlanders had
built a small fort they called New Inverness at the mouth of the Altamaha River. In Roswell's time, New Inverness was called Darien, and
what had happened there before his arrival would have seemed almost
too improbable to be believed at the end of the eighteenth century. In
1732, the "imperial idealist" James Edward Oglethorpe and his twenty
fellow trustees had established a province named for George II as a British bulwark against Spanish Florida and a utopian settlement of free-
holders uncorrupted by chattel slavery. Although my professional need
to know Georgia's colonial history had never been more than impressionistic, to know more of Georgia's founder offered this retooling historian, however superficially, a deeper contextualizing of an American
counternarrative.

Oglethorpe was a star of Georgian England's Enlightenment, a rare
combination of social reformer and military tactician. After Oxford's
Corpus Christi and military school in Paris, followed by election to Parliament, he used his chairmanship of the Committee on Prison Reform
to redress the ghastly corruption and lethal conditions of England's
debtor prisons. His reforming zeal grew until it embraced not only England's unfortunates but Europe's persecuted Protestants as well. He
brought debtors and paupers, together with expelled Protestant Salz-
burgers, Moravians, and Sephardic Jews, to the province in January 1733.
They were to be hardscrabble farmers settled on fifty-five heritable acres
each of corn, cotton, and livestock. Though he was once an investor in
the Royal African Company, the remarkable memoir of Ayuba Suleiman
Diallo, a West African Muslim carried off by slavers, decisively intensified Oglethorpe's philosophical aversion to the traffic. Against the advice and protest of most of his contemporaries, chattel slavery was
prohibited in Georgia "as against the Gospel, as well as the fundamental
law of England."[3]

Given what was to follow with grim certainty between European settlers and Native Americans, Oglethorpe sustained from the outset a
policy of cohabitation with the Yamacraw Creeks that was unusually am-
icable. The Creeks' trusting chief, Tomochichi, gave the land on which
Savannah, North America's first planned city, was built. Augusta and
Ebenezer, as well as the fortresses Frederica, King George, and St. Andrews, were generously accommodated on Yamacraw land as well. When
Oglethorpe returned temporarily to England the next year, the Yamacraw chief, his wife, his nephew, his war captain, and six chiefs of other
tribes sailed with him and unwound at the family estate until their presentation at court. When Oglethorpe came back to Georgia with the
Yamacraw chief, he brought the evangelizing Wesley brothers, whose
Methodist ministry was later reinforced by the sulfurous George White-
field, North America's first superstar preacher. In 1739, the pragmatic
relationship of settlers and original Americans so carefully effectuated
by Oglethorpe and Tomochichi would be memorialized upon the latter's
death with a military funeral and burial in Savannah's Percival Square
(later renamed for Sir James Wright).[4]

Supported by the sojourning John Wesley, who preached from a Savannah pulpit the Methodist creed to North America, Oglethorpe fought
to preserve his remarkable antislavery agrarian experiment, even as his
authority among the trustees was sabotaged by inveterate Georgian foes
petitioning Parliament to admit slavery. No matter General Oglethorpe's
high-wire success repulsing Spanish Florida's major 1742 Savannah
naval assault, Georgians wanted Oglethorpe and his trustees out of their
affairs. Georgians wanted slaves. From the New Inverness Highlanders,
however, had come a high-principled but eventually futile appeal against
lifting the slavery ban. "It is shocking to human nature that any Race of
Mankind, and their posterity, should be sentenced to perpetual Slavery,"
these common folk protested, "nor in Justice can we think otherwise of
it, than that they are thrown amongst us to be our Scourge . . . and as
Freedom to them must be as dear as to us, what a Scene of Horror must it
bring about."[5]

The truth was that the New Inverness Highlanders minded honest labor not at all, whereas a large group of settlers matter-of-factly spelled out their contrary demands to London. Unhappy at having to work without slaves, "even though their constitutions are much stronger than white people," the malcontents could see no reason not to have slaves, since "the heat [is] in no way disagreeable nor hurtful to them." Oglethorpe, supported by Wesley and a few others, strove mightily to inculcate their gospel of free labor, egalitarian ideals, and abstinence from rum. But South Carolina's slave labor system sinuously corrupted the province's settlers and ultimately incited open revolt against Oglethorpe. His authority was sabotaged by a petition brought before Parliament in 1741. Nine years later, after Oglethorpe's sixteen-year antislavery ban was lifted, Georgia, now British North America's thirteenth royal colony, ceased being the Lower South's exception.

The very next year a sect of learned Puritans who had come in 1630 from Dorset, England, resumed its quest for hallowed space to pray and prosper after having enjoyed some sixty years of both in colonial South Carolina. Seeking yet greener pastures for themselves and their bondspeople, these Puritans struck out for the Georgia coast. Colonial historian Erskine Clarke's ironic portrait of antebellum Protestantism memorably visualizes their arrival. "In this way a colony of 350 whites accompanied by their 1,400 slaves began in 1752 a southward trek to what would become Liberty County."[6] Between Darien and Savannah, at the center of Liberty County, midpoint between the disappointed Highlanders' Darien and the disparaged Oglethorpe's Savannah, rose Midway Congregational Church (Presbyterian by creed), several times rebuilt through the years.

Midway Church became known, said its worshippers, as "the cradle of Revolutionary Georgia." Yet church and county were encased in irony. Georgia's Liberty County became slavery's beachhead within a score of years after the Puritan wanderers arrived. Two of its leaders were signers of the Declaration of Independence. Two were generals of the revolution. Four would be governors of Georgia. One Midway daughter would be Theodore Roosevelt's grandmother. Another Midway daughter would be the wife of Woodrow Wilson. "This astonishing record was based not only upon the virtues of God-fearing Calvinists," said Erskine Clarke, "but also upon the labors of black slaves." On plantations whose thousands of acres were cleared by enslaved Africans who made possible the growing surplus profits from sea-island cotton, riverbank rice, and indigo, property-holding Englishmen Paul Revere into patriotic Americans indignant at royal taxes and impatient with trade restrictions and—as heterodox historian Charles Beard wryly disclosed—"southern planter[s] . . . much concerned in maintaining order against slave revolts."[7]

None would complain more bitterly than Georgia's Pierce Butler. Two hundred of his bondspeople fled to British forces after Savannah's capture, an injury to pride and property much on the major's mind at the Constitutional Convention. Little wonder, then, that when asked by a Liberty County schoolmaster to write an opinion on the subject, a schoolboy opined that "slavery is one of the most invidious though at the same time beneficial things that ever was introduced into the United States." The schoolboy's answer came twenty years after the Treaty of Paris capping the new Americans' victory at Yorktown, almost the year Roswell King Sr. became Major Butler's St. Simons Island overseer.[8] Georgia, the last of the thirteen royal colonies, had experienced the revolution free of the emancipatory tremors troubling many northern consciences. She entered the federal union in 1788 with her constitution unambiguously proclaiming, "All freemen are born equal."[9] Yet faced with the stark demographic challenge presented by the original owners of the land— Oglethorpe's Creeks—she allowed her nonvoting free colored population to grow by 300 percent after 1800.[10]

From the 1.5 million pounds of cotton grown in Georgia and the Carolinas in 1790, the total only ten years later was an astonishing 35 million, with no ceiling in sight. Whitney's invention plus short-staple bulbs picked by thousands of enslaved hands on seemingly inexhaustible fields of cheap land occupied by Native Americans foretold the dilemma of forceful Native American removals. The first president of the new United States and his secretary of war watched the looming troubles in Georgia with more wisdom than many of their successors would exemplify. Liberty County, by then a model fiefdom of slaveholders, had few concerns about the land's original occupants. Georgia's vast interior, however, with its Chickasaws, Choctaws, Cherokees, and Creeks, was a migratory powder keg. To Secretary Henry Knox, expressing President Washington's views in 1790, "the Indians being the prior occupants possess the right of the soil" and should be removed only with their consent or the necessity of war.

Given time and exposure to the white man, Washington and Knox, channeling the most philanthropic ideals of their time, wagered that these "prior occupants" could become sufficiently Europeanized while bargaining away their tribal lands in good faith until finally they disappeared.[11] By contrast, the "prior occupants" who resided south of the Ohio River anticipated a far more permanent relationship with the new American republic. In the summer of 1790, twenty-six chiefs of the Creek Nation, accompanied by an assimilated tribesman with the dodgy name McGillivray, were received with fanfare in New York's grand Federal Hall by our nation's Cincinnatus. Contemporary newspapers recorded a good time had by all, gifts exchanged, food and libations, fulsome speeches, and our marmoreal President Washington exuberantly embraced at the conclusion of the first treaty between the president of the new United States of America and Native American tribes: the Treaty of New York.

These Creeks ceded to Georgia two thirds of the land the latter laid claim to; in return the federal government guaranteed the Native Americans perpetual sovereignty to the remaining third. McGillivray received an annual $1,200 salary, a brigadier general's commission in the U.S. Army, and a trade monopoly.[12]

YAZOO IS SAID TO BE THE NAME OF AN INDIAN TRIBE THAT THE seventeenth-century French explorer Sieur de La Salle gave to a river—"*la riviere des Yazous*"—somewhere near the mouth of the Mississippi. Based on a British monarch's cartography, Georgia's incommensurable colonial boundaries ran west all the way to the Pacific.[13] Unknown to the trusting Creeks or even to George Washington, Georgia's first state legislature had already sold some 35 million acres to which it had no title to three "Yazoo" land companies months before the Senate ratified the Treaty of New

York. The title to all this unspoiled, rich terrain belonged (Native Americans excepted) to the federal government, the understanding being that Georgia had relinquished its surplus territory upon entry into the Union.

Five hundred thousand dollars at two cents per acre went to Governor Edward Telfair and fellow solons, with yet more acreage auctioned before the books were closed. Patrick Henry was a partner in the Virginia Yazoo; Charleston grandees formed South Carolina's; Pennsylvanians James Wilson of the U.S. Supreme Court and Robert Morris, once America's richest businessman, were ultimately ruined through such speculations. Both died not long after their stints in debtors' prison.[14] That the greatest real estate scandal in our history primarily interests only a few historians and economists today committed Yazoo and its considerable consequences to the entropy of national greed. Less from shame than from retributive envy, however, a new Georgia legislature annulled all the Yazoo contracts, burned the records in 1796, and left the messy constitutional problems it had created to John Marshall's Supreme Court to resolve, which, twenty years after the forgotten Treaty of New York, it finally did.

Fletcher v. Peck denied Georgia or any state the right to "impair the obligation of contracts." The Yazoo contracts were ruled as enforceable, whether illegally procured or not—a good thing, indeed, for eastern bankers and southern planters rewarded at par value for larceny. To Georgia's Creeks, however, Yazoo signaled errant manipulation and revealed a European calculus of elimination that the tribal-consolidating Shawnee chieftain Tecumseh and his messianic brother Tenskwatawa adamantly denounced. The onrush of white people into the Northwest Territory above the Ohio River Tecumseh calculated in ever fewer unstoppable moons. "Sell a country!" Tecumseh laughed when whites offered money. "Why not sell the air, the great sea, as well as the earth?"[15] Meanwhile, his one-eyed, recovered-alcoholic bother Tenskwatawa syncretized a great vision of sobriety, regeneration, and unity for his people before the Master of Life fell silent.

The future of the Shawnee people had been written in the ominous

Treaty of Detroit, where thirty northern chiefs signed away most of southwestern Michigan and a slice of Ohio to the territorial governor of Michigan in 1807. Jefferson's impatient designs for their people had been conveyed to the ambitious governor of the Northwest Territory, William Henry Harrison, early in his administration. "When they withdraw themselves to the culture of a small piece of land," the president assumed, "they will perceive how useless to them are their extensive forests, and be willing to pare them off in exchange for necessaries for their farms and families."[16] Madison's administration and territorial governor Harrison confronted a militant Tecumseh and a much-aroused Shawnee people. Tenskwatawa's redemptive visions at his Prophetstown drew more tribes to Tippecanoe in Indiana than ever would assemble again, even during the time of Sitting Bull and Crazy Horse more than sixty years later.[17]

Tecumseh's pan-Indian vision was of a vaster geopolitics, of a unity of all Indians everywhere in a geographical collaboration with white America's nemesis—the British in the War of 1812. With his party of seven Shawnees, six Kickapoos, six Winnebagos, and two Creeks, Tecumseh descended below the Ohio River in the summer of 1811 to sway the loyalty of the four nations of the old Southwest—Chickasaw, Choctaw, Cherokee, Creek—to his brother Tenskwatawa's creed. Tecumseh's contemporary biographer describes this magnificent warrior's inspired eloquence and matchless diplomacy, inescapably doomed by the acculturated realpolitik of the southern tribes. News of his brother's defeat and the destruction of Prophetstown by Harrison at Tippecanoe ended Tecumseh's "remarkable but largely unavailing six-month, three thousand mile recruiting drive."[18] "Tippecanoe and Tyler too!," a presidential campaign slogan recited by future generations of schoolchildren, ended a people's chances of survival. Tecumseh's death near the Battle of the Thames on Lake Erie doomed the pan-Indian confederacy's struggle against the United States during the War of 1812.

The half-white leader of Georgia's Lower Creeks gambled on a bribe. Chief William McIntosh signed the First Treaty of Indian Springs, ceding yet another four million Muscogee acres east of the Flint River to

Georgia for $250,000. Mcintosh walked away with a $40,000 commission, a thousand virgin acres, and the handsome hotel he immediately built overlooking the Creeks' sacred springs. But Tecumseh's spirit still lived among the Upper Creeks. Their National Council parsed McIntosh's collaboration as treason and decreed further tribal land sales a high crime. Veterans of Tecumseh's pan-Indian crusade dared the whites with their enslaved workers to march any deeper into Muscogee territory. When six chiefs of the Lower Creeks defied the National Council and signed the Second Treaty of Indian Springs, the outraged Upper Creeks scalped McIntosh and burned his hotel (restored today).

Soon after New Year's Day 1826, Opothleyahola, chief of the Creek National Council, rode into Washington, accompanied by the Upper and Lower Creek leaders, to denounce Georgia's treaty claims. The 1826 Treaty of Washington voided the baldly exploitative second Indian Springs compact and appropriated funds to send an authorized team of Lower Creeks to explore suitable lands west of the Mississippi for permanent relocation.[19] Great Father John Quincy Adams acknowledged the Creeks' legal possession of their lands, but only until New Year's Day 1827.

Even Andy Jackson could have been satisfied after the Creeks surrendered to the United States all their lands east of the Chattahoochee River for a quarter million dollars. Not Georgia's impatient governor, however. January 1827 was too long a wait for the rich cotton lands beyond the Flint River. Governor George Troup completely ignored the 1826 Treaty of Washington, commenced the Creeks' expulsion, and even mobilized the Georgia militia when John Quincy Adams threatened federal intervention—a standoff resolved by presidential pusillanimity confronted by racial avarice.

THE SOUTH CAROLINA BELVINS, BRASSFIELDS, AND REMBERTS HAD COMmingled their blood before Georgia became a state. "Pete," the Belvin family historian, traced their origins to either the French or maybe the Scots. The elegant horses splashing the Belvin family crest were probably suggestive of invention rather than of gentry, though years in Sumter and Bishopville had served these God-fearing Methodists and sizable slaveholders well. Wiley Belvin, the patriarch, left considerable wealth in land, real estate, and the enslaved when he died in 1831. To oldest son James Wiley Belvin ("J.W."), age twenty-two, fell the heavy responsibility of executorship for siblings and Brassfield grandmother, an eleven-year duty he discharged until the last was grown and the estate settled finally in 1842. Meanwhile, twenty-six-year-old J.W. had married raven-haired Eliza Judith, daughter of James Rembert, prosperous slave owner and state legislator. Three years later came their Belvin daughter Martha Elenora. Their first son, James Peter Coladen, arrived on June 5, 1840, precisely at 1:00 a.m., according to family historian Pete.

Through the years, Georgia's blandishments were catnip for South Carolina Belvins and Remberts. After the first Indian Springs treaty opened all the territory from the Ocmulgee to the Flint River, Scarboro Rembert returned to Bishopville to dazzle Cousin James about "wonderful plantation country that could be had for $1 or $2 per acre," recalled Pete the chronicler.[20] Andy Jackson's 1830 Indian Removal Act was in its fifth year of ethnic cleansing—three more to go until the Cherokees, regardless of their acculturation, invented alphabet, and written constitution, would be force-marched on a "trail of tears" to the Oklahoma Territory. James Rembert's Houston County timing was very good. The state's white population was more than 33,000 after 1830, with "just under 25,000 slaves." Where Georgia had raised 20,000 bales of cotton thirty years earlier, toward the end of the 1830s enslaved workers produced a copious 326,000 annually. James Rembert's own Houston County enslaved raised a significant portion of the 50,000 bales yearly shipped down the Altamaha from the Macon fall line.[21] "Within scarcely a generation," says Houston County's Joseph Reidy, "the Macon area had emerged as the heartland of King Cotton's Georgia domain."

Six slaveholding counties pivoted from central Georgia's Macon city in the 1840s: Bibb, Crawford, Monroe, Jones, Twiggs, and Houston. Houston, where the number of slave-owning households had risen more than 50 percent, was bigger and richer. So thirty-two-year-old James Wiley Belvin took his share of his father's estate, packed up family and

possessions, and headed for Houston County in either October or November of 1841, driving thirty-two enslaved men, women, and children
of all ages. He settled family and unfree people on 1,154 prime acres
bought from father-in-law James Rembert for ten thousand dollars, pay-
able a thousand dollars a year for ten years. He gave his thirty-two slaves
as a mortgage. In upstate New York or Ohio, say, only land could be used
as security for loans. J.W.'s quick and easy transaction was standard slavery economics: securing credit with slaves to buy land to produce cotton
requiring more labor for more cotton was a credit cycle fed by "capital-
ized wombs."

County tax rolls would list some of the thirty-odd Belvin slaves as a
Tom and a Peggy and a Sam. "Tom was overseer for Grandpa," specifies
historian Pete. This Sam must have been within a month or so the same
age as James Wiley's year-and-a-half-old son, James Peter Coladen. Sam's
mother having died in childbirth, J.W. gave the enslaved boy Sam to his
own son to grow up as a Belvin.[22] Pete lets us know early on, "Sam grew
up with Papa ["Papa" being historian Pete's own father, James Peter Coladen Belvin] and was with him all during the [Civil] War." Belvins were
quick to measure their new neighbors. "Georgia crackers" were the wrong
sort of white people. Some good people came from Virginia and North
Carolina, but the finest came from South Carolina "under different skies,"
boasted Pete. It was said that the right people were the Methodists who
lived between the county seat at Perry and the Flint River to the west—
Pete's "wealthy, educated and refined Haslems, McGhees, Felders, Toom-
ers, and Cobbs."

It occurred to me that the wrong sort of white people—"crackers
under different skies"—were those who, despite an otherwise advantageous pigmentation, were doomed to fail the test for right whiteness in
the consolidating southern social order. An issue of the new *De Bow's Review* spelled out this fail-safe prescription: "The non-slaveholder knows
that as soon as his savings will admit, he can become a slaveholder, and
thus relieve his wife from the necessities of the kitchen and the laundry
and his children from the labors of the field."[23] Black people were authen-
tic white people's sine qua non. As Pete Belvin said, the right whites "had

plantations ranging from 1,000 to 1,500 acres, with Negroes to cultivate the land."

J.W. settled into a low-key social prominence almost immediately. Eliza Judith and the children, Martha Elenora, two-year-old James Peter Coladen, and newborn Thomas Sumter, nestled in a proper clapboard house on several acres the enslaved cleared for them. Cotton prices were slow to recover from overproduction during the late 1830s, but the fertility and volume of the yield "made everything work out," according to Pete. Master Belvin became a trustee of Minerva Academy, the county's highly respected young women's school. His educational views were enlightened for his time and class; the Belvin daughters and sons would matriculate at college. Given the size of J.W.'s human property, federal appointment as Minerva postmaster and election to the legislature in nearby Milledgeville, the state capital, were predictable distinctions in 1845. Election merely required annual attendance at brief sessions. His and Eliza Judith's fine oil portraits were most likely done during the noted portraitist Thomas Sully's southern circuit that year. J.W. affects a mien of uncomplicated command, Eliza Judith a concerning frailness.[24]

Georgia slaveholding politicians no longer had much cause to worry about Spanish Florida's escape hatch for their unfree labor, since the Onís-Adams Treaty with Spain twenty years earlier had all but nailed the lid shut. In effect, of primary concern now to J.W.'s fellow legislators was how best to exact a steady increase in cotton productivity from their peculiar institution's labor force. During the late 1820s an English traveler was distressed to find "slaves seated in the same room as masters"—a plethora of violations, underscored Reidy, rarely seen in coastal Georgia and South Carolina.[25] A decade after the English traveler's astonishment, however, the dynamic of overproduction and steep depression in prices during the 1830s caused a reverse Gresham's law, a consolidation of cotton planters into omnipotent agrarian capitalists with whom J. W. Belvin caballed in the Milledgeville legislature. His eleven hundred acres, on which he and his thirty-odd enslaved workers anticipated yet another good yield, were not to be slighted.

Sven Beckert's *Empire of Cotton* reminded me that most of the South's cotton picked in 1860 would be grown on farms of more than a hundred acres; that "the planters who owned those farms owned 91.2 percent of all the slaves."[26] J.W. was a coming contender among them.

THE MOST EFFICIENT MODELS FOR THE MANAGEMENT OF THE ENSLAVED were in contested flux in the Deep South after the late 1830s. The "pushing system" increasingly found favor as the Cotton Kingdom spread from Georgia to Louisiana and remorselessly onward to Alabama, Mississippi, and (after a war with Mexico) Texas. If its mortality rates were far lower, the pushing system nevertheless did, as historian Stanley Elkins noted, rival Nazi concentration camps in raw brutality. By 1850, under the pushing system the increase in cotton picked by each enslaved worker was up a staggering 400 percent from forty years before.[27]

Old Tom, the African American overseer who served J.W. for just shy of two decades, is not recorded to have pushed his people beyond measure. In Pete's version, his grandfather had early grasped an axiom of his business that Solomon Northup soon vouched for in his memoir, *Twelve Years a Slave*. "It is a fact I have more than once observed," the literate, illegally enslaved Northup insisted, "that those who treated their slaves most leniently, were rewarded by the greatest amount of labor." Yet Northup's insightfulness was also belied by the vicious arbitrariness and self-destructive economics he routinely observed. Witness the disincentivizing commonplace of the "gin-house," a grim reckoning a hundred thousand slaves faced each day. "If [the enslaved] has not performed the full task appointed him," sighed Northup, "he knows that he must suffer. And if he has exceeded it by ten or twenty pounds, in all probability his master will measure the next day's work accordingly. So whether he has too little or too much, his approach to the gin-house is always with fear and trembling."[28]

Historians' interpretations of enslavement—"inhuman bondage," as David Brion Davis called it—seem always to defeat satisfactory generalization. Struggling valiantly through this interpretive thicket to explain how North American enslavement functioned for more than two centuries, Erskine Clarke, that conscientious scribe of the white South, settled on the formulaic straddle of "negotiated relationships" attributed to historian Ira Berlin. That the eminent African American sociologist Charles S. Johnson and his pioneering Fisk University slavery narratives team had anticipated years earlier a version of negotiated relationships as the pernicious system's glue deeply troubled Clarissa's great-grandson. In their forerunner volume, *The American Slave: A Composite Autobiography*, Charles Johnson, J. Masuoka, and Ophelia Settle Egypt summarized a tragic dyad: "The slave developed within the system a set of attitudes and sentiments, habits and conduct which were complementary to those of the master. Both sought to attain maximum satisfaction of their wants and needs; each had his status; each discovered the goal he expected to pursue, and each sought the means to achieve these goals."

The dubious neatness of "negotiated relationships" somehow reminded me of the Enlightenment's clockwork models of human behavior. Newtonian negotiations did prevail in much of the older South, but as Richard Dunn's thoughtful *A Tale of Two Plantations* (viz., Jamaica and Virginia) also found, where the demand exceeded the labor supply, negotiation was a one-way street at best.[29]

James Wiley Belvin, believed grandson Pete, appeared to skew toward uncommon moderation in a climate of regional immoderation. J.W. made it a rule not to buy slaves or sell them, with the result that their robust increase through natural reproduction went unrelieved by sales in the market.[30] Prime "field hands" might fetch a thousand dollars by the end of the 1840s. Profits in the fully internationalized cotton market were soaring, making J.W.'s fellow planters in the six counties encircling Macon and in the advancing Black Belt some of the richest Americans. James K. Polk, the Jacksonian Democrat in the White House, gave these agrarian capitalists every reason to believe that their territorial ambitions trumped those of the North or West. The great Irish publicist of their cause—John L. O'Sullivan—ballyhooed "Manifest Destiny" as the justification for a war with Mexico, only awaiting a manufactured incident. Both Polk and O'Sullivan wanted war in 1846.

In January 1846, Eliza Judith presented J.W. with their second daughter, Eliza Jane Calhoun (for the South Carolina nullifier). A month or two later, Cousin Caleb Rembert volunteered for the Macon Guards, galloped off to the Mexican-American War, and perished somewhere below the Rio Grande. Besides noting Caleb's disappearance, the Belvin family historian wrote nothing about the military occupation of Mexico's capital or the confiscatory 1848 Treaty of Guadalupe Hidalgo carving out Texas, California, and the remaining third of the North American continent from Mexico. Nothing said of an inflammatory new national Fugitive Slave Act, or of old ex-president John Quincy Adams's dire verdict of a "most unrighteous war," Emerson's high-minded lamentation, or Thoreau's civil renunciation. Once again, Thomas Carlyle pronounced a matchless verdict on a national government that "openly declared itself the patron, the champion, and the upholder of slavery."

Still, Pete's silence notwithstanding, a reasonable hypothetical might label J.W. a cautious, troubled Whig in the firestorm aftermath of the Mexican-American War with its legislatively creative but ultimately unworkable second national compromise with slavery. Like as not, Belvin welcomed Alexander H. Stephens's Georgia's Constitutional Union Party and banked on Henry Clay's jury-rigged Compromise of 1850 quieting "the spirit of disunion and revolution" of southern secessionists.[31] The Compromise of 1850 fatally compromised the health of John C. Calhoun and Henry Clay. A decade remained until the full damage to the health of the republic manifested itself.

TO THE BELVINS, LIKE MOST OF THEIR PLANTER CLASS, THE DECADE WAS to bring "the finest ten years of plantation living that anyone could possibly wish for," limned Pete. The Mexican-American War years did leave their mark on Eliza Judith. Caleb Rembert's loss in Mexico, followed two years to the month later by the death of their first daughter, Martha Elenora, had been but partly mitigated by the arrival of their last child, Eliza Jane Calhoun. The people whose welfare depended on sensing the minutest domestic vibrations must have gossiped among themselves about their mistress's slow demise. Whether it was said of her as of some other local mistresses, "They wouldn't even turn down their bed to get in it," her wizened, gray appearance may well have become a cross for her devoted, active husband.[32] Their Thomas Sully portraits presented a contrast in élan vital. All the better, then, that Eliza Judith and James Wiley had spent 1850 in Perry, the county seat, until their new plantation house near Minerva Academy was ready, with its promise of a fresh beginning.

J.W. acquired seventeen-year-old Clarissa sometime in early October 1852. Elaine DeNiro believed "that Barrington and James Wiley Belvin knew each other." Barrington King and J. W. Belvin probably did know each other, even though neither slave master's records identify Clarissa King's purchaser.[33] I decided she was sold in a transaction that shrouded the mutuality of the real actors' motives. Great-grandmother, then, would have been a prime specimen whose price in the $1,425 three-person total should have been a bargain. William was likely hired out eventually to the Roswell Manufacturing Company. Elsie's place in the scheme of things was special, however. She would become Barrington's daughter's "mammy" — little Eva's doted-upon "maum."

Much has been written about the objective conditions of enslaved women like my great-grandmother, but rarely, with no more than a handful of exceptions, has a Clarissa spoken for herself. The antebellum South kept its sexual history secret by enforcing the illiteracy of all but 3 or 4 percent of its almost four million enslaved people. Given the large absence of antebellum African American memoir and autobiography, the record of interracial abuse and affection, accommodation and agency, was the privilege of master-class distortion. She didn't "care to dwell upon this subject," wrote Elizabeth Keckley, Mary Todd Lincoln's enslaved seamstress, "for it is one that is fraught with pain."[34] But even had Great-grandmother wished to dwell on this subject, her great-grandson was never to know whether, like Keckley or Harriet Jacobs, she was capable of writing about it. Like Sally Hemings, my great-grandmother entranced by her silence.

I believed I already knew the future awaiting her, but I needed to un-
pack the foundational question posed by feminist historians such as Adele
Alexander, Brenda Stevenson, and Daina Ramey Berry: "How were enslaved people able to form families amid a system that limited autonomy
so dramatically and violently?"[35] Harriet Jacobs's caveats certainly low-
ered my expectations of charity from masters. "The slave girl is reared in
an atmosphere of licentiousness and fear," Jacobs knew from bitter experience. "The lash and the foul talk of her master and his sons are her
teachers. When she is fourteen, her owner, or his sons, or the overseer, or
perhaps all of them, begin to bribe her with presents," and there was
more, said she. "If these fail to accomplish their purpose, she is whipped
or starved into submission to their will. . . . Resistance is hopeless."[36]

I could remember no account of hopeless female resistance more
graphic than British actress Frances Kemble's *Journal of a Residence on a
Georgian Plantation*. Her witnessed experience of sexual exploitation on
her husband's island rice plantation was so appalling that President Lincoln might well have addressed Kemble, but for her journal's secrecy, as
"the little woman who wrote the big book that started this great war,"
rather than Harriet Beecher Stowe. Fanny's *Journal* featured Barrington
King as a retired Alabama planter visiting her rich-as-Midas spouse, Pierce
Butler, grandson of the turncoat Major Butler. Fanny, appalled by Barrington's abuse of one Judy, mother of his mulatto son, describes how he
beat Judy "for having resisted him, and then sent her off as a further punishment to Five Pound—a horrible swamp . . . to which slaves are sometimes
banished for such offenses as are not sufficiently atoned for by the lash." I
thought of Clarissa's mother, Elsie, Barrington King's daughter's "maum."[37]

James Peter Coladen Belvin was five months shy of his thirteenth
birthday when his mother's new seventeen-year-old servant girl arrived
at the new family home near Minerva, the town everyone said "was never
really born from an embryo." Not as tall as his fifty-year-old father, ram-
bunctious James Peter Coladen Belvin already exuded the drive that
would make him an exceptionally capable Confederate officer. Several
clues caused me to regard him to be a plantation menace, of concern to

the able Tom, his father's overseer. Peter Coladen's dismissal three years later from Milledgeville's Oglethorpe College (for a "Halloween prank," according to Pete) fit my conception of antebellum sexual abuse—of the master's heir loose among myriad temptations—to which my great-grandmother would have been especially vulnerable.[38]

To be sure, the future Captain Peter Coladen Belvin's world on the Flint River had grown exponentially into an embarrassment of riches. From the original thirty-two enslaved workers brought fourteen years ago from Bishopville, South Carolina, their natural increase stood at seventy-six souls on the 1856 Belvin tax returns. The Belvin plantation now spread across 3,480 acres valued at $10 per acre. A pound of Belvin cotton sold for $12.05. The "prime field hands" J.W. prided himself on never selling could have yielded $1,500 individually. Pete estimated they comprised about half the enslaved, the remainder being "either old people or children." In the spring of 1858, J.W. and Eliza Judith made a quick

Drawing of Belvin Plantation House, 1850

visit to Bishopville. They returned with money and twelve unfree people bequeathed them from James Rembert's estate.[39] Unsurprising that Pete Belvin's family history called the decade of the 1850s "the finest ten years of plantation living that anyone could possibly wish for." After the Rembert bequest influx, J.W.'s plantation recorded ninety-six enslaved men, women, and children on the 1860 tax rolls. They planted eight hundred acres of corn and three hundred acres of other crops "to support the mules, hogs, and the people," said Pete. Only a hundred acres went for cotton—two hundred bales worth about $10,000—"enough cash money to buy what was necessary," according to Pete.

His ancestor made lots of money, "but mostly he and his family and slaves lived well and were happy." With "everybody work[ing] from about six years old to seventy-five years old" on 4,035 acres, cotton still selling at $12, Pete Belvin's history matched Margaret Mitchell's fiction. Based on income per capita, Georgia was the richest state in the union that year, and Houston, as historian Joseph Reidy notes, was among the richest counties.[40]

MY GREAT-GRANDMOTHER LIVED THIS HOUSTON DECADE. WHEN I LO-cated her on the 1860 U.S. Federal Census—Slave Schedules, I saw how sadly different must have been her perspective of Pete's celebrated decade. The year after J.W. finally replaced his faithful overseer and coachman Tom with a Caucasian named Bryant, Macon's *Georgia Journal and Messenger* reported gruesome Belvin plantation news that rippled across the becalmed surface of the six counties: "An old negro woman and a young girl, servants in the house, assaulted the overseer's wife, hitting her about the head and shoulders with an axe." Although Pete made light of the incident, Mrs. Bryant's mutilation by Belvin Negroes in April 1858 had to have been especially unnerving to planter families increasingly defensive about Garrisonian abolitionist propaganda and Fugitive Slave Act embarrassments in the North. Old Tom's retirement marked a major development as well for Clarissa. One of the two twenty-four-year-old females on the 1860 Houston slave schedules had to be Clarissa, mother of a two-year-old female baby with her color identified as "M" on that same census.[41]

I surmised Clarissa's two-year-old to be Adela, the first of her two children born before the Civil War. Although his birth the previous year should have placed him on the 1860 slave schedules, Charles, her second, was missed somehow. Like his older sister, he arrived a shade or two lighter in color than his mother. Both, obviously, were fathered by a white who enjoyed access to J.W.'s human property and whose identity was as yet unknown to me. Harriet Jacobs's verdict upon herself, upon my great-grandmother, as well as on countless other unfree females doubly demeaned by color and sex echoed in my mind as I filed away the Belvin slave schedule. "No matter whether the slave girl be as black as ebony or as fair as her mistress . . . there is no shadow of law to protect her from insult, from violence, or even from death," lamented Jacobs, with the unflinching coda that "all these [insults] are inflicted by fiends, who bear the shape of men."[42] The fiend who came to mind was James Peter Coladen, the now twenty-year-old son of my great-grandmother's master and mistress.

"What's Love Got to Do with It?," asks Brenda Stevenson's unforgiving essay "Concubinage and Enslaved Women and Girls in the Antebellum South." Still, there were exceptions where love did have much to do with southern coupling, as with the miscegenating South Carolina Balls, the white and black North Carolina Hairstons, the ambiguous Georgia Logans. Kent Anderson Leslie's stunning biography of Amanda America Dickson (bequeathed her white Georgia father's entire fortune) documents the notorious case of paternal affection that grew from maternal rape. Rare exceptions aside, though, customary sexual relations between masters and property were the almost routine temptations of men like Georgia's Supreme Court judge Joseph Henry Lumpkin: "Which of us," mused the distinguished jurist, "has not narrowly escaped petting one of the pretty little mulattoes belonging to our neighbor as one of the family?"

First Adela in 1857, then Charles three years later, I took as living proof that J.W.'s oldest boy was progenitor of my assaulted great-grandmother's children. Ancestors are predetermined, but not their descendants' admiration. To know Peter Coladen's future seemed rather like holding a no-return ticket to a dead end. Perhaps, given her predicament, Great-grandmother may not have found her Belvin heir repulsive. During the early months of 1861, as the southland's political barometer signaled war, military cadet Peter Coladen may have presented a sufferable masterfulness. It seems that while J.W. saw the secessionist fury as a mistake, both his sons raced from Oglethorpe College to military service after Confederate batteries fired on Fort Sumter.[43] Younger brother Thomas Sumter was to die in federal captivity twelve months before Lee's surrender at Appomattox.

Peter Coladen's military service, however, was the acme of his problematic life: four years as a quartermaster officer in Company K of the Eleventh Regiment with Brigadier General George T. ("Tige") Anderson's Georgia division under the Confederacy's most brilliant corps commander, Lieutenant General James Longstreet. Unless flattened by jaundice at Richmond in December 1861, delayed on the way to Chickamauga in September 1863, excused to marry at Milledgeville in May 1864, Peter Coladen was present at Mechanicsville, Old Cold Harbor, Harrison's Landing, Fredericksburg, Gettysburg (where Lee wrecked his army against Meade's superior numbers), Missionary Ridge, and New Cold Harbor. On orders to forage supplies for Lee's doomed army, Captain Belvin missed the Confederacy's surrender at Appomattox Court House.[44] He honored the treason of a cause of which he boasted at every opportunity in later life. That he lived to do so had been due to Sam, the enslaved alter ego born the same year as Peter Coladen.

Sam was the shadow who searched through the night for his badly wounded master at Antietam/Sharpsburg, carrying him four miles to the field hospital, where Captain Belvin would regain consciousness to hear of Abraham Lincoln's Preliminary Emancipation Proclamation. Henceforth, the Civil War was a war to free the enslaved. Rules of engagement barred Sam from actual combat, but according to Pete's history, Sam got "boots off a dead Yankee quicker than anyone in the Confederate army."[45] It was Sam's remarkable discovery (bringing joyful exultations from the ranks) that the Yankees "were making shoes to fit either foot." In May of 1864, Captain Belvin obtained release to marry, taking Sam with him. Both men wedded their Houston County fiancées: Sam jumping the broom with Louisa on the Belvin plantation; Peter Coladen marrying Mary Elizabeth Walton of Milledgeville. What, if anything, passed between Clarissa and Coladen is uncertain, except to note that Great-grandmother bore no children during the war. When the captain rejoined his unit, Sam, despite his master's advice, insisted on returning with him, to remain by his side until the last taps were bugled.

On Christmas Eve 1864, bondsman and master were photographed together near Richmond, Virginia. Their remarkable Christmas Eve photograph—a seated Captain Belvin stiff as his saber, a handsome man-servant Sam tall as an oak—seemed to me to channel perfectly the iconography of their lost world. As a testament to their symbiosis, Peter Coladen gave the photo to Sam, who left with it for Houston County as soon as the captain was discharged in early April 1865 after Appomattox. This gift would remain with Sam and Louisa Belvin's descendants for many years into the twentieth century.[46] Sam Belvin became one of the necessary tropes of the Lost Cause: the good Negro. Two weeks before he followed Peter Coladen home, the Confederate Senate narrowly voted to conscript all able-bodied males, irrespective of color and on promise of freedom. A philosophical absurdity that should have bewildered both men.

PETE'S FAMILY HISTORY SPEAKS OF "EMANCIPATION FEVER" AFFLICTING Houston County's labor forces in the last year of the war. "When Sherman came along," complained a bitterly deceived planter, "every last skunk of 'em run away." Houston County whites and blacks experienced an overnight reconfiguration of their socioeconomic order. More than 400,000 Georgians soon became accountable under federal law only to themselves for the first time since General Oglethorpe's departure. People began working when they wanted to on some plantations. On others, workers roamed off entirely. Calculated in early twenty-first-century values, the South's enslaved people had represented a market value of $38 billion, a fifth of which belonged to Georgia. Frederick Law Olmsted's Cotton Kingdom was bankrupt.

At Milledgeville, fifty miles north of the Belvin plantation and where the occupied state's first Reconstruction General Assembly convened in December 1865, defiant planters voted to send Alexander H. Stephens, their defeated Confederacy's vice president, along with a former senator, to represent them in the Senate of the United States.[47] Like as not, James Wiley Belvin, a good Whig and almost certainly present at Milledgeville, would have been surprised to see such legislative defiance immediately approved by Lincoln's disastrous successor, Andrew Johnson, while Congress was in recess. When Johnson precipitously restored Georgia and her ten seceded sisters to the union on December 20 and proceeded to declare the Civil War ended on April 2, 1866, the war for the soul of the nation finally began in earnest.

"The result of the war," ordained W. E. B. Du Bois, "left four million human beings just as valuable for the production of cotton and sugar as they had been before the war."[48] "Major" James Wiley Belvin, the title a distinction conferred after his voluntary cavalry service to protect the area from Andersonville's fourteen thousand Union prisoners, emerged from the war as Houston's fourth-largest former slaveholder. The 1864 tax receipts were impressive: 115 slaves; cotton sales at 32 cents per pound. Cotton bales worth $300,000 were ready for transit from Macon down the Altamaha to Darien.[49] Determined to keep his people, Major Belvin risked an unpopular proposal. Before the war he and his people had worshipped together under Asbury Methodist Chapel's roof. Now he offered to build his people a church of their own.

To Belvin's planter classmates, however, the choice of the African Methodist Episcopal Church—a northern-born denomination that preached black pride, a denomination famously expelled from South Carolina for suspected collusion in the Denmark Vesey slave conspiracy—was both reprehensible and dangerous. But the major knew that Savannah's cultured black Methodists had voted to affiliate with the evangelizing AME

Church, that several AME pastors, among them the eloquent James Lynch and William Porter, had traveled the state fundraising for schools and mobilizing the emancipated to prepare for political engagement. Moreover, Belvin had to have been impressed when freeborn Henry McNeal Turner, chaplain of the First U.S. Colored Regiment, major officer of the Freedmen's Bureau, and powerhouse of the AME Church, arrived from Washington with the blessings of President Johnson as well as Secretary of War Edwin Stanton and Senator Charles Sumner, one of Radical Reconstruction's fiercest advocates. Turner, a freeborn South Carolinian, had become an AME pastor in St. Louis, where his eloquent preaching quickly earned him an assignment to the District of Columbia's influential Israel Bethel Church on Capitol Hill. His forceful personality amazed Stanton, who persuaded Lincoln and then Johnson to appoint Turner the first black chaplain of the United States Colored Troops.[50]

Given its hierarchical structure, its freeborn northern bishops and pastors mostly recruited from the small class of urban craftspeople, Major Belvin must have wagered that his and his people's upended future would be more secure with Turner's rising bourgeois prelate-politicians. "A wooden building was erected," Pete records, "and the Belvin A.M.E. Church was founded." Charles Henry, the second King born and reared on the Belvin plantation, was to master reading and writing under a teacher-preacher in this first wooden structure. He would profess carpentering as a trade during his time in Reconstruction Atlanta, and his later steady ascent in the AME clergy in North Carolina surely benefited from Henry McNeal Turner's patronage.[51]

Pete confessed ignorance of the labor arrangement the major made but believed "it must have been satisfying to both parties as most . . . stayed" and were still there in his time. "As fine a group of people as you would want to meet," of that he had no doubt. Mostly, it seems former slaves returned to duty with the major and most other planters as tenants on shares. By summer 1865, encouraged by AME preachers and ordered by Freedmen's Bureau officials, "most of the black refugees had returned to the plantations," claims a respected Reconstruction historian.[52] The question was whether Emancipation had merely been an interlude between serfdoms. I expected to know the answer when I finished this family history's chapter on my father's family.

My need to know much more about the Belvin imprint on Houston County would finally introduce me to DeNiro's archivist associate Ellie Loudermilk on the morning of September 1, 2019. Perry, hometown of retired U.S. senator Samuel Augustus Nunn of Nixon impeachment prominence, was the regional site for the money-earning Perry Fair and the domain of the prominent Loudermilk family. The Perry Area Historical Museum presided over by archivist Ellie Loudermilk conducted business on a scrutinized need-to-know accessibility deeply cognizant of William Faulkner's admonition about the past.

"We will meet you there at 9:30," said my instructions as I checked my watch again in Perry's Rodeway Inn's lobby. A tiny white man no more than four feet high suddenly appeared ten minutes late. Wayne Chapman, Ellie Loudermilk's assistant, explained that his superior's absence was due to the regional fair business, that she might find time to meet later, but that neither she nor he "exactly understood" what had brought me to Perry from New York. The people I mentioned were all dead. The long-ago places I listed were gone. Both surprised and amused, I conceded that although my antebellum concerns might prove unrecoverable, I would be obliged to have Chapman accompany me on a drive from Perry south toward the next settlement. After which, I said that he and I could hope to rendezvous with archivist Loudermilk.

The road south was Route 224, which led, as I later realized, to Montezuma, a sleepy township of decrepit columnar structures fit for a Civil War docudrama. "Stop! Stop!" shouted Chapman some twenty miles from Perry. "Looks like the place!" "The place" was guarded by a gleaming white wooden fence, above which I read "Belvin A.M.E. Church, Sunday School on Wednesdays." I shouldered the Herz, crossed the road, followed by Wayne Chapman, who began shouting. "Can't go in! Can't go in! Property's under observation by the Dukes" was what I remember hearing him protest. "Mr. Chapman, you can come or stay, but I'm climbing this fence and you can squeeze under it."

A quarter mile before us loomed a steepled structure at the horizon. A clearing for imposing gravestones gave way to high grass and tall pines along the graveled way as we reached the locked, handsome brick church. The Loudermilk assistant whispered that the local people called it "the cathedral in the woods." He obliged me by taking my photo standing next to a shoulder-high marble monument I found curiously incised with *Gone With the Wind* sentiments standing next to an African Methodist Episcopal house of worship: "In Memory of Sam Belvin, a loyal and faithful black man who served his master during the War 1861–1865 and saved his life on the battlefield. Born June 1840 in slavery. Died about 1909 a free man."

Two nights booked at Perry's Rodeway Inn I had counted as sufficient for Houston County research. Although Wayne Chapman suggested a visit to Montezuma and a side trip to Minerva, our deferred meeting with Ellie Loudermilk decided a prompt late-morning drive to the Perry Area Historical Museum without further delay. Ms. Loudermilk, a large bustling presence, offered reasons for being almost too busy to find an appropriate time for me. As we repaired to her inner office, she offhandedly called attention to a framed sketch of a pleasant mid-nineteenth-century country house. It was the Belvin manor house, she said. Reflexively, as I raised my camera to capture the drawing, Ellie Loudermilk displayed no concern.

Once seated in her book-lined office with an assistant, however, her concerns were unadorned, direct: Why was I there and what did I want? Ellie Loudermilk's interrogation seemed almost communitarian—a question much less about dusty records, slave censuses, property taxes, secession politics, or memory echoes than about my own personal quest to file some claim against antebellum wrongdoing. My sense of the situation strongly suggested that the appointed guardians of the Perry past assumed that I knew as much about myself as they did and that it could even matter as much to me as to themselves. To display embittered feelings about the long wrongs of Caucasian abuse of my African ancestors would have spoiled the Houston County research opportunity by making these whites feel as angry about their guilt as they ought to. The general tenseness dissipated when Ellie, momentarily called away, returned with news that her husband asked to meet with me for lunch.

Heading for Atlanta early the next morning, I felt considerably buoyed after my lunch the day before with both Loudermilks. Lunch with people of color seldom happened in Perry, where white waiters served white diners. Informed that I had written a successful biography of Martin Luther King Jr., William Loudermilk eagerly told me of his special connection to Dr. King. His construction bid on the outdated Atlanta elementary school attended by Martin King might be forthcoming any day, he thought. Whatever they could do to make a Pulitzer Prize winner's sojourn agreeable would be good business, proffered James Loudermilk. We three had strolled back to the historical museum in the jolliest of moods. A parting handshake with Bill Loudermilk wonderfully predisposed Ellie to photocopy the entirety of James Peter Belvin's remarkable typewritten family history. Too large to transmit by email, her thumb-drive version arrived by mail several days later.

The major had settled his war hero son and bride "right east of the mothership plantation." There was a good log cabin on six hundred acres, with fifty head of hogs, ten mules, some sheep, cows, chickens, "and everything else to start a good plantation," in Pete's judgment. No slaves, but Sam and Louisa had their house nearby.[53] Clarissa, assisted by Old Tom's daughter Dinah, enabled the major's fragile Eliza Judith to spend her days in serene indifference to the great changes that passed her by. However, Great-grandmother's pregnancy during the last quarter of 1865 should have surprised her former owners. My great-uncle James's arrival and complexion, I was certain, were explained by Peter Coladen's visit while on leave to marry the previous May. Did new wife Mary Elizabeth's pregnancy, I wondered, temporarily distract all the Belvins from another of those classic southern embarrassments presented by my still-captive ancestor? "Sexual chaos was always the possibility of slavery," Du Bois reminds us.[54]

For all my reasonable enough assumptions, it was Major James Wiley Belvin who ruled the roost at his plantation. Executive decisions had had to be made about Clarissa's service to Eliza Judith, about the cut of the lives of Adela, Charles, and James. And Clarissa's leverage in these arrangements needed reassessing. Clarissa King and Sam Belvin had good reasons not to leave Houston County after the war. Not only did their property-owning prospects appear dim, but life in the Belvin biosphere offered reasonable comforts, manageable routines, and a privileged inferior status in a stable hierarchy. Houston's careful Joseph Reidy believes that white owners and black workers fought one another to a standstill by 1876, existing thereafter in a top-down equilibrium a large percentage of which consisted of impoverished whites as well.[55] Major Belvin's church-going workforce may have felt itself better off than most others.

The 1870 federal census showed my great-grandmother living as a servant next door to the major and his wife; daughter Adela and sons Charles and James lived with her. Although nothing in Pete's history or otherwise speaks of boyhood bonding of my great-uncle James King with Peter Coladen and Mary Elizabeth's James Milton Belvin—born within a year of each other—given southern mores, the boys likely grew compatibly together until yellow fever killed eight-year-old James Milton in December 1874.[56] Two years before death took the captain's male heir, my forty-three-year-old great-grandmother presented the Belvin plantation with my maternal grandmother, Alice King, the woman in the stained glass window.

Whatever reactions Alice's advent provoked, no notice of it was ever taken by the Belvin family historian. Indeed, as to what the major or the captain made of this delicate, hazel-eyed, café au lait child, one should recall the judgment of an especially sensitive white southern historian "that the majority of whites ignored their mulatto offspring, as did their white families and the white community."[57] Elsie Givens's arrival more than a year or so after Alice's birth, however, speaks volumes for Clarissa's maternal forward thinking. Elsie's William died in Nashville sometime in 1875. Her grown Givenses, Thomas, James, and Jemima, stayed behind when Elsie left for Houston to care for Clarissa's unexpected Alice.[58]

THE 1880S BROUGHT MOUNTING TROUBLES TO CAPTAIN JAMES PETER Coladen Belvin. The headstrong scion acquired the reputation of a compulsive Civil War raconteur. His idle presence in Montezuma or Perry Township, where he bought drinks for fellow veterans and enticed civilian audiences, appears to have competed increasingly with farming and financial responsibilities. Moreover, memories of the extraordinary rebound of the early 1870s cotton economy encouraged a profligacy on his part that finally led to disastrous risk-taking in cotton futures and the loss of his farm in 1883. "This got the fat into the fire, with Papa and the rest of the family," writes Pete resignedly. The following October, Coladen lost Mary Elizabeth, leaving three children ages eight, ten, and twelve. "It was quite a blow to Grandpa and Grandma losing their only daughter-in-law," grieved Pete.[59] "Grandpa had decided that Papa was not able to do anything for his children. He made his will to provide for Grandma and her maid, Claricey King." She—Claricey—had finally been mentioned in "The Story of James Wiley Belvin, His Ancestors and Descendants."[60]

Peter Coladen traded planter for lumber inspector and took his children to Dooly County, where he married Willie Todd Clark, a sixteen-year-old life force who produced nine more, and where he was remembered as a cheerful Lost Cause fabulist of whom his 1917 *Valdosta Times* obituary said, people stopped "to listen to some tale he loved to tell of the Sixties." Eight decades passed before *The Valdosta Times* would run "Sam Belvin, One Family's Hero"—the poignant family story of Captain Belvin copiously weeping on the back porch after learning of Sam's death sometime in 1909.[61]

After his son's run of misfortunes, James Wiley, with Eliza Judith's presumed concurrence, had made a painful decision around 1886 about their estate. By the terms of his last will and testament, dated November 29, 1886, the major's executors were instructed to invest the proceeds from the sale of his plantation into securities for the benefit of his estate. His "beloved wife" was given all kitchen and household furniture and to receive "two hundred dollars in cash" from their estate each November 1. "After the sale of all [his] estate," his son's three surviving children of his first marriage were to receive equal shares once the youngest child reached twenty-one. By the terms of his July 4 codicil of the following year, the executors were to pay "Claricey B. King annually on the 1st of November the sum of fifty dollars . . . for six years after my decease, as a testimonial for her services to myself and wife."[62] Seventeen thousand dollars in today's money every November for six years was a bare-bones recompense for four decades of competent service.

The major died in March of 1888, a year after signing his codicil. His widow survived him by ten years. They lie beside each other in the old Felton Cemetery in Marshallville, an antebellum time capsule thirteen miles south of Perry. "In the latter 1800s, Marshallville was the most desirable place in the whole world to live," enthuses Pete. He recalls that in those days, "whenever a prominent citizen died, a Negro servant with a black horse would go around to each house and knock on the door." Sam Belvin knocked on Marshallville's doors the day James Wiley died.[63] The major's will obliged Clarissa to remain as Eliza Judith's companion until 1894.

My great-grandmother might well have honored the old planter's request, I thought. Still, as she would then have just turned a healthy sixty years, I knew disappointingly little about how she might have lived her last decade or more. As far as the family historian seems to have known, Clarissa's role in Houston County was as the dutiful, efficient servant of the senior Belvins. Nothing was ever hinted in Pete's Panglossian chronicle about her finding herself predictably and periodically used, compelled, or desired by a young master who perhaps occasionally even loved her when it pleased him to substitute the constraints of his married life to a belle on a pedestal.

TO THE BEST OF OUR MEMORIES, IT HAD BEEN SOMETIME IN THE FALL OF 2018 that my partner Dolores's curiosity about the Belvin indenture yielded an interpretive epiphany. She and I read together the indenture's *whereof*s, *whereas*es, and considerations in the October 1881 handwritten document endowing my great-grandmother with prime property located between Atlanta's Old and New Wheat streets. Clarence White, my father's devoted biographer, and Carol Preece, the genealogist Annapolis friend, had been waiting to hear the backstory of the indenture, James W. Belvin's conveyance for "five dollars cash in hand paid by the said Clarisa [*sic*] B. King (colored) for her sole and separate use during the term of her natural life and . . . on her decease, to her granddaughter Alice Lee Belvin for her sole and separate use during the term of her natural life, and to such child or children as she may have."

Suddenly, what should have been too obvious to miss became self-evident on reading the major's characterization of Alice King as her own mother's granddaughter. Had not James Peter Coladen's father finally provided definitive corroboration of his son's paternity of Clarissa's children? Clarissa's children were indeed Belvins. The remaining ancestral curiosity, however, was Great-grandmother's unshaken possession of the King patronymic, an identity, notwithstanding the major's renaming, that her last child, Alice King, would also proudly retain. Was there a controlling origin story in which a thirteen-year-old Elsie conceived Barrington King's Clarissa?

Carol's recommendation was to result in a radical narrative revision of Clarissa King's biography and of my lineage. Carol still thought I needed to work with a professional genealogist, "in order to protect yourself from some critique about your methodology in this day and age."[64] Finally persuaded, I sought the advice of Mary Helen Thompson, a genealogist friend. It seemed the DNA variables of my ancestral quest might be better served by Through The Trees, a genealogy enterprise with impressive "through line" capabilities. "My problem," I explained to the genealogist: "According to family history . . . my maternal lineage derived from the Kings of Roswell, Georgia." Explaining that I had had no knowledge of Belvin antecedents until recently, I stressed that my compelling concern was to falsify my mother's belief "that her mother was a King."

Nothing was heard for an anxious month. The report came back: "While this project began as an investigation of Alice King's ancestry, any genetic evidence of Alice having descended from a documented King family member at this time is inconclusive."[65] Although deeply disappointed by the genealogist's finding, I cannot say that I was completely surprised. Indeed, recalling the solipsism that "absence of evidence is not

evidence of absence," I found solace in believing that Mother could still
have been right.

However, the next revelation practically reduced me to several days
of incoherence. "Further analysis of the unweighted amounts of DNA
David Lewis shares with the DNA-tested Belvin family members," his
written report decreed, "suggests that James W. Belvin—the father of
James P. C. Belvin—is statistically much more likely to have sired Alice
King." The short of his findings was that "far too little autosomal DNA
was shared" between Coladen and me—no Rembert genes for David Levering Lewis.[66] Belvin federal census schedules, family wills and property
deeds, tax receipts, local newspapers, James Peter ("Pete") Belvin's impressionistic chronology, Roswell Historical Society and Perry Area Historical Society archival evidence, and historical monographs—none of
it, alone or in combination, unmasked the cloaked bloodlines of history's
dominant and subjected.

MAJOR BELVIN'S ATLANTA TRIP PROBABLY LASTED ONLY A FEW DAYS
during September 1879. Given the nature of his business, it's possible
that Great-grandmother Clarissa accompanied him because his business
there was for her. The veil separating the races, memorialized thirty-odd
years later by a young Atlanta University professor, was more like a loose
garment three years after the end of Reconstruction. A well-dressed
woman of color in the company of a white gentleman whose ship-like dimensions rolled along with them might have been an unusual sight,
though not a rare one. The business of that September 19, whether or not
she was present, was the purchase for Clarissa of a parcel of land occupied by a large two-story frame dwelling on Wheat Street four lots from
the Jackson Street intersection. The seller, Moses Frank, was a prominent Jewish businessman.

A century and a half later when Clarence White and I located the bill
of sale for seven hundred dollars in the basement of the Fulton County
Superior Court, we wondered instantly if this Moses Frank might not be

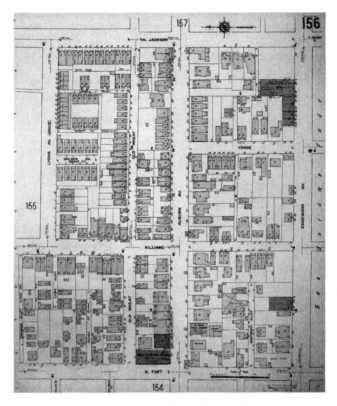

Sanborn Fire Insurance Map from Atlanta,
Fulton County, Georgia. Sanborn Map Company, 1911.

a relative of the Leo Frank whose 1913 mistrial and mob murder disgraced Atlanta's gentile leadership, scandalized much of the country, yet
also represented a broad skein of antisemitism previously contained.[67]
We did indeed confirm that it had been Moses Frank who invited his ill-
fated nephew to Atlanta to invest in a match factory. Fourteen years after
Moses Frank sold his property, Wheat Street became Auburn Avenue,
the prized artery of African American commercial, religious, and social
associations affectionately called "Sweet Auburn." It would have been a
good bet that the property James Wiley Belvin bought Clarissa King in
1879 would maintain its value and probably appreciate, even if Moses
Frank undoubtedly exercised savvy timing by selling just as his neighborhood opened to the "better class of colored people." Clarissa's eight-

room domicile, set imposingly back from the street, she must have thought was fit for Kings.

Obtaining Wheat Street was the first of a two-part plan that spoke volumes about the depth of J.W. and "Claricey's" quarter-century time line of discreet involvement. The final indenture transferring Wheat Street to Great-grandmother was different from the original. In the first version (1879), the major had retained a reversionary interest to his estate should Great-grandmother's daughter Alice die without issue. That this reversionary clause was eliminated two years later, however, reflected Clarissa's persuasive powers of correction. After all, as the 1880 federal census for Atlanta showed, all but one of Clarissa's children (her firstborn, Adela, lived with husband and three children nearby) were with their grandmother Elsie at 276 Wheat Street under the name of King: Charles, twenty-two; James, fourteen; and Alice, eight.[68] The final indenture the major filed with the court in October 1881 must have been, in his eyes, an equity dispensation for the many years of Clarissa's captive sexual service and their parallel family history.

With this second indenture, the major and his former enslaved solemnized their coexistence: "Entered into this first day of August eighteen hundred and eighty-one . . . between James W. Belvin . . . and Clarisa B. King (colored) . . . for and in consideration of the former services and fidelity of said Clarisa B. King while a slave and the further consideration of the sum of five dollars cash in hand paid by the said Clarisa B. King," the indenture declared that 276 Wheat Street, "with all and singular the rights, members and appurtenances thereof," belonged to the "said Clarisa B. King and Alice Lee Belvin during their natural lives." The self-serving reversionary clause had disappeared. Had Alice Lee Belvin died without issue, "then the property hereby conveyed . . . shall revert to the other children of the said Clarisa B. King."[69] The major's indenture retained a significant exclusion, however, to my great-grandmother's property rights. To wit: "the marital rights of 'her present or any future husband'" were excluded from Great-grandmother's property rights.

James Wiley Belvin lived some thirty years as master of two families: the white one wealthy, respected, legally separate from the other and superior to it, the black family formally ignored and unacknowledged in the written record of the other, but whose subordination ultimately transformed their master's estate. Clarissa King had finally secured independence for herself, education for her children, and an endowed future for some of my immediate family.

Alice Lee Belvin lived on as Alice King in her home at the renamed 300 Auburn Avenue. In 1891, she wed John Henry Bell, whose family origins derived from Charleston, South Carolina. They had two children: Alice Urnestine, my mother, born in 1893; and John Levering, my uncle, born in 1897. Clarissa King must surely be the Clara King listed with her son James in the 1890 Atlanta city directory at 276 Wheat Street. No further information as to her whereabouts or demise would be discovered until much later; she died intestate in Georgia's Glynn County on November 18, 1919, aged eighty-two.[70] A curious fact about my great-grandmother's five younger half siblings: none ever used the surname King.[71] They were Givenses. Alice King Bell's memorial window was the Woman in the Window whose ancestry inspired her grandson's unfinished family history.

3

. . .

AN IDENTITY
OF THEIR OWN

The Bells of Goose Creek
and Auburn Avenue

I remember Alice King Bell and John Henry Bell from a couple of old
studio photographs showing them forever poised in the prime of
bourgeois confidence. In the gendered language of their generation,
Alice, educated, refined, attractive, propertied, had to have been quite a
catch for Grandfather. Education at the Storrs School and Atlanta University's Normal Department endowed her with a solid New England
mastery of letters, math, music, and domestic science, more than enough,
quite probably, for the equivalent of a good finishing school education.[1]

My grandfather was Atlanta-born the year after the Civil War, but
his family lines ran back to colonial South Carolina. Of him, too, it was
likely said that twenty-four-year-old Grandfather was quite a catch. I
knew something of his early years: his advantageous federal job as postal
deliveryman; his distinguished service as First Congregational Church
deacon. Not only did he possess in that racially stringent era the security
of a federal salary, but John Henry Bell's South Carolina lineage claimed
the then enviable distinction of descent from African American people
who had not been enslaved. My grandparents' match was auspicious: education, property, professional security, looks.

Although Grandfather's family's position in South Carolina's historic

three-tier caste system had been decidedly less grand than my mother
and uncle remembered, his ancestors were traceable as free people of
color in the Carolina Low Country all the way back to the colonial origins
of the federal union. According to family lore and the earliest federal
censuses, the Bells had originated in Charleston County at about the
time Major Pierce Butler, George III's renegade officer, inserted a fugitive
slave clause in the U.S. Constitution. According to Adeline (or Adalaide),
my grandfather's mother, their story was said to have begun with one
Martha Jemima Bell, a formidable matriarch whose existence could be
followed decade by decade up to the Civil War. That she was alive in a
quaint place called St. James Parish, Goose Creek, at sixty and with six
offspring had early on been corroborated by the 1840 federal census.[2]
Not only had the Bells not been enslaved, but my mother confessed that
they were supposed to have been small slaveholders themselves. Moreover, John Henry's daughter proudly presumed that one had even belonged to Charleston's elite old Brown Fellowship Society, which she
sometimes referred to as the "blue vein club."

I've come to appreciate my Atlanta Bells as singularly instructive of
the aspirational limitations within the social order on which racialized
North America was built. Professionally, this history had never been of
primary interest to my scholarship, yet I had had to concede its tangen-
tial salience with Jean Toomer's lineage in my *When Harlem Was in Vogue*
or Ridgely Torrence's splendid John Hope biography. Even so, I still recall
my figurative shoulder shrug when an excited Federal City College colleague stopped to tell me about his manuscript that would appear four
years later as *Slaves without Masters*, Ira Berlin's classic.

My first published work had come four years earlier. It was a 1970 biography of Martin Luther King Jr., a topic profoundly antipathetical to
Berlin's marginal subjects squeezed into impotence between the South's
white master class and its enslaved. One got the impression that even
Berlin didn't care much for his "slaves without masters," most of whom,
he wrote rather unfeelingly, "lived in the countryside, where they squat-
ted in shanties on scraps of land that no one [whites] seemed to want." A
combination of preoccupation and shelved curiosity precluded for some

years my critical reading of the fine antecedent monographs of both Luther Jackson and John Hope Franklin on free Negroes in Virginia and
North Carolina, respectively. To my chagrin, somehow I missed entirely
notice of *A World in Shadow: The Free Black in Antebellum South Carolina*.
Unsatisfied by my seminar's summary treatment, Larry Koger, a somewhat older college undergraduate, went off on his own to research and
write the astonishing *Black Slaveowners: Free Black Slave Masters in South
Carolina, 1790–1860*. At Rutgers University, a teaching assistant brought
Mr. Koger's niche monograph and surprising personal acknowledgment
to my attention.[3]

When I learned that Koger's free person of color named James Bell
with eleven slaves on the Charleston Neck must have belonged to an unrelated family line, I now had a professional need to know these people
whose interstitial place in the South's "peculiar institution" had long
remained uninvestigated anomalies for me. Koger's revelation that 75
Charleston free black masters had been ordered to free their 241 enslaved
people at the end of the Civil War supported my mother's memory. But
another Koger revelation had not only corrected Mother's belief but also
severely rebutted the canonical assertion of Carter Woodson and even
John Hope Franklin and Berlin that many of the enslaved belonging to
South Carolina free blacks were in reality family members or protected
friends. "[B]y 1850," as the unforgiving Koger found, "free blacks were
holding slaves as investments and commerce."[4]

Obviously, then, a great many of the South's free black persons (census identified as "F.B.") had been as exploitative as the dominant class of
whites. Woodson, indeed, conceded that black slave owners sometimes
"would sell their wives [just] as other slaveholders disposed of Negroes."
A decade before the Civil War the total number of persons of African descent in the United States numbered some 3,369,000. More than a half
million of these were free persons. For the first time, the 1850 census also
counted the number of "people visibly mulattoes" as 406,000 or 1.8 percent in the total national population of 23.2 million. Those both free and
mulatto numbered 159,000—"free persons of color" (FPC), as a great
many South Carolina free blacks identified themselves. These FPCs or

mulattoes comprised half the Palmetto State's population of free persons. A decade later, in 1860, they amounted to 25 percent of Charleston's total population.[5]

Whether it would be possible to locate my grandfather's Bells in what Marina Wikramanayake described as their "world in shadow" remained to be seen. Of one thing I was certain, though: calling these South Carolinians masterless slaves minimized both the complexity of their indeterminate color and the pragmatism of their civic participation. In a word, these Bells promised one of history's best proofs of the circumstantiality of racial identity. Indeed, as the oft-cited ruling of Judge William Harper disclosed, upper-class antebellum South Carolinians had known this reality all too well. "We cannot say what admixture of negro [sic] blood will make a colored person," opined Judge Harper in 1835. "The condition of the individual is not to be determined solely by distinct and visible admixture of negro blood, but by the reputation of his reception into white society and his having commonly exercised the privileges of a white man. . . . It may be well and proper, that a man of worth, should have the rank of a white man while a vagabond of the same degree of blood should be confined to the inferior cast."[6]

THE CITY OF MOTHER'S GAUZY MEMORY BECAME A GREAT PRIORITY ONLY after my family history project had seemed to resolve the conundrums of Clarissa in Georgia's Houston County. But to my greatly annoyed surprise, just as I'd planned to begin reconstructing the Bells from their antebellum ecosystem, access to Charleston's venerable Avery Research Center for African American History and Culture became excruciatingly uncertain. The well-regarded director had resigned, followed by the center's temporary closure in 2018 due to extensive renovation. The Avery Institute, organized by the colored alumni of the prestigious old Avery Normal School, was no conventional records center and museum. Affiliated with the elite College of Charleston since 1985, the institute's holdings of family, social, institutional, and material culture of the South Carolina African American Low Country were indispensable.

Charleston was the 2019 venue for the annual meeting of the ASALH, Carter G. Woodson's renamed Association for the Study of African American Life and History. Charleston was, after all, a major landing site of the New World's transformation, the place where until late in the nineteenth century North America remained an extension of Africa rather than of Europe. "To me, Sullivan Island is like Ellis Island to most whites," I'd chortled to Dolores as we left the airport. She knew that, as historian Peter Wood noted, "well over forty percent of the slaves reaching the British mainland colonies between 1700 and 1775 arrived in South Carolina." They were quarantined there until being sold on the auction block. Seeing Sullivan Island from the battery, the enormity of the twenty-year extension of the Atlantic slave trade felt as contemptibly present as when first reading Du Bois's *The Suppression of the African Slave-Trade to the United States of America*. That young Calvinist historian with his Germanic reinforcements had fairly spluttered in his Harvard dissertation that "it behooves nations as well as men to do things at the very moment when they ought to be done."[7]

In an all but empty Avery Research Center, Dolores and I canvassed the FPC city directories from 1803 to the Civil War. We bagged her discoveries of a Benjamin Bell, carpenter on Rutledge Street, along with John W., another carpenter and presumed sibling, as my probable ancestors. My own Bell quests went unrewarded. Horace Fitchett's dissertation, "The Free Negro in Charleston, South Carolina," yielded no consanguineous Bells. Debra Newman's *List of Free Black Heads of Families in the First Census of the United States, 1790* was a major disappointment: Ms. Newman had somehow missed Martha Jemima Bell, putative matriarch of the line.

Our hurried wrap-up at the Avery was followed by a scrupulous day in the college's special collections, where the question of the Bells' modest rank in Charleston's pseudoaristocratic social scheme had seemed to be settled. My three microfilm reels covering forty decades disclosed not a single Bell capitation payment (an annual tax exacted from all free black persons). Had they been too poor to pay this tax or were they habitual scofflaws? Finally, unsurprisingly, none of Martha Jemima's children could my microfilm search find as having been accepted by the august Brown Fellowship Society, the affluent, color-conscious sanctum sanctorum, guarded since its founding on November 1, 1790, by fifty free men of color. "This Society shall be brown," declared the original five subscribers, some of whose veins probably really were as blue as Mother claimed.

No trace of my Bell ancestors appeared among the darker-skinned members of the rival Humane Brotherhood either. Not only were they excluded from the colored crème de la crème, but my South Carolina ancestors probably never saw the inside walls of Thomas Bonneau's or Daniel Payne's schoolhouses, Charleston's premier academies for free people.[8] Thomas Bonneau, whose house, we learned, stands prominent and well preserved today at 70 Nassau Street, self-financed his eponymous school for promising children of ambitious free black and colored parents. The orphaned Daniel Payne, who was fostered by Bonneau's Brown Fellowship Society, had headed a comparable academy until South Carolina's legislature, spooked by the Denmark Vesey conspiracy, definitively outlawed schools for nonwhites in 1835.[9]

As for my South Carolina Bells, their place in the historical record did appear to have been elusively minor. Berlin's *Slaves without Masters* described them as "southern free Negroes balanced precariously between abject slavery, which they rejected, and full freedom, which was denied them." Searching for a category name for southern FPCs, some scholars were satisfied with the label *denizens*, a limbo status imitating citizenship. Indeed, scholarship on free persons of African descent in North America varies troublingly across time and place, albeit finding them with greater freedoms in the North after the revolution until the Missouri Compromise made black labor feared above the Mason-Dixon line. Other scholars (outstandingly, Joel Williamson in his book *New People*) have discerned antebellum race relationships in South Carolina and Louisiana akin to the three-tiered structures of Latin America and the Caribbean.

A more careful inspection of difference, however, presents the more persuasive profile of free people as enjoying substantial civil rights of which the free persons of the Palmetto State were steadily deprived until they possessed no more than a simulacrum.[10] New Orleans *gens de cou-*

leur enjoyed almost the full range of rights of white men—bearing arms, literacy, testifying in court, unrestricted travel—whereas the shadow of inferiority fell ever more darkly upon Charleston's denizens in the quarter century leading to the Civil War.

When *Social Relations in Our Southern States*, an authoritative reference, appeared on the eve of the war, author Daniel R. Hundley constructed a regional pyramid of eight classes descending from aristocrats past yeomen to poor white trash on top of obedient slaves. "Nowhere did he find a place for the South's free Negroes," observed the accomplished biographers of South Carolina's William Ellison, cotton-gin maker and probably the richest man of color outside Louisiana.[11] The time had passed when free Africans, and especially those whose pigment bespoke Caucasian white affinity and whose skills and services earned respect, were regarded as necessary buffers between the master race and the enslaved black majority.

I HAD READ THAT THE EIGHTEENTH CENTURY HAD BEEN A TIME WHEN mulatto heads of South Carolina free households had felt not merely comfortable with whatever socioeconomic advantages pigment afforded them, when a good many self-defined their standing as the natural, superior ordination of quasi whiteness. Those with a smattering of property had voted until the colonial legislature restricted the franchise to white men after 1721. Men who were neither black nor white had served as emergency backup, as it were, for dangerously outnumbered white men. By the time their numbers peaked in the early 1830s, many free people of color—if not a majority—had long ago embraced a consciousness of kind alienating them from the regime's enslaved black majority. As to whether my unextraordinary Bells had been mulatto chauvinists was a conclusion I had yet to reach. However, the taint of family slaveholding emerged as a thankful case of mistaken identity that must have deceived my mother. A Martha Bell, mulatto, free, but mercifully unrelated to us, I found in the second federal census as the owner of sixteen enslaved men, women, and children in Upcountry Fairfield County.[12]

Robert Olwell, as near an unerring guide to his subject as I know, opined that if the nineteenth-century free black community was "'a world in shadow,' its eighteenth-century predecessor was cloaked almost entirely in darkness." From its inception as Charles II's 1663 proprietary grant to Anthony Ashley Cooper (future Earl of Shaftesbury) and seven other royal favorites, South Carolina was called the "colony of a colony" in economic and cultural fealty to its Barbadian and Saint Kitts founders. In 1670, the *Carolina* brought the first settlers bearing philosopher John Locke's profoundly reactionary *The Fundamental Constitutions of Carolina* to Albemarle Point on the Ashley River. Soon after, Izards and Middletons claimed considerable acreage along the Cooper River near a tributary earlier called Yeamans after the first proprietary governor but to be known permanently as Goose Creek.[13] Huguenots followed after Louis XIV's revocation of the Edict of Nantes in 1689: Bonneaus, Prudhommes, and Duponts.

Parliament's subsidies of naval stores (tar, pitch, and turpentine) and indigo kept the place afloat until rice replaced ridiculous efforts to grow sugar after 1720. As with the introduction of vaccination to New England, the present historical consensus holds that West Africans brought *glaberrima* rice culture to South Carolina. "All that is necessary is to point out," insisted Charles Joyner in his cognizant *Down by the Riverside*, "that none of the Europeans, whether from the British Isles, Western Europe, or the Caribbean, had any experience with rice culture at all." Fast-forward to sometime in the early seventeenth century after the sale of captured Indians to Barbadian and Jamaican sugar planters led to the colony's near extinction at the hands of allied Indians in the 1715 Yamassee War, or to its close-call comeuppance in the 1739 Stono slave insurrection.[14] Dolores would remind me that I had grasped this inflection point in race and labor on our last day before leaving Charleston.

AT MANICURED MIDDLETON PLACE PLANTATION, A MASTERWORK BY ANONymous enslaved builders on the Ashley, our jovial tour guide drawled that "violations of the Negro Act were frowned upon." South Carolina's 1740 statute – "An Act for the Better Ordering and Governing of Negroes and Other Slaves" – was a revelation, revealing how much I needed yet to know. "Other slaves" in the Negro Act referred to those large numbers of Native Americans whom the early settlers had sold into Antillean slavery at discounted rates. By 1740, the dwindling supply of Native Americans was being prodigiously allayed by Africans, notwithstanding the previous decade's avenging slave insurrections in Antigua and Jamaica in 1730, the Bahamas in 1734, and Guadalupe in 1737.[15]

The Stono slave revolt of 1739, one of the largest and costliest and most consequential in North America, very easily could not have happened that year in St. Paul's Parish, South Carolina. The insurrection's leader, an Angolan the whites called Jemmy, was a Portuguese-speaking Catholic warrior of unsuspected battlefield experience who led his eighty men toward Spanish Florida on a September Sunday morning. News of formal hostilities between Spain and England had reached the colony only days earlier. Seizing the moment at the Stono Bridge, twenty miles southwest of Charles Town, Jemmy and his followers broke into a general store for guns and powder, then killed twenty-five white men, women, and children along their way, spiking heads on the Georgia road as they marched and sang until the militia tried to head them off. "Consistent with the tactics of the battlefields of the Kongo" (in the recent judgment of a noted Africanist historian), the Angolans several times retreated and re-formed to surprise their pursuers.[16] Several groups sustained the insurgency until late November. Thirty rebels reached freedom in Florida. The last rebel surrendered only in 1742.

The Negro Act of 1740, twenty single-spaced pages of doleful *whereases*, not only codified white supremacy in South Carolina but became the ur-statute of the North American slaveocracy. The right of masters to manumit their bondspersons was abolished. Henceforth, freedom reposed exclusively with the colonial assembly, though manifold evasions would be discovered and created. To slow the dangerous African influx, higher import duties were enacted, though the two-to-one black-white ratio sped along unabated until ninety thousand enslaved surpassed forty thousand whites by 1765. Africans were denied all civil rights understood under English common law. The murder of an enslaved person by a white person became a misdemeanor. All and any assembly of the unfree was prohibited without a written pass. Their possession of guns was banned. To read was permitted; to write was a crime. "Negro" cloth of special design and color was ubiquitously mandated.

Perhaps the act's most consequential deprivation for enslaved people was its virtual embargo of even minimal economic independence, in stark contrast to Brazilian feudalism and British absentee capitalism—no Sunday markets, no personal livestock, no personal property.[17] In the valuable essay collection *The Slaves' Economy*, an astute contributor observed that "by keeping slaves out of the marketplace slaveowners implicitly acknowledged the power that slaves had earlier wielded." The Negro Act proclaimed definitively that "it shall always be presumed that every negro . . . is a slave." With a stroke of the pen, the worrisome racial intermediacy in law and practice of Latin America and the Antilles was deemed abolished. But textual ambiguity defeated textual definitive. Freedom—squelched—somehow survived. A half century before her birth, Martha Jemima Bell and her people would survive as "negroes . . . who are now free," even as South Carolina's slave owners set seal to their Magna Carta of dual identity.[18]

YESTERYEAR'S EIGHTEEN MILES FROM CHARLESTON TO MARTHA JEMIMA Bell's probable Upper Parish origins would have taken the better part of the morning. A naval air base, military housing, the Department of Homeland Security, and the new Goose Creek township transform the wetland landscape into an obliterating sprawl. Still, the Oaks Plantation, the historic St. James Episcopal Church, and the Otranto Clubhouse make it just possible for a late-seventeen-hundreds conjuration of my ancestor's time and place. She was a free colored denizen of unknown parentage, likely the incidental issue of either white charity or white guilt. Then, as unusual as the South Carolina origins of Henry McNeal Turner, Martha could have been the issue of a free white woman and an enslaved mate. She appeared, in any case, sometime after 1785: another racially mixed soul added to a small but growing number in the Lower South.[19]

Their special presence had early on had to be rendered by the state's own census takers as *M* for mulatto well before their specific color identification in the 1850 federal census. Martha Jemima Bell would be so described in the state census for St. James Parish, Goose Creek. This great-great-grandmother gave her age as sixty in 1840, which if roughly accurate meant that she was born in the decade before the 1790 first federal census. A dribble of enslaved emancipations occurred between 1737 and 1774, but, as historian Olwell's determined findings unearthed, in the ten years following 1775 there were twenty manumissions annually— a total of 199 or 53 percent of the total 379 recorded manumissions in nearly fifty years. "The most favored group were mulatto, female, children," he found.[20] All in all, it seems more likely that my generations-removed great-great-grandmother probably materialized near the end of Olwell's emancipatory wave.

The first federal census enumerators in American history counted the 1790 Goose Creek majority as numbering 2,333 enslaved people and 454 male and female whites. Surmise or circumspection may explain enumerators counting "fifteen other free persons" as neither white nor black. In the newest part of Goose Creek—the "Upper Parish" of unclaimed land and many small farmers—enumerators recorded a mystery in the "all other free persons" column. "[A]nd one was a free black female who claimed no family member other than her two slaves," as Goose Creek's perplexed Michael Heitzler noted.[21] Give or take a year, Martha Jemima would have reached the arguable age of five on the 1790 census. If she was the nameless little female whose safekeeping two slaves assured, her owner's identity and motives will probably always remain unknown, especially if the owner was free, white, and female.

This much Martha's twenty-first-century descendant ascertained with a fair certainty: In 1820, her nearest Upper Parish neighbors were the free persons of color James Fludd and Sally Johnson, both listed as household heads. This same Sally Johnson had already presented a mysterious ancestral coincidence. My examination of the digital Inventory of the Bell Family Papers at the Avery Research Center disclosed that Sally (Sarah) Johnson was the matriarch of a Bell "free family of color" unrelated to mine.[22] Martha Bell's part of Goose Creek was filled with free mulattoes, according to the parish historian. This rice-growing sprawl of a place settled by seventeenth-century Barbadian adventurers and eighteenth-century black Africans would shelter "an increasing number of 'free colored' overseers by the nineteenth century." "Some of these managers," Michael Heitzler added, "were assertive black women who carried the title of 'Maum.'"

I thought it likely that my ancestor would have merited the assertive title of *maum*. But I also saw that the glory days of St. James Parish, Goose Creek, were memories. Easily the eastern third of the parish had lost its appeal to wealthy planters. The removal to Charles Town of Ball dynasty founder Elias "Red Cap" Ball (black mistress in tow) had been an early example of growing cosmopolitan preferences among Goose Creek grandees.[23] Goose Creek, like several of Charleston County's original eight parishes, had become a backwater where the Middletons' great Oaks Plantation or the St. James Episcopal Church and the Otranto Clubhouse still announce the bygone accomplishments of masters who learned to grow rice from their slaves.

My early Goose Creek Bells have been described as people who preferred to say little about themselves, people who sought obscurity in a world of shadows where they were widely demeaned (as in the 1840 federal census) as parasites upon their communities. According to data supposedly derived from the viciously skewed fifth federal census, free Negroes north and south were infinitely worse off without the stabilizing regime of slavery. In Maine, every fourteenth Negro was said to be "either a lunatic or an idiot"; in New Hampshire "every twenty-eighth." Unlike the antebellum South's begrudged "Plain Folk" or "Common Whites" (agrarian whites on marginal subsistence) at the bottom of Hundley's *Social Relations in Our Southern States*, free people of color earned unmitigated contempt if they proved self-sufficient, and experienced lethal resentment if seen as enterprising. One sees why Ira Berlin found the logic of alienation irrefutable: "The inability of whites to live with free blacks made their removal necessary."[24]

Whatever Martha Bell may have thought about the place of her off-spring in the Palmetto State, no written expression of hers survives. She and her children kept away until the 1850s from Charleston's hothouse of aspiring cobblers and seamstresses, to say nothing of proud merchants and craftsmen hoping for membership in the Brown Fellowship or the less elite Humane Brotherhood. Martha and her fair-skinned neighbors preferred the anonymity and safety of the rural outback. Rather than Berlin's masterless slaves "forced to live and work under conditions barely distinguishable from those of the mass of slaves," historian David Dangerfield described the Bells of Goose Creek as more often masters of themselves. "They owned their land," says he, "sometimes had a few slaves, but were themselves the primary laborers of their farms."[25] Mostly, it seems, they raised corn, sweet potatoes, a bit of upland rice, and some pigs and cattle.

As isolated as they were, some of the earliest stories heard by my ancestor and her neighbors must have been about racially mixed people migrating, as it were, into whiteness. The surge of Haitian *gens de couleur* from that island's racial irruption during the 1790s had already exacerbated South Carolina's pigment complications. In 1806, John Holman Sr., an English slave trader on the Sierra Leone coast, cashed in his profits and relocated to a fifteen-thousand-dollar rice plantation on the Santee River with slaves, African spouse, and five mulatto children. Property and intermarriage eventually secured Holman's descendants a place in polite society. A similar story of the upper-class whitening of Sierra Leone slave merchant James Cleveland's mixed descendants in St. John's Berkeley Parish probably swayed Justice Harper's reasoning in that notable 1835 ruling on pigment.[26]

SOMETIME IN THE LATE 1810S MARTHA BELL HAD AN UNNAMED SON, who must have died very early because no mention of him exists in the 1820 federal census. Given her age, thirty (give or take a year), my great-

great-grandmother might have lost an earlier child or two. Conceivably, from what Heitzler's *Goose Creek: A Definitive History* tells us, Martha's likely role as a maum or plantation overseer took precedence over maternity. To have spent the decade of her twenties managing the property of an absentee rice lord, say, evinced a business shrewdness quite in keeping with the rare survival IQ that distinguished her midthirties. John Wilson Bell, the son she presented to her protector and mate in 1820, would cement a twenty-year relationship that produced five free sons and a daughter. John Wilson was followed by James N., 1821, Henry J., 1823, Benjamin, 1826, Jeremiah, 1828, and Elizabeth, 1829. Martha was thirty-five when John was born. Thereafter, she performed with clockwork regularity until Elizabeth's arrival in her forty-fourth year.[27]

This great-great-grandmother worked as a plantation overseer, probably managing a workforce of enslaved females tending flooded twenty-acre rice "squares" by the task method. She herself was overseen by one of Goose Creek's wealthier notables and political activists, a then thirty-six-year-old planter named Isaac Bradwell, son of Nathaniel Bradwell Sr. (1690–1748). Indeed, it's quite likely that Bradwell's land near Four Hole Swamp had long been her responsibility, but that she had regarded its master as another absentee Charleston grandee unlikely to chance the fevers, pests, and tedium of the Low Country outback.[28] The 1820 federal census locates him no longer in Colleton County, however, but as residing at Four Hole Plantation in Goose Creek Parish with first wife, Mary Ann Faulling.[29] The plantation took its name from an enormous blackwater swamp of ancient cypress trees and rare wildlife. Four Hole Swamp's multiple braided streams fed the Edisto and Cooper rivers, virtually guaranteeing rice bonanzas on downstream plantations.

To the best of my knowledge, neither planter Bradwell nor Great-great-grandmother Bell left a sketched or painted image of themselves. Nothing he may have written about her survived; nothing she could have said about him could she write. But some hundred years later when the New Deal's WPA ethnographers recorded their memories, the bonded workers on plantations like Four Hole told how Martha's and Bradwell's survival was owed them. "All dem rice field been nothing but swamp" was a refrain of many. "All been clear up for plant rice by slavery people." Still, Martha Jemima would have set Four Hole's daily task, which usually was said to be "as much work as the meanest hand can do in nine hours, working industriously."[30] The South Carolina "task system" may have been generally less arduous and more regulated, in keeping with the Negro Act of 1740, but Martha's overlord Bradwell almost certainly favored the controlling suffocation imposed on the enslaved as specified by slave master James Hammond's *Plantation Manual*.

Martha and Isaac's firstborn, Great-grandfather John Wilson, should have been a fine specimen of a boy. Between the births of Martha and Isaac's sons James in 1821 followed two years later by Henry, Charleston County would be shaken to its foundation by the third-most-threatening slave insurrection in nineteenth-century North America since Gabriel Prosser's close-run 1800 Virginia conspiracy, followed in 1811 by the armed march to New Orleans of the enslaved from the German Coast.[31]

CHARLESTON'S INSURRECTION ELEVEN YEARS LATER WAS SET FOR THE fourteenth of July, a historic French date chosen by a free person of color liberated from all doubt as to the sanctity of his conspiracy. When Captain Joseph unloaded 360 enslaved at Haiti's Cap-Français in 1781, he also sold his teenage cabin boy, Telemaque, to a local planter. On the captain's next delivery, the planter returned the cabin boy as an epileptic. From cabin boy to junior partner, Telemaque sailed the Atlantic slave triangle for more than a decade, mastering languages and negotiating human traffic, until both captain and partner settled in Haiti during its revolution. Sometime before 1800 Telemaque, or Telemachus, and his master relocated to Charleston, where, as Denmark Vesey, the former cabin boy established a reputation as carpenter and superior craftsman.

A prince's sum of fifteen hundred dollars came his way in the 1800 East Bay Lottery. Denmark Vesey purchased his freedom, moved with his wife to Bull Street, and joined the recently established AME Church, Charleston's largest house of worship, white or black. Aside from fondness for scripture praising deliverance and decided hostility to Liberian

emigration ("as long as my brothers are slaves, then I am too"), nothing outwardly signaled Vesey's churning detestation of the slave regime.[32] Morris Brown, Emmanuel Church's eloquent free person of
color pastor, would convince authorities later that he knew nothing of
Denmark Vesey's stealthy recruitment and indoctrination of five stalwart lieutenants among his congregation—all slaves and none free persons of color.

Six years earlier five groups of once enslaved northern black men had
come to Philadelphia from Baltimore, Wilmington, Salem, and Attlebor-
ough to form a new religious denomination based not upon doctrinal issues of faith but on their common racial insult. The meeting ended on
the eleventh day of April 1816 with all voting finally for Philadelphia's
Richard Allen as the first bishop of the new African Methodist Episcopal
Church. Even as the American republic was emergent in 1787, Richard
Allen and fellow worshipper Absalom Jones—pushed out of their pews—
hurried from Philadelphia's Caucasian St. George's Methodist Episcopal
Church that year, angrily muttering, "We shall trouble you no more." African Methodism, spreading sinuously deep through the slaveholding
South to Emmanuel Church, brought a powerful early rebuke to obedient,
passive Christianity. African Methodism, a church historian boasts,
"was the first clear, active voice . . . that was heard in the Western world
against discrimination and segregation based on color."[33]

Larry Koger blamed Vesey's failure on one of his lieutenants' violation
of a single ironclad rule. By the end of May 1822, the conspiracy's scope
had reached well more than three hundred unfree men in the city and on
several plantations. Ned and Rolla Bennett, Monday Gell, an Angolan
called Gullah Jack, Mingo Harth and son, and defiant Peter Poyas, who
would call on others to die silent ("as you shall see me do!"), coordinated
the concealed manufacture of hundreds of pike heads, bayonets, and
daggers. A duplicate key to a master's storehouse gave access to muskets
and a powder keg. Vesey's secret plantation visits eighty miles from
Charleston garnered standbys ready to block roads on July 14. Himself a
free man of color who understood the psychology of two suspect species,
Vesey pledged his confederates to unequivocal silence with mulattoes

and free black slaveholders. The politics of pigment and property, as well as the blacks' inculcated theology of obedience, threatened the conspirators' every move every day.

On May 25, a Monday, one of Vesey's men urged Peter Desverneys, an enslaved mulatto house worker, to join their conspiracy. This frightened bondsman's free mulatto friend, William Penceel, urged Desverneys to report Vesey's activities to his skeptical master, Colonel Prioleau. Peter Desverneys told all he knew, implicating rebels Mingo Harth and Peter Poyas, whose convincing denials, however, saved them. Vesey advanced his uprising's date to June 16, a Sunday when his men could blend with the market crowd, secrete themselves until nightfall, then fall upon the sleeping city. A written declaration of his intentions was carried to Haiti by an enslaved seaman.[34] Vesey's plan of last resort called for sailing captured ships from Charleston to the black republic. Meanwhile, a slave recruited by suspicious officials, one George Wilson, revealed the plot's alarming dimensions in time for Secretary of War John C. Calhoun to supply federal troops.

On the morning of the sixteenth, five military companies patrolled the streets of Charleston. Between the nineteenth and twenty-seventh of June, authorities arrested 131 suspects, among them Vesey's original conspirators together with the leader himself on the last day. Tortured, tried, and convicted, Vesey and his stalwart five denied their executioners the satisfaction of confession or contrition.[35] Thirty-five in all were executed and thirty deported. Vesey's sentencing judge's words bespoke a wounded consternation beyond his grasp that seemed almost personal. "It is difficult to imagine what *infatuation* could have prompted you to attempt an enterprise so wild and visionary," he intoned. "You were a free man; were comparatively wealthy; and enjoyed every comfort compatible with your situation. You had, therefore, much to risk and little to gain."[36]

That relative material success, that calculating respect of white people, that great legal, cultural, and pigment difference between himself and the enslaved were all sacrificed in the name of humanity's right to be born free and equal made Vesey's stunning "infatuation" the deadliest of heresies that threatened the slaveocracy's survival. The regime chanced no public martyrdom of Vesey and his confederates. Their betrayers were celebrated and compensated: Desverneys was manumitted and awarded fifty dollars annually; Penceel received a thousand dollars and exemption from the special tax on free persons; Wilson, the spy, was given his freedom and an annual fifty-dollar compensation. Koger's *Black Slaveowners* tracked these men's pre–Civil War community standing to find one of them even admitted to the Brown Fellowship Society. However, another's freedom as a black man with enslaved relatives proved too much for his sanity.[37]

Denmark Vesey's conspiracy shattered South Carolina's racial triad, although the concept of a third group available on call by the master class to control the Palmetto State's enslaved majority was both too valuable and too ingrained (nor was it a fiction) ever to be relinquished altogether. Henceforth, free people of color (individual cases excepted) came to be regarded and resented after 1822 as an untrustworthy class whose movements must be carefully policed and their tolerated liberties steadily pared back and eventually eliminated. As the perusal of Charleston city directories at the Avery Research Center had revealed, listings of FPC businesses were abolished for a decade. Nonpayment of the capitation tax, required in law but spottily enforced, provoked heavy fines. Free persons begged their wealthy white contacts for updated letters of commendation.

The Negro Seamen's Act of 1822 barred all free persons who left the state from returning on pain of reenslavement. A clear violation of federal law, it imposed temporary shore confinement of free black sailors. Emmanuel AME Church was ordered shut and Reverend Morris Brown (probably aware of Vesey's designs) was finally permitted to abandon the city for Philadelphia. The precocious Daniel Payne's academy survived a few years longer until hardening white opposition to schools for free people forced Payne to leave for the North. The first large Liberian emigration occurred just prior to Payne's departure as 180 people, free and enslaved, sailed from Charleston aboard the American Colonization Society's *Jupiter* in 1832.[38]

THE LONG-TERM IMPACT OF DENMARK VESEY'S FAILED UPRISING IM-
printed upon Martha Bell's free people of color an enduring stigmata of
tribal disloyalty. Her great-great-grandson wished that his ancestor might
have wanted a different outcome for Denmark Vesey. It seems utterly unlikely, however, that such a conspiracy made any more sense to her than
to her partner. She lived, as did most of her caste, in an inescapable dynamic of co-optation, collaboration, and unacknowledged indispensability.
Isaac Bradwell would have found the elimination of the Vesey conspirators a deplorably close call for the neighborhood as well as an augury of
formidable internal and external challenges that would face the entire
South because of the nation's new political map. It hardly escaped him
that the birth of his and Martha's first son and my great-grandfather,
John Wilson, coincided with the splitting of the United States into two
parts north and south of the Mason-Dixon parallel—into a free North
and a slave South.

To Isaac's political acumen, the inherent instability of the Missouri
Compromise guaranteed recurring sectional tensions a solid South must
never lose and a probable ultimate denouement in which she must triumph
decisively. The inflammatory "Tariff of Abominations of 1828" presented
just such a tension to South Carolina's fire-breathing John C. Calhoun,
seventh vice president of the United States, and to Isaac Bradwell, his
politically ambitious local imitation. Seven years earlier, Isaac had stood
at the forefront among Goose Creekers in Wassamassaw Chapel protesting a tariff that favored New England industries at the expense of the
agricultural Lower South.

But the much worse 1828 tariff mobilized speakers across South Carolina against "abominable" duties on British manufactures. "Let the
New England beware she imitates the old!" echoed from South Carolina
to Louisiana. Vice President Calhoun published his "South Carolina Exposition and Protest" that December, an apologia for "interposition,"
meaning the right of states to abrogate objectionable federal laws. When

President Jackson approved the revised tariff of 1832, conceived to placate the South, the unplacated Calhoun (Richard Hofstadter's "Marx of the master class") upped the ante of defiance. Calhoun called on South Carolina to nullify an act of Congress. Andrew Jackson famously vowed to hang Calhoun and invade South Carolina, and the nullificationists realized that history was not yet ready for them.

A combination of executive steel and political guile on the part of a slaveholding president preserved the union for the time being.[39] The so-called Compromise Tariff of 1833 mollified South Carolina's dignity enough for prudent unionists and pragmatists to repeal the nullification ordinance. Martha's restless protector and lover would live to vote the irrevocable secession of his state from the union twenty-eight years later. But Isaac had been astonished by the strength of the opposition to Calhoun's nullificationist extremism. To be sure, a clear majority of unionists agreed with him on the slavery question, an issue recently broadcast by northern abolitionist "fanatics" whom both he and they were resolved to combat unconditionally. Like as not, few copies of William Lloyd Garrison's new *Liberator* ever reached Goose Creek. This uncompromising screed, whose editor pledged "not [to] retreat a single inch," blowtorched the slaveocracy with a polemical righteousness and abolitionist immediatism not heard since the early days of Quaker dissent.

Furthermore, that David Walker's revolutionary 1829 *Appeal to the Colored Citizens of the World* may have circulated among some of their literate enslaved laborers truly alarmed Goose Creekers. David Walker was a North Carolina–born free AME preacher known to have met Denmark Vesey in Charleston before moving to New York City. Like Prosser's and Charles Deslondes's and Vesey's, Walker's abolitionism was inflected with a bile that stood Caucasian racism on its head, calling whites an "unjust, jealous, unmerciful, avaricious, and blood thirsty set of beings" and in the *Appeal*'s final issue warning them that unless slavery ended, "you and your country are gone!!"

Hardly unexpected, then, to find the 1835 *Charleston Mercury* reporting on September 18 that Isaac Bradwell, Esq., my misbegotten great-great-grandfather, was chairman of the Goose Creek vigilance committee.[40]

Nat Turner's spectacularly sanguinary slave rebellion in Southampton, Virginia, four years earlier surely hardened Isaac's resolve to protect his family (white and free), his parish, and the institution through which he and his class derived so much surplus capital from the sweat of the economically impoverished and politically impotent enslaved.

TO BE SURE, BECAUSE CLASS PREROGATIVE UNDERGIRDED THE SLAVE South's very raison d'être, exceptions lived side by side wherever enforcement of laws and the boundaries of freedom and enslavement intersected— above all in the Palmetto State, where racial fluidity defied legal rigor. As one of South Carolina's legal cynics advised, "Nothing will more assuredly defeat our institution of slavery, than harsh legislation rigorously enforced."[41] In so ruling in *Carmille v. Administrator of Carmille*, South Carolina Supreme Court justice John Belton O'Neall rendered virtually the state's last lenient personal manumission verdict. The 1841 Act to Prevent the Emancipation of Slaves effectively quashed the occasional increase of those manumitted by trusts, wills, and other fictional emancipatory devices. Henceforth, the state reserved to itself alone (as once before) the right of special release from racial bondage.

Although twenty years earlier, migration into whiteness of trusted and successful free persons of color had been tolerated by the planter aristocracy, the specter of Vesey, northern antislavery propaganda, and zero-sum competition forced rich whites increasingly to placate poor whites at the expense of the free people—light-skinned or dark. But Charleston's masters yielded no significant concessions to white laborers' demands for a reduction in the large numbers of enslaved plasterers, printers, boatmen, sailors, firemen, wharf holders, and railway men. After all, by property law and custom, an agreed-upon portion of the wages of the enslaved went to their owners from occupations whose pay scales undercut most of the common white competitors. As for the historical white-versus-nonwhite animus of organized labor that would bedevil postbellum America, one finds no better example than Charleston's last pre–Civil War decade.[42] Meanwhile, embittered and balked white mechanics, masons, and journeymen targeted Berlin's soi-disant slaves without masters.

"The more the utility of slavery is contested," Alexis de Tocqueville observed as he traveled below the Mason-Dixon line, "the more firmly it is established." Marina Wikramanayake noticed the forty-two free blacks who left for Liberia in 1842, the first in a decade since those who sailed on the *Jupiter*. Others would follow as the electoral power of white mechanics, construction workers, and Upcountry farmers surged in the 1850s.[43] During his famous fourteen-month Mason-Dixon exploration, Frederick Law Olmsted was both fascinated and appalled by a proper Virginia dowager's lament. "One great evil hanging over the Southern slave states" she summed up in a "single word—amalgamation." It was a crime lying "like a black cloud over the whole South," she whispered.[44] Olmsted's informant would have obliterated the flesh-and-blood evidence of her social order's sexual hypocrisy, but a commensurate punishment for the miscegenating Balls, Grimkés, Hammonds, and Bradwells never occurred to her.

Today, a plaque honors the approximate 71 Broad Street spot where Jehu Jones Sr., FPC, Brown Fellowship Society member, wealthy property owner, and the Lower South's premier innkeeper, presided. Fanny Kemble, as did William Thackeray and most visiting celebrities, dined and slept at the Jones Hotel. After Vesey, however, only the governor's legislative intercession enabled Jones to return home from a Philadelphia business trip.[45] His accomplished and prosperous son, Jehu Jones Jr., ran afoul of the state's reentry restrictions permanently after his disguised visit to a daughter in New York was exposed. The ever-grimmer reality of the two decades before Fort Sumter was that the Palmetto State's white working-class resentment of the free Africans and their "working aristocracy with callouses" so intensified as to seriously undermine the slaveocracy's political pyramid of planters atop descending grades from whites to the enslaved.[46]

Edward Laurens, whose family wealth originated in the Atlantic slave trade, lamented the rising success of FPCs. "Walk through the streets of our ill-fated city," he lectured his peers in 1832, "and see how certainly—

and how surely, and . . . how rapidly, all the mechanical arts, and all the ordinary avocations [were] becoming overstocked by persons of color" to the detriment of the "bone and sinew of our population." When white working-class impatience finally reached its peak in the wake of "bleeding Kansas" and Harpers Ferry, the Columbia legislature tabled twenty bills in the 1859 session imposing new restrictions or expulsion or reenslavement of "free Negroes." Yet as historian Bernard Powers, whose Avery Research Center intercession had proved indispensable, writes, "by 1860, 76 percent of all free black workers were still engaged in either skilled or semi-skilled occupations."[47] As butchers, tailors, barbers, coopers, and carpenters they carved out a defiant slice of the city's economy.

Men like Thomas Bonneau, Anthony Weston, Francis Cardozo, and Robert DeLarge wanted to be seen, as biographers Michael Johnson and James Roark described their protagonist William Ellison, as "not a black man but a man of color, a mulatto, a man neither black nor white, a brown man." William Ellison, cotton-gin designer, slaveholder, cultured family man, apotheosis of his class, and probably the richest man of color outside Louisiana, would die at seventy in his commodious yet unpretentious Stateburg manor house eight months after Fort Sumter was bombarded. If Isaac Bradwell said nothing about Denmark Vesey, the better to have him forgotten, Ellison said nothing, the better to have his own standing sustained. Much was at stake: the average real estate wealth of Brown Fellowship members (counting enslaveds) was $8,910.

Combined with the newer, darker-skinned Humane Brotherhood, their numbers turned Charleston's Coming Street neighborhood into an FPC preserve.[48]

Nevertheless, new mayor Charles Macbeth rode into office in 1860 with the first poor white majority in Charleston's history. A trove of remarkable letters discovered in 1935 underneath a Stateburg house captures the angst of the FPCs as the curtain of exceptionalism descends on an imperiled class. The Ellison son-in-law James Johnson maintained a lordly sangfroid as late as December 1859, writing from Charleston that "nothing would be done affecting our position." Using their kinship network and associations that defined their community of some 120 families, one hears them as they "stood up to policemen and bullies; they called on the mayor and demanded that he quash damaging rumors; they kept in touch with the whites who remained their friends."[49]

When news from Columbia reached Charleston's Coming Street on October 8 that mechanics and Upcountry farmers elected James Eason to the legislature on his pledge to eliminate free persons from white men's jobs, Ellison's son-in-law diagnosed a fatal condition: "The higher class is quite incensed but it is too late. The power is into other hands & when they have got rid of the cold [colored] population they will try to make them subordinate."[50] James Johnson signed off with a dire report: "Those who are now hunted down . . . are wisely leaving by every streamer & railroad too." Almost one thousand free persons fled Charleston for Philadelphia, New York, Canada, and Liberia after James Eason's reenslavement bill was introduced to the legislature.[51] Fort Sumter precluded the actual reenslavement of those who hadn't yet fled or couldn't. Before the hostilities began, the Haitian government hired abolitionist James Redpath to agitate among the FPCs for emigration to Haiti.

CONJECTURE BASED ON FRAGMENTARY EVIDENCE BRINGS THE SOUTH Carolina history of my Goose Creek Bells to its finish. Almost certainly Martha Jemima never left Four Hole Plantation, even after several of her six children relocated to the city. We had found her youngest, Benjamin, on Rutledge Street in the Avery's Pease index files, and her oldest, John, nearby. Both fit the profile of succeeding free artisans. The 1850 federal census, as had the previous ones, placed Martha still in the parish managing the rice, the crops, and the enslaved. Either because she really didn't know or from the venial sin of vanity—or due to the frequent indifference or incompetence of census takers—her age in 1840 and in 1850 was given as sixty. Her children's father, Isaac Bradwell, had remained with Martha until shortly after 1840, when he moved into Charleston, married second wife, Tabitha Rudd, and fathered another family.

The DNA link of Bradwell to me was sealed in blood only by genealogist Shannon Christmas: a confirmation of the reality that one can choose friends or enemies but not ancestors, however obnoxious. The 1850 census found him in Goose Creek again, perhaps called there out of lustful habit for the last time. The second wife died shortly thereafter, leaving the widower with another white son and daughter and whatever affection for Martha Jemima was bred from more than thirty years of asymmetrical symbiosis. Historian Heitzler mentions Isaac's resumed antiabolitionist prominence in the parish, whose population never dropped below 70 percent enslaved.[52] You can imagine the summary punishment he would have inflicted upon any reader of *Uncle Tom's Cabin*, if any existed in Goose Creek.

Although her political mind remains unknown, Great-great-grandmother can't have remained sanguine about her children's future in the darkening racial climate of the 1850s. The sons' trades and skills lay squarely in the crosshairs of white American and immigrant resentment. John Wilson, my great-grandfather and her oldest, supported Adeline, married fourteen years earlier, their three dependents, and his siblings with a successful carpenter's wages. Benjamin and Henry plied the same trade, and James may have been a Charleston tailor. The youngest Bells, Jeremiah and Elizabeth, probably helped their mother on Four Hole Plantation. Fair to say, all these Bells adhered to the political reticence of mulatto denizens, people who came and went quietly and competently in the city but whose traditional comfort zone was the backcountry.

In the fall of 1856, Goose Creek magistrate J. J. Browning arrested twenty-eight-year-old Jeremiah Bell for the murder of John Sparks, also a free person. The homicide's details are no longer recoverable. W. H. Hendricks, deputy sheriff of the Charleston District, transported Jeremiah to Summerville for trial, some distance from Goose Creek. The victim's family and friends probably came to Summerville to watch the trial, which might explain why John Wilson risked traveling, armed with pistol and slingshot, from Charleston to observe the proceedings. Conceivably, even if Sparks's death portended a blood feud, for a free person of color to defy the state's firearms embargo meant serious prison time.

Some Palmetto State historians have observed with keen appreciation the significance of Jeremiah's brother's recklessness. Apprehended "as a white man" and marched to the police court, where he claimed other business for his presence in Summerville, Great-grandfather paid his not insignificant two-dollar fine and lived to "pass" again when necessary. As for Jeremiah's fate, no advantage of whiteness mitigated the jury's verdict of capital punishment. He was hanged the following year.[53] Yet as I understood with a twenty-first-century ethnographic suppleness, his older brother's assumed identity represented an inflection point in the reconstitution of whiteness—a fortiori its imminent post–Civil War democratization.

It must have been a source of some concern to Goose Creek Bells when farmer Moses Jackson, their St. John's Berkeley Parish neighbor, aroused identity concerns. Ten years earlier, Jackson's 361 acres had produced corn and an impressive 1,800 pounds of rice. Jackson, listed previously as mulatto, would claim to be white on the 1860 census, a year of raw public emotion over abolitionism and social status. On a Sunday in May 1859, Jackson's three sons were ordered to vacate pews reserved for whites or be "beaten out of the church, if necessary." The boys stood their ground and were tried for rioting and assault and battery. Five years earlier, *Abby Guy v. William Daniel*, an Arkansas race identity case involving a hung jury, two retrials, and two state supreme court rulings, had exhausted opinions below the Mason-Dixon line.

The Jacksons' trial judge's incorrect jury charge was a masterpiece of illogic:

> The defendants had the legal status of white; they could vote, muster, and be members of the Legislature; but that did not necessarily confer upon them the social rights of the pure white; and that if it was a fact that the defendants were tinged with African blood, though their legal status was that of white person, that they, the [congregation], had a right to assign them positions in the church inferior to the whites, though not among the colored persons, if there were those in

the congregation who objected to sitting with them, that they could assign them positions of inferiority though not of degradation.[54]

The jury deliberated from Friday afternoon until the following evening but could not decide. The case was terminated as a mistrial. Eventually, however, the judge convicted the Jackson boys and fined them—but for assault and battery or for an inability to be "pure white"? I don't doubt that news of their St. John's Berkeley Parish neighbor's legal embarrassment troubled Martha Jemima's household, what with Jeremiah's execution and John Wilson's Summerville evasion. If, as I believe, what distinguished these ancestors was hardly that they were close observers of their times, or that they concerned themselves much with slavery's systemic injustices, or that they had any sense of a great impending crisis, but that they were ordinary practical folks whose situations—liberty, literacy, pigment—were unusual and advantageous.

When General Beauregard's cannon reduced Fort Sumter's garrison in April 1861, only a fourth of the South's white families owned a single slave. As one's undergraduate *From Slavery to Freedom* text iterated, a mere 4 percent of southerners owned more than twenty slaves. The settled historical fact was that the South's master class fought to keep its slaves, so it was that Du Bois's "wages of whiteness" underwrote the class solidarity of four years of supreme martial sacrifice. Until Appomattox, the gospel of the 1740 Negro Act that "it shall always be presumed that every negro . . . is a slave" was the opium of a cause that would be lost. After Black Reconstruction's end, White Redemption's new gospel ordained that anyone with a drop of African genes must be a Negro.

ISAAC BRADWELL EXPECTED NOTHING LESS FROM THE BROWN FELLOW-ship Society than its address to the governor several weeks after South Carolina's vote to secede from the union, a vote he probably cast enthusiastically in Columbia. "In our veins flows the blood of the white race, in some half, in others much more than half white blood," professed Robert

Howard, the two Dereef brothers, and Anthony Weston. "Our allegiance is due to South Carolina and in her defense, we will offer up our lives."[55] Certainly, after Appomattox, the newly freed common people would remember the silence of these mulatto and brown men when Denmark Vesey was hanged.

Were she still living in 1860, Great-great-grandmother's managerial usefulness on Four Hole Plantation would have reached its term. The father of her children resided in Berkeley County now. He would die there eight years later, wives Mary Ann and Tabitha buried by Isaac's sides. Carpenters and tailors were expected to be in great demand when the war stimulated the state economy. Martha, if extant, should have been relieved that her sons would survive the expected short but bitter conflict. All in all, the family would have been wise to maintain its customary watchful low profile, alert to opportunity, but now with a much heightened awareness of its vulnerability as a class.

I found Martha Jemima on the 1850 federal census, where she restated her age as sixty, though my best calculation supports an approximate sixty-five years. Ten years later, Great-great-grandmother's absence at more than seventy from the federal census is persuasive evidence of her demise. Given her role as overseer at Four Hole, a presumption of literacy seems reasonable.

The end of the Confederacy where it began, in Charleston Harbor, on April 14, 1865, cannot have been missed by the four brothers and sister Elizabeth. On February 17, Beauregard's rebel forces evacuated the city. The following day, troops of the colored Fifty-fourth and Fifty-fifth Massachusetts Volunteer Infantry Regiments reached Charleston. On the twenty-first, they marched through the oddly silent, then hesitantly jubilant city to the Neck. Lee was yet to surrender at Appomattox and a degree of building joy in the presence of the city's new occupiers continued until Lincoln's secretary of war, Edwin Stanton, ordered a grand memorial ceremony held at Fort Sumter. Martha Jemima's Bells surely knew that the same commander who had surrendered Fort Sumter, Robert Anderson, raised Old Glory there four years to the month after the fort's bombardment on April 12, 1861, with Denmark Vesey's son Robert, Daniel

Payne the schoolteacher, and Robert Smalls of *Planter* fame present as honored platform observers.

My ancestral narrative becomes cloudier after Reconstruction commenced under a former Confederate politician appointed provisional military governor by Andrew Johnson in June. Governor Benjamin Perry affirmed the abolition of slavery in almost the same breath as black codes de facto restored the institution together with a franchise restricted to property-owning whites. The reaction from Charleston's brown aristocracy, combined with congressional unhappiness with President Johnson, augured the modus vivendi of black and white moderates that coalesced in the new year.[56] A reasonable reading of how Martha Jemima's offspring saw their future in a South Carolina dominated by black and white elites suggests an impatient disaffection on John Wilson's part, a questing readiness for a much more congenial socioeconomic space.

He and Adeline must have gone to Georgia with their six children not long after Major Anderson hoisted the Stars and Stripes above Fort Sumter. James, a year younger than his brother, probably went with them, or followed soon after. Benjamin and spouse Ella stayed at home, where the Charleston city directory finds them at 33 Warren Street in 1915. The youngest Bell, Elizabeth, remains unaccounted for in my research. How long John Wilson and Adeline and children resided at Atlanta's 352 Crew Street can only be guessed, but the 1870 federal census gave this address along with the name and age of their youngest: John, age four. John Henry Bell had taken his first breath on September 27, 1866, in Sherman's destroyed city. Alice King was yet to be born on James Wiley Belvin's postwar plantation.

4

• • •

UP FROM SLAVERY

The Black Belt Lewises

I remember the framed photo as a quaintly amusing image hanging from my parents' bedroom wall in our Atlanta home. Harriett Virtue Cunningham Smith Lewis, my father's mother, was a little brown-skinned woman whose no-nonsense expression and upended corncob pipe stared at me from beneath a tilted bowler hat. The world of this nineteenth-century figure seemed all the more remote to a son who was the fifth issue of a fifty-year-old father, his concession to his second wife. Indeed, what little curiosity I permitted myself about Grandmother Harriett "Hattie" Lewis amounted to minimalist queries that elicited, in their turn, canned responses from my imperious, busy father.

My father and I coexisted much in the manner of a new hire alternately praised or ignored by some preoccupied manager of an overextended business. Instead, my older half siblings' teen years earned most of his attention. Later, their war years in uniform, followed by marriage, children, career building, put their concerns center stage for his first wife, and, when the baton passed, my capable mother. Meanwhile, I passed through puberty in a postwar family whose healthy sibling tumult gradually subsided as suave John Jr., feral James Walker, introspective Milton (all GI Bill funded), and redheadedly independent Anita went off to have their own families. As my mother's only offspring, I came of age effectively as an only child whose preoccupied, well-known father had never found the time to bond with him. Nor had I, his precocious son, ever found the time or motivation to know him. For both of us, mutual understanding would come better late than never, toward the end of the smug Eisenhower decade.

Soon after relocating from a dusty little south Georgia township, Susie Celeste Jenkins, my father's widowed oldest sister, died peacefully after seventy-five-odd years of selfless Methodism in her neat, new Atlanta home five days into 1957. Aunt Susie astonished Lewises far and wide with a typed ten-page document discovered among her papers. "The History of the Sim and Hattie Lewis Family," a multigenerational chronicle of luck, survival, and hard-earned success, was seen as an almost providential gift to a clan full of self-esteem yet lacking information on much of its own past. It became a wonderful treasure-hunt map of Lewis places forgotten, unknown, and imagined.[1]

The sway of reminiscences possessed our house that summer. My father found many of his sister's revelations refreshing, remembered some as poignant, but agreed a few were too long forgotten to credit. I came home from New York City in 1958 a newly credentialed twenty-two-year-old historian immensely pleased with myself and scheduled to sail in a few weeks for further graduate study abroad. I was later to regret my graduate school condescension that dismissed as almost useless Aunt Susie's lost world of what I saw as armpit place-names and stereotypic personages. Ellaville, my father's presumed birthplace, was situated in a void. Oglethorpe signified escape from wretchedness, agrarian and racial. Then, as if out of the red clay, my father's remote past summoned both of us.

Today, Schley County, Georgia, has the distinction of bordering Plains County, birthplace and periodic residence of James Earl ("Jimmy") Carter, thirty-ninth president of the United States. In that July of 1958, Schley County observed the dedication of the John H. Lewis Consolidated High School at Ellaville, the county seat. My father had shared news of this seeming distinction with the usual wry composure he re-

served for unanticipated breaks in the color line, now less rare since
Martin Luther King Jr.'s triumphant 1955–1956 Montgomery bus boycott. He was proud that even in a backwater place 125 miles due south
from Atlanta enough people were stirred by the times and a local son's
renown to wring a long-overdue concession from Schley County's Board
of Education.

My best memory of the school dedication is of an early Saturday
morning start, myself at the wheel of our Buick Roadmaster as Dad and I
headed down U.S. Highway 19/41 for the Ellaville known to me only from
Aunt Susie's family history. Ours was a time-stopped Saturday afternoon
never erased from my memory after seeing the eponymous brick structure sprawled across twenty hilltop acres. The heavyset gentleman hur-
rying to our parked car prompted my father's brusque exit, exclamatory
salutation, and effusive embrace. Frederick Douglass ("F.D.") Harrold
had been an outstanding undergraduate athlete from Cotton Belt Georgia when young John Lewis was president of Morris Brown College thirty-
five or more years prior. It was obvious that Harrold's lifetime service as
Schley County teacher, principal, and all-purpose coach had somehow
conjured the race relations wizardry that made this dedication ceremony
and our presence possible.

I learned much later that until the John Lewis high school was built,
Ellaville's only public school for black youth had been a 1928 wooden
structure with a seven-month school term for grades one through ten.[2]
For most black males, public school had ended after third or fourth grade.
But on that day, our arms interlocked, Principal Harrold propelled my
father and me before a congregation of local worthies distributed into
two racially separate receiving lines of curious black and white inspec-
tors. We walked as through a biracial gauntlet of greetings, extended
hands, questions, and biblical exclamations. One voice above the com-
motion, black and regal, broadcast a boyhood memory of my father; another, white and authoritative, boasted its delight that "John's made us
all proud down here." I banked in my memory compliments paid my sep-
tuagenarian father by several mature ladies before he appeared at the
speaker's platform. A supremely satisfied Frederick Douglass Harrold

stood ready to introduce Dr. John Henry Lewis. My father's speech was pure Horatio Alger–joins–the–NAACP, climaxed by an uncharacteristic fatherly notice of me, all well received. We departed after an attentive tour of the library, classrooms, basketball court, and assembly hall, and the sizable luncheon spooned by sizable ladies. Dad's facial expression signaled enough toleration of choreographed biracial backslapping—Jim Crow etiquette, as it were.

We discussed Aunt Susie's family history on the road out of Ellaville back to Atlanta. She gave us a Proustian opportunity to share a lost time that I intuited would, given Dad's weak heart, probably never return. How had he surpassed his past? was what I needed to know. I had learned from Aunt Susie's history that grandparents Hattie Smith and Sim Lewis produced seven children, "namely, Susie Celeste, John Henry, Jessie Mae, Smith Milton, Mazie Willard, Uriah Jackson, and Henrietta." Of Berry Lewis, John Henry's and her paternal grandfather, Susie knew little, except that he "owned a good home in Oglethorpe."[3] To my question, Dad answered that it had been most unusual for Berry Lewis to emerge from slavery a property owner. That fact, he said, enabled his father, Simeon, or "Sim," to acquire considerable Cotton Belt farmland. But it seems the law of mortgage perpetuity finally ruined Sim, Dad sighed, then followed his thought train to Oglethorpe, where his defeated father moved with his family and died aged forty-four in 1903.

His thoughtful mood turned uncharacteristically confessional within a few miles of the capital. I learned that Hattie and the chronicling Susie had financed both his and his physician brother's educations—starting early with African Methodist Episcopal schools or American Missionary Association schools for the boys. Hattie compensated for her sixth-grade education with a banker's acumen, whereas her oldest child, self-sacrificing Susie, put her future on hold for the family. Americus, a few miles farther south, offered them more opportunity. Dad recalled how his mother and sister's corner store sold provisions and farm supplies, made loans, and served as Americus's black labor exchange.[4] Rereading Susie's family history a day later, several passages struck home: "Deeply interested in my brothers and sisters, [I] gladly gave up the most of my earnings toward their education." Susie quotes her sister Mazie's praise: "Sister, holding to God's Almighty hand, and working side by side with Mother, did not let go until Brother John finished Morris Brown College, Yale University, and the University of Chicago, and Smith had completed the medical course at Howard University."[5]

Short lives in Ellavilles or Oglethorpes had been the fate of most southern black men until the Second World War. My father had always been an exception all of us took for granted. Now I saw how John Henry Lewis's future happened. Three weeks later, I boarded the student exchange ship SS *Arosa Kulm* in Brooklyn, New York, and sailed for England. I never saw my father alive again. John Henry Lewis survived several seizures before he fell to a massive heart attack that fall.

A few years later, when I returned to fulfill compulsory military service, I was told by an official of Schley County's education board that my father's school had been destroyed by a tornado. I shared the revelation with my half siblings, who, like me, probably parked this sad memory among the vicissitudes of an anomalous backwater occasion. Then, in

John Henry, Yale Divinity School, 1913

the spring of 2005, my family's history would bring me back to Ellaville
more than fifty years after driving my father there in the summer of 1958.
I was astonished to learn that, like Faulkner's undead past, John Lewis
High had never been destroyed, that it had delivered its last class of graduates in May 1970, that it had even lived on as a demoted elementary
school for a few years until its final decommissioning in 1973. The eponymous structure still stood, intact and forlorn, with many alumni devoted to its repurposing as a community center.[6]

The serendipitous 2005 new news had come from a then unknown
Clarence D. White in Chicago. A Lewis High School graduate, Morehouse
College alumnus, and financial consultant, Mr. White introduced himself as my father's Schley County biographer—unauthorized. His typed,
single-spaced four pages traced my father from birth in Macon County's
vanished Spring Hill community to Ivy League education and academic
administration until burial in Atlanta's old South-View Cemetery. Although I had sent grateful email thanks for his biographical profile—"Rev.
Dr. John H. Lewis (1884–1958): Eminent African-American Educator
and Methodist Minister from Schley County, Georgia"—I had soon let
correspondence lapse with my Chicago source. A decade later, my solici-
tous cousin Bettye Lovejoy Scott phoned from Atlanta to establish the
bona fides of a total stranger who astonished her with his detailed knowledge of our respective ancestors.

Clarence White, now retired in Atlanta, had been intrigued by our
mutual Lewis and Lovejoy roots in southwest Georgia. He regarded us, it
seems, as exemplary descendants of Jim Crow's unvanquished minority.
Furthermore, as we would soon observe firsthand, Clarence possessed
both a visceral and a historically contemporaneous understanding of
Georgia's Black Belt. Our curiosity about the many unknowns in our
Lewis and Lovejoy origins proved irresistible. And so he persuaded my
cousin and me to spend a long, full summer day with him and a copilot in
Macon, Schley, and Sumter counties.

We stopped on Clarence's command almost at the Schley/Macon
line, where oaks lined the red clay nowhereness of a vanished neighborhood we learned was once called Spring Hill community. We turned

onto a tree-lined dirt road, arrow straight past abandoned tires and rusted farm equipment, until our veteran local historian halted us at a clearing holding a long-abandoned frame structure. As Clarence White revealed the meaning of this place, I photographed the humble, weather-beaten Spring Hill AME church-school where my four-year-old father had learned his ABCs. It was in this clearing that John Lewis and his siblings (probably marched daily there by the stern Hattie) began climbing out of serfdom some twenty years after the Emancipation Proclamation. It occurred to me that I had been five or six years old when Mother showed me Dad's *Who's Who in America* entry, one of my childhood talismans. My car companions observed a considerate silence while I mastered my emotions.

Whether or not John H. Lewis Consolidated High School would have survived a real tornado, its longevity had been fatally compromised almost from inception by local, bitter, petty racism, certainly widespread in rural Georgia but, as Clarence reiterated during our trip, mean-spirited and endemic to Schley County. From Reconstruction to World War II, the county's record of racial violence and systemic oppression had exceeded its neighbors'. Tax-supported public schools came belatedly to Georgia after 1870, proposed by the lone remaining Black Reconstruction assemblyman. After *Plessy v. Ferguson*, separate racial schools were supposed to be equal, but their existence had been historically so barely tolerated by whites in Black Belt counties like Schley, Sumter, and Dooly that Atlanta Chamber of Commerce moderates decided after World War II that attention finally had to be paid. In June 1949, *The Atlanta Journal* headlined its staff writer's surprisingly honest article SCHLEY COUNTY JUSTLY PROUD OF ITS MODERN WHITE SCHOOLS; SETUP FOR NEGROES SUFFERS FROM OVER-ALL LACK OF FUNDS.[7]

Two thousand whites had denied three thousand blacks a single school bus to carry 775 pupils to fourteen "Negro school buildings range[ing] from poor to bad," reported George Goodwin. "Of the total 26 colored teachers, eight never went to college, and only seven are college graduates." The best of the fourteen schools was Simmons Chapel, with two teachers and one hundred students, reported Goodwin. Schley County's

Caucasian school superintendent boasted, "This year the school board provided a new water pump in the back yard" for the school. For the title of the county's worst school, Goodwin learned the winner was "the old, unpainted, rundown Negro High school located in Ellaville." Its 135 elementary and 46 high school pupils sat on "crude homemade wooden benches with an occasional manufactured desk, long since abandoned by the white schools."

Staff writer Goodwin found Frederick Douglass Harrold, my father's future sponsor, conscientiously at work as a skimpily paid Ellaville principal whose only office was "the desk at which he teaches a full class schedule daily." In one room Goodwin noted a wall "painted black [that] serves as a blackboard . . . If you can turn your back on the Negro picture in Schley County," George Goodwin winked, "everything else looks rosy." "The little county, located just north of Americus, is justly proud of its single consolidated white school; of its well qualified white teachers; of its wide program of white student activities; of its white transportation system; of its extra payments to white teachers; and of the outstanding record its white graduates have made in college. For its Negro schools it offers only apologies and promises of future improvements, 'if we can get the money.'"[8] Six years later, however, the Supreme Court's enforcement decree certainly never registered with Schley County Caucasian taxpayers, most of whom dismissed the Atlanta newspaper's reporting as wickedly uncalled-for.

The unanimous first decision in *Brown v. Board of Education* on May 17, 1954, like the Supreme Court's second unanimous opinion of "all deliberate speed" the following May, struck the deep white South like double Appomattoxes. Hardly had Chief Justice Earl Warren read the uplifting opinion invalidating *Plessy v. Ferguson* when the South's senior bigots, Virginia's Senator Harry Byrd and Mississippi's Senator James Eastland, proclaimed that "racial integration is not going to be accepted in the South."[9] With some encouraging exceptions in the border states (Delaware, Kentucky, Tennessee), Mason-Dixon line America gambled and won a half decade of massive resistance to civil rights progress. After a Gallup poll had reported only a bare majority of Americans favoring

the Warren court's decision that their president evinced scant enthusiasm for, the neo-Confederate doctrine of "Massive Resistance" gained a
momentum that seemed almost unstoppable. Asked by reporters two days
after the court's first decision whether he had any advice for the South,
Dwight Eisenhower replied, "Not in the slightest."

After sixty years of separate-but-equal noncompliance under *Plessy*,
at which Schley County excelled, "equity" public schools financed by
guilt-ridden bond issues that pretended to be "separate but equal"
sprouted like mushrooms in the southland. In Ellaville, Georgia, the un-
wonted clamor of black families motivated by *Brown* and the successful
Montgomery bus boycott finally closed Principal Frederick Douglass
Harrold's half-century-old, dilapidated firetrap in the spring of 1957.
Funds appropriated by the state built John H. Lewis Consolidated High
School, completed by the end of 1957. I never knew, nor did it even occur
to me to ask in the summer of 1958, whether an accompanying county
bond issue to equip the impressive building had been defeated by most
white voters. Even more embarrassing was the realization that my then
twenty-two-year-old's civil rights acumen had virtually ignored the South's
vast, rushed investment in equity racial education—i.e., permanent de-
ferral of racial integration in public instruction. But I was certain that
my father had to have been aware of the intrinsic fraudulence of what
had been committed in his name that summer. And that John Henry Lewis
had abided a chimera for the sake of a possibility—hence his courtly impatience I sensed that afternoon.

On the 2005 trip with Clarence, a small group of well-dressed black
people awaited us outside Ellaville's decommissioned high school. Clarence had excelled at John Lewis '64, Morehouse College '69, and Northwestern University School of Business '72. Between junior year and senior
year in college was a fellowship year spent in France. Introductions of my
cousin and me by Clarence commenced, and then I begged these accomplished men and women, whose long years of active devotion to their high
school were so exceptional, to share their stories. Everyone had experienced John Lewis High as four precious, almost unexpected, transformative years, I heard.

Notwithstanding the new desks, lockers, finishings, industrial shop, and even gymnasium eliminated from the Atlanta architect's design, church collection trays, ingenious community artisans, parental sacrifices, and classmates' fundraising had somehow defied the county board. Above all else had been F. D. Harrold's dedicated faculty: Mrs. Thelma Walker, the social science teacher, who organized voter registration in Americus in 1965; science teacher Mrs. Bobbie Smothers Balkcom, whom Clarence credited for his first prize in chemistry at the 1963 state science fair at Fort Valley State College. It certainly seemed that, until its curious closure after 1970, John H. Lewis Consolidated High School had been a fine educational success. Bettye and I marveled at the remarkable esprit de corps of these two dozen earnest people.[10] We followed the group into the old assembly hall to learn of its decade-old plans for repurposing and rehabilitating its beloved school.

Schley County's equity high school was dealt a mortal blow in December 1969 when a federal district court ordered Georgia's public schools racially integrated. The following September what had been my father's brick-and-mortar eponym received its first racially integrated grades three through seven as the renamed Schley County Elementary School—a titular metamorphosis to which Ellaville's black citizens finally acquiesced only after the moniker John Lewis Campus was informally attached.[11] My father's building had lain abandoned on its twenty acres since 2000. Instead of the donation as a community center, the county school board priced the campus at a take-it-or-leave-it $100,000. The aging Lewis High School alumni had assumed a local bank note to prevent demolition. The local bank loan was repaid, but the alumni contemplated another loan to complete designs for a community center.

THE SEEDS OF THIS UNFAIRNESS WERE PLANTED MUCH EARLIER, OF course. My father's Schley County Reconstruction history began in a flash of freedom to be followed by widespread immiseration. Writing of Black Reconstruction's disappointments, of the struggle of blacks for a share of power in Reconstruction Georgia, Edmund Drago, echoing W. E. B. Du

Bois, decided the outcome was "a splendid failure." With numbers on their side and literate men as leaders, Thomas Holt's gamely titled South Carolina monograph, *Black over White,* culminated with blacks permanently disempowered by whites. Eric Foner's exhaustive canvass carried the grand national impasse to its climacteric year, 1876, "mark[ing] a decisive retreat from the idea, born during the Civil War, of a powerful national state protecting the fundamental rights of American citizens." Joseph Reidy chose *Illusions of Emancipation* as the elegiac title of his final Reconstruction opus.

In his great book's penultimate chapter, "Back toward Slavery," Du Bois judged the years from Appomattox to the 1876 national election a tragedy of Aeschylean proportions:[12] Trust Du Bois to score Reconstruction in the key of D minor. To ask why enslaved Africans who emerged as elated freedpeople, who struggled doggedly as Negro citizens until reclassification as separate but equal colored people, who then morphed into blackness that finally extolled their African American hyphenation in a land settled by European tribes to which they came as the first involuntary immigrants, is to interrogate the conundrum of a great nation's greatest failure. Accounts of calculating planters fostering mutually beneficial labor arrangements can be found in Reconstruction literature. Davis Bend and Mound Bayou were two Mississippi settlements so successfully worked by brothers Joseph and Jefferson Davis's freedpeople that President Grant credulously extolled them as a "negro paradise."

But examples of equitable economic collaboration between former masters and former enslaved—to the extent they ever really existed—had so far vanished after Emancipation's first planting season that the cynical augury of one white Alabama planter encapsulated his region's racial paradigm for the coming century. "The nigger is going to be made a serf sure as you live," he gloated. "It won't need any law for that. Planters will have an understanding among themselves: 'you won't hire my niggers, and I won't hire yours.' ... They're attached to the soil, and we're as much their masters as ever. I'll stake my life, this is the way it will work." That was the way it worked. That Alabama planter anticipated a future that a Texas freedman had been equally certain could never come to pass. "We

thought we was goin' to get rich like the white folks," Felix Haywood recalled. "We thought we was goin' to be richer than the white folks 'cause
we was stronger and knowed how to work, and the whites didn't have us
to work for them anymore." After almost three hundred years of building
the South and the rest of the nation, his people's time ought to have come.
"But it didn't turn out that way. We soon found out that freedom could
make folks proud but it didn't make 'em rich."[13] The record, in other
words, is what the Alabama planter predicted and the Texas farmer endured. Serfdom and jury-rigged voting rolls lay in a future that my paternal Georgia ancestors defied while Reconstruction lasted in the Black
Belt counties encircling and radiating from Macon.

Henry McNeal Turner, thirty-one, South Carolina freeborn, AME
Church–ordained, and Freedmen's Bureau first nonwhite chaplain, told
an amusing story soon after his December 1865 arrival in occupied Georgia: that an epidemic of fear seized white people that the freed black people were plotting to kill them en masse on Christmas Eve. As ridiculous
as it sounds to contemporary ears, reports of white fears of black ven-
geance on that first postbellum Christmas are documented throughout
the defeated South.[14] Yet to have made light of Caucasian hallucinations,
as did so many of the new freedpeople (as did even Turner at first), risked
missing an ontological reality deeper than politics, deeper than economics, deeper than class or religion—as deep as the color of their fear of the
bottom on top.

On December 9, the Thirteenth Amendment, abolishing slavery without compensation for the loss of the South's two billion dollars, had just
been ratified by the General Assembly in Milledgeville.[15] Four days later,
appalled by the president's restoration of Georgia and the other Confederate states to the Union, the U.S. Congress overrode Andrew Johnson's
veto to appoint the Joint Committee of Fifteen on Reconstruction, a fear-
ful first step on the road to Charles Sumner's and Thaddeus Stevens's
Black Reconstruction soldered to the Fourteenth and Fifteenth Amendments. But the sibylline Turner, who introduced himself in the winter of
1865 as the "unordained Bishop" of Georgia's African Methodist Episcopal Church, couldn't have been more reassuring to a political realist like

Major James Wiley Belvin of Houston County. During Turner's first eighteen months, this future firebrand paid scant attention to the needs of the black landless.

A believer in beneficent market forces and the saving grace of the work ethic, Turner, like most of his Methodist ministerial peers, predicted better conditions as almost a matter of course. "Now as labor is popular, and it being man's normal position, let us now show the world we can perform it," he sermonized. As did his contemporary counterpart Frederick Douglass, who only asked of the laws, "Give him [the ex-enslaved] a chance." Harsh judgments on the laissez-faire ideology of a Turner or a Douglass and other postbellum black leaders deserved some mitigation. Black disciples of John Locke might have conceded the logic of that ex-enslaved man who challenged his Union Army deliverer: "If you had the right to take Master's niggers, you had the right to take Master's land too."[16]

In fact, the year 1865 had begun almost providentially with respect to available land for the newly emancipated. Asked by Secretary of War Edwin Stanton for wisdom in unsnarling thousands of ragged, hungry freedpeople from General Sherman's march to the sea, a well-spoken seventy-year-old representative Garrison Frazier, his freedom recently self-purchased in North Carolina, answered, "The way we can best take care of ourselves is to have land." Sherman's Special Field Order No. 15, issued January 16 — the joke of Dunning School historians — though not a panacea, was the substance of the solution to the South's land question.[17] Almost half a million acres along the Atlantic coast of Georgia, South Carolina, and Florida, thirty miles inland, were confiscated to settle some forty thousand freedpeople on forty-acre individual plots. General Oliver Howard's Freedmen's Bureau offered a mule to every homestead.

John Wilkes Booth's liquidation of Lincoln on the night of April 14 aborted Sherman's land experiment at birth as Andrew Johnson hurried to pardon Confederate veterans and restore their property. The accidental president dismissed General Rufus Saxton and overruled General Oliver Howard, officers who tried to protect "Sherman's land." "President Johnson may hold almost unconquerable prejudices against the African race,"

Illinois representative Elihu Washburne feared.[18] By December 1865 federally confiscated land for the formerly enslaved people who had hoed, plowed, diked, and harvested it had been rendered a solution too radical for most Radical Republicans. The land question, then, had by early 1865 already become a third-rail question for Henry Turner and his confederates, ambitious men who had to make political sense of Andrew Johnson's negrophobic Reconstruction of Georgia. The prolific Wesley J. Gaines, historian of the AME Church's Reconstruction years, extolled Turner as one "so much needed in those early days at the close of the Civil War."[19]

The almost plaintive political modesty of the forty black men assembling at Augusta's Springfield Baptist Church in early January 1866 set the tone of their leadership well into the next two years. If not drafted by Turner himself, the Georgia Equal Rights and Educational Association memorial addressed to the planter-dominated Milledgeville General Assembly channeled the petit bourgeois advancement agenda of his ministerial allies. "Suffering from the consequent degradation of 246 years of enslavement," their document placated, "it is not to be expected that we are qualified to take our position beside those who for all ages have been rocked in the cradle of civilization." Milledgeville's mid-March answer to these self-effacing Augusta, Macon, and Savannah leaders was the so-called black codes, laws that begrudged the freedpeople limited rights and precluded jury service, office holding, and suffrage.[20] There matters stood stymied throughout 1866 as three or more varieties of congressional Republicans battled with their chameleon president for control of American history and the subsidiary destiny of more than three million newly freed African Americans.[21]

The November Republican landslide empowered the congressional Radicals to such a degree that in the follow-up elections after March 1867 there came a troubling Democratic rebound among northern whites. That Georgia and all the ex-Confederate states except the president's Tennessee had rejected the Fourteenth Amendment hardly surprised the party's Radical leaders, who rightly blamed Johnson. Far more alarming to senators Charles Sumner and Ben Wade, together with representatives Thaddeus Stevens, George Julian, and Henry Wilson, were the outright or delayed rejections of votes for African Americans by Ohio, New Jersey, Maryland, Delaware, Kentucky, and Oregon. The *Cincinnati Enquirer*'s contemptible editorial spoke for millions of white voters throughout the union: "Slavery is dead, the negro is not, there is the misfortune." Northern and western malaise about votes for blacks threatened the Fourteenth Amendment's ratification unless the votes of the new freedmen themselves ensured its passage.

The stunning Reconstruction Acts of March 1867 reduced the ex-Confederacy to five military districts.[22] On April Fools' Day 1867, General John Pope assumed command of Georgia and abolished its postwar government. It was then that Henry McNeal Turner's high-risk design for both races to live and vote together advanced from concept to experiment. Much about his Abbeville, South Carolina, origins as a freeborn offspring of a white mother explained Turner's affect among white men—his self-confidence, their tolerance: assure them of his regard in return for fair play. His Georgia Equal Rights and Educational Association gingerly commended ballots for all, reasonably recommending, "As we have got to live together, let us learn to vote together." "The really remarkable features of the Negro leadership was the small amount of vindictiveness in their words and actions," a leading Reconstruction authority believed.[23]

TWO YEARS TO THE MONTH AFTER MY SECOND SCHLEY COUNTY RETURN and with three chapters of the family history written, Dolores proposed a family history research trip. Our good fortune was that Clarence White, whose volunteer research input repeatedly bolstered the family project, had enthusiastically paused his own affairs to come with us. Pfizered and masked, as were we, Clarence waited to meet us at Atlanta's Hartsfield-Jackson's auto-rental satellite. Having known him only by voice and remarkably informative emails until then, Dolores found Clarence White's tall, old-fashioned graciousness delightful. We drove away on a fine Thursday afternoon, heading south-southwest for Americus, the snappy little city my father chose as birthplace for his *Who's Who* entry. Americus was a much tonier place than Ellaville.

Our good roadway to my father's putative origins passed near Marshallville and Oglethorpe, unique stops in my family genealogy. With Clarence as pilot we took a shortcut to the town Pete Belvin celebrated as "the most desirable place in the whole world to live." Marshallville's luster had dulled with time. The rows of colonnaded mansions shaded by magnolias in my imagination actually amounted to a few substantial antebellum residences and a good number of 1950s ranch-style structures in brick. The major and Eliza Judith reposed under impressive granite covers, an arc of evergreen shading them. After Dolores and Clarence feigned surprise that Clarissa was not entombed next to my genetic great-grandfather, we three took leave of a scene consummating a social order's endemic miscegenation.

En route to Oglethorpe, Clarence confessed several failed tries to find my father's parents in the town's black cemetery. Each of us trudged off in a different direction to find Hattie and Sim Lewis in what seemed a filled-to-capacity graveyard separated from the whites' by a well-tended hedgerow. At the end of an hour under the late afternoon Georgia sun, with no trace of my paternal grandparents, Clarence agreed that we should carry on to Americus. Then, espying Dolores off at a great distance and gesturing, we drove to her. There she stood, triumphant, between two ancient tombs: Sim's beneath its flat white stone; Hattie's covered by rustic conglomerate. Their discovery made them feel real to me for the first time.

The roadway brought us into a much more impressive Americus than Dolores and I had expected. Sumter's county seat looked fashionable and prosperous thanks to Jimmy Carter's Habitat for Humanity headquarters, a major assembly entrepôt for RVs, and the phoenix of a new regional university that was part of the reason for our two-day visit. In its heyday, the turreted grand old Windsor Hotel, upscaled not long ago, accommodated rich northern industrialists and local cotton, timber, and peach barons. Southern charm enveloped us at check-in, not an eyebrow raised. When Clarence rejoined us on the screened veranda for a humungous American dinner served by white waiters, he seconded my observation that such well-paid, secure service jobs had been integrated to the disadvantage of our brothers and sisters.

We arrived early for our 11:00 a.m. meeting with Evan Kutzler, Georgia Southwestern State University's stellar associate professor of U.S. and public history. But first we had cruised the impressive campus of the erstwhile Agricultural & Mechanical School, a colonnaded brick-and-mortar learning colossus since 1996 and, as we learned, racially reflective of the regional black and white population. Professor Kutzler's youthful appearance belied his publication accomplishments and considerable local authority. Kutzler had partnered with five historians from the University of West Georgia and the University of Alabama to complete the seven-chapter digital opus *In Plain Sight: African Americans at Andersonville National Historic Site, A Special History Study*.

Fair to say, until the Kutzler team's *In Plain Sight*, African Americans had remained historically all but unnoticed at this southern version of Arlington National Cemetery. Deployed over twenty-six terraced, manicured acres that speak today of tax dollars and federal opulence, Andersonville's serried rows of marble tombstones bookended by carved obelisks and twenty granite state monuments virtually obliterate the memory of its humble origins. The first Andersonville was built by some two thousand enslaved blacks, "supplied with axes, spades, and picks," at the place where one third of the 45,000 Union Army inmates died from scurvy, starvation, exposure, and Captain Henry Wirz's unmerciful regime. Wirz was the sole Confederate officer hanged by a military court after the war. Later that same day, Clarence showed us nearby Andersonville Village, settled by Lost Cause families and where a soaring obelisk still defiantly honors the disgraced Captain Wirz.

Once the U.S. military confiscated its Confederate acreage for construction of a national cemetery, notes Kutzler's team, "Sumter County's deserted prison quickly became a symbol of emancipation and freedom." Two hundred fifty emancipated wage earners hired their labor to convert the rebel Camp Sumter or Andersonville into a shrine to martyred freedom.[24] Andersonville National Historic Site placed the Kutzler historians in the vortex of Reconstruction Georgia: ten miles from Americus and Oglethorpe, fifteen more to Schley, and twenty to Macon County. Hardly surprising that *In Plain Sight* begins with lines from Du Bois's

The Souls of Black Folk: "Of the Black Belt"—"that strange land of shadows, at which even slaves paled in the past, and whence come now only faint and half-intelligible murmurs of the world beyond."[25]

Word of Andersonville wages for reburial and retrieval of Union remains spread like wildfire to the dispossessed and landless.[26] Natural leaders of men like the future work foremen Floyd Snelson, James Haygood, and Robert Dinkins asserted their semiliterate black selves in a time of fluid power dynamics. The hoard of skills needed for digging, clearing, landscaping, masonry, and carpentry, not to mention the army of women and children tending animals and raising crops essential to the encampment's care and feeding, appeared to secure these twenty-six acres and the expanding "Freedom Village" nearby for a future guaranteed under the new Fourteenth Amendment. The consequences that November of Georgia's rejection of the amendment had already seemed to be nullified by fast-moving developments in Washington as well as on the ground at Andersonville by the spring of 1867.

Senator Sumner and Representative Stevens (Reconstruction's "Robespierre") had all but supplanted Andrew Johnson's authority. The reformed Freedmen's Bureau, enacted over bewildered Johnson's veto, established a presence in nearby Americus and a headquarters in Macon. The American Missionary Association's so-called Gideonites organized the Sumter School for Freedmen (children and adults) in Andersonville's abandoned Confederate hospital. Very likely the African Methodist Episcopal Church had already begun common schools near Americus and in Ellaville. Hunger for learning exceeded hunger for land, but that extraordinary local learning hunger documented *In Plain Sight* aroused opposition memorably flagged by Du Bois: "Attempts at education provoked the most intense and bitter hostilities as evincing a desire to render themselves equal to the whites."

AMA "Yankee school marm" Mary Battey marveled at the swelling student population "in spite of threatenings from the whites."[27] The Sumter School began with twenty-seven in late 1866, trebled numbers in a month, and taught day and night students, with majority girls in day classes and majority adult males at night, until 1873. Sumter School transformations profited Floyd Snelson, Robert Dinkins, James Haygood, and scores of others scrambling to master the ABCs of citizenship suddenly within reach.[28] Snelson (who would matriculate at the new Atlanta University) and his men memorably faced down Andersonville's former rebel landowner and armed vigilantes when they mounted a nighttime attack on Sumter School. Suddenly also within reach was a permanent black franchise after General John Pope's military regime registered almost 200,000 acceptable black and white males to vote up or down a new constitution and delegates in statewide elections at the end of October 1867.

Irrespective of character, literacy, property, almost 100,000 black men born enslaved inscribed Xs on different-colored ballots for the first time in the history of the United States. Dunning School historian G. Mildred Thompson, punctilious and courteously racist, counted 95,214 white voters and 93,457 black voters, of whom 102,283 called for a constitutional convention and 169 delegates—momentously, 37 of these delegates were black. Atlanta, site of the convention's December 9 opening, shifted the state's political center away from the secessionist Milledgeville of the old "master class."[29] New York–born Republican politician Rufus Bullock—working with "scalawag" whites and freedmen political neophytes backed by Yankee bayonets—ensured an outcome favoring the Republicans.

Two months later, when the finished state constitution emerged from Atlanta for ratification, a Reconstruction historian described the ministerial leadership as hobbled by "an ideology of deliverance." That 80 percent of the freedmen delegates were born enslaved and no more than 10 percent were literate understandably led some to hesitate to "take our position beside those who for all ages have been rocked in the cradle of civilization." A calculating Henry Turner not only opposed the constitutional provision guaranteeing freedmen the right to hold office and sit on juries, he went so far as to favor a full pardon for Jefferson Davis as well as tax relief for distressed planters as concessions in the spirit of interracial solidarity.[30] Two black northern politicians, Aaron Bradley and the Sea Islands "governor" Tunis Campbell, objected vociferously

that a consensus that ballots for black men would come in time was patently false.[31]

During four days in late April 1868 black and white men voted ratification of Georgia's Constitution of 1868. Even though the issue of the
ballot remained unresolved, twenty-nine blacks took seats as Radical
Republicans in the lower chamber, with three in the senate. Georgia's
carpetbagger Rufus Bullock defeated former Confederate general John B.
Gordon and claimed his six-year gubernatorial term of service. Black
leader James Simms's prediction that Bullock's victory meant the fall of
"the Jerichoian wall of prejudice" showed the grievous political myopia
of his ministerial class. These black Republican men were obviously ignorant of Joseph Brown's sigh of relief. Georgia's last Confederate governor and current chief of the state's supreme court knew that the wall of
prejudice was still standing: "We got a constitution which soon placed
the State under the permanent control of the white race."[32]

MAZIE WINGFIELD, AUNT SUSIE'S YOUNGER SISTER, ASSURED MY MOTHER
that a Lewis had served in Georgia's Reconstruction government. How-
ever, no Lewises or Smiths are to be found either in the constitutional
convention's prolonged January to March 1868 deliberations or among
holders of house and senate seats in the new Atlanta legislature. Yet Aunt
Mazie's presumption was understandable. In fact, the feisty politician
Robert Lumpkin of Macon County was virtually a family member.
Lumpkin's son Lucious married Harriett, daughter of Berry and Martha
Lewis. To be sure, Lewises and Smiths knew most Sumter, Schley, and
Macon County delegates. The larger significance of Mazie Wingfield's
claim, however, was its temporal truth. My aunt's memories of her imme-
diate family were hardened in the fires of white retribution that engulfed
Georgia's Black Belt from spring to winter of 1868.

The ever calculating Henry Turner and one George Washburn had
shared a rousing equal rights platform in Macon on the last night in
March. Washburn, one of black freedom's most dedicated white activists,
was brutally murdered in bed by a white mob egged on by Ku Klux Klan

founder Nathan Bedford Forrest. On General George Meade's orders, the presumed assassins were rounded up and tried. By the time they were acquitted, Washburn's killers would take their place in a galaxy of honored white felons. The drumbeat of statewide violence shocked and benumbed military and civil authorities. Agent W. C. Morrill at Americus bemoaned a "reign of terror" in Schley County. "Some six or eight freedmen shot and a dozen or more brutally beaten," he warned a county justice of the peace. "The perpetrators . . . are well known. Yet . . . no action or trial has ever been held before any competent court." Reports of "murder and assault to kill freedmen" accumulated from January 1 through November 15 of 1868.[33]

Meanwhile, Georgia's blacks and whites were impacted from May to July 1868 by politics in faraway Washington and Chicago. By a single possibly purchased vote the Senate acquitted the impeached Andrew Johnson in mid-May. A week later in Chicago, the Republicans nominated Ulysses Grant for the presidency. In the last week in June, the GOP congressional majority enticed Georgia and the querulous, obdurate South with the Omnibus Act of 1868: union reentry on condition of ratification of the Fourteenth Amendment and guarantee of black suffrage in their constitutions. On the authority of General Meade, Governor-elect Bullock convened the state assembly on July 4. A week later, Georgia ratified the Fourteenth and on the following day Rufus Bullock was inaugurated governor under the Constitution of 1868. Meade then dissolved the Third Military District a few days later, thereby enabling Georgia's return to the union upon approval of Congress.

Hattie Smith's father probably lived to speak of more Reconstruction savagery than many freedmen who tried unsuccessfully to survive its epidemic violence. I've imagined him a cagey farmer, illiterate and proud. "Our Grandfather stood for things that are high and noble," Susie's family history certified. This maternal great-great-grandfather of mine, George Wesley Smith, seems to have negotiated enough prime acreage from an unusual local white landowner to maintain a productive family farm near Ellaville. The Schley County farm still belonged to Smiths, according to Susie. Carpenter and property holder were distinctions enough for his time, place, and race, but George Wesley Smith's inestimable historical value was to vocalize the aspirations of humble people brand new to liberty and desperately determined not to forfeit it. His eyewitness descriptions of the Black Belt "reign of terror" would eventually find their way from Andersonville to Senator Sumner himself in letters transcribed by an outraged, credentialed observer.

Had Hattie's father's opinions been sought by alert officers of the Freedmen's Bureau or General Meade's staff, they would have heard some of her father's alarming facts that a roving emissary of the American Bible Society was then scrupulously transcribing. The torching of Andersonville's "Freedom Village" a day after ratification of the Fourteenth was one such example.[34] Pastor Hamilton Wilcox Pierson was appalled by the difference he saw in the treatment of black people in the Civil War's immediate aftermath. Before the war, this former president of Kentucky's Cumberland College had visited "thousands of plantations as representative of the [Bible] Society." But now he saw a transformed Black Belt where restraints based on property ownership, labor skills, paternalism, and genetic mixture were trumped by the omnipresent enmities of the white underclass. Those tens of thousands had once been confined to pine barrens, tolerated as slave patrollers, used as labor fodder, and mocked by the enslaved, who were elevated above them by cash value. Georgia's plantocracy had survived, to be sure, but it was the venom of Du Bois's "Poor White" that infused the coming relations between the two races.

A coalition of unremorseful Democrats and calculating Republicans voted for the expulsion of the house's twenty-nine black representatives— Bibb County's Henry McNeal Turner and Macon County's Robert Lumpkin included—and the two remaining senators nine days later. The rationale of the bipartisan conspirators held that black citizenship failed to confer the right to hold office. For Rufus Bullock, control of his government virtually ended. For Turner, the ambush instigated the onset of his own race-based militancy, well tracked in James T. Campbell's intellectual history. "There is not language in the vocabulary of hell strong enough to portray the outrages that have been perpetrated," the "un-

ordained bishop's" outraged missive to Charles Sumner argued.[35] Turner's vocabulary did find language sufficient to execrate Reconstruction
Georgia's bloodiest racial assault, seventy miles south of Andersonville
on September 19. More than a dozen black men traveling to a political
meeting in Camilla were killed and at least thirty wounded. The Camilla
Massacre ended the strategic accommodation of one of the future religious heroes of my father's early years.

Meanwhile, Hamilton Pierson transcribed my great-grandfather
George Wesley Smith's graphic firsthand testimonials, studiously gathered for Senator Charles Sumner's benefit. My doughty ancestor told of
large bodies of men "riding about the country in the night for a month
before the election of Grant." George heard that every Radical would be
whipped who tried to vote for Grant. One night, "thirty or forty" came
for my great-grandfather. "They sent word that I was one of the leaders of
the Grant club," he said. "They looked in the night like Jersey wagons. I
supposed they were after me, and I took my blanket and gun and ran into
the woods." George Smith "lay out all night, and a good many of other
nights." Henry Davis, a near neighbor, "fired at them and escaped." Davis
hid in the woods for a week, "then slipped back in the night and got his
family and moved off."

George Smith told of Bob Wiggins, AME pastor in Schley County,
"whipped almost to death because they said he was preaching Radical
doctrines to the colored people." There were Tom Pitman and Jonas
Swanson, who opened their doors when the night riders "call[ed] them
out." They threw blankets over them, said Great-grandfather, "and carried them off and whipped them tremendously." Pierson noted that Richard Reese, president of Schley County's Grant Club, corroborated George
Wesley Smith's account. "We want the law to protect us," Reese demanded.
Federal protection was more than spotty in Sumter County. The Freedmen's Bureau sympathized with the planters' labor problems, and Union
Army detachments were thinly spread.

Great-grandfather's friends at Andersonville National Historic Site
found their authority as foremen downgraded and the availability of jobs
for freedmen greatly diminished. By the fall of 1868, Andersonville's

heady days of emancipatory democracy, its promise of a place where opportunity acknowledged self-improvement, had all but given way to bu-
reaucracy ordained from Washington and hires for white men. Floyd
Snelson, Robert Dinkins, and James Haygood had to have seen the curtain falling on their aspirations. "White U.S. government officers came to
see black workers not as agents of social and economic change," the *In
Plain Sight* historians decided, "but simply as a cheap source of labor."[36]
Reverend Hamilton Pierson's notebook was brim filled with drama on
Election Day in Sumter County.

The Andersonville cemetery workforce began assembling at dawn
on November 3 as the glowering superintendent and Democrat Henry
Williams watched impatiently. When Williams determined the men were
ready to march to the polling station, he broadcast the command that
their attendance at the Democratic meeting place would improve relations with the white community and protect them from reprisals. Hattie's father's report to Pierson that "Kluxers" would whip "every one that
voted for Grant, and would not give any work to any but Democrats" was
certainly common knowledge. It appears that after Floyd Snelson spoke
for his men in defiance of the superintendent, Henry Williams summarily fired them. When Snelson and his men filed back into Andersonville
late that evening, we know that they resumed work as always the next
day, having called their superintendent's bluff.[37] How well Snelson and
his men succeeded in voting, though, remains uncertain. Georgia voted
almost two to one for the Democrat and former governor of New York
Horatio Seymour. General Grant's 57,000 ballots would have been greater
had not intimidation, outright repression, and violence ruled the day.

Richard Reese's ordeal as Schley County's Grant Club president had
been typical. He slept in the woods "every night until after the election."
On Election Day, Reese emerged, walked to the precinct with all his
Grant tickets, and was relieved at seeing "more Radicals than Democrats
there." Hattie's father joined Reese, Pierson's notes confirmed. But precinct officials "would not open the polls at all." Reese, Smith, and the rest
of the Republicans remained at the shuttered precinct until noon, then

headed for Ellaville, where "only white and colored Democrats were voting." No man could vote unless his taxes were paid, Reese's men were
told. "Nearly every white man there went around to the colored voters
and told them that if they would vote the Democratic ticket their tax was
paid." Reese presented his ticket and was told his taxes were unpaid,
"'and if I put in my ticket they would put me in jail, and send me to the
penitentiary.'"

George Wesley Smith told Reverend Pierson that he saw "how they
treated others and did not try to put my vote in."[38] Richard Reese filed a
risky formal protest against voting officials with the Freedmen's Bureau
in Americus four days after the election. Months later he was still waiting to learn if the malefactors had suffered jail or fines when white-
sheeted night riders burned down the new schoolhouse he had built with
fellow freedmen. Hamilton Pierson's reports of travails afflicting community leaders Reese, Snelson, and Hattie's father may have stoked Charles
Sumner's New England wrath, but the senator's Radical Reconstruction
provided feeble to nonexistent protection in the Black Belt. Rufus Bullock, the "Scalawag Governor," had even fled to Washington a month after
Grant's victory to argue for his state's resubjugation to military rule. After
Congress voted his petition in March of 1869, Bullock's unsurpassed in-
famy among white Georgians would abolish a space for his portrait among
all Georgia's governors since 1850 to the present.[39]

One of Pierson's last sources, a Reverend Charles Ennis, expressed
searing despondency about his people's future. Ennis had brought his
family to Andersonville from Mitchell County's lethal Camilla township
near Albany. A thoughtful, self-educated new citizen, he calculated the
deadly odds against militancy and armed self-defense. "We had rather
died than go back into slavery," he insisted, "but we are worse treated
than we ever were before." As for the Union Leagues and Grant Clubs for
defense, Ennis was certain they represented a fatal prescription. "The
whole [white] South would then come against us and kill us off. We cannot protect ourselves." Obvious to him that Henry McNeal Turner's belated militancy was wrongheaded. "We want the government to protect

us." Ennis echoed farmer Cane Cook's earlier lament. "If we could only get land and have homes we could get along; but they won't sell us any land."[40]

Almost as Ennis spoke to Pierson that February day, the U.S. Senate debated the final version of a proposed Fifteenth Amendment. Although it ducked the federalization of voting rights and office holding, Congress would affirm that the right of United States citizens "to vote shall not be denied or abridged by the United States or by any State on account of race, color, or previous condition of servitude." Henry Adams, Harvard professor and son of the republic's second president, famously sniffed that the newest amendment was "more remarkable for what it does not than for what it does contain."[41] The Fifteenth Amendment said nothing about the right to hold office and failed to make voting requirements national and uniform. To Henry Turner, Macon's fighting new postmaster, however, ratification of the short, precise guarantee of black voting rights would mean the redemption of the Constitution.

But Macon's new postmaster, like Ennis, Henry Reese, and George Wesley Smith, must have been skeptical of any short-term civil rights amelioration in the Peach State. Senator Sumner's insightful correspondent also had good reason for skepticism. Hamilton Pierson put spurs to his horse a day after the local Klan's literate warning. "If after the said time, your devilish countenance is seen at this place or vicinity," warned its mid-February 1869 note, "your worthless life will pay the forfeit."[42] A month later, like Bourbons forgetting nothing and learning nothing, Georgia's legislators rejected the Fifteenth Amendment in their new Atlanta capitol building. To Pete Belvin, his father's KKK membership made complete sense given black people's demands. As though 250 years of unpaid labor and proscribed illiteracy explained nothing.

Congress, exasperated, again remanded Georgia a week before Christmas to military rule and compulsory ratification of the voting rights amendment. With Rufus Bullock in the general's baggage wagon, so to speak, General Alfred Terry assumed his command at the beginning of the year, purging high-ranking Confederate officials as well as problematic sympathizers straightaway from the assembly, a political prophylaxis his predecessor, General Meade, had resisted. Governor Bullock issued a January proclamation that Georgia's blacks saw as an uplifting exception to their bleak Reconstruction experience. To the great majority of whites it would stand as a unique racial insult whose repercussions are still heard in twenty-first-century Georgia. Ordered to reconvene with a full, purged complement, members of the original 1868 legislature, joined by three ousted black senators and twenty-nine representatives, assembled in Atlanta's refurbished opera house to debate approval of the Fifteenth Amendment in July 1869. Henry Turner returned bruised but politically much evolved. "We were wrong not to support [Aaron] Bradley," he had regretted to a fellow legislator. Nor did he now leave black farm workers to the mercy of Adam Smith's market. He was trying to organize black unions to demand monthly minimum wages of thirty dollars for men and fifteen for women in Macon, Houston, and mean Dougherty counties.[43]

The state's biracial majority finally ratified the fraught voting rights addition to the Constitution on the second of February, 1870. Even though the union reentry path seemed clear, the Grant administration delayed Georgia's return while Congress debated so-called enforcement acts, designed to defeat the region's epidemic of violence. Hamilton Pierson's timing was delicious. Pierson saw that northern public opinion was wholly deceived as to the South's present barbarism. What he heard and witnessed "may seem absolutely incredible," Reverend Pierson warned his readers, but statements "given to the public in regard to outrages in Georgia come far short of the real facts."[44]

On March 15, 1870, the former Cumberland College president, newly arrived in Washington, presented his printed book of "'statements' of facts" of my great-grandfather and his Union Leaguers to the puissant Charles Sumner just as the Senate debated the 1870 Enforcement Act.[45] Amos Akerman as Ulysses Grant's attorney general was to prove resolute in fighting the Klan in person. More months passed before Congress readmitted Georgia under the Reconstruction Act of 1867 for the second, final time on July 15, 1870. The impressively named Jefferson Franklin Long of Macon, Georgia's first and last black congressperson until the late twentieth century, was seated with the Forty-first U.S. Congress. His tenure lasted only six months, but his debut speech memorably denounced multiple Confederate amnesties.

This almost quixotic Bullock interval was doomed from the beginning as sidelined ex-Confederates, planters, and poor whites coalesced as avenging Lost Cause Democrats to oust alien Republicans and the Freedmen's Bureau and restore slave labor as tenantry. When Bullock tendered his resignation in secret in the winter of 1871, his departure from Georgia for New York on October 30 foreshadowed the humiliations awaiting his Radical Reconstruction epigones in South Carolina, Mississippi, Louisiana, and the rest. That his 2007 entry in the *New Georgia Encyclopedia* ranked him as the Peach State's most progressive chief executive until Jimmy Carter may finally redeem Rufus Brown Bullock from Margaret Mitchell's denunciation as a looting scalawag and carpetbagger.[46] Georgia's much-delayed system of public education came to pass due to Bullock's support of legislation reintroduced by the reinstated black Assemblyman James Porter of Savannah. With Porter in mind, Du Bois called the public school Black Reconstruction's triumph.

THEIR MACON COUNTY MARRIAGE LICENSE CALLS THEM SIMEON LEWIS and Harriet [*sic*] Smith. It was the twenty-eighth day of February 1877. Harriett Virtue Cunningham Smith was about eighteen, two years younger than her ambitious spouse. Hattie was the oldest of thirteen siblings, all of whom lived a good span except Parmelee, the youngest. Sim's parents, Berry and Martha Lewis, lived near Oglethorpe, Macon's old county seat, inappropriately named for Georgia's antislavery founder. "Of Berry Lewis, our paternal grandfather, we know little," the family history tells us. Unknown to my aunt, Berry profited from connections to his former master's Lewis business clan, access that would sometimes help his son's farming operation. Berry must have died before his grandchildren became really cognizant of his existence.[47] If the couple's nuptials were witnessed by family, more likely it had been the bride's parents, George Wesley and Henrietta Smith, modestly praised by Aunt Susie as ancestors who "reared one of the greatest families that ever emerged out of slavery." It seems clear that Smith lineage would have greater resonance in the Lewis children's memories.

The 1880 federal census finds Sim living near and probably farming with his father-in-law in the Spring Hill community, located near the Schley County line. Susie Celeste, our family historian, arrived in January 1879, followed almost two years later by John Henry in March. Jessie Mae passed soon after delivery. Smith Milton, who came in December 1884, was "small and frail," health deficits that left him a tiny ball of compensation. Mazie Willard's birth three years later was a godsend to her parents and Susie, the extra hand to manage three rangy boys after Uriah Jackson came in November 1892. Named for her maternal grandmother, Henrietta debuted in November 1896, the sibling fated to die of peritonitis early. All but two of my Lewis ancestors took first breaths in the impoverished eighties, when more than thirty Black Belt counties counted "not more than one in one hundred black farmers" who owned land. Twenty years later, historian Leon Litwack found that "only 14 percent of black Georgia farmers owned their farms."[48] Notwithstanding its unequivocal legal and personal benefits, Emancipation's economic consequence meant endemic landlessness—nonownership of the means of production even less requited than under enslavement.

Under the wing of her father, George Wesley Smith, Hattie and Sim raised Susie, John, Smith, Mazie, Uriah, and Henrietta on family-owned acreage during their impressionable early years. Add to that providential leg up the bonus of Hattie's literacy, acquired up to the sixth grade at Andersonville's AME school. Sim had had no schooling. Hattie taught him to read and write, notes Susie. "He soon learned his business very successfully." Sufficient to permit their migration to Oglethorpe before Susie and John Henry reached their teens, it seems. Her father showed his quickness by leading Sunday school lessons and eventually serving as steward and trustee of Oglethorpe's St. Paul AME Church. "They say he stood above the crowd," recalls Susie of her father's reputation. Membership in the African Methodist Episcopal Church—called by Du Bois "the greatest institution of the Negro race in the world"—was to serve as the family's

Wee School House, built 1880s

educational and social stepladder to local and in time wider professional notice. That stepladder's first rungs had started for little Susie and Dad with the Spring Hill AME Church's wee schoolhouse, whose remains I photographed with Bettye and Clarence ten years earlier.

"The sight of blacks carrying books often had the same effect on whites as the sight of armed blacks," a historian of this Jim Crow nadir warned.[49] By all accounts, Hattie and Sim prioritized book learning for their children notwithstanding the resentful disapproval of most of their white neighbors. Still, given the stakes against Sim's success, there must have been many long spells when farm work subordinated book learning. I could remember my father and uncle chortling about stubborn mules and cotton picking and an unmotivated brother Uriah last seen whittling on a log. Susie's education, unencumbered by farm labor or even domestic service to affluent whites, proceeded apace. She completed eighth grade at Andersonville's AME school, followed by graduation from

the city of Macon's AMA Ballard Normal High School. The AMA decision to appoint her to Ballard's faculty must have been an enormously
satisfying accolade.

Aunt Susie's accomplishments were the sustenance of her siblings'
progress. The Lewis family had fallen upon straitened times since leaving their Schley County neighborhood for Oglethorpe sometime in the
mid-1880s. Great-grandfather George Wesley Smith was dead. Sim struggled smartly holding on to the acreage left him by his father, Berry. He
insisted it was possible southern blacks would prosper after Reconstruction. The political situation had remained fluid for a time as the protections under the amended Constitution and Senator Sumner's Civil Rights
Act of 1875 had yet to be fully pared away and nullified. Mississippi's constitutional convention would point the way in 1890; in the years that followed, barely a trace of a once robust black southern franchise remained.
Lynchings claiming some 140 lives annually had begun.

We decided, Dolores, Clarence, and I, to spend our second research
morning in the property records office at Oglethorpe's odd-looking Victorian courthouse. Initially rebuffed by the white female clerk, who snapped
that unexpected visitors were unwelcome because of COVID restrictions, our mission was saved by her black superior, who emerged after she
recognized Mr. White's voice. We worked together in the long, narrow
shelved space with the general index to deeds and mortgages prior to
1899, A–Z Macon County. Sim, and Berry's widow Martha and sons, borrowed and repaid monies spring and winter over a ten-year period for
seeds and agricultural supplies. Among the combination of white land-
owners, grain companies, seed and supply companies, and a hodgepodge
of small merchants were significant loans from Jonathan F. Lewis & Sons
of Montezuma. I followed Sim as his hold on his land faltered badly after
1897. His last loan came from "Jno. F. Lewis & Sons" of Montezuma in
favor "of wife" on May 1, 1899.[50] Simeon Lewis would die middle-aged and
spent four years later.

We thanked the chastened clerk and headed for Americus with my
aunt Susie as our guide, along with my memory of Dad's ruminations
from the 1958 dedication visit to John H. Lewis Consolidated High

School. As the oldest child, Susie had felt it her duty "to help [her] mother shoulder the responsibilities of carrying on the program already planned and begun by [her] father and mother." Brothers John Henry and Smith Milton were said to have finished elementary school under the superb principalship of Oglethorpe's Horace T. Lumpkin (honored with a Georgia historical marker) followed by high school at Principal M. W. Reddick's Americus Institute. My research team and I believed Grandfather Sim's last loan provided the start-up capital for Hattie's profitable Americus store, which, together with Susie and similarly abnegating Aunt Mazie, paid for much of their men's professional futures.

Dolores counted on our finding century-old city directories promised her over the phone by a librarian at Americus's new Lake Blackshear Regional Library. The 1908 Americus city directory yielded Hattie Lewis at 1003 Jackson Street. As we parked midblock on Jackson, Clarence called our notice to the corner AME church, apparently a 1920s brick structure erected on the footprint of an earlier structure where Grandmother Hattie must have worshipped. A modest brick dwelling, obviously too recent, occupied number 1003. But at the end of the street was an empty corner lot of a plausible shape and dimensions for an enterprising Harriett Virtue Cunningham Smith Lewis's early twentieth-century community store. Some weeks later, after Clarence corroborated his recollection of a more recent business on this site, I became certain that we had found the place where John Henry Lewis's transubstantiation began.

Aunt Susie was an advanced thirty-one when she married a "very successful farmer" in 1910. She bore four sons with Sanders Bendross of Early County. Aunt Mazie, similarly ambitious and musically talented, was then a single twenty-three and living with Grandmother Hattie. Speaking for them both about their brothers, Mazie said she and Susie "gladly gave up the most of my earnings toward their education." These aunts were finally free to concentrate on their own professional careers as teachers.

JOHN HENRY AND SMITH MILTON DILIGENTLY JUSTIFIED THEIR MOTHER's and sisters' professional expectations and financial support. It must have been the case that my father and uncle supplemented significantly their sisters' tuition and board remittances through money earned working service jobs during vacations and summers in Atlanta and Washington, or from northern "hotel work," as "Uncle Doc" recalled. Fortunately, my professionally proud uncle paid for a page profiling him in Arthur Bunyan Caldwell's forgotten edition, *History of the American Negro, Georgia Edition, 1920*. My father must have balked at the subscription price for inclusion in this cornucopia of invaluable self-assessments, but from it one infers that both brothers made the best of their high school opportunities at the colored Americus Institute and Macon's Ballard Normal until each had the wherewithal for college and medical school.[51]

"Uncle Doc," as I would know my father's younger brother, earned his Howard University Medical College degree in 1911 at age twenty-seven, one year after Susie's marriage. He stares severely from the photo in his Caldwell biographical entry, affirms his Republican Party registration and Odd Fellows and Pythians memberships. After several trial runs in Americus and Albany, bachelor Smith Milton established a successful practice in Moultrie, Georgia, where "in the recent epidemic of influenza he lost only one case." Hardly surprising, then, that he became "local examiner" for America's two largest black insurance companies, Standard Life and North Carolina Mutual. Caldwell's almost inaccessible *History of the American Negro* reveals that Uncle Doc was actually commissioned first lieutenant in the First World War "but was not called" to duty.[52]

A few years earlier than my uncle, my father had gone ahead to attend the Atlanta college named for Bishop Morris Brown, the South Carolina AME preacher forced into Philadelphia exile after Denmark Vesey and more than thirty other members of his church plotted Charleston's takeover by hundreds of the enslaved in 1822. Morris Brown College, the fourth such AME institution of higher learning below the Mason-Dixon line, opened its doors on Boulevard and Houston streets within walking distance of First Church in the winter of 1885. The physical distance between them, however, was as nothing when contrasted with their respective social and economic origins. Unlike First Church and the Atlanta

University annex, Morris Brown emerged from working-class ethnocentrism and Big Bethel Methodist Church collection plates—no derived New England mannerisms and WASP philanthropy.[53] Larger-than-life divines like William F. Dickerson, Wesley J. Gaines, and Henry McNeal Turner infused their southern flagship, Morris Brown, with a morality of personal sacrifice and an eschatology of racial overcoming.

For twenty-one-year-old John Henry Lewis, a poor, ambitious student from the Black Belt's backwater, the new school in the state capital was a lifeline. My father enrolled in Morris Brown College in the fall of 1901. The previous year, Turner, in his dual capacity as presiding bishop and chair of its board of trustees, authorized a capital campaign that funded a large central administrative structure (Turner Hall) connecting the school's original north and south buildings. Turner's pedagogical impact would be greater than brick and mortar. That same year the college's theological department became the Henry McNeal Turner School of Theology, a separate entity imbued with the dynamic bishop's evangelical and political conceptions of ministry.[54] Elected presiding bishop of Georgia's Sixth Episcopal District in 1896, Turner now preached that the future of the race was Africa. John Henry Lewis should have found himself in sight and sound of enduring theological and civil rights developments during his four years.

Henry Turner's outsize early-twentieth-century impact upon Morris Brown College was broadly coterminal with upheavals that his emigrationist, political, theological, and reparationist pronouncements created for his denomination, his race, and his place in history. His African evangelizing instigated the 1896 merger of South Africa's Ethiopian Church with the AME Church, much to the British government's alarm. Two years later, Turner shocked many African Americans and incensed whites when he preached that "Jesus was a black man," and thus "God is a Negro." Historian of the South Leon Litwack's estimate seems incontrovertible: "Few black clerics matched Bishop Turner . . . in the zeal with which he sanctioned a new role and attitude for black people." Black people were told to buy guns and use them even before the Atlanta Race Massacre of 1906. The Louisiana laborer who famously gunned down pursuing constables, Robert Charles, subscribed to Turner's incendiary *Voice of Missions*. More than a century before *The Atlantic*'s Ta-Nehisi Coates, the bishop demanded "five hundred million dollars, at least, to begin emigration somewhere." Otherwise, he prophesied, "it will cost, sooner or later, far more . . . to keep the Negro down."[55]

5

. . .

THE ARC OF
WHITE SUPREMACY

The Optimistic Atlanta Bells,
1865–1894

The great historian of the South C. Vann Woodward saw few signs of recovery less than a score of years after the Civil War. The old order lay prostrate. Material decay he saw everywhere:

By the fall of 1879 Charleston was still unable to rebuild the great district in the heart of the city which had been burned over during the war. Commerce in almost none of the seaports was increasing and in some it was falling off. New Orleans was handling more cotton and sugar than before, but she was neither erecting new buildings nor repairing many old ones. Her streets were to remain cesspools and open sewers for years. Mobile looked "dilapidated and hopeless." Galveston's population had declined since 1873. Norfolk was "asleep by her magnificent harbor," while Savannah, Wilmington, and New Bern were "at a standstill."[1]

Omitted from Woodward's catalog of distress was Terminus or Marthasville or Atlanta, as it finally came to be known after 1844. A wreck of a place in 1879, Henry Grady's phoenix Atlanta was a braggadocious decade in the future. It was already known, however, as a start-over place for those who had either lost everything in the war or, even more appeal-ingly, never had much to lose: ruined planters; uprooted Confederate warriors; Irishmen no longer needed as "patterollers"; impoverished yeo-manry and landless freedpeople in a biracial stream of mechanics, mer-chants, craftspeople, former Grand Army of the Republic soldiers, and enterprising Jews.

Persons of color, free and formerly enslaved, flowed into the city from across the South in the aftermath of Appomattox. As the war ground down toward their probable defeat after 1863, surprising numbers of Deep South slaveholders responded positively to the Quaker and AMA designs for the postwar education of some of their enslaved. AMA field secretary and future founder of Fisk University Clinton Fisk canvassed the Confederacy, "planning," in one AMA historian's evangelical prose, "with wonderous wisdom for the system of schools in which all the years to come should give light and save life."[2] Some five years beyond Appo-mattox, the AMA's and Freedmen's Bureau's educational sweep through the ex-Confederacy would have established collegiate schools for the freedpeople in every state but Arkansas and Texas. The previously quoted AMA historian acknowledged an antebellum reality of the project, how-ever: "the proportion of pupils who were far more Anglo-Saxon in their parentage than they were African."[3]

My paternal great-great-grandmother Martha Jemima Bell seems to have passed her life in self-determined occupational circumstances. She or someone gave the federal census taker her age as sixty in 1850. By the South's perverse law of *partus sequitur ventrum*, Martha's progeny were born both free and as free persons of color.[4] But that my great-great-grandmother lived another fifteen years to see the collapse of the Confederacy with sons John, James, Henry, and Benjamin and daughter Elizabeth strikes me as unlikely.[5] It seems most likely that this octoge-narian ancestor was dead when the Confederacy imploded, and that her absence deprived her cautious, penniless offspring of the strong glue of a matriarch.

Martha's John Wilson probably foresaw long-overdue scores being settled as the legal separation of enslaved and free coloreds vanished al-

most overnight. Until Confederate batteries fell silent, many of his people had donated money to war relief. Marginal FPCs like his kind, who
virtually monopolized the urban small trades and crafts, now faced the
liberated ambitions and skills of vast numbers of freedpeople – even as
they faced the already fierce competition of the white working class.

THE EARLY BELL YEARS IN ATLANTA ARE INESCAPABLY SPECULATIVE.
What resources they brought with them; how they traveled, if overland
or sea, to Georgia; what Atlanta contact information they possessed;
what expectations went with them, defy recovery. Isaac Bradwell, who
survived three years after the Civil War, may have belatedly acknowledged concern for some of his children with Martha Jemima. Still a man
of consequence as John Calhoun's political disciple, Bradwell would have
been well informed of the AMA's redemptive Atlanta educational project. The association's Storrs School, housed in a Confederate boxcar, its
seams bursting with old and young illiterates, was barely a year old. With
means, reason, and perhaps conscience, Isaac Bradwell may have blessed
his oldest son's departure with money and advice. If so, the deed might
somehow explain my mother's equivocal memory of this old rice planter
and ancestral predatory progenitor.[6]

The Atlanta migration of Martha Jemima's oldest son, John Wilson,
his spouse, Adeline, and ten family members must have happened no
more than a year after Charleston surrendered.[7] The 1870 federal census
locates them all in Fulton County's ward 1, where little John Henry, age
four, my success-destined grandfather, is recorded as the first Atlanta-
born Bell. John Henry's six-year-old sister and my great-aunt Mary Elizabeth would have been the last Bell to open her eyes in the Palmetto State.
They, in order of seniority after John Wilson (forty-nine) and Adeline
(thirty-seven), were Anna (twenty-five), James (twenty-four), Emma (nineteen), Julia (sixteen), Minnie (fourteen), and William (twelve), followed
by Mary and John Henry. Dangling like an appendix was also a family
alliance about which I would not learn very much until my late teens,
two mysterious Careys (eight-year-old Charlotte and Archie, age two).[8]

Great-grandfather gave "blacksmith" for occupation instead of "carpenter," as regularly listed in Charleston's 1850s city directories. The census recorded *M* for mulatto, but his great-grandson was surprised by the illiteracy notation. Many Charleston FPC craftsmen who couldn't write, I believed, claimed to be able to read.

John Wilson and Adeline must have come to Atlanta just as the recovering railroad city upstaged the old center of Bourbon power, Milledgeville, to become the state's new capital and future theater of much of the South's fiercest Reconstruction combat. In March of 1867 a recalcitrant ex-Confederacy had been reduced to five military districts by an impatient Congress. It's not unreasonable to suppose that John Wilson brought his family to the city's first ward because of its promising prospects for a carpenter-become-blacksmith. Georgia's imminent military reoccupation resulted in the building of extensive federal barracks in a large corner of the ward, along with stables for cavalry. On April Fools' Day, Union general John Pope abolished Georgia's postwar government and ordained a precedent-breaking franchise of loyal black and white men to create a government under a constitution that accepted the new Fourteenth Amendment as a precondition for Georgia's readmission to the union.[9] This reconstructed franchise guaranteeing the Fourteenth's adoption would have permitted John and son James to vote for the new state constitution during Georgia's statewide October elections.

Had father and son voted for the first time in their lives, however, their satisfaction might have taken a cautionary turn when they saw that the state's July ratification of the Fourteenth Amendment was all but nullified by an epidemic of Ku Klux Klan savagery. That precipitated the collapse of the unlucky acting governor Rufus Bullock's shaky Reconstruction coalition of local Republicans, collaborationist whites, and activist blacks.[10] But politics were a secondary concern at best for the family. The respective blacksmith and shoemaking skills of father and son ought to have kept the family afloat in Atlanta's superheated economy of new housing, booming transportation and commerce, and proliferating service industries. Anna and Emma were seamstresses whose fine prewar needlework for ladies on Charleston's Battery ought to have yielded surplus household income from Atlanta's nouveau riche mistresses.

Unlike a great many grown black women compelled to service in white homes or driven to demeaning drudgeries outside the home, Adeline's census occupation of "keeping house" meant that her concerns could center on taking care of the youngest Bells, Mary Elizabeth and John Henry, as well as enforcing domestic authority over prepubescent Minnie and William. Better still for Adeline's responsibilities was Julia's recorded "at home" presence—surely meaning shared managerial and cooking duties. The "at home" citation also more frequently indicated, as it did in Julia's case, reading and writing lessons at the new Storrs School for ambitious freedpeople, to which Julia probably brought "at home" little Mary and Grandfather, although the distance to ward 4 was considerable.

Such was the urge to learn that AMA educators and Freedmen's Bureau officials had been astonished at the sums already expended by the newly freed, the number of schools early built by their Baptist and Methodist churches, and the intensity to overcome shown by a people forbidden generation to generation to learn how to read and write about a world mostly built by themselves. As a retired Storrs School teacher remembered, "To see children go away weeping because they had been refused admission . . . was too much even for my hard heart."[11] A good thing, then, that Great-aunt Mary and Grandfather John Henry were among the school's fortunate.

A careful reading of the 1870 and 1880 federal censuses shows the Bell family steadily profiting from the religious and educational opportunities funded by the American Missionary Association and significantly amplified after the Reconstruction Congress restored the Freedmen's Bureau over Andrew Johnson's veto. Historian Clarence Bacote, who lived much of the school's life as a senior faculty member, fills in the origin story of Atlanta University and its Storrs School subsidiary indispensably. That old Confederate boxcar begun as the AMA's first school became almost overnight too small. Thanks to Reverend Henry M. Storrs's generous Cincinnati congregation, the Storrs School materialized in 1866, bringing New England schoolmarms Jane Twitchell, Amy Williams, Carrie Gordon, and several more reporting for duty under Congregational divines Frederick Ayer and Cyrus Francis. Around 1875, Storrs School morphed into the larger "red brick church school" on Atlanta's Courtland and Houston streets, where large numbers of avid men, women, and children were shepherded along the missionary association's causeway to literate citizenship, children mornings and afternoons, adults evenings seven to nine.[12]

As for the Goose Creek Bells, their unenslaved experience, color, and opportunism steered them dead center into First Church and "AU." In 1905, the deacon's list of those whom First Church honored "for long terms of service and faultless records" cited John H. Bell, 1884, then age seventeen.[13] Had the Atlanta Bells been unrecorded in the 1880 federal census, as I had at first feared after a day or two of research, my only recourse would have been to narrate the lost decade across a span of speculations. But I finally discovered that the name Bell, heard as "Be-yell" by a semiliterate enumerator, had produced "John W Beall" at the wrong age of seventy, not his fifty-nine. Inaccuracy and misspelling deformed this 1880 census for Atlanta's Fulton County, ward 2, where the family now lived.

The household head was said to be "log in sight," meaning John Wilson was blind and twelve months unemployed. A[deline] Beall still "kept house" at a correct fifty-two years. Son James, whose real age was thirty-four, and Anna, thirty-five, now lived elsewhere and probably were married. Adeline's helpmate Julia, now twenty-six, was no longer "at home." The nineteen-year-old daughter figure described as "teaching school" must be the precocious Mary Elizabeth (age seventeen), a Storrs graduate and future Atlanta University Normal School alumna. The mystery Careys I'd barely noticed on the 1870 census return as "adopted daughter at school" Charlotte Carey, age sixteen, a family connection to remain forever murky.[14]

But the 1880 census revealed as much about who the Bells thought they were as about where and how they worked in ward 2. Number 110 Crew Street placed my great-grandfather's tribe midblock among a long street of houses occupied only by middle-class white families, except for the Wilsons, who also identified themselves as mulatto. The admonition "No Colored Allowed" in public spaces and even in many private businesses was still more than two decades in the future in Georgia. "Redemption," as it was called, moved somewhat cautiously in imposing naked racial repression until the South's leaders could become confident about the North's disengagement from civil rights.[15]

THE EDUCATIONAL OPPORTUNITIES FAMILIES LIKE THE BELLS HAD AL-ready taken advantage of made a boundless leap forward in September 1867. The AMA, in tandem with the Freedmen's Bureau, obtained a charter from the state to build an institution of higher education for the unenslaved on the highest hill in the city. What was to become Atlanta University had been organized two years earlier in an abandoned church building on Jenkins Street by two somehow literate freedmen, James Tate and Grandison Daniels. Presented with the experience and resources offered by the AMA, the men gratefully accepted the guidance and eventual leadership of Edmund Asa Ware, recently designated superintendent of education for Georgia by Freedmen's Bureau head General Oliver O. Howard. Moreover, with the state charter had come the singular Reconstruction award of an annual legislative appropriation of eight thousand dollars. The South's first institution of higher learning for people of color announced it was open to make a new race of people in October 1869. The best grammar students from Storrs School would feed the new Atlanta University, whose ambitious Lower Normal Department was advertised as a curriculum to be fully operational in 1873.[16]

North Hall for women rose on Diamond Hill, where Confederate ramparts still stood in 1869, where Mary Elizabeth Bell could have found her place, and where as a teenager I would harvest a Union cannonball from a fallen tree in the early 1950s. Atlanta University's Congregationalist founders and New England faculty envisioned an uncompromisingly color-blind, academically superior institution for both sexes, an asylum of brown-skinned cosmopolites in the mold, say, of James Weldon

Johnson, future poet and civil rights paragon, and Adella Hunt Logan, militant feminist avant la lettre. South Hall for men and classrooms followed thanks to twenty-five thousand Freedmen's Bureau dollars in 1872. Edmund Asa Ware, the university's first head, Yale '63, became famous for enjoining trustees, teachers, and students to "Find a Way or Make One," Ware's Yale class motto.[17]

The next year AU offered the academically rigorous Higher Normal Course as a bridge to the college curriculum from the less complete Normal Course. Great-aunt Mary Elizabeth, who had wasted no time taking the causeway to one of the school's first baccalaureate degrees, ultimately had to settle for the delayed distinction of a Higher Normal diploma. Like his motivated sister, Grandfather John Henry found the collegiate high wire of tuition and part-time employ a feat too problematic as well, although his performance was adequate during the 1880 semester. Yet no late-nineteenth-century Atlanta Bells finished the Atlanta University with the prized college diploma, their credentialed twenty-first-century family historian concluded after a thorough digital troll of all the university bulletins. One wondered, too, about how intensely they may have valorized their educational access. An AU acquaintance born enslaved let it be known how grateful he was "for the pen of Lincoln and to the sword of Grant" but was said to be more thankful "for the patient school ma'am who taught the Negro his letters and set a million of us to reading."[18]

The reality, as the first class of six graduates exemplified in 1876, was that baccalaureate success at President Ware's institution demanded great self-sacrifice matched with extraordinary discipline and a good mind—four years of ancient languages, philosophy and science, history and literature, modeled on Exeter and Yale. Henry Ossian Flipper marched on to West Point, the first of his race. William Sanders Scarborough occupied the classics chair at Wilberforce and became famous for his popular university textbook on classical Greek. William Henry Crogman assumed the presidency of Atlanta's Gammon Theological Seminary. Class valedictorian Richard R. Wright, celebrated as a Storrs schoolboy by poet John Greenleaf Whittier, accepted the presidency of Georgia's first black land-grant college and late in life organized a Philadelphia bank that survived the Great Depression.

Such a curriculum for black students would earn the earnest ridicule of Hampton Institute graduate Booker Washington not so far in the future.[19] Meanwhile, academic standards continued their rise on Diamond Hill. The trustees sanctioned the elimination of the Agricultural Department in 1881. In 1895, the meat-and-potatoes grammar division, representing an average of 60 percent of the total university enrollment, was abolished. James Weldon Johnson, graduating with a BA with the highest honors the previous year, lauded ever after an education in which "the ideal constantly held up to us was of education as a means of living, not of making a living."[20]

ARTICLE I, SECTION 8, OF THE CONSTITUTION SETS OUT CONGRESS'S POWER to establish "Post Offices and post Roads." In time, postmaster general would become one of the most powerful positions in Washington, bringing great influence within the corridors of federal power and majordomo authority for eighty thousand letter carriers. The job of mail deliverer, with its government salary and guaranteed pension, was much sought after.[21] For black people after the Civil War the postman's cap and uniform certified literacy, efficiency, and reliability. More than those attributes, the Negro postman signified approved upward mobility—an honorable family man whose advantaged children were expected to advance the race's bright promise.

John Henry Bell likely entered the U.S. Postal Service at some time during the mideighties. A single year of the Normal Course at Atlanta University in 1881 offered surplus evidence of his English literacy. As for confidence about passing the federal written test, my grandfather's active participation at First Congregational Church must have afforded him the successful example of Storrs classmate George White's father. George White Sr., a pillar of their church, was one of Atlanta's first mail carriers of color. Whites and Bells, as I would learn from my mother years later, had shared the same ancestral professional leg up: Storrs School,

AU, First Church, Auburn Avenue neighborhood, and marriage. Their familial ties steadily tightened after John Henry Bell donned the uniform of the U.S. Postal Service probably in 1884 at age eighteen. George White's youngest son, Walter, remembered that in forty-three years of infallible professionalism his father had failed to deliver the mail only once, "during the blizzard of 1888."[22] No similar memory of professional defeat appears to have survived among the Bells' lore.

First Church constancy is likely to have also brought Grandfather's first notice of my grandmother. Hers, like his, was a story of particular roots, Congregationalist nurturing and education, and fortunate resources. Alice L. B. King was completing the senior middle class of AU's Normal Course in 1889 with music instruction as her major concentration. She was seventeen, poised, and, it seemed, curiously vulnerable in her Victorian dwelling on Wheat Street in the fourth ward. John Henry couldn't have known that *L.B.* abbreviated her natural father's adamant preference for Alice Lee Belvin. Or that Alice's formerly enslaved mother, Clarissa, had proudly, stubbornly clung to her origins as an especially favored servant of the Barrington King plantation but a few miles northeast of Atlanta. Clarissa King, in defiance of the slave code's inviolable prescription and in rebuke of Major James Wiley Belvin of Houston County's sexual impunity, dared identify herself by her chosen surname. Meanwhile, until his demise the previous year in Marshallville, Major Belvin of Houston, progenitor of Clarissa's children, financed the well-being of his adored Alice, freeborn in 1872, who presented herself as an amalgamated Alice Lee Belvin King.

The somewhat sinister disappearance of most of the personal data collected by the tenth federal census has obliterated a decade of America's social past. Somehow, because of two avoidable conflagrations combined with bureaucratic insouciance and unexplained application of the "useless paper law of 1889," the surviving social corpus of the 1890 census was incinerated in February 1933. Not until 1970 would census takers again collect special separate schedule forms akin to those distributed for the last decade of the nineteenth century to every household. A great nervousness afflicted old-stock Protestant Americans at the beginning of the nineties, a spreading dread of replacement by the aliens trudging down Ellis Island's ramp. "The [1890] schedule contained expanded enquiries relating to race," a census specialist reminds us, "white, black, mulatto, quadroon, octoroon, Chinese, Japanese, Indian." It asked about immigration and naturalization dates; ability to speak English; home ownership. President Benjamin Harrison's Department of the Interior committed itself to recording the vital signs of a commonwealth speeding breakneck into hyphenation.

The 25 percent population increase in a decade totaled some 65 million citizens. Numerical data redrew voting districts and Electoral College allocations. To the best of my knowledge, all explanations for the destruction of the 1890 federal census have omitted the "one-drop rule" anxieties at play in pre–World War II racially segregated Washington, DC.[23]

Not being able to look back on the decade prior to December 1890, I have only a general sense of my paternal grandparents' late-1880s world, and of the 1890s lamentably less. A faded mortuary document I filed away early on established the 1890 demise of my blinded great-grandfather John Wilson, buried sometime that year. His Atlanta gamble had worked well enough. Daughters Anna and Mary Elizabeth found genteel occupations and steady husbands. Shoemaker James and dressmaker Minnie struggled to keep up with the younger Bells, although Minnie eventually returned to AU for academic polish. William's year at AU carried him to Minnesota as a white man with a white spouse; their daughter Willa was born in Saint Paul in 1893.

At age twenty-four, John Henry became his mother's only provider after the Crew Street chapter closed with Great-grandfather's death. The Atlanta city directory for 1892 finds John H. Bell, mail carrier, renter, at 74 Rawson Street. "Am thinking John Henry and Addie had moved to a better neighborhood by 1892," local historian Clarence White guessed in response to their grandson's query. "They were probably living well among Jewish and white neighbors in what was probably the most fashionable part of town."[24] Whatever curious professional or identity connections enabled the Bells' relocation to the Washington-Rawson quarter, their

1892 presence in Atlanta's most exclusive neighborhood had to have been makeshift and exceedingly brief. Logically, the 1892 city directory listing was already out of date, because John and Alice had taken their marriage vows the previous year.

The months from 1890 to 1892 must have entailed radical readjustments in family arrangements. The Clara King in residence at 276 Wheat Street in the 1890 city directory can only have been Major Belvin's long-suffering partner and the final legatee of the Wheat Street–Auburn Avenue indenture.[25] I believe Clarissa saw the property she legally wrangled away from Belvin in 1880 only once again. There she seems to have returned ten years later: presumably to meet John Henry Bell, to reassure herself that Alice's choice of mate was wise, and to remove any doubt from sons Charles and James that 300 Auburn Avenue was their sister's exclusive inheritance. This extraordinary great-grandmother, knowledge of whose unsuspected existence I owed to an enabling archivist, seemed to vanish so completely thereafter as to defy biographical exhumation.

John and Alice wed at First Congregational sometime in 1891. A couple of old studio photographs show them forever poised in the prime of bourgeois confidence. Alice's doe-like expression and hourglass figure were captured in gelatin on the eve of their wedding. She stands by a studio tree sumptuously clothed in a damask dress, her full brown hair in a pompadour, a thin Spanish fan in her left hand accentuating her silhouette. His hair center-parted and pomaded, his right arm uncovering a gold pocket watch, John Bell projects a photogenic gravitas that waits to give way to a triumphant smile with the last flash of magnesium.

In the gendered language of their times, Alice, educated, refined, attractive, propertied, had to have been quite a catch for Grandfather.

Atlanta's Wheat Street was an odd and confusing artery that intersected Jackson Street, then briefly split and reconnected as it ran east to Boulevard. The property James Wiley Belvin purchased from Moses Frank for his former enslaved concubine abutted Jackson. The property's substantial Victorian stood with another structure smack in the middle of the Wheat Street divide, with the result that 276 and 300 Wheat Street referenced the same house. Two years after Alice and John, with Adeline, took exclusive possession of their home, Wheat Street's principal artery was renamed Auburn Avenue in response to prominent white petitioners' clamor for more cosmopolitan street nomenclature.[26] A far more significant Auburn Avenue arrival in 1893 was the couple's first baby that August, my mother, Alice Urnestine. My mother's mother was twenty-one; her pregnancy had the benefit of her mother-in-law's half dozen successful deliveries; her physical delicacy may not have been especially concerning to Adeline or to the midwife. Baby Alice Urnestine's life signs must have been exceptional given the athleticism of her later years.

Evidentiary limitations constrain what can be securely written about the political culture of 300 Auburn Avenue. Undoubtedly, the Bells were *moyenne bourgeoisie* and color-struck, but it seems fair to grant them awareness of the systematic nullification of the great constitutional protections of the Reconstruction era. It could not have been but distressing to Alice that she and John Henry could be barred from Atlanta's new opera house. Or that managers of fine hotels could refuse access to John if his race were disclosed. Ten years before Alice Urnestine's arrival, a brace of discrimination cases involving theaters, restaurants, hotels, parlor cars, and taverns was brought by educated colored persons before the U.S. Supreme Court. In the *Civil Rights Cases* of 1883, the court's majority eviscerated the egalitarian Civil Rights Act of 1875, a comprehensive act enacted to honor the recently deceased lion of Reconstruction, Senator Charles Sumner.

Instructing the plaintiffs of their error, Justice Joseph Bradley of New Jersey ruled for the majority that the Civil Rights Act of 1875 applied only to cases where the state discriminated against their race, not individual persons. Furthermore, Bradley's back-of-the-hand obiter dicta dismissed the ails of black people as juridically tedious. It would run the slavery argument into the ground, explained he, to have the act apply "to every discrimination which a person may see fit to make as to the guests he will entertain, or as to the people he will admit into his coach or cab or car, or admit to his concert or theatre, or deal with in other matters."[27] That licensed coaches, cabs, and cars, and even theaters, were hardly personal property escaped the Supreme Court's understanding of the

Civil Rights Act. The Bells and their friends should have become even more alarmed about threats to their "political or civil rights" after the once encouraging Harrison administration deceived them.

Benjamin Harrison, bewhiskered grandson of the ninth U.S. president, sent an address to Congress soon after his March 1889 presidential inauguration that almost anticipated Great Society rhetoric. Mindful that federal court decisions in *Slaughter-House*, *Reese*, *Cruickshank*, and the *Civil Rights Cases* of 1883 had reinterpreted the Fourteenth Amendment into nonapplicability, the president asked, "When and under what conditions is the black man to have a free ballot? When is he in fact to have those full civil rights which have so long been his in law?"[28]

At that very moment, indeed, the white South stood ready to adopt the so-called Mississippi Plan, the state's 1890 charade of a constitutional convention (applauded by its lone black member) that claimed to upgrade its electorate by eliminating illiterates and indigents (identified as overwhelmingly black people). Providentially, with both the house and senate of Mississippi controlled by Republicans for the first time since 1875, AU students and Congregational parishioners joined thousands of ordinary black citizens who dared believe that Harrison's Republicans would repay their partisan loyalty by honoring the Constitution.

President Harrison did endorse two high-minded bills that envisioned an educationally and politically reinvented ex-Confederacy. Remembered by the names of their two northeastern proposers, Henry W. Blair and Henry Cabot Lodge, the former's bill envisaged an educational tsunami for the South; the latter, a voting rights enema. The education bill of New Hampshire's determined Blair, approved thrice by the Senate, possessed a conceptual and monetary logic seductive even to southern whites. Eighty percent of the country's illiterates above ten years old lived in the former Confederacy, according to the 1880 census. Seventy percent of illiterates were the former enslaved; 20 percent were the poor whites. Blair's federal education bill proposed to finance itself with the federal surplus created by America's sky-high tariff on imports—a tariff loathed by the South and West as discriminatory. Budgeted at fifteen million dollars annually over ten years, with the bulk of it going to the South, the monies were to be divided equally between the races in any state where segregation was enforced.[29]

Colored America's first historian, George Washington Williams, called the Blair bill the "grandest measure of our times." Even though the bill was flawed by sectional compromise, the new Afro-American League endorsed the senator's federal educational reform. In its original form, Blair's bill had imposed federal supervisors, annual reports to the U.S. commissioner of education, and punitive suspension for maldistribution of funds. Even though the bill had acquiesced de facto to separate but equal southern schools, Blair eventually dropped all federal supervisory requirements from his bill, except the annual report. Whether or not tony Atlanta Congregationalists regretted the stigmata of separation in public schools, the senator was reliably informed that most southern colored people pragmatically welcomed the bill as a better-than-nothing solution. By inverse logic, Georgia's Joseph E. Brown, South Carolina's Wade Hampton, Mississippi's Lucius Q. Lamar, and North Carolina's Zebulon B. Vance cautiously concurred.[30]

The transformative impact upon the South's black and white public schools of Blair's $110 million—translated as $3 billion in contemporary money—would have been so socioeconomically stunning that recent historians of the South have imagined "an alternative South." Instead, to its sponsor's surprise, the federal education bill was narrowly defeated after two months of Senate debate and unexpected presidential silence. Henry Blair's decade-old, curated coalition of liberal northern, willing midwestern, and "very best men" of the South imploded.[31] As cities above the Mason-Dixon line swelled with their own "illiterates" from eastern and southern Europe, political resentment of the bill's southern largesse had steadily grown. In Republican strongholds in the Northeast, where solace for "the Negro" competed with national economic questions, indifference mounted. Finally, decisively, southern anxieties molted into hysteria from fears that any federal beneficence, however pro forma, risked entangling their peculiar region in some future national reformist movements and policies beneficial to colored people.[32] Negrophobia trumped federal aid for public schools.

Mississippi's elimination of its black voters, meanwhile, emboldened such widespread cleansing of southern voting rolls as to menace the GOP's very existence below the Mason-Dixon line. The president and his concerned attorney general approved the potent 1890 federal election bill introduced jointly by Boston Brahmin Henry Cabot Lodge and Senator George Frisbie Hoar. While debate over the Blair education bill roiled the Senate, Lodge's so-called Force Bill battled its way to a narrow six-vote passage in the House. At First Congregational, the college on Diamond Hill, half a hundred more churches, innumerable barbershops and dives, the colored people of Atlanta and the region figuratively held their breaths as Lodge's antidote to poll taxes, literacy tests, registrars' examinations, and devious forms of intimidation reached the Senate. Once signed by President Harrison, federal circuit courts (if petitioned by five hundred citizens) could appoint federal supervisors to inspect registration lists, verify voter information, ban illegal aliens from voting, and certify the vote count for congressional elections.

The election bill's bombshell empowered federal supervisors to summon deputy U.S. marshals to guarantee election security by force if necessary. Mobilized by the specter of Black Reconstruction reborn, the South's filibustering senators fought to save "home rule," "self-government," "the solid South"—white supremacy—at any cost. "The negro [sic]," editorialized the *Wilmington North Star* eight years before the Wilmington pogrom, "will be a source of absolute danger to society and all the educational schemes in the universe cannot cure it."[33] After filibustering the Senate to a standstill for ten months, southern lawmakers masterfully traded their votes for the Northeast's McKinley Tariff Act, the Southwest's Sherman Silver Purchase Act, the populists' Sherman Antitrust Act, and other regional priorities, after which President Harrison's party complicitly tabled the Lodge Force Bill in January 1891.

LOOKING BACK BUT A FEW YEARS, MY NEWLYWED AUBURN AVENUE GRANDparents may well have judged 1891 as the year of no return from Jim Crow, a term soon to encapsulate more than half a century of national disgrace.

The cost of losing the protection of the Fifteenth Amendment was political death. Speaking in Atlanta's Bethel AME Church on Auburn Avenue
after the Lodge Bill debacle, Bishop Henry McNeal Turner, a new acquaintance of the Auburn Avenue Bells, despondently exhorted his audience "to leave Georgia and go to their own country, Africa, where they
would have equal rights and help govern and have street cars of their own."
Historians James Campbell and Kendra Field found that in South Carolina and parts of Arkansas and Oklahoma, "entire communities sold their
belongings and embarked for the coast to meet ships—sometimes real,
often imaginary—bound for the 'promised land' of Liberia."[34] That a "one-
drop rule" of racial identity could become the South's eleventh command-
ment by the second decade of the next century simply defied their mental
culture. The tenacity of a multiracial fiction so held this family, whose
special sense of self would ultimately cause them to be derided by their
African American brothers and sisters as "no-nation people" in the coming decades of white supremacy.

6

* * *

IN THE FOLD OF
WHITE SUPREMACY

The Deceived Bells,
1895–1906

First Church, as its devoted parishioners were wont to call their Congregationalist tabernacle, ended its succession of white pastors with Reverend Samuel H. Robinson's departure in 1894. AMA leadership prided itself on a mission done well enough in the twenty-three years since Reverend Ayer's pastorate that it thought the time had come when the pulpit should host an able man of color. Henry Hugh Proctor, Fisk University '91 and Yale Divinity School '94, ended up a good fit for twenty-six years. Born of emancipated parents near Fayetteville, Tennessee, Proctor had native ability that good fortune had nurtured in a solid country school. Preaching may have been instinctive. He recalled learning his letters "near this spot out under a big tree [where] I made my first speech at a closing exhibition."[1]

Fisk University's academic standards and tuition money demanded seven hardscrabble years for Proctor's baccalaureate. The faculty assembled by grave President Erastus Milo Cravath (a figure out of the Old Testament, thought some) was outstanding and some of Proctor's classmates dazzled him as well. One, who entered a year after him, in 1885, and graduated three years later, Proctor would meet again when he assumed his

Atlanta pastorate. "Coming out of New England there was something about him no other seemed to possess," admired Proctor. "He was soon to be known as the most brilliant student in the school. He was a lively, jovial chap, and a speaker of great magnetism."[2] He was William Edward Burghardt Du Bois. Another classmate who impressed the future pastor was a studious, ambitious girl named Maggie Murray, the future Mrs. Booker T. Washington.

Henry Proctor's quartet of singing Yale men not only earned his tuition but also provided a novel baccalaureate thesis, "A New Ethnic Contribution to Christianity," which rather anticipated classmate William Du Bois's numinous "Of the Sorrow Songs" chapter in *The Souls of Black Folk*. The Gospels needed irrigation with the sentiments of this world's lowly, ventured the man, who reminded others much later that he "dug his way through Fisk and sang it through Yale."[3] Proctor expected to make a name for himself at the second-oldest Congregational church in colored America, located in the capital of the New South. He could hardly have expected, however, to find himself at the epicenter of a confluence of national and racial projects the very next year.

The Auburn Avenue Bells, together with their fellow First Church parishioners, proudly awaited Proctor's arrival, even as the Panic of 1893, which would grind on four more years, made them cinch their household belts. Benjamin Harrison's 1892 defeat and the second return of New York Democrat Grover Cleveland (the unique nonsequential U.S. presidency) had deeply unsettled black voters North and South. The year of Proctor's appointment saw congressional repeal of the Ku Klux Klan Act of 1871. Still, official Atlanta pretended to be at the front of an economic and interracial wave. The final work was then being completed on the city's ambitious Cotton States and International Exposition, a two-million-dollar extravagance à la Henry Grady advertising southern commercial, technological, and agricultural advancement. Atlantans black and white winked at news that Caucasian Exposition president Charles Collier, accompanied by some twenty southern businessmen, had secured $200,000 from the House Committee on Appropriations only after a young Alabama Negro educator, Booker Taliaferro Washington of Tuskegee, eloquently described the racial adjustment boon to come from such an enterprise.[4]

As news spread of Washington's signal Capitol Hill success, many cultured African Americans solaced themselves that the deep humiliation of black people's near total exclusion from the 1893 Chicago World's Fair ("The White City")—unforgettably castigated by Ida Wells and Frederick Douglass—was meaningfully mitigated by the Cleveland administration's appropriations gesture.[5] On opening day, Wednesday, September 18, 1895, national and local newspapers ballyhooed that the president himself would open the Cotton States and International Exposition by flipping an electric switch from his summer residence in Cape Cod, Massachusetts. Pavilions and houses for six southern states and thirteen South American nations were ready to "foster trade between southern states and South American nations" as well as with the country at large and Europe. The Negro House, rising somewhat away from the main attractions, was to showcase a variety of educational and industrial products. An exposition vanguard of the more than 800,000 visitors during the park's four-month tally pawed like horses before the Ponce de Leon gates. Meanwhile, a welcoming committee of distinguished colored leaders accompanied Tuskegee Institute's new man of the hour through a wilting downtown Atlanta to the fairgrounds three miles away.[6]

Rufus Bullock was remembered scurrying from the governor's office mocked as a carpetbagger and reviled as a "nigger lover" by Georgia's white people. Twenty-four years later, as president of the Atlanta Chamber of Commerce and master of ceremonies, Rufus Bullock would soon find himself acclaimed by both races after he presented Booker T. Washington on that immemorial late afternoon. Reverend Henry Proctor sat self-importantly with his college classmate, now the third Mrs. Washington, in the exposition's racially segregated auditorium. Among several church members accompanying them might well have been the Auburn Avenue John Henry Bells. Family legend could be squared with a mail carrier's hurried after-work arrival on the city's recent Nine-Mile Trolley. Beyond speculation, though, is the positive impact awaiting Proctor and his fellow spectators. "I sat beside his wife as he leaped into fame," marveled First Church's pastor. Clark Howell, *The Atlanta Constitution*'s renowned editor and one of Booker Washington's principal boosters, anxiously twisting his hat in the whites-only section, prayerfully hoped the packed auditorium would be similarly astounded.[7]

Washington strode to the platform's edge, surveilled the spray of wide-eyed eyes in a dark sea, and broke the utter silence of his moment by thanking "the managers of this magnificent Exposition" for an occurrence that did more to cement the friendship of the two races than any (he actually said) "since the dawn of our freedom." In little more than half an hour this enslaved mother's racially mixed son, self-taught and mentored by a general, delivered one of the most compelling speeches in the American canon. For the economy of message it matched the Gettysburg Address. For accuracy of historical timing it recalled William Jennings Bryan's "Cross of Gold" nomination speech. Proctor, who had heard Douglass at Cooper Union, must have noticed the absence of the recently dead Great Frederick's noble defiance from this day's speech. Instead, on that September day in 1895, what the exposition's black and white ticket holders heard from this confident black schoolteacher was the nononsense language of a business contract.[8]

He began at the story's beginning: "One third of the population of the South is of the Negro race. No enterprise seeking the material, civil, or moral welfare of this section can disregard this element of our population and reach the highest success," he said defiantly. This Cotton States Exposition afforded the two races the opportunity to regain the lost common opportunities among us of "a new era of industrial progress." Washington ventured to elucidate frankly that both races had reached an inflection point in mutual misunderstanding. "Ignorant and inexperienced," he contended that it was hardly a mystery that his people's new life "began at the top instead of at the bottom; that a seat in Congress or the State Legislature was more sought than real estate or industrial skill." That powerful white listeners well knew that the emancipated people's real estate options had been quashed at the outset by a U.S. president Booker Washington left unsaid to guilty memory.

Tuskegee's principal then reached for a bromide in which both races were imagined lost at sea, parched and waterless. Some southern whites would water industrial growth with foreign labor, he regretted; some southern blacks imagined finding better conditions in foreign places. "Cast down your bucket where you are" was his command to both. His people must cultivate friendly relations with the southern white man, "their next door neighbor." Because in the leap from slavery to freedom, he warned, the Negro race should never overlook the fact "that the masses of us are to live by the production of our hands . . . that we shall prosper . . . as we learn to dignify and glorify common labor and put brains into the common occupations."

The lesson Washington ventured to teach white people was found in the same bucket. "Cast it down among 8,000,000 Negroes whose habits you know," a people, he reminded his chamber of commerce listeners, "who have without strikes and labor wars, tilled your fields, cleared your forests, built your railroads and cities." The point needed repeating: "[I]n our humble way, we shall stand by you with a devotion that no foreigner can approach, ready to lay down our lives, if need be, in defense of yours." Some of the Atlanta University students probably found Booker Washington's antebellum similes cringeworthy. Nor was such servile behavior common among Reverend Proctor's congregants. And mindful of ever-ready white misreadings, Booker Washington punctuated these inclusive aspirations with a signature credo that sealed the socioeconomics of his contract: "In all things that are purely social we can be as separate as the fingers, yet one as the hand in all things essential to mutual progress."

He drew this exquisitely compartmentalized regional manifesto to a close on two chastening notes—first, the imperative of white and black coexistence; second, the sine qua non of equity and justice for his people. Washington proudly broadcast that "the wisest among my race understand that agitation . . . of social equality is the extremest folly." That was followed by an applause line: that "earn[ing] a dollar in a factory just now is worth infinitely more than the opportunity to spend a dollar in an opera house." Alice King Bell, if present, must have winced, yet she would also have heard this commonsense seer say that there was no defense "for any of us except in the highest intelligence and development of all."

Studio photo of Alice King, 1890

Chamber of commerce upbraidings followed: "Nearly sixteen millions of hands will aid you in pulling the load upwards, or they will pull you against the load downwards. We shall constitute one third and more of the ignorance and crime in the South," he warned the Bullocks and Howells, "or one third of its intelligence and progress; we shall contribute one third to the business and industrial prosperity of the South, or we shall prove a veritable body of death, stagnating, depressing, retarding every effort to advance the body politic." Booker T. Washington's rhetorical coda encapsulated the cash value of pragmatic ideals. "Far above and beyond material benefit," he truly believed, "will be that higher good . . . in blotting out of sectional differences and racial animosities and suspicions, in a determination to administer absolute justice, in a willing obedience among all classes to the mandates of law. This, this," he ended, turning his gaze upon the white dignitaries seated behind him, "coupled with our material prosperity, will bring into our beloved South, a new heaven and a new earth."[9]

Even he was surprised by the ovation. Bullock raced to shake Washington's hand, violating the South's new code of racial etiquette. Washington's evenhanded biographer describes the *Constitution*'s Clark Howell leaping from his seat, shouting, "That man's speech is the beginning of a moral revolution in America!" William H. Baldwin Jr., Southern Railroad vice president, punctilious Tuskegee trustee, and New England embodiment of sectional reconciliation, survived a nervous seizure so intense that he paced about the grounds.[10] Grover Cleveland's public approbation came widely publicized after the president sent Booker Washington a congratulatory letter, "with much enthusiasm for making the address," three weeks later.

African American leaders overwhelmingly applauded what they quickly described as the Atlanta Compromise, with the alcohol-challenged T. Thomas Fortune saluting Washington "as our [new] Douglass, the best equipped . . . to be the single figure ahead of the procession." John E. Bruce, another widely read black journalist, was relieved that "twaddle about negro [*sic*] equality in the south by the negro of mixed blood" and their northern white zealots would end soon. Henry Proctor, recalling Washington's success as uncannily propitious, undoubtedly spoke for his congregation of prosperous and educated, my persuaded Bell grandparents included. Young W. E. B. Du Bois, superlatively credentialed and climbing, joined the Atlanta Compromise chorus, writing from a small college in Ohio that Washington's "was a word fitly spoken." What would surprise future civil rights generations, though, was Du Bois's follow-on Atlanta Compromise judgment published in Fortune's *New York Age*: "Here might be the basis of a real settlement between whites and blacks in the South, if the South opened to the Negroes the doors of economic opportunity and the Negroes co-operated with the white South in political sympathy."[11]

If virtually none of the African American leadership class disagreed at the time with Booker Washington's formula for racial coexistence in the South—men like Blanche K. Bruce, Charles Chesnutt, and the two Grimké brothers—partly it was that their Edwardian class myopia overtly or subconsciously read the Fifteenth Amendment as a privilege of literacy and character, not as purely a right of citizenship. Such had been twenty-two-year-old Du Bois's high Tory sense of civil rights that Fortune's *Age* had quoted him saying of the Lodge Bill, "When you have the right sort of black voters, you will need no election laws." To be sure, his was an extreme view, but many men and women scrambling away from enslavement placed exceedingly high value on civic deportment.[12] Weighing their survival options after Reconstruction's cruel deceptions and the reality of Redemption's stealthy progress, these advantaged black Americans grasped at Booker Washington's Hobson's choice—either "contribute one third to the business and industrial prosperity of the South, or we shall prove a veritable body of death, stagnating, depressing, retarding every effort to advance the body politic."

BENJAMIN RYAN TILLMAN (AKA "PITCHFORK BEN"), SOUTH CAROLINA'S senator from 1895 to 1918, boasted of his great success during the month of the Atlanta Compromise some years later. "We took the government away. We stuffed ballot boxes. We shot them. We are not ashamed of it."[13] Palmetto State voters had decided by a paper-thin margin to hold a constitutional convention in Columbia to revise the state's charter. At month's end, all but a handful of the state's 135,000 black voters were eliminated by literacy requirements, statutory recitations, poll tax payments, residency laws, a crimes registry, and the eight-box ballot, not to mention homicidal intimidation.

South Carolina whites were only copying the Mississippi model. News of their white supremacist triumph reached Atlanta and Tuskegee, Alabama, days after Booker Washington's exposition elocution and its extolling of the New South's benevolent race relations. By year's end, however, there would be 1,600 recorded lynchings during the preceding decade, 113 in 1895 alone. Tuskegee's principal put the best face on these horrors by explaining, "The men who are lynched are invariably vagrants, men without property or standing." It remained to be seen whether the Atlanta Compromise augured, as he earnestly wished, a meaningful diminishment and eventual banishment of unlawful, ritualized executions by community. What can be said of the African American franchise, however, was predictable in the short term. By 1900, with the work of the southern constitutional conventions substantially done, Louisiana would have fewer than 6,000 registered black voters, where before there had been more than 130,000; Alabama would list 3,000 after a previous registered total of some 181,000. Yet "without the legalistic machinations of the Supreme Court of the United States," bemoans an attentive historian, "the Southern colonels and merchants would have been harder pressed to complete their new order."[14]

In the wake of Dr. Washington's speech (Dartmouth bestowed an honorary doctorate), the Auburn Avenue Bells must have debated the troubling implications of the Separate Car Act decision of the Supreme Court. The Louisiana lawsuit arose from one Homer Adolph Plessy's October 1892 arrest for defying Louisiana's malicious Separate Car Act requiring intrastate nonwhite passengers to be seated in cars designated for them. Plessy, a young, self-assured Creole of indeterminate racial color and represented by legendary carpetbag lawyer-novelist Albion Tourgée, was found guilty by Judge John Howard Ferguson of the district court, a decision promptly sustained by the state supreme court.[15] The Bells and their close friends the exemplary Funderburgs, Westmorelands, and Whites, like others at First Church, shared an esteem of pigment and culture they regarded as integral to their pride as people of African descent. Indeed, one of their number is said to have coined the expression *mulatto chauvinism*. The prospect of laws denying them full participation in the country their ancestors helped build portended an injustice almost too cruel to imagine.

Plessy's appeal reached the docket of the United States Supreme Court in January 1893. There it would linger as *Plessy v. Ferguson* until April of 1896. Removed from the fray by his February 1895 death, Douglass had offered no support to the plaintiff's mostly white defense team, led by the melodramatic Tourgée. That Albion Tourgée's main argument condemned as constitutionally outrageous the reclassification of octoroons from white to black understandably offended dark-complexioned observers. An early remark Tourgée was believed to have uttered poisoned the well:

"that a single drop of African blood is sufficient to color a whole ocean of whiteness?" Then came the eleventh-hour fear of large numbers of mixed-race persons that *Plessy v. Ferguson* very well might extinguish the convenience of racial indeterminacy by a one-drop-of-blood verdict marking African Americans for decades.[16] But what was relevant as arguments commenced on that fateful April Monday in 1896 was Booker Washington's Atlanta Compromise hovering over the Supreme Court in the Old Senate Chamber on Capitol Hill.

The court's verdict was foreordained. Associate Justice Henry Billings Brown, New England educated and a GOP contributor, framed the epic case before him as a mere commonsense question of the "reasonable" exercise of the state's police power to regulate public health and safety: equal cars to achieve equitable results in the best interests of the public. Justice Brown strained to comprehend the plaintiff's argument that the Thirteenth and Fourteenth Amendments were at stake. To Homer Plessy's attorney's protest that separate railcars were a "legalization of caste" and an imposition of "involuntary servitude" in violation of the Thirteenth received a puzzled shrug. Tourgée's insistence that the arbitrary Separate Car Act violated Plessy's right to "due process" under the Fourteenth Justice Brown dismissed in light of the high court's step-by-step misinterpretation of the *Civil Rights Cases* of 1883.[17] Homer Plessy's attorney demanded that the great constitutional wrongs flowing from the *Slaughter-House Cases* be undone straightaway.

Had not the Supreme Court essentially reduced these *Slaughter-House Cases* to protecting black people from hostile laws specifically aimed at them in name only? In *U.S. v. Reese* and *U.S. v. Cruikshank*, continued Tourgée, the amendments were said to bar racially discriminatory laws but not discriminatory acts by individuals. Plessy's lawyer sensed the smug insouciance of the court's majority, but he must have hoped that he would at least be sustained by John Marshall Harlan, the independent Kentucky jurist whose lone dissent in the *Civil Rights Cases* Frederick Douglass had praised and Tourgée had carefully researched. Harlan's previous dissent Tourgée placed at the heart of Plessy's appeal, that "Justice is pictured [as] blind, and her daughter, the Law, ought at least to be color blind."[18] Tourgée's summation placed Justice Brown and his associates in Homer Plessy's separate car. "Suppose a member of this court . . . should wake up with a black skin and curly hair. . . . What humiliation, what rage would fill the judicial mind?" conjectured Tourgée. Justice Brown "would feel and know that such assortment of the citizens on the line of race was a discrimination intended to humiliate and degrade . . . an attempt to perpetuate the caste distinctions on which slavery rested."

Whether or not Tourgée was aware of Justice Harlan's cosmopolitan black half brother, Robert, reared by their white father "to take advantage of every opportunity accorded him," may or may not have been relevant.[19] Yet none of the eight justices can have denied to himself that if the law were applied color-blind, a dark-skinned, curly-headed judge could occupy any carriage of his ticket price and choice. Nevertheless, the seven-to-one adverse verdict read by Justice Brown a month later was a Jesuitical masterpiece. Complimenting the "learned counsel for the plaintiff," the majority determined "the underlying fallacy of the plaintiff's argument to consist in the assumption that the enforced separation of the two races stamps the colored race with a badge of inferiority. If this be so," opined Henry Billings Brown in one of the most insulting decisions ever rendered, "it is not by reason of anything found in the act, but solely because the colored race chooses to put that construction upon it."

Justice Harlan's famous dissent in *Plessy* was prophetic. "The judgment this day rendered will in time prove to be quite as pernicious as the decision made by this tribunal in the Dred Scott case."[20] The national press barely mentioned the decision. And judicial prescience went oddly unnoticed even within the nation's black community.

To be sure, Booker Washington was obliged to comment from his Tuskegee fiefdom. Separation was not necessarily iniquitous, he decided. The inequality of accommodations was the issue, and as for the verdict's constitutional implications, Dr. Washington observed, "the Negro can endure the temporary inconvenience, but the injury to the white man is permanent."[21] Historian Thomas Holt finds no "contemporaneous published reactions from Du Bois, Wells-Barnett, or others among the emerging spokespersons for the New Negro." In Ida Wells's case, perhaps because she had brought one of the first separate car suits in Tennessee, silence meant déjà vu. Resignation, perhaps, or a good deal of uncertainty as to *Plessy*'s meaning for black people's daily lives explained the absence of immediate recorded reaction.

After *Plessy v. Ferguson* southern people of color were banished literally and figuratively to the back of America's bus, even though in places like Atlanta, Chattanooga, Mobile, and New Orleans there was resistance to segregated public transportation that prefigured the 1955 Montgomery bus boycott. Southern blacks stepped off sidewalks in small towns when white people approached. We vanished from public libraries and public parks in cities. More often than not we were denied the ministrations of the municipal hospital. Soda fountains were racially prescribed, as Justice Harlan feared, as were fitting rooms in most department stores. When and where available, we drank from separate water fountains and used separate toilets. We climbed to "crow's nests" in municipal auditoriums and vaudeville theaters. State and local tax revenues were allocated as unequally and separately as toilet facilities. In rural areas, where John Henry Lewis somehow educated himself, what schooling there was ceased when planting and harvesting time came.

What a black sociologist called the etiquette of Jim Crow marked millions with disabilities in education, in self-confidence, and in business acumen, and enforced a chronic disjunction from the American mainstream. A recent valedictorian of Brown University who traveled from Nashville round-trip to hear Washington speak did indeed risk an unpopular opinion: "God forbid that we should get the implements with which to fashion our freedom and then be too lazy or pusillanimous to fashion it," lamented John Hope, the future Morehouse president.[22] Yet one of my childhood memories is of my mother's recitation from her own childhood of John Marshall Harlan's reported speculations about *Plessy*'s future absurdities: separate courtroom Bibles for blacks and whites; separate sidewalks, fountains, bathrooms, theaters, streetcars. "Where will it end?" Alice Bell recalled the aged jurist dreading the apartheid reality that would envelop much of her privileged existence.

John Henry Bell with his children, Alice Urnestine and
John Levering, in the aftermath of Alice's death, 1901

ANOTHER SCHOLAR'S DESCRIPTION OF THE SO-CALLED NEW NEGRO IS
too apt a description of the Auburn Avenue Bells not to borrow: "Less
anchored in the struggles of the past, they often projected an acute impression of self-fashioning, of being themselves living works of self-creation,"
wrote Thomas Holt.[23] Alice and John Henry Bell were a civically conscientious couple in a fashionable house, and parents of two representative
children. My mother, Alice Urnestine, was their first. Their second, a boy
born in 1897, they gave an inquisitive middle name. Levering's curious
middle name derived from a Philadelphia Huguenot family whose young
daughter Anna Levering and my mother became childhood pen pals by
way of my grandfather's interest in First Church's abolitionist past.

John Levering Bell, my uncle, was another of the colored race's blond-haired, blue-eyed mixtures destined for the crosshairs of anxious Caucasian inspection. Born a year after *Plessy v. Ferguson*, Levering, as his friends would call him, would meet white supremacy's first lesson soon after learning to walk. That lesson Albion Tourgée had initially disdained as absurd—"that a single drop of African blood is sufficient to color a whole ocean of whiteness?" Before Levering turned ten, he and fourteen-year-old Alice Urnestine would have drummed into their bright lives the one-drop-of-blood legal code that ordered racial life below the Mason-Dixon line. Although Uncle Levering's and Mother's phenotype, like that of their parents' many friends and associates, legally locked them out of whiteness, their degrees of whiteness sometimes advantaged them among their own people. Professional accomplishments, privileged leadership roles, and biracial cousinage compensated a class of colored people, most of whom indeed were too proud to demean themselves by "passing."

The logic of their position in the nation's evolving racial structure would continue to escape them, even as the imperium of whiteness eliminated no-nation people around them. Their self-creation would smash against a wide wall of white antipathy that not even the accommodating Booker Washington succeeded in breaching. Frederick Douglass had recognized, as would W. E. B. Du Bois, that Andrew Johnson's negrophobia channeled the historical rage of the majority of nonslaveholding whites whose legal status, cash value, military service, political impotence, educational deprivation, occupational options, and patrol duties had been subordinated by an oligarchy in which they found themselves disdained by enslaved black workers who answered only to their masters.[24] More than two centuries of the South's slaveocracy gave an angry white majority the consolation of skin privilege that rendered it almost congenitally hostile to black people. To them, the politics of accommodation invited an open season on the innocent.

Such was the reality that must have appalled my grandfather as well as his fellow postman and churchman George White in February 1898 when Frazier B. Baker, South Carolina schoolteacher and postmaster, died in a hail of gunfire. Republican recapture of the White House after Grover Cleveland's second return owed much to the South's surviving black vote in 1896. The McKinley administration had rewarded African Americans with a number of postmasterships, including Baker's near Florence, South Carolina. Pitchfork Ben Tillman called the appointment a heinous insult to South Carolinians. White petitions flooded the office of the postmaster general while irate locals boycotted Frazier Baker's Lake City post office. Finally, on the night of February 22, some three hundred whites set fire to Postmaster Baker's home and temporary post office. Baker died of multiple gunshot wounds exiting the dwelling. His wife, wounded—but their baby daughter fatally shot—reached safety with other family members.

The Charleston *News and Courier* blamed Frazier Baker's death on postal officials in Washington. Although the lynching of Dr. Washington's "invariable vagrants" could be written off as a highly regrettable regionalism, arson, homicide, and maiming of a federal appointee and his family caused widespread indignation across the country. The mob assault on the Bakers prompted the first federal intervention since the end of Reconstruction. Historian Philip Dray's detailed account of the McKinley administration's good-faith pursuit of the mob members was applauded by John Henry Bell and millions of citizens of both races. Still, federal arrests and the trial of key perpetrators failed to win convictions in Charleston after the government's key witnesses were discredited in June 1898. Well-connected Bostonians and Brooklynites did raise funds to help the Bakers and finally arrange their relocation to safety in the North.[25]

Historical coincidence played its part in the Baker injustice as well. One week before Postmaster Baker was killed, the battleship USS *Maine*'s forecastle exploded mysteriously on the night of February 15, carrying 266 seamen to the bottom of Havana Harbor. A hesitant McKinley momentarily resisted attacking Cuba while Democrats and the Pulitzer and Hearst presses bayed. What might well have been the race's cause célèbre suddenly shared the limelight with war. A Kentucky newspaper editorial urging substitution of "Remember Postmaster Baker" for "Remember the *Maine*" briefly caught the popular wind. Bishop Turner, the AME Church's combative senior prelate, warned that war with Spain over Cuba would be an immoral land grab, even uttering the heresy that "Negroes who are not disloyal to the United States ought to be lynched."[26] But the Spanish-American War narrative prevailed for the same reasons blacks would rally to the flag in 1916. Editor E. E. Cooper of the Washington *Colored American* predicted whites would become less prejudiced when blacks died for their country fighting "to free the Negro people of Cuba."[27]

Patriotism swelled among the race's leaders, most of whom believed Americans sincerely saw in *Cuba libre* freedom fighters versions of their own revolutionary minutemen. As Reverend Proctor's muscular patriotism would send him to France as an army chaplain during the Great War, it seems almost certain that his congregation, the Auburn Avenue Bells included, remembered the *Maine* as much to liberate dark-skinned Cubans as to avenge Postmaster Baker. Battlefield reports from Cuba more than justified E. E. Cooper's wager. To fight Spain's colonials, white America's readiest and best were the congressionally authorized Ninth and Tenth Cavalry and Twenty-fourth and Twenty-fifth Infantry—the veteran black "Buffalo Soldiers." It was at San Juan Hill, with Lieutenant Colonel Theodore Roosevelt finally commanding on July 1, that the battle-hardened black Ninth and Tenth Cavalry joined with the horseless Rough Riders and the white First Cavalry and, in one general officer's firsthand account, "gallantly swept over San Juan Hill, driving the enemy from the crest."[28] Roosevelt's *The Rough Riders* book would crop the Buffalo Soldiers from the original San Juan Hill photo. Later, "T.R." demeaned the black regular army units at Kettle Hill and San Juan Hill as shirkers.

Well before then, for E. E. Cooper of the *Colored American,* the Spanish-American War had already become a travesty after the battered Spanish monarchy surrendered the Philippines to what became overnight the new American empire in December of 1898. Secretary of State John Hay's "splendid little war" had liquidated the Spanish empire in sixteen weeks. Puerto Rico and Guam entered the United States' grab bag as unconsulted dependencies, Cuba as a Platt Amendment protectorate.[29] Ever-cautious

Booker T. Washington questioned his government's new geopolitics. "Until our nation has settled the Indian and Negro problem," said the Great Accommodator, "I do not think we have the right to assume more social problems." The president whose Justice Department prosecuted Postmaster Baker's assassins disappointed postman John Henry Bell after the War Department authorized the black Forty-eighth and Forty-ninth Volunteer Infantry for Philippine occupation duty. Emilio Aguinaldo's Philippine Republic would die fighting in 1903 after seventy thousand U.S. troops lost four thousand men.[30]

I can well imagine that more than a few concerned First Church congregants joined the Black Man's Burden Associations inspired by Bishop Turner in mocking reaction to "The White Man's Burden," Rudyard Kipling's hymn to U.S. imperialism.

HENRY PROCTOR'S FISK CLASSMATE WILLIAM DU BOIS, HIS NEW WIFE, Nina Gomer, and their baby son, Burghardt, arrived on Atlanta University's campus a few days before Christmas 1897. The new professor of sociology and economics had preferred the convenience of a faculty apartment in Stone Hall men's dormitory rather than living arrangements across town in the Auburn Avenue neighborhood. The Proctors were pleased to present the Du Boises to their important circle and may even have hoped that the agnostic classmate might join the First Church fold. Proctor would have known that a teenage Du Bois and mother had attended their local Congregational church in Massachusetts. It was known that the new professor was expected to direct special economic and social researches in the new year, which already elicited considerable excitement among AU's best students. But Du Bois had, as it were, preceded himself in Atlanta with the appearance in the highbrow *Atlantic Monthly* that August of "Strivings of the Negro People." In a sense, that unusual article was Du Bois's national debut, and an excited Proctor had called it to general notice.

"Strivings of the Negro People" opened with white America's diurnal question about Negroes: "How does it feel to be a problem?" Its candid personal answer in a dozen conceptually dazzling, lyrical pages said that white America was the problem's problem. Its author remembered a "wee wooden schoolhouse" in the Berkshires where a schoolboy had been "shut out from their world by a vast Veil." But life within the veil gifted a special "second-sightedness in this American world." Whence an ontological reality emerged: "One ever feels his two-newness—an American, a Negro, two souls, two thoughts, two unreconciled strivings, . . . whose dogged strength alone keeps it from being torn asunder." Comes, then, another gem: "to be a poor man is hard, but to be a poor race in a land of dollars is the very bottom of hardships."

Du Bois's *Atlantic Monthly* confession burst its seams with existential concepts, many still contemporaneously urgent. Most strikingly, "Strivings of the Negro People" proposed a dialectical solution to a perennial dispute bedeviling African American thinkers and doers—proponents of integration versus emigration; assimilationism versus ethnocentrism. Think Frederick Douglass and Marcus Garvey. Double sighted, or double conscious, Du Bois's person of color must neither reject America nor vanish into it. "In this merging he wishes neither of the older selves to be lost. He would not Africanize America, for America has too much to teach. . . . He would not bleach his Negro soul in a flood of white Americanism, for he knows that Negro blood has a message for the world. He simply wishes to make it possible for a man to be a Negro and an American, without being cursed or spit upon by his fellows, without losing the opportunity of self-development."[31]

Tuskegee's principal should have seen the troublesome implications in Du Bois's piece. Clark Howell, owner-publisher of *The Atlanta Constitution*, almost surely did. "Strivings" closed on a note neither southern leader cared to hear. "The power of the ballot we need in sheer self-defense." Retitled and slightly revised, this essay would open *The Souls of Black Folk*. Leonine John Hope, Brown University graduate and "voluntary Negro," assumed the presidency of the relocated Atlanta Baptist College (the future Morehouse) in the fall of 1898 and became Du Bois's indispensable friend and ideological ally. "Strivings" Hope saw as a godsend. "Yes, I am going to say we demand equality," he risked saying after Booker

Washington's Cotton States success. "I am going to say, we demand *social equality*."[32] Little George Towns, with undergraduate degrees from AU and Harvard College, praised Du Bois's *Atlantic Monthly* confession and thereafter was restrained by fellow professor Du Bois from dangerous anti-Washington public statements. Sixty years later, I remember as a student home on spring break holding my breath when emeritus professor Towns repaired his own roof and still took brisk early morning walks in our Diamond Hill neighborhood. Towns and Hope believed their friend's pen was going to write the epitaph for the Atlanta Compromise sometime soon.

Proctor admired Du Bois but respected Washington's influence. He was an avid and informed participant in the first Atlanta University Studies but also a source about them for the eagle-eyed Washington. Proctor's was an ideological balancing act communicated to a privileged congregation whose livelihoods, group solidarity, and primary emotions constantly risked being throttled in white supremacy's tightening coils. My grandfather's First Church trusteeship and finance committee service brought a front row seat on the action. Du Bois's second year produced the statistically significant Atlanta University Study "The Negro in Business." None other than Bourbon governor Allen D. Candler addressed the conference and assured it that as many "God-serving and God-fearing" whites as blacks lived in Georgia. Papers were read by Henry Hugh Proctor, Alexander Crummell, Ms. Minnie Perry of Atlanta's black orphanage, Mrs. Helen Cook of the Colored Women's League of Washington, DC, and Atlanta Baptist College's John Hope, plus several others.[33]

That this May 1899 conference took place at all should have been impossible. Encased in their New England bubble on Diamond Hill, Nina Gomer, Du Bois's Iowa-born wife, was mostly spared rubbing against the realities of Deep South apartheid. Six days prior to the conference, their son Burghardt, after ten enfevered days and nights, expired of nasopharyngeal diphtheria. Dead at sundown on Wednesday, May 24, he had lived just two years and one month. As word spread, a broad swath of black Atlanta wept. "Of the Passing of the First Born," the eleventh essay in *Souls*, Du Bois would write weeks after racing across the city looking for a black doctor; after walking with Nina from Mitchell Street to the train station with Burghardt in his little coffin as passing whites leered and laughed; and, finally, after rushing back from Great Barrington, Massachusetts, to preside on May 30 at the "Negro in Business" conference.

"A perfect life was his, all joy and love, with tears to make it brighter," Burghardt's father would write afterward. "He knew no color-line, poor dear—and the Veil, though it shadowed him, had not yet darkened half his sun." His apostrophe to his son allowed appalling solace: "Well sped, my boy, before the world had dubbed your ambition insolence, had held your ideals unattainable, and taught you to cringe and bow."[34] The couple's misfortune was somewhat alleviated the following year when Nina Yolande, their healthy baby girl born in Great Barrington, arrived on campus to be doted on by AU faculty and students and ogled by Bells, Herndons, Whites, and others when presented at First Church.

In March of 1901, First Church lost a much-admired parishioner, my grandmother Alice King Bell. The time Alice and John Henry were given as caring parents, popular couple, active church and community members, his growing business network, her celebrity as hostess at 300 Auburn Avenue, all that vanished in the agony of another failed pregnancy just as they seemed ready for at least another promising decade. My grandmother was only twenty-eight, but it was her fifth pregnancy in the tenth year of marriage. She left her distraught husband their eight-year-old daughter, Alice Urnestine, their five year-old son, John Levering, and the large Victorian on Auburn Avenue inherited from her Confederate father.

Grandfather buried Grandmother in Oakland Cemetery, resting place for many of the city's genteel dead. The photograph that looks to have been taken right after Alice's interment I still find disconcerting. The trio looks away from the camera, far off into the distance, a benumbed John Henry Bell is seated, my mother and uncle stand as expressionless as manikins beside him. Alice left all three too soon, and her disappearance seems to me to have erased for her children much of her life story's moral. Alice Urnestine and John Levering privileged their freeborn Bell heritage, never quite acknowledging or gradually forgetting J. W. Belvin and his enslaved Clarissa.

MORRIS BROWN COLLEGE HELD ITS FIRST CLASSES IN THE BASEMENT OF Bethel AME Church on Auburn Avenue in the fall of 1881. Four years later, Methodist bishop Atticus G. Haygood, general agent of the Slater Fund for the Education of Freedmen, president of Emory University, and author of *Our Brother in Black*, one of the New South's most pertinent books, delivered the dedicatory address on Morris Brown's new Houston Street campus the day after Thanksgiving. Bishop Haygood's presence at the AME Church's flagship college below the Mason-Dixon line spoke volumes for Henry Grady's vision of a South whose people were said to be too busy to hate. "This college is essentially a home institution, and it has been paid for only by the money of colored people," Haygood enthused. "You have set your white brethren a worthy example of energy and liberality."

Far from the good bishop's thoughts that day was a kindred example of energy also begun in "Big" Bethel's basement at about the same time. The Gate City Colored School would still self-finance the public schooling of Atlanta's black young long after Atticus Haygood's death the year after Booker Washington's Atlanta Compromise speech. To do him justice, however, when the state legislature had threatened AU's annual eight-thousand-dollar appropriation in 1889 over Caucasian outcry that faculty families and students dined in common, Bishop Haygood's wicked letter in the *Constitution* reminded those outraged that the law against interracial schools had been far more violated "by laws against interracial procreation." Wickedly, he suggested imprisonment for parents of mulatto children as a cure.[35] AU lost its appropriation the next year.

Atticus Haygood had been an antebellum fossil. His noblesse oblige likes were dying, or changing into consolidating executives of northern business or into Populists latching on to cheated debtors and angry farmers. Whether it was a Tillman in South Carolina, a James K. Vardaman in

Mississippi, a Josephus Daniels in North Carolina, or a Tom Watson in Georgia, by 1900 white politicians had reached almost unanimous agreement that the solution to their disagreements was the elimination of the Negro from public life. Oddly, Georgia still lagged behind almost all the rest of the ex-Confederacy in whitening its voting rolls. Tuskegee's Great Accommodator served as a good reason for procrastination. The so-called Gate City—Atlanta—also slowed the segregationists' final solution. Twelve railway lines crisscrossed Atlanta, where a second station under construction would surpass the Taj Mahal. Its textile mills fed the global cotton market. Coca-Cola quenched the nation's thirst. With its hundred thousand people, Atlanta's density, commerce, skyscrapers, comprised a Manhattan in utero. Moreover, a third of the city was black and it had more famous black colleges than any other city.

The chamber of commerce saw the savage 1898 killing and property destruction of Wilmington's biracial city government as hardly an enviable model.[36] The challenge for white Georgians was to invent racial concerns of such moral and economic gravity that the Protestant North, alarmed by alien European immigrants, and the West, alarmed by Asian immigrants, would empathize with the South's worsening Negro problem. In 1903, the year of the appearance of *The Souls of Black Folk*, Atlanta newspaperman John Temple Graves delivered a bloodcurdling speech before genteel northern opinion makers at the Chautauqua Circle. Describing "The White Woman" as the "empress of his civilization," Graves conjured a Fort Sumter of chastity. "To treat her with disrespect," exhorted the publisher of *The Atlanta Georgian*, "was to summon from their scabbards a thousand swords of swift defense."[37] It certainly was not the souls of black men John Temple Graves feared. White Georgians caterwauled they were mobilizing against black men's assaults upon their women.

A new myth of Negro reversion from a Christianized, disciplined, and predictable race into stubborn unaccountability and deadly lasciviousness was the white supremacist counterargument to the Atlanta Compromise. In John Temple Graves's vision, strange black males roamed the countryside and festered menacingly in urban slums. Such exagger-

ated dangers caused respectable black Baptist, Methodist, and Congregational churchgoers to recoil. Even Reverend Proctor was wont to despair
of "dives" and "dens" cluttering his city wherein drunken black males
and wanton white women abounded.

White southerners believed the Negro "was losing his manners and
his morals." Yet the truth was, as Woodward's data strongly suggested in
Origins of the New South, that black people lost their jobs to white people
more rapidly than manners and morals. That hard times caused great
changes to the black labor force was a reality tracked and historically explained to any earnest objective reader of Du Bois's new *The Philadelphia
Negro*. The New Orleans city directory for 1870 listed black occupational
majorities "as cigar makers, painters, clerks, shoemakers, coopers, tailors, bakers, blacksmiths, and foundry hands." By 1900, the New Orleans
city directory, like Charleston's for the same year, "showed not ten percent of these occupations held by blacks."[38] Black impoverishment, not
new morals, explained Graves's troubling obsession.

ALTHOUGH DU BOIS MADE NO SPECIFIC MENTION OF HIS LEADERSHIP CON-
cept in *The Souls of Black Folk*, his 1903 book became the bible of the "Talented Tenth" overnight.[39] Its sixteen essays landed like manna on the AU
campus, fueled an excited consensus at First Church, and mustered an
emergent ideological mutiny against the Atlanta Compromise. Essay II,
"Of the Dawn of Freedom," raised the curtain on an epic struggle, for, as
future millions would intone, "the problem of the twentieth century is
the problem of the color line." But "Of Mr. Booker T. Washington and
Others," essay III, demolished a regional icon. Du Bois explained the
Washington phenomenon simply. Washington came "with a simple definite program, at the psychological moment when the nation was a little
ashamed of having bestowed so much sentiment on Negroes."

His doctrine "allowed whites North and South to shift the burden of
the Negro problem to the Negro's shoulders and stand aside as critical
and rather pessimistic spectators; when in fact the burden belongs to the
nation." On the promise that someday full justice would be rendered unto

them, this leader asked his people merely to give up three things—"First, political power, Second, insistence on civil rights, Third, higher education of Negro youth." The result, adjudged Du Bois: Negroes were disfranchised; they were legal creations of a distinct status of civil inferiority; deprived of aid for institutions of higher education. *Souls* dismissed the Atlanta Compromise with the indictment "that a people who voluntarily surrenders such respect, or ceases striving for it, are not worth civilizing."[40]

"Of Mr. Booker T. Washington and Others" diminished the principal of Tuskegee's stature among important men and women of color whose existence Du Bois's essay probably made known to both races for the first time. They were a rainbow of New Negroes for whom it was difficult to see how "such as the Grimkes, Kelly Miller, J. W. E. Bowen . . . can much longer be silent." A young, brilliant Atlanta newcomer was one of those New Negroes who had every intention of being heard. J. Max Barber was coeditor of the boisterous *The Voice of the Negro*, a new literary magazine partly owned by the superbly trained Boston University PhD John Wesley Bowen, black America's first. Booker T. Washington's conciliation Barber found deeply flawed. He answered the call to the Niagara Movement's first meeting in Fort Erie, Canada, front and center among the twenty-nine men and one boy. The father of the boy, Alonzo Herndon, would become one of America's wealthiest men and a major First Church benefactor.

Their Niagara "Declaration of Principles," composed by Du Bois, crackled with resistance to white supremacy: "The Negro race in America . . . needs leadership and is given cowardice and apology, needs bread and is given a stone. This nation will never stand justified before God until these things are changed."[41] The second Niagara Movement meeting, at Harpers Ferry, West Virginia, in August 1906, larger and with women participating, channeled the resistance fervor in an even higher register. Monroe Trotter, Du Bois's Harvard College contemporary and a militant Boston newspaper publisher, and Reverdy Ransom, AME prelate and spellbinding orator, partnered with Du Bois. "The Address to the Country" was a calculus of justice that found its special notation in Du Bois's human rights scripture: "Cannot the nation that has absorbed ten million foreigners into its political life without catastrophe absorb ten million Negro Americans into that same political life at less cost than their unjust and illegal exclusion will involve?"[42]

The truth, which some had known since *Plessy v. Ferguson,* was that Georgia's whites were more than ready to bear the cost of "unjust and illegal exclusion" of black people from civil society. Six months earlier, at the Georgia Equal Rights Convention meeting in Macon, such was the anti-Bookerite mood of five hundred black delegates that Bishop Turner's keynote address received thunderous applause. Du Bois stalwarts Barber, Hope, Herndon, Towns, and Proctor cheered Turner's unrecorded remarks as summed up by *The New York Times.* Turner "declared the American flag to be a dirty and contemptible flag and that hell was an improvement over the United States when the Negro was involved."[43]

President Theodore Roosevelt wired his White House dinner guest Booker Washington for an explanation of Turner's "treasonous" statement. When warned he might be indicted for sedition, the fierce old prelate told Washington he could prove "forty times more treason perpetrated against my race under the shadow of the United States flag than they can establish against me." Tom Watson, Georgia's Populist Party vice presidential candidate, who was bitter that blacks had stuck with the party of Lincoln in 1896, editorially lynched Turner and the Georgia Equal Rights Convention in *Tom Watson's Magazine.* "The Ungrateful Negro," Watson's April Fools' Day 1906 farewell to the Fifteenth Amendment and the Negro, anticipated his influential paper's gubernatorial endorsement of former *Atlanta Journal* publisher Hoke Smith, Grover Cleveland's interior secretary and a white supremacist progressive pledged to purge the electoral rolls of Negroes.[44]

HOKE SMITH'S OPPONENT WAS *THE ATLANTA CONSTITUTION'S* PUBLISHER, Clark Howell, one of Booker Washington's principal boosters. Smith had the dual advantage of sounding like a genuine racist and a credible reformer—ruling Negroes out of politics and regulating railroads and banks. Howell, chamber of commerce friendly and convinced that the Atlanta Compromise nullified Negroes as political threats, underestimated the redneck vote. Thomas Edward Watson saw Georgia's August Democratic primary as a foundational opportunity for a new racial order. "Nothing can be done as long as the South is forever frightened into political paralysis by the cry of 'negro domination,'" his *Tom Watson's Magazine* shrieked. As Watson's tool, Hoke Smith swept the Democratic primary and pledged a constitutional referendum, once elected, to disfranchise dark-skinned Georgians. Meanwhile, Smith's master prepared the ground for a white supremacist auto-da-fé. "What does civilization owe the negro?" asked Watson's publication. "Nothing! *Nothing!* NOTHING!"[45]

On Thursday, September 20, a crowd of more than seven thousand filled downtown Atlanta to hear the "Great Commoner" and Democratic presidential candidate William Jennings Bryan speak at Ponce de Leon Park. Most were white and many had swarmed into downtown from nearby towns and even outlying counties where fast city ways, alcohol, free black people, and labor competition were unwelcome features. The news dailies were blaring lurid stories of attempted rapes of white women by black men. John Temple Graves's *The Atlanta Georgian* took pride of place in inflaming white emotions. My grandfather's postal rounds may several times have carried him past bellowing newsboys along Decatur and Marietta streets. If so, he and his fellow postman and churchman George White returned home unnerved. A few days earlier, a dozen alarmed AME ministers had published concerned newspaper messages denouncing any sexual assaults by black men.

At about 4:00 p.m. on Saturday, the twenty-second, Atlanta's busy Five Points ricocheted with shouts from a *Journal* newsboy—"NEGRO ATTEMPTS TO ASSAULT MRS. MARY CHAFIN NEAR SUGAR CREEK BRIDGE!" An evening editorial in Graves's *Georgian* challenged the milling crowd near the exclusive Kimball House: "It is time to act, men; will you do your duty now?" At 8:00 p.m., historian David Godshalk identifies a man emerging from Kimball House, shouting, "Are we Southern white men going to stand for this?" The mob of thousands of mostly young whites responded with an affirmative rebel yell. "The Atlanta riot was if anything worse than reports," Du Bois wrote to his friend Mary White Ovington immediately after returning from investigating property holdings in Alabama's Lowndes County. He sat with his shotgun on South Hall's steps, his family secluded. "Litany at Atlanta," his hysterical and heretical composition, captured the dystopian awfulness of a four-day pogrom.[46]

Trolley cars heading for Grant Park through the Marietta-Peachtree intersection were stopped by ravening mobs whenever blacks were seen on board. Trolley 207's interracial passengers attracted a swarm of enraged white men hurling past the whites to beat bloody six black women and four black men. The police rescued them. More trolleys brought more unlucky black passengers riding with whites until the transit command finally ended service around midnight. At least two black male riders had died of wounds before then. Two black barbers and a bootblack caught the attention of rioters near the post office. After killing the three men instantly, their assassins dragged their bodies to the foot of the symbolic Henry Grady Monument.[47]

Businesses employing blacks and blacks owning businesses a mile south from Five Points and in side streets along the way were searched and ransacked, like the popular restaurant on Peters Street owned by black Mattie Adams, who was bludgeoned nearly to death. She recognized a competitor's son in the mob. Milton Brown, a white establishment's faithful driver, leaving Forsyth after work, was fatally shot multiple times by a passing citizen. Heavy rainfall after 2:00 p.m. Sunday dispersed the rioters, most of whom were finally out of steam and out of victims. However, John Temple Graves's contribution that day was an article in Joseph Pulitzer's New York *World*, a long justification of white supremacy's unavoidable police action. National newspapers reported the success of Atlanta's police action. The *San Francisco Chronicle*: ALL SOUTH READY FOR WAR UPON NEGRO. The *Outlook* excused it.[48]

Several family memories seem to be corroborated by historians of the city. Joseph Terrell, known as the state's "education governor," is believed to have phoned a Darktown contact early Sunday morning to offer its black citizens militia protection. My mother's Oglethorpe classmate, thirteen-year-old Walter White, claimed years later that when the riot resumed that Sunday he and his father positioned themselves, fully armed, to defend their home when the riot passed Courtland Street on its way to attack Darktown. "You're not to fire until they cross the edge of the lawn," George White whispered to Walter. A gunshot from a nearby dwelling caused the mob to scatter along Auburn Avenue. John Wesley Dobbs, patriarch of a distinguished black family, fingered his postal service revolver, fully expecting to shoot any of the mob trespassing on his house at 446 Auburn Avenue. Higher up Auburn at 300, John Henry Bell's family remembered calm, firm instructions to remain quiet in an upstairs room with Grandmother Adeline. The master of the house, standing beside a front window, also held his postal service Colt ready.[49]

Darktown and Brownsville bore the assaults Sunday and Monday. With an arsenal of knives, pistols, and hatchets, Darktown took care of itself handily on Sunday. White marauders took careful measure of this dense settlement and wisely backpedaled on Houston Street. Darktowners' stolid courage probably saved their betters during four days of concerted white homicide. John Wesley Bowen and Henry Proctor spoke for respectable blacks when they discreetly thanked their dark-skinned cousins. One reason the final black death toll would remain uncertain was said to be because bodies were stealthily collected for decent burial by Darktowners.

Brownsville, on the other hand, was Darktown's socioeconomic opposite, an upper-middle-class village on the city's eastern edge peopled by black professionals, many connected to Christian Methodist Clark College and Gammon Theological Seminary. Monday evening an exploratory advance by police and deputized white locals coalesced along Jonesboro Road into an attack on Brownsville. Impelled by rumors that Brownsville blacks were preparing to attack white neighborhoods with guns supplied by corner grocery store owner Luther Price, the rioters encountered a group of black men who fired and killed Officer Jim Heard and injured four others. Frank Fambro, the village butcher, also died in the encounter. Three infantry companies surrounded Brownsville that evening but waited until Tuesday morning for reinforcements. Then, joined by the Governor's Horse Guard, the combined forces flooded the village and ordered Brownsvillians to exit their homes and stand under guard while searches took place for nonexistent weapons.[50]

When Yale man and physician W. F. Penn of Brownsville spoke in public days later at a chamber of commerce meeting with several influential blacks present, his language humbled and shamed some of the whites: "What shall we do? We have been disarmed: how shall we protect our lives and property? If living a sober industrious, upright life, accumulating property and educating his children as best he knows how, is not the standard by which a colored man can live and be protected in the South, what is to become of him? If the kind of life I have lived isn't the kind you want, shall I leave and go North? When we aspire to be decent and industrious we are told that we are bad examples to other colored men. Tell us what your standards are for colored men. What are the requirements under which we may live and be protected. What shall we do?" Confederate colonel A. J. McBride jumped up and pledged, "If necessary, I will go out and sit on his porch with a rifle."[51]

Good Samaritan McBride's offer was no longer necessary. On Wednesday, September 26, Gate City newspapers unanimously headlined: AT-LANTA IS HERSELF AGAIN, BUSINESS ACTIVITY RESTORED AND RIOT IS FORGOTTEN, *The Atlanta Journal*; LAST TRACE OF THE TROUBLE GONE, *The Atlanta Georgian*; NO FURTHER OUTBREAKS ARE FEARED, *Evening News*. But Max Barber's *The Voice of the Negro* guffawed at these absurdities, publishing its editor's departing denial as he headed for asylum in Chicago. "Behold! We have peace—No, not peace," denounced Barber, "but a wilderness called peace. Sixty or seventy colored people are in jail for killing one policeman while sixteen whites are in jail for the whole riot which resulted in the murdering and maiming of more than a hundred people." The president of Atlanta's Fourth National Bank had advised Barber to save himself within twenty-four hours after a local telegrapher identified Barber as author of the New York *World*'s "A Concerned Citizen," an explosive identification of Graves, Tom Watson, and a host of respected chamber of commerce riot colluders—a searing exposé of white mob action "as lawless and as godless as any savages." He castigated Watson as "a human moccasin," exposed the editor of the *News* as the instigator of "the fire-eating and reckless editorials," and went so far as to charge Smith's subordinates with having "blackened their faces." Barber's article exposed "a prominent banker" as one of the riot's engines.[52]

Two days later, the city's health office announced the number of issued death certificates: two dead whites—Officer Heard and a Mrs. Thompson, a heart attack victim. There were ten black deaths.[53] There would never be a reliable body count. That the toll of black dead would have been larger, however, both Clark College president William Crogman and Gammon Theological president John Wesley Bowen admitted in a secret message of thanks to Darktown's fighting "lawless blacks." Yet the *Georgian*, whose inflammatory editorials helped cause the riot, received a joint letter from these two credentialed colored community leaders on Wednesday that augured deepening intraracial class divisions. Bowen and Crogman deplored their city's "infamous negro dives" and condemned "black men who have stirred up hatred of the races by their crimes against the white women." Bowen and Crogman even "pledged to ferret out the man who gunned down Officer Jim Heard."[54]

JOHN HENRY BELL'S MAIL ROUNDS MADE HIM MORE AND MORE DEPRESSED over the next weeks. The shuttered, ransacked black businesses along Decatur, Marietta, and Peters looked damaged beyond repair. Moreover, the proliferation of "For Colored Only" signs was a new development throughout the city, and they were matched by "For Whites Only." People he knew, even some whites he didn't, seemed to go out of their way to greet and even halt to chat. A miasma of enforced correctness lay upon ordinary interactions. The new politics of official segregation appalled him, and coming as soon as Hoke Smith's November inauguration were ballot box algorithms removing all but a handful of African American voters.

Exactly when Grandfather decided to do so is uncertain. He and Alice had identified themselves and their two children as mulatto in the

1900 federal census. Six years later, Grandmother's presence in Oakland Cemetery suddenly became problematic for her family, whose identity as "no-nation" people was becoming illogical. Walter White, my mother's Oglethorpe classmate, experienced an identity catharsis that late September week in 1906 that he described unforgettably forty years later in *A Man Called White.* As the white mob departed his family's front yard, Walter realized, "I was a Negro." From that day, "[I] was not white. There is nothing within my mind and heart which tempts me to think I am."[55] His was a rebirth equally experienced by John Henry Bell and his children.

My maternal grandfather hired two men and a brace to remove his wife from Oakland Cemetery, a resting spot that would no longer be available to him when he died as a Negro.

7

. . .

SEPARATE AND
UNEQUAL

Bells and Lewises,
1906–1930

Drawing the greatest numbers since their historic meeting four years earlier in Saint Paul, Minnesota, members of the National Afro-American Council poured into New York City on October 9, 1906. Timothy Thomas Fortune, the versatile eccentric whose journalistic advocacy had birthed their organization, had been cast aside by what the country's black leadership now acknowledged, with either admiration or misgivings, was an all-powerful Tuskegee machine. Bishop Alexander Walters, the National Afro-American Council's youthful chief, took his marching orders, therefore, from Booker Washington.[1] That October morning's unseasonable warmth only increased the bishop's anxiety as he took the capacity crowd's emotional temperature. The long day would hardly be a credit to the Great Accommodator's leadership.

Not two weeks had passed since Atlanta's white majority terminated whatever illusions of post-Reconstruction citizenship remained to 45 percent of Georgia's population. Not a seated soul in the meeting hall believed the risible body count of only two whites and ten blacks released by Atlanta's health office the previous week. In fact, the ghoulish truth about the riot's fatalities was never to be established. Militant J. Max

Barber's accusatory report published in the New York *World* claimed "almost as many white people were killed, and as many were wounded as colored people." Longtime residents estimated that at least a thousand blacks had deserted the city.[2] My grandfather could not be with the outraged majority in Manhattan, but his sentiments must have aligned with the opposition. The National Afro-American Council virtually sprang to life in February 1898 after the nighttime immolation of the colored postmaster of Lake City, South Carolina.

John Henry Bell had joined the Afro-American Council early, kept his dues current, and greatly approved of the monsoon of condemnation roaring through the Negro press. Kelly Miller, Howard University's normally restrained academic dean, wrote "An Appeal to Reason," more animated by wrath than by reason, against "the half savage descendants of Oglethorpe's colonists." Calvin Chase's influential *Washington Bee* called on the federal government to "civilize the South"—a challenge tantamount to asking Booker Washington to call upon his dinner host Theodore Roosevelt to speak sternly from his bully pulpit.[3] If John Bell had no satisfactory answer to give his daughter and son about their president's silence, it also dawned on puzzled or disillusioned National Afro-American Council members during those three days that neither Bishop Walters nor Dr. Washington had answers as to where their race was headed.

The Atlanta Compromise postulated that the South's blacks and whites would prosper in peace in a separate but unequal mutuality. But in the eleven years since the Cotton States and International Exposition, South Carolina, Louisiana, Alabama, North Carolina, Arkansas, and Tennessee had replicated the Mississippi constitutional model of literacy tests, grandfather clauses, and poll taxes to strike black voters from their rolls. Governor Hoke Smith had sworn to amend Georgia's constitution, a commitment no one doubted would soon be delivered. That the usually buoyant Alexander Walters gave way to dire predictions from the speaker's rostrum deflated even stalwart Bookerites. "The Negro will not be the only one to suffer. . . . Business will be paralyzed, credit destroyed," declaimed the bishop of the African Methodist Episcopal Zion Church.

"Desolation and ruin will surely follow." Walters couldn't have more viv-idly evoked his audience's still-vivid memories of North Carolina's ra-cially cleansed and devastated black Wilmington.[4]

The Afro-American Council's vice president, a handsome woman first in almost every field of endeavor, aimed arrow-straight for Atlanta's real malefactors—"the better class of southern white people." Tall, one-blood-drop Mary Church Terrell, minted at Oberlin College and a vet-eran of the nation's corridors of influence, called the assembled men to action with all the signature impatience of a National Association of Col-ored Women founder. When the black pastor of Washington's Fifteenth Street Presbyterian Church followed Mrs. Terrell, he surprised the hall and quite surpassed her invective: "There is but one way . . . to deal with a mob; and that is to shoot it to death, to riddle it with bullets or dyna-mite it," prescribed the Princeton-educated and usually courtly Francis Grimké.[5]

In historian David Godshalk's judgment, this October meeting of the council marked an inflection point for Booker T. Washington's lead-ership among his own people—an approximate midway between his At-lanta Compromise address and his displacement by the Du Bois–inspired Amenia Conference of 1916. Feeling the ground giving way, the Great Ac-commodator sternly reminded his restive audience that most held return tickets to places where white people lived with whom there was no other choice than to live without provocation. Nevertheless, the Afro-American Council majority resolved to ask President Roosevelt to appoint a non-partisan commission to visit southern states "wherein these outrages and barbarities have been perpetrated."

A worried Alexander Walters proceeded to introduce one of the country's liberal activists and influential publishers, thirty-four-year-old Oswald Garrison Villard, short, balding, and opinionated. A Garri-son, as in William Lloyd, on his suffragist mother's side, Villard's father once controlled General Electric. A beaming Booker Washington expected to hear himself lauded after several days of unaccustomed criticism. In-stead, although he could not have known, Oswald Garrison Villard per-sonified modernist, corporate, demographic, and civil liberties persuasions destined to undermine a racial status quo that was Washington's bread and butter.

Reports of black resistance in Atlanta were impressive, Villard observed, but it would have been "a thousand times more effective," he counseled, "to make the South understand that its injustice to the Negro should result in withdrawing from Atlanta all trade possible, and of spreading through the whole world the story of Atlanta's shame."[6] Three years from his appearance at the National Afro-American Council, Oswald Villard would draft the call for what became the NAACP. It seems that most of the audience would not recall anything the Great Accommodator said in his closing remarks that was especially memorable. What he did say was not new: "Any policy that does not seek to harmonize the two races and cement them is unwise and dangerous."[7]

JOHN HENRY LEWIS, A NEWLY MINTED MORRIS BROWN COLLEGE BACCA-laureate, assumed the principalship of an AME high school in the fall of 1906 deep in Georgia's southwest. Cuthbert's Payne Institute was named for the revered South Carolina educator and AME bishop Daniel A. Payne. Today, Cuthbert seems a ghostly remainder of its high cotton flourish, majority black workforce, and Georgia Central Railway prosperity. But the boll weevil and the Great Black Migration were fifteen years in the future when my twenty-five-year-old father arrived, inexperienced but motivated, and single. Mazie, his young sister, came with him to finish her education and keep house. Like his undergraduate college, named for Morris Brown, the AME denomination's second bishop, my father's Cuthbert high school appointment honored another refugee Charlestonian, both men remarkable vessels of civil rights progress. By 1900, like the AME Church's flagship Wilberforce University, Morris Brown was also known for imbuing its best students with what its religious trustees called a certain millenarianism, an African-centered Methodism providentially called to uplift an abused people and redeem their persecutors.

Payne Institute provided young black men and women the secondary education that Georgia's Caucasians stonily refused to vote tax dollars for.[8] High schools for young people whose parents had money enough for private education like Payne's were almost as rare as angels on the head of a pin. In southern backwaters of the early twentieth century C. Vann Woodward estimated that "every other Negro and one in five white men [one] met could not read or write." John Henry Lewis could be forgiven if he suspected Cuthbert's racial literacy ratios suffered by comparison.[9] But he was the sort of educator to whom it would have been unforgivable not to try shaping Payne into one of the African Methodist Church's finest southwestern alternatives to a public high school.

He soon made the acquaintance of another lone educator in the county. Principal Fletcher H. Henderson Sr. of Howard Normal Randolph School, a similar private secondary institution, probably shared professional tips and an occasional welcome to the Henderson parlor. Perhaps the musical and math precocity of young Fletcher Henderson Jr., a future orchestral genius of national renown, registered with Father's sharp-eyed appreciation of unusual teenage talent. And maybe, as well, some regret that Fletcher Henderson Jr. was not attending Payne Institute.[10] The state's present political climate made his newcomer role especially suspicious, however. Local whites made known by smirks and comments their approval of the September bloodletting in Atlanta. He knew to keep abreast of the fast-moving situation in Atlanta, whence updated telegraph news was both depressing and alarming. He learned that Max Barber had fled the city, that at least thirty blacks were killed.

John Henry Lewis was deeply troubled but hardly surprised to read that black upper-class blame of lower-class blacks became the biracial placebo of Atlanta's elites. Reverend Proctor's "The Dives Must Go," a searing condemnation of lower-class sloth and lust, had been delivered on the last Sunday before the riot.[11] Bad Negroes rather than feral racists were to blame. Charles T. Hopkins, prominent white attorney and principal organizer of Atlanta's post-riot Civic League, summoned superior white people to help the best black people lead wayward black masses back to the path of respectable segregation. "The Negro race is a child race," Hopkins knew. "We have boasted of our superiority and we have now sunk to this level—we have shed the blood of our helpless wards. Christianity and humanity demand that we treat the Negro fairly."[12]

For Proctor of First Church, for Bowen and Crogman of Brownsville, as well as for a lifeboat of Methodist and Baptist divines, Hopkins's Civic League presented itself as a broad tent spread by the powerful white business community to include a black professional class willing to accept moral culpability for the riot—expiation followed by subordination. But John Lewis's agrarian origins and hardscrabble educational attainments gave him pause. Moral depravity offended his Methodist soul, yet biracial collusion of elites necessarily signaled diminished concern for the common people. He knew most of his students' families admired their Bishop Turner's civil rights reputation, the manliness exhibited by his followers at the Georgia Equal Rights Convention held in Macon just before the Atlanta riot. Yet the old lion had fallen silent lately.

A meeting at Morris Brown with James English, the banker who served J. Max Barber with a twenty-four-hour departure notice, and Charles Hopkins should have disturbed John Henry.[13] It was reported that English's ten-dollar contribution generated five hundred dollars for Morris Brown's fundraising initiative. Although I could conceive of my father indulging his bishop's canny fundraising for their college, he must have seen the slippery-slope peril of white beneficence. Godshalk's *Veiled Visions* reports Du Bois's cagey view of the Morris Brown event: "There is no use of my going over there and saying what I really believe."[14] Du Bois had taught almost a decade at Atlanta University when my father began teaching at Payne Institute.

Unlike Burghardt Du Bois, who writes amply of his early AU classroom experiences, John Henry's Cuthbert pedagogical experience vanished long ago. Yet both must have been asked early on the same soul-searching question by a troubled student. "What would you say to a soft, brown face . . . blurting out in American history, 'Do you trust white people?'" "You do not," Du Bois ruminated, "and you know that you do not as much as you want to." I believe my father would have answered, as did the AU preceptor, "that most white folks are honest, and all the while you are lying on every level, silent eye there knows you are lying . . . to the greater glory of God."[15] A sense of professional mission must have trumped whatever reservations my father held about the cruel reality of his students' American futures under *Plessy v. Ferguson*. Rather, his own striving American ideals led him to believe that Theodore Roosevelt's vaunted new Square Deal applied to black people as well.

THAT BOOKER WASHINGTON HAD DINED IN OCTOBER 1901 AT THE WHITE House en famille shortly after the Roosevelts installed themselves was widely regarded as proof of the president's racial enlightenment. He had stood fast when the white South fulminated against senatorial confirmation of a colored collector of the Port of Charleston. He had even shut Mississippi's Indianola post office after competent Minnie Cox was terrorized into resigning as postmistress. May 1903 brought earthshaking news of Department of Justice inquiries into a plague of imprisonment of southern blacks for indebtedness (peonage).[16] At the 1904 Republican National Convention in Chicago black southern delegates (denied the franchise at home) voted for Roosevelt's renomination against powerful party bosses. Notable federal appointments continued. Two years later, Teddy Roosevelt's midterm popularity among African Americans remained rock-solid.

Off in a Georgia corner, preoccupied with his administrative duties, Principal Lewis probably missed the second Niagara Movement meeting at Harpers Ferry, convened by Du Bois and William Monroe Trotter on August 15, 1906. Two nights earlier, three companies of the storied Twenty-fifth Infantry Regiment (Colored) ordered to Fort Brown on the Rio Grande were alleged to have "shot up the town," killing a white bartender and wounding a policeman in racially hostile Brownsville, Texas. Cuthbert's high school principal no doubt did hear of this Brownsville incident. Not a single soldier admitted guilt. The army inspector general conceded the evidence was inconclusive. Brownsville receded to newspaper back pages and then disappeared.

An infuriated Roosevelt arbitrarily signed an executive order dismissing without trial and with forfeiture of their pension 167 soldiers. Ordering

Secretary of War Taft to withhold his decision from publication until after the November congressional elections, the president sailed for America's new Panama Canal, where photographers captured him in full testosterone manning a huge dredging machine.[17] At San Juan Hill these infantrymen had carried the day for Roosevelt; in Manila Bay they had performed as the new American empire's shock troops. Six were Medal of Honor winners. Congressional elections approached with Republican control of the House hanging in the balance. African American votes were significant to the GOP in Maryland, New York, Missouri, Ohio, New Jersey, and Kansas.

When the Great Accommodator learned on October 30 what his friend proposed to do, he saw that Roosevelt's Brownsville fiat was fatal to his life's work—more than ten years of his wizardry, appeasement, deception, manipulation, mastery, and even courage extinguished in a fit of executive arrogance. His eleventh-hour appeal was contemptuously disregarded: "You cannot have any information to give me privately, to which I could pay heed, my dear Mr. Washington."[18] A Saturday morning telephone call emboldened an indomitable Mary Church Terrell to call upon Secretary Taft at home with apparent success. However, all finally failed—Washington, Terrell, and Taft—when faced with the absent president's rock-solid indifference. On November 7, the day after the GOP retained control of the House, the War Department released the decision to disgrace the Twenty-fifth Infantry's First Battalion. Nicholas Longworth, Teddy Roosevelt's son-in-law and a new representative, acknowledged his debt to black voters for his narrow victory.

"Once enshrined in our hearts as Moses," declaimed Reverend Adam Clayton Powell Sr. of the Abyssinian Baptist Church, Roosevelt was "now enshrouded in our scorn as Judas." The November 1906 congressional elections would expose a presidential perfidiousness that would embitter colored America and devastate Payne's student body.[19]

ALMOST FROM THE DAY AFTER J. MAX BARBER BOARDED HIS CHICAGO train, Henry Hugh Proctor had seized and reformulated an Atlanta riot narrative of purgation, resurrection, and salvation. He bested his white alter ego Charles Hopkins of the Civic League with evangelizing bromides about "Congregationalizing the Negro" along with visions of "the better city" about to "spring forth." The Great Accommodator, badly shaken by Roosevelt's racial politics, found the pastor's thoughtful game plan of turning a local political disaster into a national moral crusade ingenious.[20] Proctor proposed to erect a brick-and-mortar monument to the reconstructed Atlanta, a new First Church rising over the old.

All of Atlanta understood Proctor's turning to Booker Washington instead of Fisk classmate Du Bois to speak and turn the first shovel at the 1907 ceremonial groundbreaking. William Howard Taft, Teddy Roosevelt's uneasy successor, blessed the enterprise in person.[21] Proctor was, after all, friend to Burghardt Du Bois and Booker Washington, both of whom frequented his church, notwithstanding their competing approaches to the colored race's best policies. "But there need be no conflict," assured the Yale-educated divine. "They are right and left wings of a great movement. Just as a bird must have both wings for successful flight, so must any movement have the radical and conservative wings." Breaches were healed, the work of cooperation between the better elements of both races progressed, hummed Proctor, "and it was the unanimous opinion that the city was better afterwards than before."[22]

Proctor would spend almost two years bearing his message of moral reform and interracial peace throughout the North and Northwest. Supplied with Booker Washington's list of powerful whites in thirty-five cities above and even below the Mason-Dixon line, Proctor not only raised tens of thousands of dollars in under twenty-four months but also secured a grand pipe organ from Andrew Carnegie. A number of appearances in which the crusading prelate sang spirituals recalled his Yale Divinity School performances. His appointment as assistant moderator of the National Council of Congregational Churches served as a red carpet. At Brooklyn's historic Plymouth Church in December 1907 the wealthy congregants thrilled to stories of Atlanta's newfound racial brotherhood and assurances that their tithes would build a temple to racial pride and progress. "We are not a race of criminals," Proctor preached, "and we refuse to be judged by the vagabonds of the race who commit outlandish crimes inconsistent with the character of the race as a whole. We insist on being judged, as are other races, by their best and not by their worst."[23]

Nor was his congregation of the educated and well placed a parsimonious one. An informed perusal of the treasurer's record books for those months discloses a robust stream of Bell and Westmoreland tithes.[24] White architects Bruce and Everett of Atlanta designed the building. But Proctor and trustees Alonzo Herndon, John Henry Bell, Isaac Westmoreland, Owen Lovejoy, and others commissioned the city's leading colored contractor Robert E. Pharrow "and as many Negro artisans as possible" to erect their sanctuary. My Bell grandfather and the other trustees had memorial stained glass windows fabricated by colored master craftsmen three blocks from Courtland Street.[25] John Henry Bell, his daughter Alice, and son Levering almost certainly chose together the family window that inspired this descendant's family history.

The church doors opened in early 1909 to local biracial applause and positive national notice. Reverend Proctor's self-serving memoir claimed that future Madison Avenue advertising king Bruce Barton publicized First Church as "the church that saved a city."[26] A more accurate characterization would have been the church that insulated a privileged minority from the less fortunate citizens of color. Trustee Alonzo Herndon's gifted spouse, Adrienne, presented the morality play *Everyman* in the one-thousand-seat auditorium, the church's first production starring her with the support of her AU elocution class. Sponsored by First Church later that year, the segregated city auditorium featured Fisk Jubilee lyric tenor Roland Hayes, whose libretto of spirituals and finely articulated European songs foretold international recognition.

Atlanta had no dearth of large black churches serving its multiple faiths. On Auburn Avenue the AME's Big Bethel dwarfed Proctor's sanctuary, and the nearby Wheat Street Baptists regarded Sunday services at First Church as positively tedious. But Proctor's tabernacle excelled every Atlanta god box—black and white—in facilities such as an open library holding three thousand books, a gymnasium for young men,

and a public men's bath priced at one cent per visit. Topping these facilities was the Connally Water Fountain, Atlanta's sole outdoor "integrated
water fountain."[27] In years to come, First Church's annual Colored Music
Festival would become an irreplaceable segregated Gate City cultural
asset. With all that, Burghardt Du Bois was, nevertheless, only months
away from heading for New York City and a new civil rights organization
organized by associates of Oswald Garrison Villard.[28] Deciding that the
world remained unfazed by his remarkable social science studies, *The
Souls of Black Folk* author was leaving a city far more ready to embrace
the peace of unequal separation than the pain of civil rights progress.

   In time, however, he would see that his judgment was too severe; that
his influence among some of Atlanta's best and brightest young minds
foretold a renaissance of racial assertiveness. Some six years earlier, Atlanta University's appeal to the Rockefeller General Education Board for
a teachers' practice school had languished subject to finding an additional ten thousand dollars. "By chance," as university historian Clarence Bacote notes, "Mrs. Charles Russell Lowell, whose brother [Robert
Gould Shaw] perished in the Civil War, had just finished reading with
great interest the *Souls of Black Folk* in May, 1903." She promptly dis-
patched her check for ten thousand dollars. The new practice school
named after General Oglethorpe opened in 1904.[29] Less than a decade remained until graduates of Atlanta University's Oglethorpe Preparatory
School would spearhead a reawakened black citizenry that finally forced
Atlanta's white majority to find tax funds for a segregated black high
school.

ANY ADMINISTRATIVE RECORDS OF MY FATHER'S TENURE AT PAYNE
vanished with the school's liquidation on the eve of the Great Depression.
During his three years there the small faculty appears to have doubled,
standards were sharpened, and its curriculum became more collegiate,
to the point that Payne would be incorporated into Morris Brown College
as a collegiate annex soon after his departure. My father enabled his
younger sister Mazie to complete Payne's twelfth grade. His own welfare

benefited from what had to have been spartan conservation of his salary. To that resource the good fortune of his mother Hattie's and older sister Susie's steady monetary help from their Americus convenience store was added.[30] In Cuthbert, my father served the AME Church admirably and confirmed Henry McNeal Turner's esteem.

The world beyond Cuthbert still escaped his intellectual comfort zone, however. He could see that the new judicial diktat of separate equality presented credentialed people like himself with a range of potentially defeatist ideological options: Frederick Douglass's assimilationism; Bishop Turner's emigrationism; Booker Washington's accommodationism; Burghardt Du Bois's Talented Tenth militancy. Or was there some ideological synthesis on the order of Proctor's?[31] Somehow, he decided that a graduate degree from Yale could educationally arm him against the deceptions of *Plessy v. Ferguson*. Although Reverend Proctor's credentials probably influenced my father, his Yale Divinity School admission was pure high-wire persistence.

Prompted to explore postgraduate possibilities by a colleague at Payne Institute, Principal Lewis penned a "Dear Sir" catalog request on New Year's Eve 1908 to Yale Divinity School. Reverend Edward Lewis Curtis, acting dean, complied readily. On January 9, an excited Lewis wrote that he was "even more anxious to come to your school, having looked over the catalogue." The letter's next question: "Prof., do you think you can secure for me a work scholarship for next year?"[32] Dean Curtis's January 12 reply assured Principal John H. Lewis that he could "rely upon receiving a work scholarship," what might translate as today's diversity, equity, and inclusion beneficence. His Yale application endorsed by Morris Brown's president, his distribution of courses assured, and his financial support guaranteed, Payne's principal informed Dean Curtis on February 23, 1909, "I will come in the fall."[33]

My father's September 1910 arrival as a junior classman at Yale Divinity had been delayed by unexplained illness, misplaced documents, salary delay from Payne, a Morris Brown semester, summer resort work in Asbury Park, New Jersey, Yale's scholarship reconsideration. His late July 1910 appeal to Curtis—Father's last and written from New Jersey—

hoped Curtis "can recall that some months ago I wrote of plans to enter Yale Divinity?" To be able to do so, Curtis was reminded, "I resigned on my own volition the position at Morris Brown College." He was still determined to attend in September, even without sufficient funds, "as the season at this resort is very dull." If the dean found it "impossible to offer me assistance before leaving," Lewis hoped Curtis "can later find some way to help me."[34]

The culture shock John Henry Lewis must have experienced at the start of the Yale years, from 1910 to 1913, were the polished anecdotes of my childhood. There was New Testament Greek, which nearly disgraced him in the first semester.[35] Moving among a sea of white students for the first time came with practice to be sure. Morris Brown had stood him in good stead, though, as he modeled both presence and diction on eloquent Bishop Turner. Either my father was the lone African American in the divinity school or he failed to remember the other person. African Americans of his generation tended to avoid banding together in white educational institutions, their twofold point being exemption from voluntary segregation and exemplification of exceptional grace. Avoidance of other blacks at Yale could hardly have been easier, however.

When the confident new black fraternity founded in 1905–1906 at Cornell University reached Yale four years later, the Zeta chapter of Alpha Phi Alpha boasted a dozen men drawn from various departments of the university: among them Charles H. Wesley, Nimrod Allen, Aiken Pope, John M. Ross, William Bishop, and my father. Charles Wesley, matinee-idol handsome and the third future Harvard history PhD, after Du Bois and Carter Woodson, possessed superior intellectual suavity but, as later years were to reveal, deficient administrative judgment. Wesley's *The History of Alpha Phi Alpha* (1929) tells us that "twenty-one years of a black college group are described for the first time."[36] His book's considerable family-history value situates John H. Lewis with Alpha Phi Alpha's "teachers, ministers, physicians, lawyers, dentists, and businessmen" in a swelling Talented Tenth brotherhood that formed the basis of both the National Association for the Advancement of Colored People and the National League on Urban Conditions Among Negroes.[37]

Some thirty-five years later, John Henry Lewis and Charles Harris Wesley, the first black Guggenheim recipient and author of a dozen monographs, found themselves well-intentioned antagonists in the AME Church's great educational crisis at Wilberforce University. My father would admire his Yale classmate Wesley's *The Collapse of the Confederacy* (1937), but he was not at all surprised to find that the ethnocentric American Historical Association, to make no mention of the Mississippi Valley Historical Association, bridled at Wesley's interpretive presumptuousness. "Dr. Wesley has upset a tradition," Carter Woodson once observed of the profession's prejudices. "Negroes are supposed to talk and write about the affairs which are particularly their own history."

Wesley was an important New Haven acquaintance. George Williamson Crawford, Yale Law School's second African American alumnus, was as well. There was even a physical resemblance in color, trim body type, and bespectacled intensity, although George was senior by fifteen years. My father's hard-earned supplemental earnings from New Haven waterfront jobs came in large part thanks to George Crawford. An Alabama striver with a bachelor's from Talladega College, George had finished Yale in 1903 with the prestigious Townsend Oration Prize, settled permanently in New Haven with family, and eventually served as the city's corporation counsel.[38] George was a Niagarite and charter member of the NAACP. His was a household name of permanent significance my parents would press upon me.

The new divinity school dean must have admired his African American scholar's professional drive, his determination to learn the best from the best. Another more relevant impression is that Yale's then dean of the divinity school, Charles Brown, strongly recommended John Henry Lewis's divinity application to the Graduate School of the University of Chicago.

It was hardly surprising that John Lewis gave prosperous Americus as his birthplace at Yale and Chicago. That he arrived at Yale and Chicago three years younger than his 1880 census age was certainly a surprise. To be a competitive twenty-eight-year-old graduate student, he matched the average age of precocious white student populations at the great northern research universities. It must have seemed only fair that John Lewis readjust the starting line of his professional life as fixed under *Plessy v. Ferguson* to become an even more precocious Morris Brown BA, an illustrious Yale BD, a cutting-edge Chicago MA, and a prospective sociology PhD from Chicago.[39] His term at Chicago began in the autumn quarter of 1913 with high marks in "Church and Society" and "The Family." By spring quarter 1914 "The Class Struggle in Society," bookended by "The Evolution of Philanthropy," curiously prefigured courses to be taught by the legendary Robert E. Park, who arrived from his ghostwriter service at Tuskegee the following year to make Chicago the cradle of American sociology. My father easily passed his field examination, and his master's thesis, "Social Service in the Negro Church," was accepted in August 1914.

Chicago, weather excepted, fascinated Professor Lewis. The Great Black Migration from the South was beginning. Lynchings, endemic and irrepressible, were driving an early wave of black folk with means northward. The great infestation laying waste to the South's sole marketable crop enchained both white landholders and black tenants in a survival-of-the-fittest fury neither understood nor withstood. Georgia's *Tifton Gazette*, hardly a world away from Cuthbert, called for restraint before all black labor headed north. "They have allowed negroes to be lynched, five at a time, on nothing stronger than suspicion; they have allowed whole sections to be depopulated. . . . They have allowed them to be white-capped and to be whipped, and their homes burned, with only the weakest and most spasmodic efforts to apprehend those guilty." The head of Chicago's new Urban League stated a sad fact: "Every time a lynching takes place in a community down South," explained T. Arnold Hill, "you can depend on it that colored people will arrive in Chicago within two weeks."[40]

Professor Lewis read *The Chicago Defender* and watched as the Illinois Central transformed a city. Chicago was a long way from being the Eden painted by the *Defender*, but its reputation as a good place to find employment and live without fear of arbitrary arrest and redneck harassment had attracted tens of thousands in recent years. As many as 300,000,

Le Petit Journal–European Notice
of 1906 Race Riot, 1906

and possibly more, African American farmers, unskilled laborers, and domestics would leave for Chicago, Detroit, Pittsburgh, and Indianapolis before 1920. But there was one other development without which the Great Black Migration might not have materialized. In 1914, the year he was awarded his master's degree, the number of immigrants arriving from Europe to the United States numbered 1,218,480.

In a historical coincidence his son would find meaningful, the University of Chicago approved his father's master's degree on August 2, the opening week of the Great War unforgettably described in Barbara Tuchman's *The Guns of August*.[41] The numbers from Europe plunged to 326,700 in 1915, leaving a demographic vacuum to be filled by hundreds of thousands of black people as bewitched by the American dream as John Henry Lewis was. He assumed a professorship at Atlanta's recently renamed Morris Brown University as Europe's civil war commenced.

Professor Lewis returned to a city deeply altered eight years after the 1906 race riot. Colored Atlantans knew better than to bother themselves about the vote. Municipal ordinance seated them at the rear on public transportation. Department stores sold clothes on a no–fitting room and no-return understanding. "Colored Only" signs directed people to safe or forbidden spaces depending on pigment. No ordinance officially segregated elevators, but both races observed a policy of exclusive use. Benjamin Davis Sr., publisher of the black news weekly *The Independent*, called early on for separate lift conveyances. Suppose a colored man stumbled and fell against some white lady while getting on or off the car, Benjamin Davis warned, "what would be the outcome?" John Temple Graves, whose *Georgian* probably did most to fan the riot fires, had editorialized a white supremacist's triumphant advice: "These two opposite antagonistic races can never live together in the same government under equal laws—never. Help us to separate!"[42]

On his way to Morris Brown University at Boulevard and Houston streets, John Lewis found a much different commercial landscape. With the notable exception of Alonzo Herndon's palatial midtown barbershop, the dense, vibrant black businesses near Five Points and Peachtree had either relocated or been driven west to Auburn Avenue. This relocation of commerce brought with it dangerously deep living arrangements that guaranteed in a few years the greatest conflagration since Sherman's visit. His Morris Brown had inflated to become a university. It appeared to be the conceit of President William Alfred Fountain Sr., fortyish, variously educated, and with a 1901 bachelor's from the college. Lewis and Fountain had overlapped enough to develop a mutual if guarded respect. Fountain Sr., after obtaining honorary degrees from Wilberforce University and Turner Theological Seminary, was elected fifth president, the first Morris Brown College graduate in that role, in 1911.

Consideration of the college's new name arose almost immediately and became official with the original charter's amendment in April 1913.[43] That Morris Brown University emerged as the AME Church's most ambitious institution in student size and geographical location may have been the consequence more of ecclesiastical ambition than of prudent institutional planning. Reading the school's official history between the lines, President Fountain's executive decisions do seem heavily weighted by the designs of Bishop Joseph Simeon Flipper, Atlanta University alumnus and Morris Brown's third president. Flipper, brother of the first African American West Pointer and something of an academic visionary, was elevated to the bishopric in 1908. Three years later he declared himself chancellor of Morris Brown and Fountain's superior; both chancellor and president soon boasted a mammoth institutional success: Morris Brown University, composed of Turner Theological Seminary, Payne College of Cuthbert, Central Park Normal and Industrial Institute in Savannah, and almost one thousand students. A powerhouse football team outperformed most of the southern competition.

Supported by a substantial slice of the tithes of one million black Methodist faithful, the restructured Morris Brown University advertised an affordable education to working-class and generally darker-skinned young men and women who were underrepresented at neoabolitionist-endowed Atlanta, Fisk, Morehouse, and Spelman, and even at Howard and Lincoln universities.[44] The new Morris Brown excited John Lewis. By turns, he taught literature, education, and sociology, the latter a subject that most appealed and in which he intended to earn a PhD after returning to the University of Chicago to study under Robert Park. I thought it was significant that he offered no courses in theology at first. His next academic year brought major news to the campus as well as the nation. Bishop Turner's death that May silenced a defiant voice long since become unsteady.

That November, the removal from the scene of an embattled and unwell Booker T. Washington at age fifty-nine surprised the nation much more. The Springfield race riot of 1908 had shown the advancing movement north of the so-called race problem. Reading his December 1915 *Crisis*, John Lewis probably nodded approvingly of Du Bois's Booker Washington farewell. "This is no fit time for recrimination or complaint," editor Du Bois condoled. "Gravely and with bowed head let us receive what this great figure gave of good, silently rejecting all else."[45] Washington's death, as Du Bois rightly gauged, coincided with the beginning of a new epoch in African American history. On a sprawling estate in the Berkshires a banner coalition of officers and sympathizers came together in the Hudson Valley, where Burghardt Du Bois and these impatient men and women debated and strategized for three remarkable August days in 1916 the NAACP's new civil rights master plan.[46]

Whether or not the death of Henry McNeal Turner affected my father's decision is unknown, but it seemed fitting that he decided that year to seek his AME Church ordination. Unlike the protected tenure his professor's credentials could have guaranteed him, pastor John Lewis forfeited his liberty. Ordination in the most hierarchical and authoritarian of black religious denominations, where general conventions elected bishops who controlled presiding elders who commanded pastors who approved deacons, could mean summary assignment anywhere in the United States. In Father's case, however, ordination came with assignment to Atlanta's Trinity AME Church, nicely supplementing his faculty salary. Professional calculus also entailed marriage. Pastor Lewis married twenty-four-year-old Eva Brown Walker of Americus early in 1916, "an accomplished musician," said Aunt Susie.[47] President Fountain readily approved Professor Lewis's request for the talented Mrs. Lewis's appointment to Morris Brown's music department.

His student preparations and the inevitable faculty committee must have constrained Father's extramural activities. But disengagement from civic activities should have been out of character. After all, he would have been conscious of his standing in the larger black community, being of what historian Nell Painter describes as "the representative colored men."[48] In the very year of Booker Washington's death, President Woodrow Wilson's White House praise for D. W. Griffith's *The Birth of a Nation* inflamed racists everywhere. In nearby Marietta, Georgia, Leo Frank, the Jewish factory superintendent on whose uncle's property the Bells resided, was lynched that August. And on Thanksgiving night, a peripatetic Methodist preacher, extolling the Lost Cause, resurrected the Ku Klux Klan on Georgia's gigantic Stone Mountain.

The new Morris Brown University professor had foreseen a race relations disaster after Theodore Roosevelt's egomaniacal destruction of the

Republican electoral majority in the 1912 presidential election. After the East Saint Louis, Missouri, bloodbath in April 1917, whose black fatalities remain uncounted till today, sociologist Lewis understood that the nationalizing of racial hostility was the predetermined spawn of white supremacy. Much more immediate reading was found in the local press. In the national press, Woodrow Wilson's dismissals of black officeholders, segregation of federal employees, and voluble silence about lynching were frequently excused when reported.[49]

No frayed class syllabi have survived from these Morris Brown years, yet it seems certain that Professor Lewis made his students familiar with the best literature and social science monographs produced by their own people in order to counter the white supremacist pseudoscience scholarship flooding highbrow publications, influential churches, university lecture halls, and legislative chambers. Assigned canonical life histories— Douglass, Daniel Payne, B. T. Washington, Du Bois's John Brown, perhaps Archibald Grimké's Sumner and Garrison—stimulated hypothetical race-progress scenarios. A few years later, Benjamin Brawley and Carter Woodson would produce standard Negro history texts such as Brawley's *A Short History of the American Negro* and the latter's *The Negro in Our History*, but before the 1920s and Woodson's Association for the Study of Negro Life and History, black history was not yet history.[50] Notwithstanding George Washington Williams's earnest *History of the Negro Race in America from 1619 to 1880*, antebellum history and Reconstruction were the preserves of white scholars. Measured against the canonical Dunning School and the Anglo-Saxon eugenicists, John Lewis's resources seemed regrettably meager even when arguably superior.

His Morris Brown students made do with Du Bois's pathbreaking *The Suppression of the African Slave-Trade to the United States of America*, along with mimeographed copies of his almost forgotten 1909 American Historical Association presentation, "Reconstruction and Its Benefits." John R. Lynch's recent *The Facts of Reconstruction*, a candid first-person narrative was as though never written when compared with the public's indelible image of James Pike's *The Prostrate State: South Carolina under Negro Government*, a virulently racist tract masquerading as eyewitness journalism. That Albert Bushnell Hart, Du Bois's dissertation adviser, even threw black people under history's bus was symptomatic of the times. "Race measured by race, the Negro is inferior, and his past history . . . leads to the belief that he will remain inferior," *The Southern South* concluded.[51] Because Hart saw his exceptional student as a rule-making exception, he failed to see that the social-science findings from *The Philadelphia Negro* as well as from the remarkable Atlanta University Studies empirically measured racial behavior as a function of inequitable socioeconomic opportunity.

EVEN THOUGH PROFESSOR LEWIS WAS AMONG THE SUPPORTERS GATHERED in the new Odd Fellows Building on Upper Auburn Avenue on April 2, his son has always been disappointed not to find him photographed among the NAACP's original members. The issue bringing Pastor Lewis to Auburn Avenue was of utmost urgency to his Trinity Church parents. In November 1913, the Atlanta school board had arbitrarily ended eighth-grade schooling for black children. The black community's leaders had made a formal protest, then capitulated from general inaction. Religious schools and private academies such as AU's Oglethorpe Preparatory School almost certainly muffled community resistance at that time.[52] But now, four years later, the board announced in February the elimination of seventh-grade public education for black students as an outrageous economy measure to enlarge the number of white schools. The local issue before them spoke powerfully to the former Cuthbert principal.

George White's second son, Walter, AU 1916, corralled his powerful Standard Life Insurance Company fellows to agitate within the community. One among them urged that someone reach out to the new NAACP. Walter is credited with the early February SOS letter to the NAACP. Organize and the association will send help, was the reply sent. The white-run school board's blatant disregard of *Plessy v. Ferguson,* meanwhile, mobilized some of the city's colored leadership to demand a civil confrontation. Harry Pace, Standard Life Insurance's secretary-treasurer, Benjamin Davis Sr., *The Atlanta Independent*'s publisher, John Hope and activist spouse Lugenia, and William Penn, the Yale-educated physician who had shamed the white "respectables" after the riot, risked a prickly confrontation with the school board whites in mid-March of 1917. Astonished Mayor Asa Candler, the Coca-Cola mogul, was blindsided when a board member announced, "Gentlemen, I want to plead guilty to every word these men have spoken."[53] James L. Key was a politician with a conscience and a calculation about the future. "We have not given them a square deal and I do not propose to do anything that will any longer keep them from a square deal."

Field Secretary James Weldon Johnson arrived two weeks later to establish the Atlanta branch of the NAACP, a startling 1917 development well publicized by Benjamin Davis's *Independent*. A "monster mass meeting" of some fifteen hundred organized by Walter White awaited him in the Odd Fellows Auditorium. Johnson's loyalty had died with Booker Washington and been publicly finalized at the NAACP's 1916 Amenia Conference. "Gentleman Jim," as his associates called him, had been the first lawyer of his race admitted to the Florida bar and, opined a knowledgeable scholar, "the first Floridian ever to compose an opera (with J. Rosamond, his New England conservatory–trained younger brother) . . . followed by 'Lift Every Voice and Sing,' which came to be called the Negro national Anthem."[54] Johnson impressed his relatively young Atlanta audience as a more adroit NAACP recruit than the distinguished Du Bois. Atlanta University educated, he took the pulse of a new militancy barely if ever felt since the terrible riot. He masterfully buoyed the new members, took the measure of Standard Life's Walter White, and returned to New York to lobby successfully for a twenty-three-year-old insurance agent as the new NAACP assistant secretary. Now wary of adverse national publicity, the Atlanta school board shelved (temporarily) its excision of the seventh grade.[55]

New NAACP member John Lewis's involvement with the Atlanta branch was terminated at year's end with his assignment to a brief pastorate in Springfield, Missouri, followed immediately by Pasadena, California. Bishop Flipper, presiding bishop of the church's sixth district and impressed by my father's administrative initiative, decided to test his general adaptability. The Lewises headed for Los Angeles on the Santa Fe Limited sometime in late 1917, his second assignment Pasadena's First AME Church, established in the early 1880s and much in need of revitalizing. Eva gave birth on October 18, 1918, to their first child, John Henry Lewis Jr. Their second son, James Walker, arrived in August the following year. The family was to live in Pasadena two full years, until Reverend Lewis's Methodist superiors summoned him back to Georgia.[56]

ALICE KING BELL, THE GRANDMOTHER WHOSE MEMORIAL CHURCH WINdow instigated this family history, died before her children really knew her. Alice Urnestine was fifteen; John Levering was four years younger. When Grandfather John Henry remarried Mamie Westmoreland in December 1908, his precocious daughter and pensive son had moved well into their teens more or less molded by their South Carolina grandmother, Adeline. From what little is discernible of his personal life, John Henry must have found his unattached years agreeable enough after Alice left him. Then, five years later, the terrible riot brought Alice back into his life. Like great swaths of the city cleansed almost overnight of black people, her Oakland resting place had been threatened by the cemetery's designation of new grounds for the exclusive burial of whites. Grandfather arranged for her reinterment in South-View, the cemetery established some twenty years earlier by relatively prosperous colored families.[57]

When John Henry Bell had wished to refinance 300 Auburn Avenue in 1900, Alice's signature, as required by Major Belvin's indenture, was mandatory. My grandfather understood that legal possession of the Bells' valuable Victorian passed directly to the heirs of Clarissa King, to the exclusion of husbands. During Reconstruction, the house between Wheat and Auburn sheltered James Wiley Belvin's emancipated offspring in the care of their emancipated Givens grandmother. Come the 1880s, Major Belvin and Clarissa King, his emancipated concubine, favored their freeborn last child, Alice (Lee Belvin) King. The South Carolina free person of color heritage must have complicated this family tree.

"[A]mong many Negroes in the South there was a self-imposed silence about the past," Pauli Murray's endlessly revealing family memoir
Proud Shoes reminds us. "When the former slaves passed from the scene,
their descendants were apt to blot out the family experience: it was too
painful to live with."[58] Bell identity—the antithesis of bondage—considered
enslavement a historical humiliation, descent from concubinage a moral
humiliation. Three years after Grandfather and Mamie wed, Adeline's
death buried the last surviving memory, other than her son's, of Clarissa's resilient existence. Yet, like recessive genes, there must be recessive
memories that carnally reenact themselves across the decades. The day
Urnestine and Levering stood curled and pressed in the parlor, when it
was most probably Captain James Peter Coladen who came to inspect
them. Was Alice still alive, or was the presentation orchestrated by a not
so pleased John Henry Bell?[59]

My mother's "Aunt Mamie" is a more tactile family memory for me,
her step-grandson, thanks to an accretion of biographical puzzle pieces
through the years. "Mamie Westmoreland, the second daughter of Isaac
and Emma, spent her life in Atlanta, Georgia," a California Westmoreland responded some years ago. "She married a widower . . . and raised
his two children by an earlier marriage: Ernestine and John Jr. Mamie
did not have any children of her own. The Bells lived in a big house on
Auburn Avenue."[60] Mamie's father's midtown shoe store, like the Herndon barbershop, was a Gate City testimonial to bootstrap business success out of slavery. Isaac's white physician father had secured the spot on
Whitehall Street together with the vocational training. Ten years after
Emma died, Isaac Owen still worked at his trade because he wanted to.

The Bell-Westmoreland synergy might have occurred as the two
families became deeply linked in the final construction phase of First
Church. The Bell and Westmoreland memorial windows doubtless engaged the families in a common psychic and aesthetic enterprise. Mamie's parents were pillars of the Congregational Church and progenitors
of eleven surviving sons and daughters, most of whom funneled through
Oglethorpe Prep and AU, entered professions, and parented teachers,
physicians, business executives, and two Tuskegee airmen shot down

over Italy in World War II. At thirty-six, Mamie Westmoreland was a handsome elementary school teacher and night school principal. Marriage entailed resignation and domestic dependency in her day. Her acceptance of Grandfather's proposal strongly suggests compatibility.

The Bells welcomed an empathic, educated woman from a leading black family whose executive prowess would help organize the prestigious local Chautauqua. Moreover, this marriage decidedly enhanced the Bell family's cousinage extensions—Careys, Funderburgs, Neals, Whites. That "Aunt Mamie" was an aunt of my mother's Oglethorpe Prep classmate Walter White would attain a special significance. Because they had known her some years before she became the new mistress of Auburn Avenue, fifteen-year-old Alice Urnestine and eleven-year-old Levering probably adjusted seamlessly—even gratefully—to stepmother Mamie, who buffered a maternal void. Of another void the Bells had said almost nothing for many years.

THE NAME OF THE UNDEREDUCATED HOUSTON, TEXAS, NEWCOMER MEANT nothing at first to my grandfather. Certainly, though, his mail delivery route made him aware sometime in 1909 of a new occupant of the new Rucker Building at 160 Auburn Avenue. Henry Allen Rucker, President McKinley's collector of internal revenue for Georgia, personified to Redemptionist whites all the loathsome federal patronage once accorded special southern black men. Henry Rucker deigned to meet with only those deemed rich or powerful. The man at the Rucker Building, Heman E. Perry, thirty-six, was neither. Yet he was at the very beginning of a fifteen-year run of phenomenal black commercial success unrivaled elsewhere in America. One of nine children of hardworking John and Lucy Campton Perry, Heman had a smattering of elementary schooling and a few years as a cotton sampler, followed by undocumented midwestern and New England roaming and selling insurance to black customers as an agent, perhaps, of Massachusetts Mutual Life and perhaps one or two other white companies.[61]

One student of his remarkable legacy called Perry "the commercial

Mother as a flapper, 1915

Booker T. Washington," an apt characterization of his philosophy but certainly not a description of Perry's modus operandi. The genius who conceived the Standard Life Insurance Company in 1908–1909 possessed none of Washington's shrouded prudence, his painful success calculus. Heman Perry was an honest visionary who never saw a risk not worth taking if the risk leapfrogged obstacles to black economic progress. As he was virtually unknown to the colored men with means who mattered, his original life insurance scheme was dismissed outright as preposterous, Grandfather no doubt included. Georgia's recent mandatory minimum required a $100,000 deposit within two years in order to obtain a charter as a legal reserve insurance company. In January 1909, Perry secured his conditional insurance company charter and set up headquarters in Henry Rucker's building. In the quite likely event of failure to meet the state's January 28, 1911, deadline, Perry pledged a refund of all monies subscribed plus 4 percent.

His two-year stock-selling calvary took Perry to virtually every significant city from Virginia to Texas, a signed letter of commendation from Booker Washington's former secretary Emmett Scott in hand. The year 1910 closed with more than sixty thousand dollars. Almost shameless pleas produced an additional ten thousand dollars. After two white bank loan refusals, and a Hail Mary trip to New York, he admitted failure and surrendered the Standard Life Insurance charter on the deadline. Harry Pace, perhaps Heman's closest Atlanta friend and ultimate best adviser, reported that "every subscriber had been sent a check for the invested amount plus 4-percent interest" by February 3, 1911.[62] The effect on stunned recipients was such that when Perry announced a second run for a legal reserve insurance charter a few months later, his rebounded reputation across the South yielded all but thirty thousand dollars of the mandatory hundred-thousand-dollar deposit. The last-minute purchase of insurance stock authorized by Alonzo Herndon secured the legal reserve charter on March 22, 1913. Among the second set of confident subscribers was John Henry Bell.

To enter into the weeds of Perry's final success invites a tangent and a migraine. But without a crucial infusion of money from Atlanta Mutual Benefit's purchase of Standard Life stock, Heman Perry's second marathon would have failed. Three large barbershops (one famously profitable), all run with the scruples of a Swiss bank, had afforded Alonzo Herndon the surplus capital to buy Atlanta Mutual Benefit in 1905. The odds seemed against a Herndon-Perry business collaboration: model businessman versus assets gambler—indeed, only one sepulchral photo of them at work together has ever been found.[63] Atlanta Mutual Benefit's recent and unusual entry into Kentucky's insurance market was prompted by racial solidarity and business opportunity. Perry's offer to manage Herndon's suddenly onerous Kentucky obligation in return for an Atlanta Mutual Benefit loan benefited them both. The Herndon-Perry entente dissolved in less than a year. Later, Atlanta's black business community was to regret the stillbirth of the speculatively powerful duality of Atlanta Life Insurance resources and Standard Life Insurance imagination.

Some contemporaries saw in the widespread success of Standard Life the hexed promise of the Freedman's Savings Bank, a criminal Reconstruction misadventure that still haunted black business confidence. Widespread confidence in Standard Life continued well into the twenties, however. Officers of its board, economist Alexa Benson Henderson notes, "read like a blue book or social register of Negroes at the time."[64] Many, like Robert R. Moton and Emmett Scott of Tuskegee renown, Robert Reed Church Sr. ("wealthiest Negro in America"), and John Hope of Morehouse College are still familiar. As Standard Life surpassed its early prospects, it became an opportunity magnet for the new generation of college-trained men of color—and some few women—who had no lived memories of enslavement. Future bank manager Lorimer Milton headed for Atlanta after Brown University. Harry Pace, the AU valedictorian and Du Bois condisciple who founded the first jazz recording studio, was an early Perry collaborator. Georgia's first black CPA, Jesse Blayton, honed his skills at Standard Life. New AU honor graduate Walter White began hawking life insurance there before selling civil rights.

Confidence soared through the decade as the company expanded its business to twelve states and the District of Columbia. By 1922, Perry's Standard Life held $22 million of subscribed insurance. North Carolina Mutual, followed by Mississippi Life in third place, were Standard Life's rivals: the sole legal reserve life insurance companies under black control. Perusal of A. B. Caldwell's popular *History of the American Negro and His Institutions, Georgia Edition*, discloses page after page of men of affairs like my father's physician brother, Smith Milton, who were proud holders of Standard Life insurance policies.[65] Standard Life's vanished records preclude precision about John Henry Bell's exposure to Heman Perry's multiple business elaborations. Family lore insists they may have been significant. After some thirty years in service, Grandfather Bell is believed to have taken his federal pension sometime after 1920. His grown children and their stepmother, Mamie, shared his confidence in Heman Perry as Perry's legal reserve life insurance company morphed into a huge, interlocked, hydra-headed corporation with power enough to bend *Plessy*'s Jim Crow into equality.

Standard Life transformed what came to be called Sweet Auburn almost without noticing the sharp, sustained loss of Georgia's black population, the South's largest, during the Great War from 1916 to 1919. Charles Wesley estimated a total of some 400,000 southerners outmigrated for northern factory work during the first migratory surge, with another 400,000 after the closing of Ellis Island. The exodus of more than 50,000 Georgians during the Great War depleted church congregations, reduced bank deposits and insurance payments, drained farm laborers, and left desperate doctors, lawyers, dentists, morticians, and merchants either impoverished or with the choice of following their people wherever they went. Notwithstanding the Great Black Migration, by 1919, Auburn Avenue would hold seventy-two businesses where twenty professionals maintained offices. As the vital corridor of more than 40 percent of Atlanta's people, it headquartered the National Urban League, both Ys, and the Atlanta State Savings Bank. Much of the state's black spiritual and organizational activity derived from the Baptists' Wheat Street and Ebenezer churches, the Congregationalists' First Church, and the AME's Big Bethel.[66]

Benjamin Davis Sr., grand secretary of the United Order of Odd Fellows, had overseen construction of the Odd Fellows headquarters and the grand 1915 opening of its auditorium and roof garden at Auburn and Butler. First Church and the Odd Fellows matched each other's vituperation over Proctor's sermons against evil public dancing on Davis's rooftop. Davis's weekly *Independent* denounced the new Congregational church as "a waste of money better spent improving . . . the slums and alleys." The quietus soon came when Proctor, endorsing classmate Du Bois's controversial "Close Ranks" editorial, eventually took leave of First Church to accept a chaplaincy in Woodrow Wilson's war.[67] On the drawing board were Atlanta Life Insurance plans for its grand Auburn Avenue headquarters. Meanwhile, Standard Life's new Service Company was by far the most enterprising operation on the block. The word on the street was that Perry had purchased several hundred acres of undeveloped land to build a colored residential neighborhood on the city's West Side.

HEMAN PERRY'S VISION FOR ATLANTA WAS MY MOTHER'S ADULTHOOD.
She became aware of Perry's fabulous insurance speculations in the
home or from her university friends. Alice Urnestine earned her two-
year normal degree at eighteen from AU ("the old AU," she always said)
in 1911.[68] That she was never happy about not having a BA degree she several times showed by pursuing college credits until she actually satisfied
her ambition with the college-level diploma. My mother's mere normal
degree was puzzling. It seemed unlikely that her father and my grandfather had thought that even bright daughters ought be content with just
enough college training to teach elementary school or merely enough refinement for an appropriate marriage. While the family was not rich, family
finances certainly appeared adequate to meet the marginal costs of the
baccalaureate course. The records of the church treasurer for the decade
show Bell family tithes among the congregation's most generous.[69]

What is obvious about Alice Urnestine is that her considerable gifts
molded her. Her brilliance at math was matched by musical prowess. Her
flawless memory made languages easy. Whenever paths crossed years afterward, Oglethorpe classmates remembered help with Latin and French.
Her essays for George Towns's AU literature class were of almost suspect
clarity. Her bosom friend from Oglethorpe days, when both marveled at
new Professor Du Bois's omniscience, described my mother as both proud
and shy, a mixture Kathleen Adams attributed to family history and
Caucasian appearance. For all Mother's assets, Adams pitied Alice Urnestine's "no-nation" identity.[70] By losing their great constitutional fight
in *Plessy v. Ferguson* for a national color-blind citizenship, Albion Tourgée and Justice Harlan had foreseen white supremacy's one drop of blood
paradoxically maximized by African Americans as the ultimate valida-
tion of group identity.

Mother's shyness was her personal compensation as the people in
her world embraced what Professor Du Bois's famous book described as
lives lived in "second-sightedness and divided identity."[71] In a sense, she
lived both at the forefront and between the people she knew well or so-

cially encountered. She, her brother Levering, Mae Yates (née Pitts), Norris Herndon, and other no-nation Oglethorpe classmates emerged from their 1906 racial trauma feeling as unshaken in their sense of self as had Walter White, who famously recorded his antipathy for a dominant majority whose ace in life was only skin privilege.[72] But Mother's embarrassment at being mistaken for white several times ultimately caused her to decide to never ride public transportation. She was famous for striding long-legged across the city. But she also found that her cosmopolitan culture could prove disadvantageous among uneducated black people and dangerous among similar whites.

Bell family connections helped Mother obtain a much sought-after teaching post in Atlanta's badly funded, crowded, tatterdemalion black public grammar school system, where white salaries averaged forty-three dollars and colored twenty. She had been quick to become an NAACP member in 1917 when the Atlanta school board tried to abolish seventh-grade instruction for colored children. Her admiration of another no-nation woman had earlier attracted Mother to the quietly dynamic Neighborhood Union founded by Lugenia Burns Hope the year of her college graduation. The Neighborhood Union with its gendered motto, "Thy Neighbor as Thyself," had begun about five years earlier when Chicago-born and Hull House–influenced Burns Hope organized the first Gate City kindergarten in a notoriously deprived neighborhood near her distinguished husband's Atlanta Baptist College campus. Four Gate City Kindergarten Association facilities followed, financed by Heman Perry, Alonzo Herndon, Hugh Proctor, and mortician David T. Howard. What had started as an elitist outreach to poor working-class black mothers became the 35,000-member needs-based women's Neighborhood Union by 1918.[73] Alice Urnestine recalled early years in the Neighborhood Union helping and learning from struggling families in Beaver Slide, an unpaved escarpment deprived of running water near Diamond Hill.

As they were born in the same year and related by marriage since John Henry and Mamie Westmoreland's union, Alice Urnestine championed Walter's part in bringing the NAACP to the city as a family triumph—doubly so after Walter's resignation from Standard Life Insurance to become NAACP assistant field secretary in early 1918. Yet even before Walter's relocation to New York, Mayor Candler and his chagrined white school board majority resumed their attack on minority education. Feeling the white public backlash for conceding the seventh-grade argument, a school board official snarled at the black leadership delegation—"[not] one nickel more for the education of the Negro children as they were already getting more than they deserved."[74] The city government announced a bond issue to improve and enlarge the white majority's public schools. Atlanta's recently founded Commission on Interracial Cooperation (CIC), with a galaxy of liberal white panjandrums and "thoughtful educated Negro leaders," should have been consulted, but instead the city announced that the revenues would go exclusively to white children.

The Independent announced that Negroes' patience was exhausted. The battle of the Jim Crow school bonds would roil Atlanta's whites and blacks as nothing had since Bishop Turner's Georgia Equal Rights Convention militancy. This time, however, Woodrow Wilson's war, the mobilization of black working-class women by black upper-class women, and the shift from leadership by respectable black males to multiclass mobilization promised positive educational results. The nation's war declaration occurred the same April week that James Weldon Johnson had warned black Atlantans of the two existential futures before them: "One is for American citizenship and the other is almost a state of servitude. . . . [Whites] will force the Negro down into a permanent secondary standing in this country . . . unless we take steps to prevent it."[75]

Out of the blue came the unexpected patriotic appeal of Burghardt Du Bois's controversial "Close Ranks" editorial in The Crisis. The Bells, Harry Pace's NAACP, Lugenia Burns Hope's Neighborhood Union, and Benjamin Davis applauded Reverend Proctor's pledge to display the American flag above his pulpit. "In a crisis like this," Du Bois's Fisk classmate asserted, "there are two classes only—Americans and traitors [and] Negroes are Americans." John Levering Bell reported for basic training at Camp Gordon during his senior year. He was one of the 400,000 African American doughboys. Five thousand African Americans attended the NAACP's war rally in the city auditorium. "Measured against its promise to create a foundation of interracial cooperation rooted in a shared patriotic citizenship, World War I was an utter failure," decides Atlanta historian Jay Winston Driskell Jr. He cites the 147 nationwide lynchings in 1918 and 1919, "thirty-nine of which took place in Georgia."[76]

When John Henry and Eva Lewis read in a Pasadena newspaper that almost "two thousand homes had been destroyed and more than ten thousand Atlantans, mostly blacks, were homeless," their first reaction probably evoked the horror of the 1906 race pogrom. "The Great Atlanta Fire," beginning in an alley off Auburn Avenue on the morning of May 21, 1917, "exploded out of the Darktown neighborhood that defied the 1906 white marauders, swept like a burning scythe down Auburn, crossed Boulevard, Rankin, and leaped across Ponce de Leon, incinerating fine old Victorians owned by white people. Mayor Candler ordered houses dynamited to stop the conflagration. "The flames literally raced through the Negro section," said a fireman. "There wasn't a chance to head them off among the closely packed houses."[77] When the fire stopped, seventy-three city blocks and three hundred acres were cinders. Property loss equaled five million dollars, and four thousand were homeless.

The Neighborhood Union women suddenly faced their organization's cruelest duties as they understood the linked causality of the race riot and the Great Fire. Lugenia Burns Hope and her faithful volunteers would be morally liable for the minimum food and clothing, psychological mending, material recovery, temporary housing, all of it absent the tax dollars embargoed by Gate City's white power structure for emergency care and feeding of the city's whites. "That no [southern] black neighborhood enjoyed access to city service well into the twentieth century," Professor Driskell reminds us, was an outrage so violative of civic equality that only those respectable elites of the Proctor and Bowen stripe, disdained by the irascible Ben Davis Sr., believed the simulacrum of leadership allowed by powerful whites was worth having.[78]

Three hundred Auburn Avenue owed its survival to a fortuitous location. That it and one other dwelling stood alone where obliteration wiped away a block-long stretch astonished my Bell ancestors. For the most part, Henry Grady's modern new city had stopped well short of the relocated black commerce. My inspection of the 1918 Atlanta city directory showed 300 Auburn Avenue vacant! Two years later, the family dwelling held its full complement, any damage apparently repaired by colored architect/builder Henry Cooke Hamilton at Grandfather's expense.[79]

Whether Grandfather himself filled water buckets from the lone Jackson Street hydrant, commandeered willing firemen, or was joined by Wheat Street parishioners, the waterlogged structure would survive until after its sale twenty-seven years later. It would have stood at Jackson and Auburn at the corner across from Wheat Street Baptist Church, where the Martin Luther King Jr. National Historical Park begins today.

ATLANTA'S NEXT MAYOR AFTER THE GREAT ATLANTA FIRE WAS JAMES L. Key, the businessman councillor who had pressed his colleagues not to quash seventh-grade education for black children. After three years in which the city's white majority had refused to increase taxes even when faced with a comprehensive assessment of the city's needs after the conflagration, outgoing Asa Candler decided to roll the dice for an $800,000 budget fed by four different bond issues for 1918. The three new schools for white students plus their additional improvements for a total of $515,000 was said to be justified by the providential survival of three black grammar schools in the maw of the fire. Bonds for streets and sewage, hospitals and fire control, parks and police, amounted to a modernizing commitment that beggared Henry Grady's dreams. Atlantans had refused to let the city indebt itself in 1915. Passage of Candler's bond issues required a two-thirds affirmation of all registered Atlanta voters whose poll taxes were uninterruptedly paid since 1877.

Registered black voters—68,000 in 1906, now 11,285—scarcely figured in the council's calculations.[80] To enhance the likelihood of passage, the bond election was set for July 10, 1918, coincident with the city's Democratic primary. A furious Benjamin Davis summoned his *Independent* readers to "vote against every bond issue; it matters not whether it is for water, street improvement or what not." It was past time for the city "to build up-to-date modern school houses for Negroes."[81]

Color, class, religion, and the poll tax usually constrained African American unity. That the Atlanta NAACP had recently overcome a deep leadership schism, however, should have considerably increased its numbers. Reverend A. D. Williams, pastor of storied Ebenezer Baptist Church, treasurer of the National Baptist Convention, and father-in-law of Martin Luther King Sr., had recently suppressed his deep enmity. Fortunately, the local branch leader, nimble Harry Pace, had followed James Weldon Johnson's advice to mask the NAACP's Talented Tenth and GOP origins by inviting every significant Methodist and Baptist personality to a mass meeting. A new executive committee made up of "all shades of differences and local factions resulted," after which Pace offered Williams leadership of the association.[82] The new NAACP supported Ben Davis's call to the black population to boycott the bond election.

With the solid defeat of the July bond election, Atlanta's white leadership faced a dilemma it could not explain. The chamber of commerce, Atlanta Federation of Trades, Bell Southern, the four newspapers, and even the release of Camp Gordon's soldiers brought only 3,881 of the two-thirds 8,881 necessary votes for the four bond issues. That a significant percentage of white males was in military service overseas might explain the low poll numbers. Absent railroad men on special runs, mechanics at work on special projects were hypothesized as causes. The whole outcome was just mysterious. But that black people—Negroes—had upended the city's solution to its myriad problems was inconceivable. "It was quite another thing to organize the city's black registered voters to publicly undermine the development plans of the city's most powerful white men."[83]

W. E. B. Du Bois would have wagered Jim Johnson that the affliction of white supremacy precluded the Atlanta power structure from risking even a guess as to why the 1918 bond election failed. Instead, when James Key entered office in January 1919, his decision was to authorize the reintroduction of substantially the same defeated bond election. He pledged to raise teachers' salaries and fund the building of new schools, but, re-membering the blowback from previous moderation, Mayor Key offered black voters merely the bromide of patience rewarded. Still, old habits of special access for well-behaved elites led Hugh Proctor and several prom-inent ministers deeply committed to the politics of respectability to in-vite Mayor Key to a bargaining session. News traveled through black Atlanta of the mayor's eloquently meaningless promise that his city "should not be content until it has placed itself in a position to furnish a comfortable seat in a comfortable schoolhouse for every child." Mean-while, the state legislature's sleight of hand the previous August—an ap-proval requirement of two thirds only of those voting in the announced March 5 election—seemed to guarantee the mayor's unchanged 1919 bond project.[84]

Seven days before the March 5 ballot, Alice Urnestine Bell must have reported for duty at the NAACP's new Women's Registration Committee. Forged from the ranks of Lugenia Hope's Neighborhood Union, the Regis-tration Committee called "men forth to do their duty." Votes with poll taxes paid were sine qua nons for defeating Mayor Key's 1919 agenda. NAACP president A. D. Williams marveled at the success of the Women's Registration Committee. "Night after night people came forward and paid their dollar," said he with a sexist aside. "That was largely done because the women were allowed to make speeches." Walter White's autobiography recalls a poor man paying thirty-two years of back poll taxes. Branch vice president Truman K. Gibson, later famous as Joe Louis's business man-ager, messaged black voters and taxpayers an eleventh-hour summons: "The hour has struck for all of the Negroes in Atlanta, high and low, rich and poor, to drop everything and rally to this cause."[85]

The March 1919 bond election, with almost two thousand poll-taxed African Americans voting against it, failed. March winds whipped a heavy downpour that literally dampened turnout. Someone records that a panic-stricken alderman sent volunteers to find more white voters, but the polls finally closed with a stopgap school tax failing by a narrow mar-gin. The extent of the catastrophe was greatly compounded by the 1918 bond failure causing retrenchments, suspensions, and cancellations of city agencies and functions. Vital police, fire, and hospital services were worn thin by the Great Fire. The white public school system was bursting at the seams while the shamefully deprived black public school system festered. The bewildered city attorney tried to make a case for the narrow passage of all the bonds. Even with the new two-thirds majority rule, however, it became clear that the margin of registered affirmative voters was insufficient.

As white voters had overwhelmingly approved the bonds, Mayor Key, with the council majority, appealed to the state legislature to ignore the election results. The shameful argument was that the blacks "flock[ing] in droves to vote against the tax rate . . . may have been misinformed."[86] That Henry Rucker and Benjamin Davis—two crafty leaders who could have owned the victory—took pains to mock or deny the reality of a black vote showed that the specter of 1906 must have hovered over both. But it would be the spirit of the Georgia Equal Rights Convention and the Niagara Movement that informed the Atlanta NAACP's well-thought-out endgame after the city was permitted to rerun the bond election. The Atlanta Crackers, the local minor league baseball team, was famous for winning most of its games. A number of sports enthusiasts were said to be unwilling to bet on the city's chances in this third round.

Perfect weather blessed the city's third bond election on April 23. White mass meetings had continued throughout the weeks. White schoolchildren had performed plays demonstrating classroom needs. Neighborhoods were saturated with *Constitution* and *Journal* articles and photos depicting civic life after the bond victory. The segregated teachers' union hinted that raises for its black colleagues were acceptable. When the election day ended, notwithstanding a major increase in registered voters (women having been enabled to vote for the first time), somehow each bond fell short of the required vote, whereas the special tax increase lost by a margin of nine hundred votes. A chasm of some $350,000 anticipated revenue now played havoc with the city's development plans. Some two thousand black voters organized by the NAACP suddenly materialized in the minds of white Atlantans.[87] The NAACP's April manifesto ("an eight-point plan") awaited serious consideration. It stated a willingness to support a bond issue, but only on the condition that it contained "specific and unalterable provisions for a division of the funds so that the colored schools will be amply taken care of."[88]

First, however, the Gate City needed a face-saving way to lose. Harry Pace, now in the music recording business in New York as president of Black Swan Records, urged Mayor James Key and his chamber of commerce to invite the NAACP to hold its annual meeting in Atlanta in 1920. The city that claimed to be too busy to hate swallowed its defeat in a celebratory welcome of a new black leadership contingent. Finally, on March 8, 1921, Atlanta voters held a fourth bond election. "In the end," as historian David Godshalk summed up this Jim Crow travesty, "nearly half of the $8,850,000 raised from the new bonds was spent on black and white education, including the construction of four new black elementary schools and Booker T. Washington High School which opened in 1924. . . . For the first time since the riot, Atlanta's African Americans had planned a successful political strategy and secured the victory that had long been denied them despite interracial cooperation with white elites."[89]

Atlanta's first high school for black youth was sited on twenty acres bargained at a fair price from Heman Perry's Service Realty Company in 1921. The huge, architecturally eclectic brick structure was slated for completion sometime in 1924. It was obvious that it would be the fulcrum of Atlanta's new West Side, which Perry's Service Realty Company was already transforming into a middle-class black residential bonanza. On several acres, neat two-story brick houses along paved lanes showcased a modern lifestyle many whites would envy. Moreover, thanks to Standard Life Insurance and Citizens Trust Company, Perry promised that his modern communities, with houses sold for between three and eight thousand dollars, were affordable through time-payment-plan loans.[90] One can understand my mother's excited determination to be one of Booker T. Washington's first teachers. This high school at the center of motivated students and striving parents in a new part of the city was professional nirvana.

Booker T. Washington High School, built 1924

Competition for teaching posts would be intense, she knew. In a real sense, though, Booker Washington was their school, families like hers from First Church who sustained the NAACP and were Standard Life stockholders. Harvard's Graduate School of Education, summer session 1923, must have enhanced Mother's placement chances. For occupation she wrote "Math Teacher, Junior High," indicating either confirmed appointment or aspiration. Among forty registrants listed on page six, Mother was one of only three southerners, two of whom were Virginians.[91] Rather curiously, no Cambridge address was given. But this author recalls mention of a lively week in snobby Oak Bluffs on Martha's Vineyard. Although grades for the two courses—"Education for Citizenship in a Democracy" and "Problems of Citizenship"—are no longer retrievable, her son presumes Mother aced her finals. Question 6 of the final examination titillates in our contemporary pedagogical confusion: "Assume that you are free to teach American History in the junior high school in your own way."

Alice Urnestine's way of teaching math as head of her department was as a strict disciplinarian. Hers was a reputation smart students felt good about pleasing. At this distance most of her professional colleagues are names without personality. Fair to say, her artistic and thespian sensibilities brought admiration from both sexes as she passed into her thirties remarkably unchanged. On the 2022 centenary of Sigma Gamma Rho sorority, founded at Indiana's Butler University, several sorors informed me that Mother founded their Atlanta chapter in 1923. Local news from *The Independent* found her motoring to a Saturday Tuskegee football match with a Theodore Goosby and his sisters Janie and Kate. Alice Urnestine's midtwenties profile of professional and social joie de vivre described a racially separate life in circumstances of relative equality.[92]

A cover story in the February 2, 1924, issue of *Forbes* electrified black and white Atlanta. Several friends of the Bells had met the Afro-Caribbean author during the warp-speed visit to Standard Life headquarters and on circuits across the city where the insurance giant's "twelve subsidiary corporations" (Service Realty Company, Service Construction Company, Service Pharmacy Company, Citizens Trust Bank, etc.) were transforming the urban and social landscape. Besides the certainty that he knew Walter White and the well-respected Charles S. Johnson, editor of the National Urban League's new *Opportunity* magazine, Eric Walrond, twenty-six, British Guiana born, and future Harlem Renaissance novelist, was a somewhat curious choice for the country's leading business magazine.[93] His *Forbes* article exuded an unbridled enthusiasm soon de rigueur to Madison Avenue yet a pitch fabulous for insurance regulators, traditional businessmen, and certified accountants. *Forbes*'s Standard Life Insurance president was "the brainiest Negro in the South . . . earn[ed] $75,000 annually . . . and is said to be worth $8,000,000."[94]

"The Largest Negro Commercial Enterprise in the World" presented the amazing story of H. E. Perry, "commercial Booker T. Washington, founder of $30,000,000 Standard Life Insurance Company." Entering Perry's headquarters at 180 Auburn Avenue, Walrond, after comparatively diminishing Harlem, "could not imagine Negroes owning or operating anything like it (the office equipment alone costs $100,000)." With thirty million dollars of insurance in force, branches in twenty-two cities, "the company employed 2,500 people—all colored—on its payroll." Moving to the Service Construction Company with striking photos of actual houses, *Forbes* readers noted the remarkable financing made possible by Citizens Trust, currently boasting "$250,000 capital, $264,037.14 surplus, $1,438,182.4 reserve, and 15,600 accounts."[95] Atlanta's emergent West Side, with its Atlanta University, future Morehouse and Spelman, together with the great eponymous high school, Walrond visualized as a "Negro El Dorado."[96]

Business historian Alexa Henderson delivers a sober judgment on the Standard Life Insurance Company failure, whose consequences were deeply personal, socioeconomically transformative, and profoundly historic in the long civil rights half century. Perry knew that Standard Life "was unable to invest directly in many of the projects that he desired to serve the black community," explains Professor Henderson. Perry solved his problem simply. He used the funds from his black policyholders accumulated by his company to "serve" the black community by depositing them in his Citizens Trust bank. Perry's bank loaned $600,000 to his Service Realty Company "to invest in Atlanta real estate, which it then sold on the time payment plan."[97] When the Standard Life deposits were soon depleted, Perry covered them by issuing shares of new stock.

The Service Company then purchased the entire issue of new stock, "giving the Service Company 1/2 interest in the Standard Life." Depletion of the insurance reserve and withdrawals from Citizens Trust spelled doom. "Working to stem the immediate cash flow problem, Perry struck a deal with Southeastern Trust Company, a white-run company," which Du Bois later called a pawn brokerage house. Harry Pace dissented violently, explaining afterward that Perry was "arrogant and fixed in his opinions" and not "apt to seek or to accept the advice of his friends or employees."[98] Southeastern committed to furnish funds to Citizens Trust as needed to make bank clearings. Management of the Service Company "passed to whites," followed by the fatal ruling of the Georgia Insurance Department in 1924 that Standard Life Insurance was impaired by its large amount of nonadmitted, undeveloped real estate.

"Probably no business venture had so stirred the financial ambitions and dreams of the Negro nor given him confidence in his ability to handle commercial affairs," bemoaned the prestigious *Baltimore Afro-American*, "than did Standard Life under the direction of Heman Perry, its founder and guiding genius." It seems Alonzo Herndon's opinion of the *Forbes* magazine exposure—"it is often wise to keep our hand hid"—found consensus among Gate City colored men of affairs.[99] My grandfather must have agreed with his fellow First Church member. Still, the National Negro Business League had by no means written off the seriously impaired Standard Life. Robert Russa Moton, its tall, black, imposing president and Booker Washington's Tuskegee successor, appealed with such efficacy to Julius Rosenwald of Sears & Roebuck that a provisional agreement with Rosenwald, John D. Rockefeller Sr., and AU trustee Trevor Arnett was reached by August to save Perry's insurance company. The philanthropists had learned enough, however, to insist on "someone other than Perry to manage Standard Life," a capitulation the outraged Perry rejected outright.[100]

In January 1925, Standard Life Insurance Company and its remaining assets merged with the white Southern Life Company of Tennessee to become the Southern-Standard Life Insurance Company. A suit filed in Fulton County Superior Court by minority stockholders in late June of 1926 claimed that Standard Life had been the victim of a sinister takeover by the Ku Klux Klan, "not only to intimidate the Negro with the rope and torch, but also to strike at the foundation of his economic strength." Perry declined to take part in the litigation. Afterward, he left the city with plans to begin another reserve life insurance company in Missouri.

The bitterness aroused by the failure of Standard Life was noted by John Hope, Atlanta University's president, in a speech to a National Interracial Conference in 1929. "The unfortunate happening to that insurance company was one of the awful shocks to Negro society," recalled Hope, a policyholder himself. "[And] all the while there stood by a group of perfectly nice people, the businessmen, a Chamber of Commerce and the like, and there was an interracial commission functioning. But there they stood, and watched and waited for months and months. It seemed impossible for Negroes to make a step to the white people or the white people to make a step to the Negroes that would result in that great organization's being righted and allowed to function."[101]

There were policyholders like Burghardt Du Bois who sent letters protesting the lost value of their policies as late as 1927. With the most macabre timing, John Henry Bell had devastated his family four days past Christmas, a Tuesday afternoon in 1925. *The Atlanta Constitution* announced his death "in his fifty-ninth year at his residence, 300 Auburn Avenue." No mention was made of suicide by gunshot wound to the head.[102]

8

◆ ◆ ◆

NEGOTIATING FAMILY AND WHITE SUPREMACY

The Lewises

The blinding truth of it survives today's overuse within academia. But when Burghardt Du Bois uncloaked the phenomenon a century ago, the novelty of an idolatrous whiteness as described in *Darkwater: Voices from within the Veil* appalled sympathetic Caucasians. His New Negro readers coming of age after the Great War marveled at the caustic truth of what their great thinker denounced as the dead-end pigmentocracy of a new world order. He who had opened the twentieth century with the exhilarating *The Souls of Black Folk* two decades later confounded his people's progress with an eschatology of an all-encompassing, brutal whiteness. "The discovery of personal whiteness among the world's people is a very modern thing—a nineteenth and twentieth century matter, indeed," warned the new book's startling second chapter, "The Souls of White Folk."

"The ancient world would have laughed at such a distinction," Du Bois reminded readers. "The Middle Ages regarded skin color with mild curiosity and even up into the eighteenth century we were hammering our national mannikins into one, great, Universal Man, with a fine frenzy which ignored color and race even more than birth. Today we have changed all that, and the world in a sudden emotional conversion has discovered that it is white and by that token, wonderful!" Some special angle of vision enabled Du Bois to recognize an alien new species whose supreme ethnocentrism held that "every great thought . . . was a white man's thought, that every great deed . . . was a white man's deed; that every great dream the world ever sang was a white man's dream."

The original version of "The Souls of White Folk" had appeared in embryo before the Great War in New York's progressive weekly, *The Independent*. Ten years later, it came roaring back as a full-blown indictment packaged within Du Bois's pulsating *Darkwater: Voices from within the Veil*, his collection of essays, fiction, poetry, and allegorical squibs.[1] The nineteenth century's last decade and the twentieth's first few had spawned books and laws deeply insulting to people of color everywhere: Kipling's "The White Man's Burden" beckoning America to the imperial jamboree; the one-drop rule of racial identity following the high court's *Plessy v. Ferguson* decision; Thomas Dixon Jr.'s *The Clansman* sparking the Atlanta riot and inspiring Griffith's film *The Birth of a Nation*; Madison Grant's *The Passing of the Great Race*; and Oswald Spengler's *The Decline of the West*. Lothrop Stoddard's *The Rising Tide of Color: Against White World-Supremacy* appeared almost simultaneously with *Darkwater*.

Astute readers, black and white, might have surmised that the author, who stunned the board of the NAACP and much of educated colored America, as well as pacifists and isolationists everywhere, with "Close Ranks"—his 1918 editorial prioritizing patriotism above racial justice—now bitterly regretted that naivete. It was a privileged intellectual exceptionalism that now caused Du Bois to weigh the souls of white people on the scales of postwar injustice with a frightful temerity. "Conceive this nation, of all human peoples, in a crusade to make the 'World Safe for Democracy'?" he asked Americans. "Imagine the United States protesting against Turkish atrocities in Armenia, while the Turks are silent about mobs in Chicago and St. Louis; what is Louvain compared with Memphis, Waco, Washington, Dyersburg, and Estill Springs?" he demanded. "In short, what is the black man but America's Belgium, and how could America condemn in Germany that which she commits, just as brutally, within her own borders?"[2] Du Bois wrote these words after what James Weldon Johnson had called the "red summer of 1919" in which some twenty-six race riots exploded across the country from South, North, Midwest, to far West.

Until the unaltered reality of foreign war and domestic racism became undeniable, Du Bois himself had tried on a bold face. "Returning Soldiers," exhorted a *Crisis* editorial, "Make way for Democracy! We saved it in France, and by the Great Jehovah, we will save it in the United States of America, or know the reason why."[3] But the reason why came quickly and his *Darkwater* book seemed to seal the status of the author's people with such depressing finality that they would spend the remainder of the twentieth century transfixed by subordination, defiance, marginality, and alienation. Du Bois had returned from Flanders Fields devastated by an undeniable truth. "We darker men said: This is not Europe gone mad; this is not aberration nor insanity; this *is* Europe; this seeming Terrible is the real soul of white culture—back of all culture—stripped and visible today. This is where the world has arrived." "Whiteness," announced the NAACP's great arbiter, meant that the "new" white people of whom America was "heartily ashamed" were being trained to despise "'niggers' from the day of their landing, and they carry and send the news back to the submerged classes in the fatherlands."[4]

Harcourt, Brace & Howe released *Darkwater: Voices from within the Veil* in February 1920. Atlanta's Chautauqua Circle archives make no mention of it, but *Darkwater* must have been prime reading at one of the ladies' third-Monday monthly meetings—perhaps at 300 Auburn Avenue, where Mamie Westmoreland Bell was the chapter's acting secretary. Just as certain it was that much of literate colored and white Atlanta discussed this terrible collection of poetry, fiction, and twentieth-century prognostication wherein civic inferiority was indissolubly soldered to skin color no matter one's wealth, profession, education, or morals. Du Bois's publisher and an astonished *Literary Digest* reported an unprecedented interest of southern farmers, sharecroppers, northern domestics, and janitors in buying *Darkwater*—"a veritable groundswell of common folk."[5] For all its hieratic language, the book's many sections of familiar verisimilitude could sound the emotional depth of a whole people. Its sales far exceeded those of *The Souls of Black Folk*.

That the author was honored only months after the book's publication with the distinguished Spingarn Medal in Atlanta, where the NAACP held its eleventh annual conference by invitation of Mayor James Key and the chamber of commerce, broadcast a conundrum of mixed signals that year, to say the least. The power brokers of white Atlanta had bitten the bullet of solid black opposition to a twice stymied multimillion-dollar municipal bond issue. Of $4 million, $1.2 million were committed to build black public schools. To the women of the Neighborhood Union, to the newest Deep South branch of the NAACP, to the Standard Life Insurance's West Side expansion, and to the Bell family's professional prospects, the racial purgatory forecast by *Darkwater* was not yet inevitable.[6] In his new *Journal of Negro History*, fellow Harvard PhD Carter Godwin Woodson described the book as written by "a poet" whose scholarship was inadequate to the task of "scientific treatment." William Colson, former lieutenant of the black 367th Infantry and a contributor to A. Philip Randolph's socialist *Messenger*, admired Du Bois's great learning yet found the book floating above the needs of "the man farthest down." Colson also regretted that there was too much Hegel and not enough [Eugene] Debs. *The Nation* conceded that "no other colored American has ever written like this and few white," but publisher Oswald Villard deplored the author's "note of bitterness, tinctured with hate."[7]

Even so, there were enough colored people who saw their future predicted in "The Souls of White Folk." They were among many colored families throughout the country who fixated upon the elimination of the category of mulatto after the 1920 U.S. Census closed. To those with phenotypes offering "safe passage" out of their race, *Darkwater* was an existential wake-up call. James Weldon Johnson's furtive novel *The Autobiography of an Ex-Colored Man* had captured the gnawing dilemma denied or resisted by so many of them. Harry Herbert Pace, a Du Bois disciple and 1903 AU valedictorian who organized the Atlanta NAACP branch and founded Black Swan Records, would die in July 1943 as a

wealthy white man in Chicago. Young Walter White ventured a guessti-
mate of more than a hundred thousand African Americans who "passed"
by 1930. Sociologist and census consultant Caleb Johnson reached a similar conclusion, reporting that "scientific investigation indicated that the
Negro race is not dying out from infertility but is bleaching out through
admixture with the white race." John Hope, Du Bois's friend and professional collaborator, had politely declined well-intentioned offers from
prospective benefactors to remain in Providence as a white man after
graduating from Brown University.[8] He volunteered his service to the
uplift of his people, not white imposture.

JOHN HENRY LEWIS, HIS SPOUSE, EVA BROWN, AND THEIR TWO BOYS, JOHN
Henry Jr. and James Walker, returned to Atlanta in the fall of 1920. Pasadena and neighboring Los Angeles had afforded racially easier city envi-
ronments than comparable places below the Mason-Dixon line, like
Birmingham, Wilmington, Charleston, or Tulsa. Even so, the family
learned early that racial segregation ordered their lives. Starting in July
1914, white Pasadenans had imposed a "Negro Day" at the Brookside
Plunge, the new municipal swimming pool. The pool was off limits to
black citizens every day but Tuesday, after which it was drained, then
refilled for whites. Mexicans, Asians, and Negroes existed apart and segregated from the Caucasian majority.[9]

Pasadena's black business district thrummed with potential, however, and there were schools and cultural outlets that future sports
heroes Jackie and Mack Robinson and later science fiction writer Octavia
Butler benefited from. Of several churches serving the community, First
AME, organized in 1880, seemed to march ahead due to Pastor Lewis's
expanded Sunday school, refinancing and remodeling program, much-
increased membership, and appealing sermons. The Atlanta summons
terminating my father's Pasadena assignment was not unexpected. Morris
Brown University's capable president William Fountain Sr. was elected
bishop at the denomination's 1920 General Conference. At the declared
age of thirty-six, John Henry Lewis was now the sixth president of the

AME Church's second-largest educational institution, ambitiously rechartered since 1913 as Morris Brown University. "In this the greatest effort of my life," he wrote proudly to Yale's dean, Charles Brown, "I shall from time to time seek counsel and aid from you."[10]

The considerable promise of the Lewis presidency was to be complicated by a power dynamic common to AME colleges and universities. Ultimate decision-making generally resided with resident bishops. His earlier Morris Brown College service should have made my father aware of the risk of rapid institutional growth propelled by what might best be described as episcopal megalomania. Joseph Simeon Flipper—Atlanta University alumnus of 1876, third Morris Brown president from 1904 to 1908, bishop of Georgia's sixth district from 1912 to 1928—would preside first as board chair of the college and then as chancellor of a grandiose Morris Brown University largely conceived by himself in 1913: "a total identity of seventeen years with Morris Brown College/University," notes the school's hundred-year history.[11] The senior Fountain, my father's immediate predecessor, seems to have marched in step with his bishop.

Henry McNeal Turner, my father's mentor, had liquidated a large Morris Brown indebtedness twenty years earlier with a mobilizing call to the faithful that also brought enough money for Turner Hall, a five-story stone structure holding classrooms, dormitory rooms, administrative offices, a dining hall, and an auditorium. Since those years when Morris Brown was nourished by tithes from thousands of humble black Methodist believers, the war, the boll weevil, lynching, and the Illinois Central Railroad had begun to cream off the migrants headed north. Between 1915 and 1930 some 1.5 million black people were to seek better lives outside the South, calculates John Hope Franklin's indispensable source, *From Slavery to Freedom*. The needs of the Methodist school now outpaced the means of those who stayed behind (too often because they had to), because ecclesiastical vision and deficit financing had been allowed to continue, "occasioned largely by the acquisition of land and buildings one brick the other frame," opined the school history later.[12]

President Lewis inherited, then, what was described as the "Morris Brown System," consisting of Morris Brown University in Atlanta; Turner

Theological Seminary at Morris Brown University; Fair Haven Hospital in Atlanta; Payne College in Cuthbert; Central Park Normal Industrial Institute in Savannah; a 653-acre farm outside Macon purchased as a prospective future site for Morris Brown University; and farmland cultivated to supply the school's boarding department.[13] Yet even as he was daunted by the challenge of finding the dollars to keep this broad and heterogeneous educational platform afloat, the new president sensed that his school possessed special curricular assets that the relatively new great white educational foundations might find worthy of their financial support. Unlike the costlier collegiate institutions founded and funded by northern WASP charities, African Methodist Episcopal colleges were homegrown entities, self-financed by proud and poor black people themselves. For the most part, moreover, AME schools had remained aloof from what had become a noisy, no-holds-barred ideological war of vocational instruction champions (Washington) versus classical education exponents (Du Bois).[14]

At Morris Brown, as at five other AME colleges below the Mason-Dixon line, a potpourri curriculum offered animal husbandry and masonry with Greek and philosophy along with nursing and physics and military science. Bachelor of arts, of pedagogy, and of divinity were granted. My father assumed his presidency just as the all-powerful General Education Board—an eleemosynary octopus—broadcast the end of humanities and social science education in the Negro missionary or mission colleges founded during Reconstruction. The great gaggle of such colleges and universities established by the white Christian missionaries of the North—like Congregationalist Atlanta, Fisk, and Talladega; Baptist Morehouse and Virginia Union; Presbyterian Biddle and Knoxville; Methodist Clark, Morgan, and Rust—had subsisted into the early twentieth century barely recognized and universally unfunded by the newer secular philanthropies created by genteel corporate capitalists of New York and Boston in concert with the so-called southern progressives of Atlanta, Durham, and Richmond. Tuskegee trustee and railroad magnate William H. Baldwin Jr. famously summed up these men's educational philosophy in 1898 with his advice that Tuskegee students would do well to reject the Yankee teaching that educated their parents out of their "natural environment."[15] No doubt John Lewis recalled Baldwin's admonition.

The John D. Rockefeller Sr. General Education Board, which materialized in 1902, would determine thereafter institutional winners and losers in education, science, and medicine for the next sixty years. Reverend Frederick T. Gates, spiritual counselor to the Baptist Rockefellers, had warned the family patriarch that, absent some institutional means of shielding his obscene millions, a legion of taxing muckrakers would prevail upon an aroused Congress to tax Standard Oil and its robber-baron fraternity. A head-spinning $52 million in Rockefeller dollars filled GEB coffers between 1901 and 1909, with steady accumulation of more through the decade.[16] Atlanta and Fisk universities would plead for dollars in vain. When Henry Morehouse (famous for his "Talented Tenth" idea) and fellow white Baptist educators asked the GEB for funds for Virginia Union salaries, dormitories, and faculty quarters in 1908, "all requests were denied." Education historian James Anderson reveals that of the one hundred black colleges and normal schools in 1914–1915, "two-thirds had no endowment funds; and the remaining third had a combined total of only $8.4 million"—the bulk of it owned by Hampton and Tuskegee Institutes."[17] To say that by 1920 President Lewis's Morris Brown University endowment was almost infinitesimal broached hyperbole.

Dr. Washington's much regretted demise, followed by the impatience of urban blacks, did encourage the philanthropies to take a new look at the Negro problem after 1915. The new look began on the morning of November 15, 1915, at the General Education Board's Manhattan headquarters on Broad Street. Foundation stakeholders had convened to judge the public relations efficacy of Hampton Institute professor Thomas Jesse Jones's "scientific" draft report on Negro higher education. Two black educators joined eleven whites. The former duo, Robert R. Moton of Tuskegee and John Hope of Atlanta Baptist College (Morehouse), were essential cover for Thomas Jones and a dogmatically committed new GEB secretary, Abraham Flexner, author of a revolutionary new report on American and Canadian medical and scientific education. Professor Jones was a naturalized Welshman whose knowledge of African American colleges and normal schools had been rapidly acquired, seemingly without the benefit of the analogous Atlanta University Studies conducted by W. E. B. Du Bois.[18]

My father would have known little of these historic developments at that time, but what Du Bois learned from Hope that John Lewis would later learn from *The Crisis* channeled Hope's profound disillusionment. John Hope had spoken of his people's growing suspicion that the GEB had in mind "actually a different kind of education for Negroes." Chiefs and senior representatives from the Peabody Fund, the Slater Fund, the Phelps-Stokes Fund, the Anna T. Jeanes Foundation, the Southern Education Board, and several more held their breaths until Flexner answered Hope. "It was very important to distinguish between what it is worthwhile doing for no better reason than that the white schools are and have been doing it," stated Abraham Flexner sternly. Take women's education, he exclaimed. "A costly mistake had been made in granting women the same educational opportunities as men."[19] It had been painfully obvious to Hope that Negroes would not benefit from "mistakes" made in the case of white women.

John Henry Lewis undoubtedly read the *Crisis* review of Jones's two-volume 1917 book before leaving Pasadena for Atlanta. *Negro Education: A Study of the Private and Higher Schools for Colored People in the United States*—sponsored by the Federal Bureau of Education and financed by the Phelps-Stokes Fund—he must have seen as both an opportunity for Morris Brown University and an insult wrapped in pseudoscientific racism.[20] The Jones findings established that only 33 of 653 black private and state schools deserved collegiate classification. Even those were said to cling to an ossified curriculum of Greek, Latin, and philosophy bequeathed by earnest nineteenth-century Yankee preceptors. Instead of racially tailored instruction in cooking, carpentry, tailoring, laundering, and animal care, as at Hampton and Tuskegee, Jones despaired that everywhere he probed administrators and faculties succumbed to student demands for college subjects leading to careers in law, medicine, preaching, and business.[21]

Du Bois's blistering February 1918 review of *Negro Education*, while conceding institutional unevenness, pretentiousness, datedness, even preposterousness, aimed straight for the foundation mandarins who had invented *Negro Education* as "a master plan to bring about the restriction and replacement of 'academic and higher education' . . . by a larger insistence on manual training, industrial education, and agricultural training." Washington himself had never meant to insist, Du Bois quoted him as saying, "that the education of the Negro should be confined to that alone, because we need men and women well-educated in other directions."[22] *The Crisis* put a finer meaning to proliferating "bogus colleges and anemic academies" that must have resonated with a former Cuthbert high school principal. Not merely did they show "a people's edifying desire to escape the dead end of being hewers of wood and drawers of water"; Du Bois identified "the real problem" was not that there were too many bad African American schools—"with merely a silly desire to study Greek"— but that the emergence of "a few excellent ones" had been systematically impeded by white philanthropy.[23]

JOHN HENRY LEWIS FROM SCHLEY COUNTY AND AMERICUS, GEORGIA, perhaps knew better even than the editor of *The Crisis* that Rockefeller education millions were as much at the mercy of the South's explosive race-class politics as had been the Blair tariff millions in the early 1890s. An entire class of southern whites stood ever ready to send the General Education Board packing should its resources ever encourage "niggers" to see the world beyond *Plessy v. Ferguson*.[24] If equivocation in the service of endowments describes the genus University President, then my father's unprecedented GEB dalliance was modestly successful. After all, the 1885 dedicatory address of Bishop Atticus Haygood—Emory College trustee, Slater Fund general agent, and author of *Our Brother in Black*— had saluted Morris Brown College as a towering example of Negro philanthropy. So long as colored people showed "this good spirit of self-help," exhorted the venerable bishop, "you may be helped by other people without harming you."[25]

The earliest mention of my father in the records of the General Education Board, in July 1920, cites Secretary Eban Sage's approval of $3,500 for faculty salary increases for the fiscal year ending June 30, 1921. At the same time, a Morris Brown University request was under consideration for the repairs the new president had found it "absolutely necessary to make" due to the physical deterioration at the Boulevard and Houston Street campus. Sage's response was to send one of the GEB's most able "circuit riders" from Richmond to discuss Morris Brown's long-term needs in person with John Lewis.[26] Jackson Davis, a Tidewater-bred, thirty-eight-year-old, cultured segregationist soon destined for GEB peerage, introduced himself to an equally driven black administrator sometime in mid-November of 1920. This first of several future meetings, extensive but cordial, must have lifted my father's spirits. "He knows what is going on and has definite ideas," Jackson Davis wrote to Secretary Sage, "commending the spirit and ability of the new president J. H. Lewis." One large apprehension concerned the GEB officer, however—"whether Bishop Flipper would let President Lewis carry out his ideas."[27]

"Detailed estimates of cost" to put the Morris Brown plant "in good physical condition with the requisite amount of equipment" were expedited before Davis's return to Richmond. Eban Sage initialed President Lewis's request as "recommended one half" for $5,630.00 in early December.

More GEB encouragement arrived four months later. Addressing "My dear Dr. Lewis" (honorary Wilberforce title), Dr. Sage was pleased to report his executive committee's decision to duplicate all Morris Brown University cash receipts "not to exceed four thousand dollars." The care and repair of the Atlanta facilities certainly needed infusions of Rockefeller dollars. Enrollments were on track to peak at some nine hundred students by 1922. Bishop Atticus Haygood's promised beneficence seemed at hand. "At that time," as stipulated in GEB archives, "the schools of the Morris Brown System had never received money from white people."[28]

Morris Brown System requests decidedly increased, as evidenced by Secretary Sage's somewhat urgent advisory to Jackson Davis in late June 1921. Writing that President Lewis was "in my office at this time" (at 61

Broad Street, Manhattan!), Sage thought it best that Davis again visit and "confer with him about the matter." The urgent matter concerned the production of enough black teachers to service elementary and normal-level needs throughout the state. National estimates of the time gave 1 black teacher for every 334 black persons compared with a ratio of 1 to 145 for whites.[29] Finding enough trained teachers for the uplift of his people was this educator's raison d'être. Reliable sources informed John Lewis that the city might either sell outright or exchange an old white public school adjoining his campus. The Lewis administration believed it could serve as Morris Brown's much-needed teacher training department. Presumably Jackson Davis must have counseled delay after the Board of Education mentioned a sales price of $45,000. Jim Crow policy obviously ruled out consideration of a nominal sale price for the old, worn facility. But my father's commitment to his teacher-training proposal became a priority he believed was a self-evident necessity.

The president soon returned to the matter. A follow-up letter spelled out the needs and opportunities that compelled a larger campus and more buildings. "Morris Brown receives more young people from the rural sections of the South than any of the other large institutions," Sage read; if prepared "in our training school for service in their respective communities, we will have accomplished a worthy task." The alumni association and friends led by him had raised $5,000 with more subscribed. Were the GEB to commit between $20,000 and $25,000 "to stimulate our financial effort," President Lewis was confident Morris Brown could meet the Board of Education's sales price. Secretary Sage's follow-up communiqué to Jackson Davis opined that Lewis's teacher-training project seemed "out of reach," news withheld, however, from Flipper and Lewis.[30]

The Morris Brown president's opening semester 1923 appeal sounded like a Dickensian message of best-and-worst-of-times. "We find it very necessary to ask assistance" for teachers' salaries. Resources were "temporarily impaired" due to the economy and "the migration." Notwithstanding, "improvements have been made in equipment, buildings and faculty." The September term had started "with excellent prospects." Four college

instructors and two more high school teachers brought the annual aggregate increase in salaries to $2,160. The noticeably named Trevor Arnett,
the GEB's new secretary, was begged "to come to our rescue as you have
so nobly the past three years." The transplanted Englishman Arnett's
reputation at the University of Chicago as the leading fiscal authority in
higher education boded disappointment for my father's administration.
He was to learn in December of the GEB's decision to terminate salary
support of his teachers.[31]

The president's Dickensian troubles multiplied. The South's ongoing
loss of its black population had grievously curtailed the church's support
of its schools. Georgia's loss of souls was particularly harmful to Morris
Brown's sprawling system due to the seemingly unfathomable disappearance of much of what monies were still collected among the AME
faithful by Bishop and Chancellor Flipper and a host of presiding elders
at the church's annual district conferences. A decade earlier Burghardt
Du Bois's *Crisis* essay "The Negro Church" had both praised and cen-
sured his people's Baptist and Methodist organizations. "Before such an
organization one must bow with respect," acknowledged this lapsed Congregationalist. Yet John Henry surely remembered a wrathful Du Bois's
negative judgment of the race's ecclesiastical leaders. "The paths and
higher places are choked with pretentious, ill-trained men and in far too
many cases with men dishonest and otherwise immoral."[32] Nor had
Morris Brown University significantly benefited, it was recalled, from a
$250,000 educational campaign nationally advertised at the quadrennial
AME General Conference of 1920, just as the Lewis family returned to
Atlanta.

Funding his university on a wing and a prayer, so to speak, Lewis
somehow found a solid "New Negro" faculty of credentialed and mostly
urban men and women of Emancipation's second generation. "President
Lewis was highly successful in recruiting young and able people to serve
as faculty members," confirms Morris Brown University's *Morris Brown
College: The First Hundred Years*.[33] While success lasted, law faculty recruit Belford Vance Lawson, whose several future U.S. Supreme Court
appearances would legitimate business boycotts and desegregate railroad

dining cars, joined Harold D. West, a future Meharry Medical College president, Mary L. Stokes in mathematics, Ann Cochran for Normal School development, Eugene Bailey in chemistry, and Howard D. Gregg as church historian. Morris Brown alumnus Cornelius Vanderbilt Troup, head of the commerce department, established the school's urgently needed standard financial recordkeeping system. He earned an Ohio State doctorate (a Morris Brown first), became president of Georgia's Fort Valley State College, a land-grant HBCU, and would remain among my father's closest professional friends.

When the university celebrated its fortieth anniversary on May 25, 1925, the impressive evening occasion in Auburn Avenue's Big Bethel AME Church unfolded somehow without its president. Bishop Joseph Simeon Flipper presided as chancellor and trustee chairman. Following Reverend Russell Brown's invocation, a student quartet rendering by Messrs. Wilkerson, Troup, Wingfield, and Wingfield of a spiritual, Bishop Flipper delivered the principal address. Other remarks of faculty and songs of volunteers brought the festival to a close with an appeal for funds by Benjamin J. Davis, influential popular publisher of *The Atlanta Independent*.[34] Although no explanation is found for President Lewis's absence in *Morris Brown College: The First Hundred Years*, the audience rose singing "Dear Old Morris Brown, Victory to Thee," the new school song written at President Lewis's behest.

Wherever my father was, his intramural imprint was indelible after five years—notwithstanding his bishop's presumed superior importance. The link to the Rockefeller educational philanthropy would prove priceless to his successors. In the same year, 1922, that its winning basketball team was organized, the vanity and literary student publications *Brownie* and *Âurora* emerged. That the purple and black Wolverines football team roared back under Captain "Whirlwind" Johnson to pulverize Clark College and defy AU in Morris Brown's forty-first year was the stuff of forever nirvana to alumni. I imagined Schley County's Frederick Douglass Harrold scoring the winning touchdown that year.[35] There seemed much to cheer for forty years of African Methodist educational uplift.

Yet President Lewis must have realized that his chancellor's hydra-headed creation and the funds available for its survival had become almost fatally asymmetrical by 1926. The Great Black Migration seemed unstoppable. The decimation of the South's postwar heavily mortgaged landholders was a prefiguration of the Great Depression three years ahead. Meanwhile, the General Education Board terminated Morris Brown's faculty salary subsidy and declined to assist in the purchase of the obsolescent white high school.

Sixty-one Broad Street is silent about John Henry Lewis's visit. To be sure, Secretary Trevor Arnett must have politely masked his astonishment at the purpose of the visit shortly to be publicly announced. *The Pittsburgh Courier*, the nation's premier black newsweekly, bannered John Lewis's proposition on May 1, 1926: MORRIS BROWN PLANS MILLION DOLLAR DRIVE. Seeing Morris Brown grandiloquently described by one Cleveland Allen as "the largest institution under the direct control of Negroes in the world," subscribers read that capital campaign preparations had begun a week ago when Lewis "called on the General Education Board and asked for a contribution of $100,000." According to reporter Allen, Morris Brown University experienced its "greatest growth" under President Lewis's six-year administration.[36]

Recent completion of Fisk University's million-dollar capital campaign must have served as a model, even though a most unfortunate one, as President Lewis saw it. At Fisk, formerly the citadel of Du Bois's Talented Tenth, a stealthily purged trustees' board numbered Thomas Jesse Jones, Mrs. Booker T. Washington, Robert R. Moton of Tuskegee, and trustee president Paul Cravath, son of the great Erastus, who was reliably quoted to state that "separation" was "the only solution to the Negro problem." Under President Fayette McKenzie's reign, student government had been abolished; *The Fisk Herald*, oldest of all such black student literary publications, suppressed; a demeaning female dress code imposed; dancing banished along with an NAACP branch; Greek letter societies banned; even white college undergraduates hired as instructors. The Rockefeller General Education Board had pledged $500,000 in 1923 to Fisk as an earnest of its new commitment to black higher education. The Carnegie Corporation followed with $275,000, the balance understood as a pledge opportunity for the nation and especially for progressive southern whites, with wealthy white Nashvillians in mind.[37]

When John Lewis approached the board in the spring of 1926, the catastrophe of the "Flexnerized" Fisk University should have greatly sobered the great business philanthropy by then. Eight solid weeks of student boycotts, supported by Nashville black residents and the alumni majority, had forced the resignation of Fisk's authoritarian white president in April of 1925—after which a contagious eruption upended white presidencies at Howard, at Lincoln, and nearly at Hampton. A June 1924 campus address entitled *"Diutuerni silenti"* (My silence ceases) had mortally wounded the McKenzie regime. On an invitation from the Fisk Alumni Association to speak at the June 1924 commencement, Du Bois excoriated the president, the trustees, the complicit faculty, and the Midas gift of an endowment to reward students who "learned to make peace with the reality of the caste system." Seldom since Abelard's century has a speech inspired by Cicero produced such student seisms that defied university trustee boards and toppled their presidencies.[38]

The troubled Morris Brown University president must have credited the mandarins of the GEB with superior racial and generational calculations that would elude most of them well into the next decade. Adequate financial support for collegiate institutions headed by well-credentialed African Americans was still beyond programmatic grasp. It was worth noting, however, that after a preliminary inspection of McKenzie's Fisk situation, Sears & Roebuck magnate Julius Rosenwald had cautioned Abraham Flexner about potential difficulties. "There seemed to be an air of superiority among them and the desire to take on the spirit of the white university," Rosenwald warned Flexner, "rather than the spirit which has always impressed me at Tuskegee."[39]

THE POLITICS OF HIS CHURCH ABROGATED MY FATHER'S PRESIDENCY WITH an insulting suddenness he would never quite pardon. Joseph Flipper, age sixty-nine, was elevated to the august status of senior bishop of the AME Church in 1928. William Fountain, my father's Morris Brown predecessor and presiding bishop of the Thirteenth and Eighteenth Episcopal Districts, was reassigned in early 1928 to Georgia's plum sixth, thereby ending Flipper's sixteen-year tenure as presiding bishop of Georgia, chancellor of Morris Brown University, president of the board of trustees, and de facto chief executive. To say Flipper's managerial methods were as imperious as they were inefficient seems to understate the irregularities that handicapped President Lewis's financial authority and created a chronic institutional cash-flow problem demoralizing to his faculty and finally insupportable to the school's creditors. Some $150,000 of indebtedness was accumulated by 1928.

Morris Brown's million-dollar capital campaign was a Hail Mary pass antipathetical to the racial agenda of the Rockefeller board, conceptually far-fetched in a period of deepening economic distress and profoundly unfavorable demographics and achievable, if at all, only with more time and the loyal support of my father's new episcopal overlord. Bishop Fountain returned to Atlanta with William Jr., his ambitious son, however, a new-minted holder of a degree from Northwestern University's Garrett Biblical Institute and his father's permission to replace the Morris Brown University president. The trustees' meeting convened by Bishop Fountain for May 30, 1928, appears to have been a summons to a humiliation. John Henry Lewis Sr., Morris Brown University's sixth president, offered his resignation in advance.[40] Absent the acquisition of the white public high school, he must have solaced himself that his student teachers now gained classroom experience in the public schools by special arrangement with the Atlanta Board of Education.

He was to remember the sudden coldness of some faculty members and especially the warp-speed manifestation of disloyalty of several of his administrators. Although most students had left campus, several had come to express gratitude for his significance in their promising lives. A letter from Will Alexander, the highly respected director of Atlanta's Commission on Interracial Cooperation, might, if written sooner, have helped boost the million-dollar capital campaign. "I know, personally, how unprivileged the majority of the students who come to you are," wrote the coming New Deal's genuine racial liberal. Alexander was aware of "the marvelous transformations wrought in their lives in this institution." He promised Lewis that "well-to-do Southern people would express their approval in substantial ways" once they knew "these facts."[41] But the ex-president must have been fully distracted by domestic concerns soon thereafter. John Jr. and James Walker, their oldest, were born in Pasadena, but two more, Milton Dunbar and redheaded Anita Adele, had followed early on in Atlanta, where the Morris Brown University System provided both high school and elementary schooling. My father took his proud brood to Pasadena, where his welcomed seniority enabled him to resume pastorship of the city's First AME Church.[42]

NO KNOWN RECORD OF ALICE URNESTINE BELL'S CONTACT WITH JOHN Henry Lewis exists until their marriage at First Church in August 1931. Reverend William Faulkner presided. My AME-proud father obliged my

Eva Brown Lewis, 1917

mother's upper-crust Congregationalism without a protest. From their son's ex post facto perspective, their professional careers had followed parallel lines that hardly ever socially intersected during Father's eight-year presidency—different denominations and dissimilar educations. One imagined Alice Bell attending George Washington Carver's public lecture at Morris Brown University four blocks east of Auburn Avenue.[43] Perhaps a dramatic presentation conceived by Miss Bell at Booker T. Washington High School attracted the Lewis family. Possibly, given that both were gifted pianists, Eva drew John's notice to Alice.

No great personal passion seems to have interfered with my mother's driven professional commitment. Booker T. Washington High School educated some seventeen hundred students, many of them beneficiaries of Alice Bell's mathematics department. Her reputation as exceptional for making calculus obvious survived her departure from Washington High for more than a decade. Other students remembered her as their introduction to dramatic productions. Isaac Westmoreland's precocious granddaughter performed as a twelve-year-old in a school play with Lena Horne directed by their ambidextrous math teacher.[44] The former became well known as Eva Rutland, author of Harlequin romance novels, articles in *Redbook* and *Woman's Day,* and the drama *When We Were Colored: A Mother's Story.* Lena Horne invented herself as the famous singer and actress whose Washington High School days seem scarcely recalled.

Pageants and plays I knew to have been among my mother's well-received avocations. Her "Dark to Dawn" was chosen as the commemorative pageant at the fiftieth anniversary of the Atlanta Colored Public Schools. Its title conveyed its message. Her cherished concert prowess had been sacrificed to teaching and a delayed career as wife, mother of me and my half siblings, and admired hostess of a distinguished administrator. A surprise almost as astonishing as my Confederate DNA was a Ms. Tashell Thomson's November 2019 email regarding Alice Urnestine Bell's charter membership in Sigma Gamma Rho. Thanking Ms. Thomson for print and photograph matter about Alice U. Bell's "active SGR years," I told her they were "some of the most meaningful surprises since beginning my family history project." I learned from Wikipedia that

Sigma Gamma Rho began in 1922 as a small black women's club; followed by incorporation as a sorority of schoolteachers three years later, it had received its charter at Indiana's Butler University as a collegiate sorority in 1930. "Education is a failure if it cannot be used to solve the problems that confront daily life," proclaimed volume 1, number 1 of *The Aurora*, Sigma Gamma Rho's gospel publication.[45]

As of 1923, my prim, reserved mother had been one of Sigma Gamma Rho's first Atlanta sorors. Indeed, Mother was Eta Chapter's national organizer, and she had been the face of Eta Chapter at Sigma Gamma Rho's legendary coming-of-age 1927 Grand Boule in Indianapolis along with old friends and AU alumni Madeline White, Janie Goosby, and Clara Pitts.[46] Greek letter rankings are fiercely contested. The brothers of Alpha Phi Alpha, my father's fraternity, and sisters of Alpha Kappa Alpha are said to brook no debate about ascendancy. Most meaningful to me, however, was the disadvantaged socioeconomic tier served by Soror Bell's Sigma Gamma Rho Eta Chapter. Clara Pitts, much admired by my mother, bore the title "Mother of the Motherless" because of money begged and secured from the city in order to rebuild Atlanta's Carrie Steele Orphan Home, one of the country's oldest black foundling institutions.

Mamie Westmoreland Bell, former night school principal, Chautauqua cofounder, and lifestyle sustainer, seems to have been her family's anchor after my grandfather's December 1925 suicide. John Henry's demise must have stymied his daughter's and son's growth. Yet Mamie bolstered Alice and Levering with the proud valor of we're-all-right-and-don't-bother-to-ask affect. Uncle Jack's companionable temperament and handsome looks helped him rebound from his father's sudden exit with a seemingly smooth career imitation in the postal service and an even more prestigious assignment to its rail mail service. Three years later, twenty-four-year-old Emma Davis from Mississippi accepted Levering's offer and they married at First Church. For the rest of her life, Aunt Emma's Native American genes, naturally silver hair, and Blanche DuBois sashaying earned acclaim as Gate City's most irresistible distaff personality.

Uncle Jack with pipe, c. 1940

The Chautauqua Circle's worn, thick, leather-bound book of barely legible pages of meeting minutes found at Clark Atlanta University's Robert W. Woodruff Library is a family historian's catnip. Educated women interpreting society's flow in a forum of their making permits an indispensably holistic perspective on time, place, and race. In September 1913, one hears Mrs. Bulloch argue the affirmative and Mrs. Johnson the negative of women's suffrage at the circle's first meeting. With the United States at war in 1918, votes for women seemed assured; topics that year were "Women and the State" followed by "Egypt in the Limelight," then discussion of the "Bahai Movement." Mamie Westmoreland Bell's and her stepdaughter Alice Urnestinc's voices animate these circle happenings. On June 16, 1922, circle secretary Clara Pitts writes, "We took a most pleasant trip to California with Mrs. Bell. And many of us really thought that Mrs. Bell had been to California." Although she was absent the month after her husband's death, it's noted that Mrs. Bell "sent her treasurer's report which was read in part."[47]

The May extravaganza that filled Carrie Johnson's North Boulevard lawn on May 28, 1928, was called "Heart O' the Rose, a Pageant of the Coming Spring." Written and directed by Chautauquan Alice Bell, it brought the flower of Gate City's black bourgeoisie to celebrate itself. This "most brilliant and beautiful affair," exuded the secretary, showcased "the children, nieces, and grandchildren of members of the Circle." A sense of accomplishment, facile of appearance yet painstakingly orchestrated, had become the signature of Miss Bell's work. "Too much cannot be said in praise of Miss Bell's ability as a writer," judged the secretary, "for the play was the work of an artist—the children acted well their parts." This well-dressed gathering epitomized a civic satisfaction if not unique to their city (North Carolina's Durham and Chicago were close contenders) more than justified after the second coming of Heman Perry acolytes. A formidable cadre of college men such as Brown University's Lorimer Milton, Michigan's Jesse Blayton, AU's Clayton Yates, and Hampton's Walter Aiken had picked up and set going again pieces of the imploded Standard Life. Such a lovely scene as the Chautauqua spring pageant the year before the Great Depression defied the coming immiseration of millions of fellow African Americans yet also prefigured the biracial, business-class power structure of Atlanta's next thirty years—a top-down biracial synergy expertly deconstructed by Bancroft Prize-winning historian Tomiko Brown-Nagin.[48]

Two years and four months after my mother's memorable 1928 pageant, Chautauquans gathered in the home of Mrs. Charles H. Johnson, spouse of her much-respected physician husband, to pay "high tribute" to an original founder, Mrs. John H. Bell. My step-grandmother had passed peacefully after a short illness in the old Auburn Avenue Victorian (renumbered as 384). To say that "her presence and influence will be greatly missed" unintentionally beggared a noble person's family and civic significance. Alice Urnestine would leave relatives, friends, her teacher's position, her church, and her world in less than another year. Yet even this tenacious historian had failed to discover if, when, or how Mother may have known Father before they decided to marry.

Atlanta University—"Old Atlanta U," alumni remorsefully called her—disappeared with its final convocation in June 1929. Dr. James Porter and Ms. Clara Maxwell Pitts, both class of 1886, apostrophized the South's last undergraduate college open to blacks as well as whites and where the racially integrated faculty and their children lived and ate in common. Because of the Rockefeller patriarch's deceased wife's affection for the Atlanta Baptist Female Seminary, a handsomely endowed Spelman College emerged as the fulcrum of the Atlanta University Center after 1924. This large story of ongoing philanthropic overhaul in black higher education remains to be discussed elsewhere.[49] Atlanta University's rebirth as a graduate school, however, persuaded Alice Bell to complement her normal school diploma with a bachelor's degree obtained from all-male Morehouse College. Today's Spelman College bears scant resemblance to the Rockefeller-appointed President Florence Read's straitlaced finishing school of the twenties. By special arrangement as a nonresident evening student, my mother, together with a dozen other women, graduated with a BA as a Morehouse woman in 1929.

MORRIS BROWN UNIVERSITY'S EX-PRESIDENT AND FAMILY RETURNED TO Pasadena in 1928 only to uproot themselves for Little Rock, Arkansas, less than two years later. He was never to accept the judgment of those who called his presidency a costly failure. He was certain the double misfortune of episcopal misprision followed by episcopal nepotism had preempted all the probable national and local subsistence he might still have secured for Morris Brown. The General Education Board had commended his policies, while the new Commission on Interracial Cooperation seemed disposed to cultivate furrows of white Atlanta wealth. The Arkansas opportunity had come quite unexpectedly and even as a source of some concern as Eva's diabetes grew more troubling. Circuit rider Jackson Davis had recommended John Henry Lewis for a prominent part in the GEB's new focus on black secondary education.

Historian James Anderson cites the month and year—April 1925—when Rockefeller and Rosenwald millions had combined to provide the southern Negro with significant and regionally acceptable high school training. "It should appear that people of the community themselves are doing the thing," decreed the board's often benevolently presumptuous Wallace Buttrick. "The thing is to control it and direct it into the right channels."[50] To Buttrick and his class, my mother's behemoth new Booker T. Washington High School was seen as an unwelcome complication for the GEB's master plan for Negro secondary training. Atlanta's three-year African American boycott of educational bond issues had finally ended in a biracial compromise followed by a 1921 municipal bond issue of nearly nine million dollars, from which were built four black elementary schools and the Washington High School on land donated by Heman Perry—all without GEB involvement.[51] The mandarins at 61 Broad Street shifted their attention to Little Rock and New Orleans.

Little Rock was conceived as a linchpin of their national scheme of vocational industrial training for black youth. The Lewis family—an ailing, game Eva, three sons, and a daughter—arrived in Little Rock soon after Rosenwald son-in-law Alfred K. Stern's November 1928 letter to the city's superintendent of schools. "We have selected Little Rock," Superintendent R. C. Hall was informed, "as the first of the cities in which we are willing to participate in the experiment of providing an industrial high school for Negroes."[52] The Julius Rosenwald Fund, in obedient conjunction with the lordly Rockefeller General Education Board, envisioned a $300,000 trade academy modeled on Tuskegee—viz., a Little Rock Negro School of Industrial Arts. The Rosenwald Fund commitment of one third of the construction cost of the new school was intended to guarantee an outcome consonant with the GEB's educational paradigm—so much so that the fund would persist in ignoring official white reservations as well as furious opposition from much of Little Rock's black community.

"The schoolboard [sic] and I have given them [Negroes] as much industrial education as it is wise to give," Superintendent Hall suggested to Edwin Embree, the Rosenwald Fund's WASP president. Local Negroes required no special training to become "chauffeurs, janitors, draymen, seamsters, and laundrywomen, etc.," explained Hall further. Moreover, the cost of equipping an industrial plant would prove excessive. Indeed, R. C. Hall had already expressed a chagrin hardly characteristic of Jim Crow public school officials, writing to GEB official Frank Bachman, "We, like most other southern cities, have not provided for the negroes [sic] as they should be provided for."[53] What could be more exemplary of the school board's chronic denial of educational equality than its three-year-old Central High School, a white supremacist fortress that would become the civil rights cause célèbre of the Eisenhower presidency? Little Rock's white high school, brand new and majestic, was three years old.

Undoubtedly, Hall was also politically mindful of influential attorney W. A. Booker and his association of black attorneys. Informed of the high school's proposed name, Booker's chastisement of the proposed Rosenwald school was unanswerable. "Our people here have been waiting patiently over a span of years for a real high school, one that would not be a subterfuge; one that would give a thorough educational training and literary background, and a curriculum upon which a college education could be well predicated."[54] The small M. W. Gibbs School near Ringo Street had long since exhausted its secondary school shelf life. Notwithstanding its name, black middle-class Little Rock understood that Atlanta's Booker T. Washington High School offered a full-fledged platform of collegiate courses.

The racial relations awaiting the new high school principal seemed at first surprisingly propitious, as reflected in a reassuringly upbeat September 1930 letter to the *Crisis* editorial board from John Lewis: "Interracial relations here in Little Rock seem to be improving as indicated in the erection of the half million-dollar high school and junior college." Referencing his appearance before the city's Rotary Club, Principal Lewis also noted his Lions Club speech before "leading business and professional men of the city." He added, "Any publicity given this matter will be appreciated by the local people."[55] My father's satisfaction derived from what actually seemed to be a bait-and-switch success of black and white Little Rock vis-à-vis the GEB and the Rosenwald Fund. Five months earlier construction had begun on what the board and the fund insisted was an industrial school but the black community called the Paul Laurence Dunbar High School. No such struggle developed five hundred miles away in Columbus, Georgia, where simultaneous construction proceeded on the Rosenwald Fund's William H. Spencer Industrial High School. Both white education superintendent and black principal concurred that "we should give little attention at this time to academic education for black high school pupils."[56]

The architectural firm responsible for Central High School, Wittenberg & Delony, delivered a virtual Art Deco replica reduced by a third to accommodate some twelve hundred students. The wing-shaped brick structure spread itself block length along Ringo Street with thirty-four classrooms, physics, chemistry, and biology laboratories, a one-thousand-seat auditorium, a cafeteria, and seven industrial shops. The rounded construction cost topped $400,000, including $67,000 in construction costs from the Rosenwald Fund. The GEB allocated $30,000 over five years for teachers' salaries.[57] "Clearly things were developing contrary to the philanthropists' plans," concludes education specialist Anderson. Rosenwald president Embree himself recognized early the reasonableness of the local opposition to an industrial training program. "In the long run Dunbar was to become a model of academic excellence," opines Anderson, as would Atlanta's Washington High School.[58] Jackson Davis, my father's insightful GEB sponsor, fully expected that Little Rock "will be a great step forward."

For the new school principal already troubled by his spouse's medical condition and lingering prospects of a black boycott on April 14 opening day, an appeal for an assuaging pronouncement from *The Crisis* must have seemed strategically helpful. "Since there is some doubt in the minds of some as to the correct way of spelling 'Laurence or Lawrence,'" Father wrote Burghardt Du Bois, "a little light from the *Crisis* will clear up the matter." "Paul LAURENCE Dunbar was very keen about the spelling of his name," Dr. Du Bois ruled. *The Crisis* followed up in the next issue with notice of Little Rock's new high school and Morehouse College president John Hope as the dedication speaker. Alfred Stern spoke as well, good-naturedly praising an instructional outcome that deviated from the philanthropists' paternalistic master plan. Attorney Booker's curriculum "upon which a college education could be well predicated" was well satisfied with a junior college wing and a library of eight thousand volumes. "When it was built in 1930," states the University of Arkansas's authoritative John A. Kirk, "Dunbar High was reputedly the best equipped black school in the United States."[59]

EVA WALKER LEWIS SUCCUMBED TO DIABETES FIVE MONTHS AFTER HER husband's successful dedication ceremony. Her loss had to be a terrible blow, but my father displayed stunning self-control and geographical mobility in the months that followed. A man with four young children, facing the professional expectations inherent in heading the South's newest collegiate high school, truly faced difficult decisions. Relatives of his or of Eva's must have enabled his return to the University of Chicago for a class in test evaluation and another in administration during the summer quarter of 1930. Somehow, my father and his children survived until the following summer, when John Lewis and Alice Bell became husband and wife in First Church as previously mentioned on August 11, 1931.[60]

Although I was not to join this large family until five years later, what I know of her management of young people, her appealing self-confidence, her canny intuition, and her unalloyed pleasure in her husband's ambition must have made those initiating weeks at 1204 Ringo Street more a promise than an intimidation. In any case, her math department dignity fast receding, Mother was to spend the decade winning and shaping my father's high-spirited dependents in the large white Ringo Street house, where much was recentered by my arrival. And, in a sense, because both Mamie Westmoreland Bell and brother John Levering had so recently gone away, Little Rock seemed the right new beginning. Moreover, their circumspect mutual circles may not have been surprised by the nuptials.

Arkansas's Grif Stockley, one of his state's most original unaffiliated historians, sees the Little Rock black elite, "teachers, college professors, doctors, lawyers, and certain members of the business community, readily accept[ing] the notion of a black aristocracy based on education, skin color, or wealth, or any combination of these." Small in number, the elite "comprised only 3 percent of Little Rock's black population." To meet

Judge Stockley in person, as I did more than twenty years ago, meant spending hours rehearsing the full dimensions of the Elaine Massacre, the Arkansas Delta's 1919 bloodletting of more than two hundred black sharecroppers by constabulary, vigilantes, U.S. Army troops, and local white planters. Twelve of seventy-six corralled men were summarily sentenced to death. Walter White's incognito surveillance and *Nation* report astonished the country and certified his indispensable value to the NAACP. Such was the mental shock of Elaine, a hundred times more severe than that of the Atlanta Race Massacre of 1906, that most black Arkansans had blotted out its memory by the 1930s.[61]

Wilmington, Tulsa, and Elaine, like Atlanta in 1906, were the cultural scars of Jim Crow that induced amnesia, subservience, collaboration, or imitation of the oppressor. As if white supremacy's chastising efficacy needed reinforcement, some 22,000 Little Rock African Americans witnessed an unsurpassed auto-da-fé in May 1927, but months before the GEB and Rosenwald Fund addressed Little Rock's public education deficiencies. The lynched, bullet-riddled body of John Carter, who was accused of attacking two white females, was strapped to a car and driven through the city by a white mob to West Ninth Street. There the mob stopped, built a makeshift funeral pyre with pews torn from historic Bethel AME Church, and consummated its ritual by fire.[62] A thousand jubilant whites had to be dispersed by the National Guard. Ninth Street, like Auburn Avenue, was the preserve of doctors, dentists, barbers, lawyers, undertakers. West of Ninth the Mosaic Templars met and proud students attended Philander Smith College and Arkansas Baptist College. Dunbar High School opened three years later in April 1930. Although John Carter's immolation was never publicly acknowledged by Little Rock's white establishment as a reason, a collegiate high school serving the black middle class was probably the result.

Life for the Lewises of Little Rock was privileged within segregation's bubble. The principal's status placed them at black society's apogee. His early Depression salary of $1,625, supplemented by pastoral income from a local AME church, ensured the family's secure lifestyle. A University of Arkansas colleague of Judge Stockley's describes the all-too-prevalent

Paul Laurence Dunbar High School, built 1930

class conformity of the black elite, in which segregation "provided black businesses and black professionals with an exclusive black clientele for their services that they remained reluctant to sacrifice in a push for social equality." To be sure, the capital city's black majority applauded the existence of Dunbar, but for the most part the energy to make the collegiate high school a reality was an upper-middle-class imperative that defined its raison d'être. That the nationally celebrated civil rights couple Daisy and L. C. Bates, publishers of the militant *State Press* newspaper, were cold-shouldered at first as uneducated scolds was a snarky judgment of the black elite.[63] The local NAACP, phlegmatic but socially distinguished, relied upon aging attorney Scipio Africanus Jones to represent its concerns.

Attorney Jones, born enslaved and racially mixed near Tulip township, educated himself at Little Rock's Philander Smith and its Shorter College, read law with local white judges, passed the Arkansas bar, and then achieved national renown by successfully defending the Elaine Twelve. The U.S. Supreme Court's unprecedented *Moore v. Dempsey* decision of 1923 was rightly credited to Jones. Scipio Jones, like my father, remained loyal to the Republican Party even when, with Hoover, the party sponsored the South's lily-white faction. John Lewis had applauded the symbolism of Jones as Arkansas head delegate at the 1928 GOP National Convention.[64] It's certain that neither Scipio Jones nor newly arrived John Lewis expected the Arkansas Negro Democratic Association (ANDA) to pierce the veil of the white Democratic primary, the U.S. Supreme Court's ineffectual recent white primary decision in *Nixon v. Herndon* notwithstanding. Really, as John and Alice took the measure of their people's options, the status quo seemed best. The Democrats' so-called New Deal program certainly looked dubious: a physically impaired Franklin Roosevelt with a Texas negrophobe as his running mate.

I WAS BORN THE YEAR AFRICAN AMERICAN VOTERS FINALLY EXITED THE Republican Party. Robert Lee Vann, *Pittsburgh Courier* publisher and acquaintance of my father, had shocked Negro leadership with a call to turn the image of Lincoln to the wall in 1932.[65] Mother failed to persuade Dad to vote for FDR in 1936, but she prevailed on him in their fifth year of marriage to increase the number of Lewises, which happened on the twenty-fifth of May. I was their second robust eight-pound attempt, my brother James told me many years afterward. At her advanced forty-four years, I suppose repetition was altogether ruled out. Lucky David, the third Levering after Uncle Jack's nine-year-old son. Dr. G. W. S. Ish, a black Yale contemporary of Father's, delivered me at Tenth Street Hospital.[66] No doubt my half siblings accommodated me with good spirits in our good-size, white, two-story frame home on Ringo Street, within walking distance of Dunbar High, where John Jr. and James Walker flourished, and Gibbs Elementary, where Milton Dunbar and Anita Adele survived. I sensed from earliest cognition Mother's adoration, offset by Father's distracted notice.

Memories until our leaving Arkansas for Ohio in 1944 remain largely impressionistic with several inchoate shocks. I escaped a nearby Catholic school at about age five. My parents agreed that I was a better fit for home-schooling, since my slowness in reading disappointed the businesslike nuns and retarded the march of classmates to literacy and arithmetic. School with Mother was an indulgent osmosis in which every question

was answered, every puzzle and problem explained, history and literature conjured with names and places, and my exceptional memory compensated for the bother of reading. Tommy, a neighborhood white boy
my age whose parents were too poor for bigotry, was like an alter ego.
Years later, when I met Ernest Green, one of the Little Rock Nine, who
integrated Central High School, I learned that older friends of his remembered my quirky precociousness. My first heartthrob at eight years,
Joyce Martin, the elementary school principal's smart daughter, also
confirmed their judgment when we met as adults. Life was mostly affirming on Ringo Street behind Du Bois's veil, despite the 1941 National
Urban League survey that found housing for most Little Rock blacks of
"the lowest extremes of poverty, primitiveness and squalor."[67]

When the time came to wear dress shoes, I went with both parents to
a downtown store, where an early inchoate shock happened. Dr. and Mrs.
Lewis were accorded respectable Negroes' courtesy. I must have found
several questions to ask the salesman as he fitted a couple of sizes. After
my satisfied strut before a floor mirror, we bade the manager a courteous
goodbye and went on our way. We were immediately overtaken by a blond
female customer—stopping us excitedly yet apologetically. Speaking directly to my mother, the shoe customer pleaded that they leave Arkansas
with their boy as soon as possible. "They will kill him," she whispered before heading back to the shoe store. My stunned father covered his emotions with a whispered "The woman's crazy!" Mother looked oddly thankful.
The next inchoate shock, later that year, seemed to validate the shoe customer's fears. As we descended the city bus to attend some long-forgotten
Ninth Street event, Mother waited below for me to follow. The rear door
slammed shut and the conductor gunned his bus with my leg pinned fast
as she ran, holding my leaning torso while passengers inside screamed.
Mother sprinted half a block before the bus halted.[68] I see her even now in
tears, gasping for breath as both of us recovered on a rough-hewn bench.

Daisy Bates reached the Sunday afternoon scene on Ninth Street minutes
after army sergeant Thomas Foster was shot dead with five bullets by

policeman Abner Hay. The white policeman had holstered his weapon and lit his pipe while standing over his black victim. Foster had been angered that policemen Hay and George Henson had clubbed drunken Private Albert Glover instead of letting military police carry the soldier back to Camp Robinson. According to Bates's popular *State Press*, Foster was "one of the most popular and respected soldiers on the post." The United States had been at war less than five months since Pearl Harbor. A large, dumbstruck crowd watched as the dead soldier's ambulance pulled away on March 2, 1942. "A Negro soldier standing next to me was crying openly," wrote Bates. "Why should we go over there and fight? These are the sons of bitches we should be fighting!"[69] Although my parents understood this sentiment, which they were too responsible to share publicly, John and Alice arranged to show our outraged solidarity with the community by opening our home one Sunday to Camp Robinson's black officers.

THE NINTH STREET KILLING OF SERGEANT FOSTER AND FRAUDULENT exoneration of the policeman by a federal grand jury finally shattered black Little Rock's acquiescence. L. C. and Daisy Bates's *State Press* broadcast screaming headlines about the biracial power structure's insouciance. Church meetings prodded demands for black policemen on Ninth Street. A new Negro Citizens' Committee of credentialed leaders released its shocking findings about the Ninth Street homicide. "[O]ne need only compare the response . . . to the massacre of blacks in Phillips County twenty-three-years earlier," Grif Stockley remembers. "Then, a hand-picked delegation of the . . . black elite had sat on their hands in silence at a bi-racial meeting as . . . Governor . . . Brough extolled . . . whites as heroes who had averted a riot of blacks."[70] Young lawyer William Flowers and his band of young black professionals had formed the Committee on Negro Organizations (CNO) at the town of Stamps in March 1940. They pledged a statewide departure from the old leadership order. New Deal philosophy and defense-industry economics stealthily encroached upon southern folkways — even those of racially buttoned-down Little Rock.[71]

John Lewis's Dunbar teachers had already caught the spirit of courtly defiance. When news reached them in June of 1940 that Melvin Alston, president of Virginia's Norfolk Teachers' Association, had prevailed on appeal with NAACP representation, Little Rock's black teachers bestirred themselves. Taking counsel from Norfolk's Alston and the NAACP's White, the city's entire membership of eighty-six black primary and secondary teachers of the Classroom Teachers Association (CTA) formed a Salary Adjustment Committee (SAC) to uncover the remuneration schedules of white and black instructors. The SAC quickly found that white high school instructors earned an average salary of $1,216. At Dunbar, the average was $724. Apprised of their concerns in a petition requesting immediate adjustment, Little Rock superintendent of schools Russell T. Scobee passed the black faculty document to the Board of Education, where it remained ignored throughout the summer of 1941. Insult to injury came when Dunbar's faculty discovered

Family trio at Dunbar

that white teachers were given an undisclosed increased average that summer.[72]

My father would have known of attorney Scipio Jones's correspondence with the young Thurgood Marshall about the Classroom Teachers Association's grief.[73] Nor might he have been surprised that the NAACP's thirty-three-year-old new litigation chief expressed reservations about involvement with Little Rock. A similar salary suit in Nashville appeared likely to be satisfactorily resolved early the next year. The NAACP was also hopeful for an equitable ruling against the Orleans Parish School Board and the New Orleans city superintendent. South Carolina's contemporary salary equalization suit was dead, however, due to the absence of a suitable plaintiff. Walter White's opinion of the entire six-hundred-member Arkansas NAACP was almost derisory. Thurgood Marshall had advised Jones and his associate Robert A. Booker to delay filing their case when news came that the CTA teachers refused to sign their new contracts. "Boy," Marshall is always remembered to have exclaimed, "these southern teachers have acquired brand new backbones!"[74] But the character of the Little Rock teachers remained to be tested.

Thurgood Marshall joined Jones and Booker the last week of February, met with CTA leader John H. Gipson, reassured himself about the plaintiffs' unity, and chose Sue Cowan Morris, Dunbar's English department head and an NAACP stalwart, as Superintendent Russell Scobee's named adversary. John A. Kirk, a knowledgeable student of Arkansas race relations, captures Marshall's transformative impact. "Importantly, it helped to forge links between local black activists and the NAACP"— the younger militants like the Stamps lawyer Harold Flowers and both Bateses, Professor Kirk had in mind. "He sure did shoot them some straight dope as to their part and membership to be played in the NAACP cause," Kirk heard an awakened elite concede. "Little Rock is 'agog' over him."[75] Scipio Jones filed suit in federal court on February 28, 1942, on the grounds that the Classroom Teachers Association members were denied their rights under the Fourteenth Amendment.

Thurgood Marshall's approval of Sue Cowan Morris as the suit's principal plaintiff exemplified those legions of model litigants used by

NAACP attorneys in the future. A child of educated parents who curated her private Mississippi schooling, shaped her seventh and eighth grades at Spelman in Atlanta, and capped her secondary and collegiate matriculation at Alabama's Congregationalist Talladega College, Sue Morris was hired as English department head in 1935. Encouraged as she must have been by Principal Lewis, she perfected her pedagogy in the summer of 1940 with As in "Methods of Teaching English" at the University of Chicago. Demure, if nervous, Morris presented superbly during the February preliminary hearings in federal judge Thomas C. Trimble's courtroom. Superintendent Scobee's wounded protestations set the proceedings' tone: Little Rock had the "best educational system for Negroes in the entire South."

Lawyers for the school board condescended to recite the impartial criteria used to rate all the city's teachers: "special training; ability; character; experiences; duties; services; accomplishments." Judge Trimble, widely believed to have influenced the Sergeant Foster grand jury, upheld the innocence of the school board and ruled that the Fourteenth Amendment was inapplicable to the issues raised by the Classroom Teachers Association's complaint. Indeed, Trimble dismissed the salary suit as altogether improper, since the CTA was an unincorporated organization barred on a technicality from bringing suit in federal court. So ruled, it must have seemed that nothing should detain the NAACP's unsurprised young chief counsel from leaving Little Rock. Less as a lifeline than, perhaps, as a southern courtesy, Thomas Trimble agreed to hear Sue Morris as an individual plaintiff sometime in the future. The Dunbar teachers' case would be the last case argued by that remarkable jurist Scipio Jones. It had been his prepared brief, argued before the U.S. Supreme Court by aged Moorfield Storey, the NAACP's honorific white president, that finally freed the Elaine Twelve in *Moore v. Dempsey*. My father's friend died in March of 1943.

Judge Trimble and Superintendent Scobee expected to find a deflated CTA and chastened plaintiff Morris after nineteen months of contemptuous delay. The summons to trial on the twenty-eighth of September and second of October, 1943, was supposed to be an embarrassing judicial ritual. Marshall, assisted by Booker and a younger John A. Hibbler, reprised the Fourteenth Amendment violation of equal salary remuneration. Clearly, neither the CTA teachers nor Morris and her attorneys objected to *Plessy*'s separate-but-equal status quo. Little Rock's black teachers demanded only *Plessy*'s correct application under the Fourteenth Amendment. What Thurgood Marshall proceeded to demonstrate was the irrefutable equality of his superior plaintiff, Sue Morris.

With Dunbar's establishment thirteen years earlier had come a supervisor of Negro schools, initially salaried from General Education Board funds. In Charles R. Hamilton, Caucasian principal of white Garland Elementary School, reposed the supervening judgment call as to the merits of individual Negro teachers. Albeit merely routinely conferring with his racial counterpart, Principal Hamilton's submitted statement found that Dunbar High School's Miss Morris fell short of classroom qualities that made her an exceptional teacher. With the court's permission, Marshall called my father to offer his sworn opinion of his teacher's professional qualities. The family had understood when Thurgood discussed the matter with Dad that we faced a livelihood decision that was bound to be inconvenient at the very least. Mother said proudly that much was expected of Lewises.

Morris "ought to be a Group 1 teacher," stated Lewis before Trimble's court. "A teacher in the upper brackets."[76] Asked by Marshall to say more, my father respectfully revealed that Garland's principal had declined to study the standard evaluation criteria in use at Dunbar. Marshall noted the difference in credentials between the Dunbar principal and the high school degree of Principal Hamilton. Sue Morris memorably justified her principal's confidence in a fine statement. Principal Hamilton's professional chagrin augmented when Marshall extracted his admission of no more than "two or three" annual Dunbar visits.[77] The burnish of September's performance faded in October, however, as the school board's Rose Law Firm (of Hillary Clinton fame) presented a 1941 "merit ratings sheet" of specious objectivity.

My father must have agreed with Marshall's characterization of the Rose Law Firm's "lousy" tactics when "well respected" Miss Annie Giffey, with thirty-one years of white primary school supervision, declaimed, "regardless of college degrees and teaching experience no white teacher in Little Rock is inferior to the best Negro teacher."[78] Judge Trimble took the parties' arguments under review. His decision in favor of the school board would come in January 1944.

CHRISTMAS SEASON OF 1942–1943 CHANGED THE LIVES OF THE CTA PLAIN-tiffs. The school board informed Sue Cowan Morris without explanation that her services were terminated. John H. Gipson was dismissed from the school system, which left the CTA leaderless. John Henry Lewis received word of "definite dissatisfaction" among the city's powerful white people. "Be sure to give Susie Morris and Prof. Lewis a break in the story," Marshall had urged Walter White, "because Lewis really put his head in the lion's mouth."[79] Lewis decided not to wait for the inevitable and submitted his resignation. His Sunday pastorate in North Little Rock would have provided a subsistence living for a family of four, now that my brothers were in military uniforms. Thurgood Marshall informed Dad that the NAACP Legal Defense Fund—Ink Fund, as it was now called—intended to appeal the Little Rock salary case to the Eighth Circuit Court of Appeals. It seemed the NAACP was not optimistic, however, as Marshall told fellow attorney Myles Hibbler. "It's going to be tough any way you look at it."

Meanwhile, a professional cushion came from Dad's hierarchical AME denomination: the presidency of Arkansas's determined little Shorter College of North Little Rock. Marshall wrote a boosting congratulations. "All of us here . . . are more than happy that you received this appointment which you richly deserve." More than that, the good letter added, "Negro teachers especially, and Negroes in general who are interested in securing justice in the courts, will forever be indebted to you for your courageous stand in Little Rock."[80] Dad's grateful response praised Shorter College's potential. Gipson had come with him to Shorter. He would remain in Arkansas "for the time being to assist in whatever way possible in seeing that salary equalization fight through." Dunbar's now former principal repaid Marshall's compliments with an earnest foresight history would justify. "We are under many obligations to you for the leadership and ability which you exhibited in this case. Whatever may be the outcome, the defendants will never forget Thurgood Marshall," he insisted. "In you, the race has a champion of no mean ability."

Yet he worried that the people were fickle. "With me and Gipson out of the equation, most of the colored teachers have surrendered and 'run from the scene.'"[81] My father added that he would find work for Sue Morris. This was a promise he somehow failed to keep. While the salary case was being appealed to the Eighth Circuit Court of Appeals, the school board voted a $140,000 increase in salaries, with a significant portion used to close Little Rock's racial salary gap. Sue Morris would remain anathema to Little Rock's whites even after the unanimous decision of the appellate court in June 1945 severely reproaching Judge Trimble. Mark Tushnet, legal historian and former law clerk to Justice Thurgood Marshall, rates the Little Rock victory "very significant because challenging merit-rating systems had to be heavily fact-based."[82] To achieve their appellate victory, Thurgood Marshall's Little Rock plaintiffs meticulously exposed mountains of hidden salary disparities for which the three Eighth Circuit justices found no credible explanation other than chronic racial bias. Finally, at the insistence of my father's successor, Mrs. Sue Cowan Morris Williams ultimately returned to her Dunbar High School position after offering an apology. The Lewis family had long since relocated to Wilberforce, Ohio.

9

◆ ◆ ◆

STRIVING FOR
EXCELLENCE

The Wilberforce Years

N orth Little Rock's Shorter College presidency and Union AME
Church pastorate would have sufficed the material needs of the
Lewis family. Also it seems my parents proudly discounted the
new social nervousness of some teachers and clergy, who had scant confidence that the salary equalization defeat would be reversed on appeal.
The surprisingly scrupulous *Encyclopaedia of the African Methodist Episcopal Church* credited Reverend John H. Lewis with liquidating Bethel
AME's twenty-year mortgage and rebuilding Union AME during his
twelve-month pastorate. Meanwhile, Shorter College department chair-
persons prepared self-study reports as part of its new president's plan for
an institutional overhaul. Lewis's role in the teacher salary litigation had
redoubled his impatience to gain whatever greatly diminished rights and
liberties were left to black people under *Plessy v. Ferguson*. With the remarkable Shorter College alumnus Scipio Jones in mind, my parents were
the earliest readers of a new university press book that appeared during
the last weeks in Little Rock before our *Green-Book* drive to Ohio.

Certainly, no two books influenced a gradual change in the national
racial order as meaningfully as *What the Negro Wants* — one my parents
devoured as mandatory — and *An American Dilemma*, whose accusatory

title troubled much of literate America and would serve as a steady reference book in the Lewis library. William Terry Couch, distinguished editor of the University of North Carolina Press, had meant *What the Negro
Wants* to serve the cause of better race relations in the South. His sincere
gesture had resulted in deep editorial heartburn, however, after reading
the opinions of the contributors, thirteen black men and one woman, invited by Professor Rayford Whittingham Logan of Howard University's
history department.

Editor Couch moaned that none of Logan's contributors—Du Bois,
Mary McLeod Bethune, Wesley, Sterling Brown, Roy Wilkins, A. Philip
Randolph, Langston Hughes, George Schuyler, or even former Tuskegee
Institute president Frederick Douglass Patterson—had understood what
the UNC Press properly expected of them. "What problem would be
solved if the white South dropped all barriers and accepted amalgamation?" Couch asked about an issue the book's contributors barely introduced. "The things Negroes are represented as wanting seem to me far
removed from those they ought to want," Logan found himself reproached
by the editor.[1]

PROFESSOR LOGAN, FIFTH BLACK HARVARD HISTORY PHD AND CONSUL-
tant to the NAACP in international relations, finally threatened civil action after the university press editor balked at publishing opinions certain,
in his view, to promote interracial misunderstanding. *What the Negro
Wants* emerged from a compromise. Chapel Hill's Couch distilled a repul-
sion for Gunnar Myrdal and a dismay at his fourteen book contributors
into a preface of fourteen bilious pages of white supremacist condescension.[2] The problem that vexed the South's soi-disant racial liberals Vir-
ginius Dabney, Howard Odum, Mark Ethridge, and even Father's Jackson
Davis (and certainly many northern whites) was their deep fear that social equality inescapably followed political equality.[3] "If it were not for
the sex-caste foundation," Odum was sure "it might have been possible to
make adjustments."[4] The southern liberal reviewer chosen by *The New
York Times Book Review* squirmed at the mere mention of intermarriage

but conceded some benefit from such a collection of essays.[5] *The Nation* and *The New Republic* afforded black scholars E. Franklin Frazier and J. Saunders Redding, respectively, higher ground from which to present fair appreciations of the contributors' demands.

Leslie Pinckney Hill surpassed his collaborators in nutshell summation: "There is little doubt now as to what the American Negro wants," declared the Pennsylvania college president, with a positive nod to Eleanor Roosevelt and Wendell Willkie, among others. "Negroes want to be accepted by our American society as citizens who in reality belong, who have the respect of their fellow man and the equality of opportunity for life, liberty and the pursuit of happiness. Negroes want what good men want in every democratic society. If they wanted less they would not deserve the status of citizens."[6] President Lewis of Shorter College applauded. Several of the collection's contributors—Burghardt Du Bois, Charles Wesley, and Roy Wilkins—were family acquaintances.

HISTORIAN JAMES CAMPBELL'S *SONGS OF ZION: THE AFRICAN METHODIST Episcopal Church in the United States and South Africa* saw the late-nineteenth-century academic village of Wilberforce as a bucolic refuge of credentialed originals privileged to attain and sustain personal and professional fulfillment more or less unconstrained by white people. "A remarkable elite community had coalesced," he found, "around the university, representing some of black America's most distinguished families." Springy elocutionist Hallie Quinn Brown settled there and organized a chapter of the exclusive National Association of Colored Women. "Two other founders of the NACW, Anna Julia Cooper and Mary Church Terrell, also taught at Wilberforce in the last decades of the century," Campbell tells us. Cooper's *A Voice from the South* "was published in [nearby] Xenia." Martin Delany, erstwhile emigrationist and former Civil War warrior, "spent his retirement in Wilberforce." William Sanders Scarborough, America's first published black classicist (*First Lessons in Greek*), headed the classics department.[7] The author could also have noticed a very superior young Wilberforce University professor Du Bois who made two fast campus friendships with Major Charles Young of the military science department and poet Paul Laurence Dunbar, a frequent visitor from Dayton.

Wilberforce University in Greene County, Ohio, had survived intact as an ethnocentric oasis of collegiate achievement at midtwentieth century. But its antebellum origins, as I was to learn walking daily to school, had been literally as fabulous as they were racially problematic. An eight-year-old's blurred memory of driving two days in a wartime Plymouth with the family dog from Little Rock to Nashville, Louisville, the Appalachians, and from Cincinnati east to Xenia, still retains my parents' proper professional remonstrance—that the new divinity school dean's son please learn to read. Introduced at the preparatory school for faculty children, family dignity was saved when I declaimed perfectly after being asked to read from the class lesson. Every day walking to school thereafter I shortcut across the deep ravine dividing the campus roughly in half. Eons before the Europeans came, this vestigial canal channeled the spring waters known to the Shawnees as the Tawawa ("clear or gold water").

Some ninety years before the Lewis family's arrival, Tawawa Springs was a luxurious spa for southern planters who brought their enslaved concubines and mulatto children from Virginia and deep south Mississippi to their imposing resort hotel (Tawawa House) encircled by cottages on fifty-five shaded acres adjacent to the flowing Tawawa canal. This seasonal display of opulent license and sexual subordination, offensive to Ohio Quakers and troubling to Methodists, soon instigated the purchase in 1855 of Tawawa Springs by the Cincinnati Methodist Conference joined by bishops of the AME Church. An unholy alliance of planters and antislavery Methodists converted the hotel into classrooms and offices, the cottages into Wilberforce University dormitories for enslaved mulatto children and numerous escapees brought to Greene County by the Underground Railroad. Remarkably, Tawawa Springs or Wilberforce University briefly survived Secession; the student trust fund established by planters and supporters was not depleted until 1862. Wilberforce University, honoring William Wilberforce—educational flagship of the AME Church—emerged in 1863 from the purchase of Tawawa Springs by the entrepreneurial Daniel Alexander Payne, his fellow AME bishops, and the abolitionist largesse of Salmon Chase, chief justice of Abraham Lincoln's Supreme Court.[8] The learned Payne became the first African American university president of the first institution of higher learning owned by African Americans. The day following Lincoln's assassination Wilberforce University was burned to the ground by white arsonists, the cruelest of Reconstruction harbingers.

"It was to this rich background that the Board of Directors, in 1944, called Dr. John H. Lewis" to the deanship of Payne Theological Seminary, the trustees' minutes disclosed. "His reputation as a conscientious, hard-working administrator undergirded by firmly implanted Christian principles made him truly the man for the job."[9] Fulsome endorsements in exceedingly underresourced situations was the lot of African Methodist preachers, as the new dean and professor of homiletics and his spouse would soon discover. Payne Theological Seminary was the almost single-handed achievement of its South Carolina namesake, the autodidactic teacher whose secondary school for Charleston's free colored students had been shuttered in the long white backlash from Vesey's revolt. Expelled from South Carolina in 1835, the small, delicate AME convert battled his way up the church hierarchy to the overlordship of correct homiletics—arbitrator of educated preaching, ringmaster of worship purged of primitive reflexes. Payne's "Education of the Ministry," stern epistles written during the 1840s, deplored such African survivals as "the singing and clapping ring" and "fist and heel" worshipping. "One of [Payne's] first priorities as a minister," Campbell reminds us, "was to replace the music congregations loved with more edifying fare." That even the venerated if less educated Bishop Morris Brown, Denmark Vesey's former Charleston pastor, linked homiletic arms with Payne was enough to silence untold numbers of unsophisticated preachers. From its establishment at Wilberforce in 1863, followed twenty-seven years later by its official baptism as Payne Theological Seminary, the Wilberforce institution

Payne Theological Seminary building, 1951

would boast some seventy years later of sending more than a thousand well-trained men "throughout the United States and even into foreign fields to render Christian service."[10]

The seminary's meticulous admission requirements honored Daniel Payne's elevated expectations. Without regard to sex or Protestant denomination, bachelor of divinity applicants must hold a bachelor's degree or its equivalent from an accredited college. Greek and Hebrew awaited all first-year students, ambitious fare, certainly, in light of a contemporary *Howard University Bulletin* statistic that of the three larger denominations of the race, "79% of the ministers have neither college or seminary training." Tuition at twenty-five dollars per quarter, twenty dollars quarterly for (scarce) dormitory space, and "meals at a reasonable rate in the university dining room" made the school astonishingly affordable. Moreover, a unique if not unconstitutional late-nineteenth-century funding arrangement between the AME Church and the Ohio General Assembly sustained two different educational institutions known as Wilberforce University.[11]

Wilberforce University, the African Methodist Church's "flagship institution," was a cohabitation of dual trustee boards, two academically complementary campuses, and an expanding physical plant nourished from the Buckeye State's tax roll revenues. West of Tawawa ravine stood the church side's historic Victorians and Carnegie library; east, the state side's modern masonry and recreational complex. West was the college of liberal arts and divinity school; east, the college of education and industrial arts. The time was coming when the divisive question arose as to whether Ohio's legislatively funded Wilberforce University might be a Faustian ploy to divert African Americans from attending predominantly white Ohio State University—a prospective intraracial and civil rights crisis imbroglio that neither episcopal bishops nor elected officials deemed sensible to acknowledge at that time. Charles Harris Wesley, my father's Yale University contemporary, was in his third year as the highly regarded president of Wilberforce University, comprised of the College of Liberal Arts and Payne Divinity School and the College of Education and Industrial Arts.[12]

THE MANTLE OF PAYNE LEADERSHIP HAD RESTED WITH THE DISTINguished Dr. Charles S. Spivey Sr. from 1937 to 1944. He was a 1919 Payne alumnus and a Yale Divinity graduate whose death brought the Lewis family to Wilberforce and to yet another of my father's notable institutional overhauls. It seems that the new dean's impact was immediate on what had become Payne's ingrown and somnolent institution of five professors. "The work at Payne is progressing nobly under his direction," the first memorandum informs Payne trustee board chairman Bishop John A. Gregg, the enterprising successor to Henry Turner's evangelizing mission in Africa. Classrooms and offices housed in a grand old manor house willed to Daniel Payne had long accommodated a growing student cadre in cluttered corridors and bursting seams. "The basement of the Seminary building has been reclaimed and made into a classroom," Bishop Gregg learned.[13] New electrical equipment arrived for an administrative office to serve the dean's capable new secretary, my mother. The War Department supplied two military barracks for single men and married couples.

At the close of his first academic year, Payne Theological Seminary's Council of Bishops ratified Dean Lewis's new Department of Rural Church Affairs, an initiative promptly financed by the Phelps-Stokes Fund. "In all of this has been seen the philosophy of Dean Lewis, *viz.*, 'take whatever you have and make the best of it!'" another literate trustee communiqué lauded.[14] Two new ventures spoke to initiatives intended to be self-sustaining and relatively affordable. The inauguration of the annual Daniel A. Payne Lectures, calendared for the second week in April, debuted with lectures by Bishops Richard R. Wright Jr. and Reverdy Ransom. Yale Divinity's emeritus dean Charles R. Brown was scheduled to present the 1946 Payne Lecture, "The Art of Preaching," a considerable institutional coup as well as a deep personal gratification for Dr. Brown's erstwhile student. Pari passu with the Payne Lectures was a new *Payne Theological Seminary Alumni Journal* with a "Dean's Page" and "Book Review" section. Among the first titles reviewed were George Santayana's *The Idea of Christ in the Gospels* and John Rylaarsdam's *Revelation in Jewish Wisdom Literature.*

The *Alumni Journal* and Payne Lectures forecast a largeness of Dean Lewis's designs that some may even have viewed as grandiloquent. The dean did give an impression of running to keep up with lost time. "For the past fifty years, Payne has been housed in an inadequate building formerly used as the dwelling of one of its sainted founders, while scores of majestic buildings have sprung up on the Wilberforce campus," the new Dean's Page observed. "The church in its Post-War planning can adopt no worthier project than the building of a great theological seminary on this historic spot," his faculty and students were told. "We owe it to the fathers to preserve and enrich the great heritage which is ours." That September the new dean had publicly confessed to having sought strength in the "basement of Mother Bethel in Philadelphia," where "I prayed for the spirit of the founder of African Methodism."[15]

Fortunately, Bishops John Gregg of the Fourth Episcopal District, Reverdy Ransom of the Third, Richard R. Wright Jr. of the Thirteenth and First, and Sherman Greene of the Eighth as well as a portion of the First my father knew to be among the church's most scrupulous divines.

Reverdy Ransom was ex officio trustee member of Payne Theological Seminary's governing board. As presiding bishop of the Third District, he selected the majority of trustees of the Wilberforce College of Liberal Arts and School of Theology and six of the nine trustees of the College of Industrial Arts and Education. Ransom's luster at eighty-plus years was unrivaled among fellow divines and, in his mind, absolute at Wilberforce University, where he seemed merely to tolerate the executive authority of President Charles Wesley, raised as an AME and respected as the author of *Richard Allen: Apostle of Freedom* (1935).

In light of the institutional catastrophe that would badly cripple my father's ambitious plans, Wilberforce's commencement of May 1946 stays with me as a golden coming-of-age afternoon. A technically triumphant panoramic photo seemingly captures the Wilberforce universe: Charles Wesley and John H. Lewis front and center with every faculty member present in a great flood of the race's best and brightest graduates. That year Ransom and Wesley had finally and fully retired the $89,000 Wilberforce indebtedness, with the bishop and president ceremonially burning the mortgage.[16] That year saw the oldest university college in black America reach its apogee.

The inaugural Daniel Payne Lecture, delivered by Yale's retired dean Charles Reynolds Brown, was for Mother and me enjoyably memorable. Three decades after awarding my father the bachelor of divinity degree in 1913, emeritus dean Brown spent the night in our Wilberforce home to deliver an endowed lecture to seminarians the next morning. The special camaraderie of my dad and the dean was still vibrant after so many years. Dean Brown's jovial morning salute to me at the foot of the staircase was delivered as a matter-of-fact eventuality: "Well, I suppose we'll be seeing you at the school?"[17] I got the impression there and then at age eleven that legacy was a privilege kept available in a drawer. Dean Brown's "The Art of Preaching" left the larger northern AME community well disposed to Father's expensive initiative.[18] The Council of Bishops met in executive session shortly after Thanksgiving on a cold Ohio afternoon in 1946. The council's chairperson, John Gregg, was my father's older friend from Morris Brown days and, as I needed reminding, also my distinguished godfather. As Gregg was a former Wilberforce University president who had twice declined the Howard University presidency (in 1924 and 1926), his influence with his fellow divines Greene, Wright, and Ransom was beneficently considerable. They unanimously approved Dean Lewis's plans for the renovation of Daniel Payne's outmoded seminary residence and erection of two new structures at a robust cost of $150,000 each—a men's dormitory and a combined chapel and administration building.

Architectural designs prepared by the "noted architectural firm" headed by Rial T. Parrish of Cincinnati were accepted. None of our family could have imagined that architect Parrish, liberal and professionally patient, would become a frequenter over the next five years of the construction site just off Wilberforce's Clifton Road, which twisted all the way to Antioch College at Antioch, Ohio. Fair to say, Mother's attentiveness was almost as indispensable as the architect's. A necessary feature of the bishops' deliberations was her requested episcopal revenue figures, tallied and assessed to pay for each brick, beam, and unionized worker to turn Father's ambition into a $300,000 fait accompli. Her funding quotas were $35,000 each for the First, Third, and Fourth Episcopal Districts. Five thousand dollars from the Eighth District. Alumni and friends $10,000 each. Two thousand dollars each from the Thirteenth and the First again. "Century Club and other donors = $7,056.49."[19]

Her calculation of some $251,000 certainly sufficed to begin construction. John Lewis's six-page pamphlet with Parrish's drawings—"A Justification of Our $300,000 Building Program"—mailed to Wilberforce alumni, black newspapers, charitable associations, and Greek letter organizations, was tantamount to a race-wide summons: "Surely, we must have a religious leadership great enough for this Atomic Age; we must have a program attractive, vital, progressive," challenged the impressive pamphlet.[20]

The groundbreaking ceremony happened the following year, a March morning on the Payne campus in 1947. This was to be the $150,000 administration building, housing chapel, library, and offices. Several hundred Wilberforce students, faculties from the university's church, state, and theology components, visiting ministers and friends, witnessed a lively program that ran, notwithstanding the presence of credentialed observers, briefer than usual. The detained chair of the Council of Bishops and Father's reliable ally, John Gregg, wired congratulations from South Africa. Remarks from the president of the Payne Theological Seminary's student council were followed by the head of the Literary Society's remarks.

Dean Lewis spoke to the point, as was his wont, then presented the august chair of Wilberforce's combined trustees' board, Reverdy Cassius Ransom. The white-maned senior prelate evoked Daniel Payne's presence so vividly that some of the audience may have departed believing the earth consecrated by the AME saint. After the Payne Singers sang, a note from the archives tells us, "the spirit of the occasion was summarized in a poem written by Mrs. J. H. Lewis, 'We Break Today,' and read by Mr. Albert L. Davis as the ground was broken." Four stanzas of iambic pentameter must have been Mother's first poetry venture in many years, since Chautauqua days.[21]

This consequential Lewis morning would be remembered not for what was supposed to rise on this day's broken ground, however. Even then, my parents were in deliberations with the architect. A sharper assessment of Mother's quotas would merge architect Parrish's two buildings into a single multipurpose structure: a stately, steepled, and columned building that promised delivery of more—chapel, library, lecture rooms, offices, fewer student quarters—with less, for $250,000. The dean's bishops and their parishioners hardly needed reminding of the great wealth that ought be available to Payne Theological Seminary. "The church of Allen with 1,000,000 members, 10,000 churches, 8,000 ministers, and with property valued at 60,000,000 dollars is able to have and should have a graduate school of theology . . . certainly the equal of Gammon or Howard"; only unity, faith, and vision were needed.[22]

CHURCH HISTORIAN DENNIS DICKERSON'S CLOSE READING OF SOME TWO decades of "internal strains" associated with AME diocesan reform cited the denomination's scholar Charles Leander Hill's judgment that too many bishops "flaunt themselves as earthly princes vested with special powers and authority." A far less kind judgment by the iconoclastic publisher of *The Young Allenite* dismissed bishops as "thieves, rogues, hogs, money hogs and grafters."[23] AMEs of an older generation remembered the 1928 General Conference where Bishop Archibald Carey, in his capacity as host bishop and Chicago police commissioner, swamped the delegates with a police band, a platoon of uniformed detectives, "the ubiquitous presence of city personnel," and Mayor William ("Big Bill") Thompson's sacrilegious blessing of the Great Black Migration.

The 1928 Chicago "carnival" provoked outrage enough to carry a majority reform vote compelling the transfer of all bishops with more than eight years of service.[24] In its final nonretroactive form (sparing Bishop Carey) the residency rule would prove highly significant. What John Lewis's Yale and General Education Board exposure told him, however, was that most of these bishops were the CEOs of corporations, captains of industry, kingpins of finance, and above all the mayors and governors many could have become in a color-blind American society.[25] In Richard Allen's ecclesiastical kingdom, driven and gifted black men achieved lifetime power, perks, and pride. "Many prominent and well-serving ministers had suffered, along with their families, at the hands of tyrannical leaders who used their power to browbeat men into submission," as Howard Gregg's history of the infamous 1928 convention would document.

Charles Wesley believed he had defied the axiom that good college presidents seldom survived bad bishops. A Guggenheim Fellow and the third black Harvard history PhD, Wesley possessed enough professional self-confidence to refuse Wilberforce's initial 1942 offer unless new rules of presidential tenure were devised. "The President was to be the major executive official of the university," Wesley assured himself in 1942, having squared a diocesan circle.

FIVE YEARS LATER, IN THE MONTH OF JUNE—WITH A SUDDENNESS BEwildering to Dean Lewis but perhaps anticipated by President Wesley—

Bishop Ransom, in his dual oversight capacity, ordered Charles Wesley to vacate his office by the end of the day.[26] That a dozen of Charles Wesley's relatives drew university salaries, that Wesley had simultaneously fired the university registrar and a presumptuous and attractive dean of women, Georgia Myrtle Teal, who was also the new wife of recently widowed Bishop Ransom, were developments that roiled the campus waters.[27] Where 1946 had closed on a collegial high note at the school's ninetieth commencement, the new issues concerning faculty and resources and even spousal additions still seemed well within the managerial skills of Ransom and Wesley.

But it was the proposed insult to the bishop's true mistress that drove Ransom to trash Wesley's hard-won presidential understanding. Machinations in the state capital augured Wilberforce's radical reconstruction. The church's trustees claimed to have been blindsided by the withdrawal of Wilberforce's accreditation that March by the North Central Association. Both church and state boards were said to be "in need of reconstitution." Of far graver concern was a bill amending the laws governing Wilberforce University's College of Arts and Industrial Education. Under its terms, the appointive power of Ohio's long-serving Democratic governor was increased from six to eight of the nine state-side trustees. Further, the legislation required that the College of Arts and Industrial Education trustees choose its own president.[28]

Like it or not, the Ohio legislature funded two thirds of the Wilberforce annual total budget, which included the university librarian's salary and book purchases, the athletic complex, and student health services. As a faithful AME, President Wesley denied (rather improbably) both advance knowledge of and preference for the Columbus legislation, insisting that "no evil at Wilberforce but cannot be removed by conference and consultation." To Ransom's public charge that he was in league with powerful state forces plotting to create a Jim Crow institution, Wesley boasted of making Wilberforce "an institution such that white students would be attracted to it."[29]

Wesley "ask[ed] only to be recognized . . . as president of Wilberforce University by both boards of trustees." He claimed that "the majority membership of these boards seems desirous to do this," and perhaps a majority of students as well. An indignant Ransom was quoted to snarl, "If the students don't like it here, let them get on away from here."[30] In hindsight, the majority vote taken to dismiss the Wilberforce president—"as of midnight, June 12th"—was seen even by the participants to have been institutionally catastrophic. Annetta Gomez-Jefferson, a bishop's daughter whose privileged AME experience informs her gem of a small monograph, recounts the hubris of one day in June.

On June 11, Charles Wesley surprised the ninety-first Wilberforce commencement: "[Graduates] will remember that you are members of the largest graduating class in the history of Wilberforce University." He proceeded to stun the assembly. "You also have the opportunity of learning that the President of the University has had his services terminated . . . as of midnight tonight. Someday I hope to stand again on this platform as President of Wilberforce University," his low-throated voice told the assembly. "I will come home if you want me to." Professor Gomez-Jefferson recounts the day's denouement. A group of Wesley supporters gathered a group of students to march to Bishop Ransom's home to burn Ransom in effigy: "The eighty-six-year-old Reverdy, Bishop Reid, Reverend Gomez, and Myrtle [Teal] watched from the front window in disbelief as the stuffed likeness blazed and shriveled until it was dust."

It was clear that my father's unannounced and much disappointed visit to "Tawawa Chimney Corner," Ransom's imposing episcopal residence, a day later marked the beginning of historic Wilberforce's humiliating decline. Mother's closest faculty friend and future Wilberforce trustee Jayme Coleman Williams would recite to me from her hundred-year-old vivid memory Ransom and his episcopal coterie's male arrogance on the day before Wilberforce's ninety-first commencement.[31] "If the bishops waited until after the commencement when the students had all gone away," she sighed, "the situation would have solved itself." John Henry and Alice Urnestine realized that their Payne ambitions had been gratuitously and seriously handicapped.

The quality—not to say even much of its raison d'être—of our Wilberforce lives altered after the summer of 1947. A June editorial in the

Chicago World stated matter-of-factly who should be blamed: "Bishop Ransom, the Methuselah of the AME Church, who should have been retired over 20 years ago." My father, having presumed to question his bishop's rationale after driving to Tawawa Chimney Corner, lapsed into an apprehensive silence fully audible to my mother. He foresaw the necessity to staunch the church side's inevitable budgetary void with money diverted from his seminary. Central State's new president seemed as sublimely confident of the future as my father remembered from their New Haven years.

Meanwhile, the Reverend Charles Leander Hill, pastor of Columbia, South Carolina's most prestigious AME church, learned that June of his elevation "to the lofty office of the acting president [of] . . . the oldest institution of higher learning for Negroes in the world."[32] The acting president, a sharp blade of a man, called what he found there at Wilberforce a "soup hound." It seemed that personnel records, registration documents, books from the library, key professors purchased with increased salaries—all had been moved across the ravine to the independent new institution presided over by Charles Wesley and eventually called Central State College. "By some sort of magic of economics," Reverend Hill was able to pay the summer school faculty "two full months' salary."[33]

ECONOMIC DISLOCATION IMPACTED MY OWN PRIVILEGED LEARNING world as well. Come September, Wilberforce parents on both sides of the ravine learned that their children were to be bused three miles away to public school in Xenia, the county seat. "Wilberforce Prep," with its intimate teacher-student ratio, Mrs. and Mr. Chips faculty, and well-known campus visitors, had died in a contemporary war between church and state. The Xenia bus looped past the deanery with its adolescent gowns on their way to town. Climbing aboard five mornings a week with book bag and violin case like my pals Billy and Alfred Carr, we and thirty aliens eventually survived among Xenia's demotics well enough for cagey camaraderie, pubescent flirtations, but never home visits. I remember few whites from the Xenia years, so the tensions involved were of class, as sharp as any later racial confrontations. Billy and Alfred, putative descendants of a Thomas Jefferson nephew, strutted as to the manor born.[34]

An age eleven infatuation with Miss Circe, my attractive, early thirties English literature teacher, lasted through Xenia High School. One day I puffed up enough gall after class to ask her if she'd like to see the new Technicolor RKO film *Joan of Arc,* starring Ingrid Bergman and José Ferrer. Miss Circe was delighted and, to my relief, Mother and Father gave permission to have the student chauffeur drive us round-trip to the Dayton movie house. It was probably my most successful grown-up rehearsal.[35] If Xenia buses offered unusual sociological experiences to young Wilberforceans, the war of the two Wilberforces also revealed how socially fragile was our split-down-the-middle Anthropocene. Crossing the ravine could be eventful. Some state-side adults glowered when I whisked past them on my Schwinn to trade comic books with the Carr boys or lingered to chat with lovely "Snicker Britches," another reminder of Tawawa's antebellum days.

Racial intrusions, mostly ignored, visited my family during this difficult time. Two chagrined white Prudential Life Insurance agents hurried to their car after a hushed half-hour closed-door meeting with my parents. The shocking news was that a policy to pay for my college education had been voided. The "friendly" white examining physician in Xenia determined my life expectancy to be too problematic. My father's rage and Mother's stupefaction were memorable. He locked the door to his study. Mother sublimated with Chopin in the music room. Some days later, Dr. Nancy Lautzenheizer indicated for nonattribution that her Xenia medical colleague was a known racist.

That my two half brothers, James Walker and Milton Dunbar, who lived in our large, ramshackle deanery, had completed graduate sociology degrees at the University of Cincinnati under the GI Bill three years earlier struck my then innocent knowledge as appropriately routine. Not until many years later did I learn from Ira Katznelson's *When Affirmative Action Was White* how few African Americans benefited from the World War II federal education assistance program. John Henry Lewis Jr., a Yale Divinity legatee, was a similar beneficiary until 1947 when he joined

IBM. Their sister—my redheaded, headstrong half sister, who defied our father to marry a Dunbar High School mechanic—graduated from Wilberforce the year we arrived, whence she followed her high school choice to the Chicago steelworks.[36]

MEANWHILE, EVER DEPLETED RESOURCES CAST A PALL OVER WHAT WE came to call the church side. Where the College of Liberal Arts had numbered more than seven hundred students at the end of 1947, this historic school now held a mere three hundred after the North Central Association's withdrawal of accreditation. When the AME peerage met in Kansas City for its 1948 Quadrennial General Conference, the report presented to it by beleaguered President Hill reserved its greatest praise for Payne Theological Seminary, "under the dynamic leadership of Dr. J. H. Lewis." The annual Daniel Payne Lecture, presented by Dr. Gaston Foote, had been "one of the intellectual highlights of the current year." And there was more. Hill extolled the dean's "completely modernized theological curriculum" and gave the impression of work well underway on a "new administration building."[37]

President Hill's praise notwithstanding, Payne Theological Seminary came away from the grand 1948 Quadrennial General Conference nigh empty-handed. As the dean's 1948 report charged, any "superficial observer" would have judged the conference "a failure." Had Dean Lewis ever attended a national political convention, he might have found that the AME's conference in Kansas in March of 1948 compared favorably with Democrats' meeting in Philadelphia in July of that year: Harry Truman written off by Gallup; Strom Thurmond's Dixiecrats ready to bolt the convention; Hubert Humphrey stepping into history's limelight; Henry Wallace too far ahead of his time.[38]

Meanwhile, at the Kansas City 1948 quadrennial, where new bishops were elected and several others moved to new districts, Bishop William Fountain Sr., my father's Morris Brown nemesis, was removed from Georgia's Sixth Episcopal District in accordance with the infrequently invoked eight-year rule adopted at the General Conference of 1928. That

Bishop Richard Wright Jr., a Payne Theological Seminary trustee, replaced the senior Fountain was not seen as particularly significant.

The photo taken of the two men is a study in contrasts: Bishop Gregg,
of a lighter pigment and with a pointed goatee accentuating sharp features
over a large frame; Dean Lewis, a classic brown ectomorph exuding all the
clean-shaven intensity of an administrator. They stand before the unfinished chapel building's just-emplaced cornerstone the very day, June 9,
1948, Payne's trustees were given the dean's impatient annual report. Both
men knew this cornerstone bespoke yet another wager against a conjunction of unpredictables. Indeed, what money they had scraped from the
districts that year had been impounded. Two ancient indebtednesses
wrought financial havoc until "lawyered down." A trustees' note states,
"Bishop Gregg and I borrowed $6000 and paid the Summers estate in full."[39]

John Gregg reached the term of his trusteeship the following year.
The 1949 annual report properly honored the bishop's "great leadership
and guidance in the building program." Even so, the annual report concluded on another tactfully sour note: "However, the contributions received from the districts fell short in some instances of respective district
quotas." The godfather I came to admire greatly at age twelve saluted
whenever I saw him. The parents told me it was his signature greeting, an
old soldier's habit from service as an officer in the Spanish-American
War.[40] Bishop Gregg's successor would preside as chair of the Council of
Bishops until the Lewis family departed Wilberforce.

SEVEN WEEKS AFTER BISHOP GREGG LEFT WILBERFORCE, IN THE COM-
pany of my parents I was presented to a goateed, nattily attired gentleman.
My father's early Alpha Phi Alpha standing and even more impressive
Sigma Pi Phi distinction evoked a civil greeting. The gentleman's response to Mother, whose student she'd been at Oglethorpe Preparatory
School, was much livelier. When asked if I was among the young people
who had performed that morning, my proud response was affirmative.
Dr. Du Bois indulged a few of my rehearsed lines, tipped his fedora, then
headed alone into Galloway Hall to deliver an electric speech to the ca-

pacity audience. A half century earlier his teaching career had begun at Wilberforce, an institution of whose suffocating Methodism he often wrote disparagingly.[41]

As I later described in Du Bois's biography, the colored "four hundred" of segregated America—"440 doctors, lawyers, college presidents, businessmen, morticians, dentists, college administrators, together with wives and children"—heard the speaker abjure the very concept of his Talented Tenth. "Karl Marx stressed the fact that not merely the upper class but the mass of men were the real people of the world," he told this stunned, class-proud assembly, which called itself the Boule. Forty-five years after its origin as the leadership class of Black America, Du Bois proposed a "Guiding Hundredth" that should increase its numbers to three thousand by the next Boule, and then to thirty thousand twelve years hence at the 1960 conclave—"the numerical one-hundredth of our race." It did seem that the "Talented Tenth Memorial Address" at Wilberforce marked the beginning of the end of Du Bois's purchase on the "political loyalty of the class whose character was synonymous with his name." After his address, I remembered Boule members leaving Du Bois "sitting alone on a campus bench."[42]

Galloway Hall insulted, enraged, traumatized, devastated a social class. Their venerated public intellectual had thumbed his nose at a safe class construct for a Marxist-inflected deviation just as the nation embarked on a frightening geopolitical tear. The attorney general's list of "subversive organizations" appeared at the end of 1947. The trek of suspect persons to the House Un-American Activities Committee (HUAC) sessions had begun in earnest. Soviet blockading of overland access to Berlin and only the narrow defeat of Italy's Communist Party seemed to confirm Winston Churchill's "Iron Curtain" prophecy. A month after the "Talented Tenth Memorial Address" Burghardt Du Bois resigned for the second and last time from the NAACP, a decision that many of the Boule expected and almost all regretted.

If by his credentials and professional status John Henry Lewis met the social criteria of the Talented Tenth, he was never comfortable with the category's valorization of family pedigree and white admixture. His mind and spirit had always found room for Booker Washington's regional political and economic common sense. His wife was a Bell, however, whose feelings for the Great Accommodator bordered on loathing. Mother dismissed Du Bois's Marxist Talented Tenth at Wilberforce as a timely scolding by a beloved professor. Although my parents represented dissimilar preferences for group progress, the shock of Galloway Hall accelerated a painful awareness that *Plessy*'s apartheid depended upon the circumscribed bargains a great many people like themselves tacitly observed with white supremacy. Finally, almost a half century after Justice Henry Billings Brown dismissed Albion Tourgée's color-blind appeal as well as Justice John Marshall Harlan's curious dissent, the social-science plates beneath *Plessy v. Ferguson* continued to shift in the postwar United States.[43]

My mother's admiration for the grand intellectual notwithstanding, she shared my father's disbelief when news reached Wilberforce that Du Bois predicted a major shift by African American voters in November to the Progressive Party. My parents' ingrained Republicanism had been dented more than a year earlier by Missourian Truman's unprecedented address from the Lincoln Memorial to the Thirty-eighth Annual NAACP Conference. Mother gave distant cousin Walter White total credit for this NAACP one-off, as well as for the Truman administration's surprisingly ambitious civil rights report, *To Secure These Rights*.[44] They must have also doubted whether the unexpected executive order desegregating the nation's armed services would survive Truman's inevitable defeat. The parents were simply dumbfounded when Harry Truman handily defeated the GOP's Thomas Dewey and Strom Thurmond's Dixiecrats, to say nothing of Du Bois's Progressives, in 1948.

Dean Lewis's next-to-last report to his bishops, in June 1950, masked futility with determination. He reported a 10 percent increase in student enrollment. Though Mother's quotas continued to languish, Father stated he was encouraged by the authority granted him at the board's previous meeting to borrow fifty thousand dollars. Moreover, as his bishops were reminded, architect Parrish suggested several cost-saving eliminations to his building, and the building contractor, H. S. Boren, had shown "great confidence in us by continuing to work even when we are unable to pay him according to our contract." Payne's determined chief was "reasonably sure" that if Mr. Boren was immediately paid at least half the fifteen thousand dollars due, "he would be willing to resume work until the building is completed."[45] In my upstairs view of Mr. Boren's construction site, our apple-tree grove, which Mother liked to say had been planted by the pioneer nurseryman Johnny Appleseed, was long gone. Father's combined administration and chapel building rose phoenixlike, awaiting roof, finished interior, and chapel windows.

Looking back, I see that the dean's June 1951 trustees' report must have been disingenuous. The report's high sanctimony was suspicious. Truly grateful "to our heavenly father for His guidance and blessings," yet the times had somewhat discouraged the dean. Still and yet, "there is every evidence that Payne Seminary will survive to fulfill its divine mission." Grateful he was that "all the bishops have met their current budgets," but the problem remained—"to meet the building budget." Because of the separation of Wilberforce and what had finally become Charles Wesley's Central State University, contributions had diminished and costs ballooned. The single building originally estimated at $150,000 was now $200,000. "We have not raised, in all these years, a million dollars for the training of ministers," solemnized the dean's report, "and yet we have sent out a number of 'million-dollar men.'"[46] One "million-dollar" person, Edward Odom, my father's favorite professor, had resigned to enter the navy as a chaplain.

This report ended on a plea that his bishops appreciate what had been accomplished and what remained in their power to consecrate. "I trust that all of you will go through this building and examine it carefully. Building experts who have examined it declare that it is or will be when completed, one of the finest buildings of its type in the country. It will stand for a hundred years as a monument to your leadership and vision." Rial Parrish urged sealing the basement and finishing the floors immediately for fifteen thousand dollars. Contractor Boren could have the structure ready at the beginning of the year. "If the five Bishops of the supporting districts would resolve to raise $40,000," an answerable prayer, "we could complete and dedicate the building next June."

Of great interest to the Payne Theological Seminary community was the report's breaking news, however, that the Dunbar Life Insurance Company of Cleveland, Ohio, an African American business consolidated fifteen years earlier, had agreed to advance the building project fifty thousand dollars. Dunbar Life's success was symbolized by its new headquarters, relocated on Euclid Avenue with $579,000 in mortgage loans to one hundred families in formerly Jewish Cleveland Heights. The dean's report omitted two vital developments: that the Lewis family would soon leave Ohio for Atlanta; and that the Dunbar Life chief executive, Mr. Melchisedech Clarence ("M.C.") Clarke, visited our home to seek reassurance about his loan. "John," Mother and I listened as the insurance mogul protested, "I'd never have given money to your bishops if I'd known you were leaving."[47] Seven years later when Payne Theological Seminary would achieve full accreditation, Mr. Clarke should have been solaced that his Dunbar Life loan enabled Messrs. Parrish and Boren to seal and roof Father's handsome building.[48]

Memory has us taking the Limited from Cincinnati's monumental Art Deco station to Atlanta sometime in late July of 1951. Cyril Butterfield, our Bermudan theology student driver, delivered us and enough luggage to survive any misadventure en route. I folded my car-wash business with the Carr boys. It earned us three a farewell pot of money and pledges of brotherhood forever. Mother called Father's and my attention to Union Station's soaring murals and the artist's name, not remembered by me until three decades in the future. Asa Randolph's Brotherhood of Sleeping Car Porters led us to our reserved compartment with what seemed special satisfaction. Some forty-four hours awaited us till arrival time, but my parents explained that once across the Ohio River and thirty miles from Cincinnati, we crossed into the segregated part of the United States. When we left our berths for breakfast the next morning, the black head steward politely guided us to our curtained rear space while arched white eyes feigned unconcern.[49] My seven-year release from apartheid ended with all the demeaning obedience worthy of a character in a Margaret Mitchell novel.

10

. . .

WITH ALL
DELIBERATE SPEED

The Lewises

Bishop Richard R. Wright Jr. (1878–1967), son of Atlanta University's first valedictorian, was black America's first recipient of a doctorate in sociology, a University of Pennsylvania distinction bestowed in 1911 after Wright's Berlin and Leipzig studies in admitted imitation of idol Burghardt Du Bois. Supremely self-confident, administratively competent, and religiously progressive, he was the church's thirty-year editor of *The Christian Recorder*, African America's oldest literary periodical. While residing as editor in Philadelphia, Richard R. Wright Jr. had joined his distinguished senior parent's Citizens and Southern Bank and Trust Company, the North's sole black-owned banking firm.[1] The younger Wright was known and by some feared for his fiduciary integrity. My father's deanship had begun midway through Wright's Payne trusteeship from 1942 to 1948, at which time the General Conference's fractious Kansas City meeting voted to replace Georgia's senior Bishop Fountain with the junior Bishop Wright.

Details of the Fountain dynasty's sudden overthrow at Morris Brown College remain shrouded in a miasma of episcopal egos and outsize family corruption—all filtered through sketchy AME histories more suggestive than explanatory. Full justice after a quarter century of institutional growth was due the father-son administration that had replaced the gravely indebted Lewis presidency in 1928. Work well done always earned my father's praise. It was the timely decision of Bishop Fountain Sr. and President William A. Fountain Jr. to move Morris Brown to West Side Atlanta in 1938. Negotiations that year between the college and the new Rockefeller-financed (and slightly relocated) Atlanta University resulted in Morris Brown's eventual physical inclusion in the grand master plan of Atlanta University, Morehouse College, Spelman College, and Clark College—*Ebony* magazine's "Black Oxford of the South."[2]

For Bishop Wright what most AMEs saw as assured fecundity had really been a decade of Morris Brown's underperformance caused by family enrichment. An early GEB appropriation for the school's endowment had gone instead for an episcopal home and residential real estate and houses in the nonacademic enclave of the Morris Brown Circle. Recent construction of a twenty-four-unit apartment building for a quarter million dollars, together with "extensive excavating" in connection with the new Alonzo Herndon Memorial Stadium, was deemed excessive. When Fountain Jr. had barged uninvited into a meeting of his trustees in June 1950, he was abashed to find that all administrative affairs were vested in a new vice president appointed by Bishop Wright. "In 1951, Dr. John H. Lewis accepted the call to return to his alma mater." The once popular Fountain died the following year in Nashville.[3]

TWENTY YEARS SINCE LEAVING FOR LITTLE ROCK AND WILBERFORCE seemed to vanish after the first week in Atlanta for my mother. The residential world she knew along Auburn Avenue was almost unrecognizably diminished. Indeed, the Bells themselves had helped fuel the large residential shift to Hunter Road when Uncle Jack Levering, acting for both of them, had sold Clarissa King's Belvin indenture in May of 1942 for less than five thousand dollars. Alice and Levering's big Victorian at 300 (later renumbered 384) Auburn had long since become a multifamily rental. Mother seemed to reenter the elite social bubble of her young womanhood. As though reserved, a place awaited her in the Chautauqua

Aunt Beulah, c. 1950

Circle. In November 1951, Mrs. John H. Lewis introduced the Friday evening speaker, a Mrs. Vishnu Gokhale, wife of an Atlanta University visitor from the Philippines. The elite organization now numbered thirty members. Among them was Mother's prominent sister-in-law Mrs. Smith Milton Lewis (my aunt Beulah), Father's physician brother's wife. That Aunt Beulah, from the small town of Buena Vista, was the acting Chautauqua president and new principal of Oglethorpe Preparatory School bespoke a certain presumptuousness, some said.[4]

Heman Perry's early-twentieth-century West Side real estate investments and construction company had stolen a strategic march to block the Caucasians far out west near Mozley Park.[5] When his real estate empire imploded, his success example and his Citizens bank survived as platforms for second acts. After Mother's best friend had moved in 1931 with husband Clayton Yates to their grand hilltop home, Hunter Road sprouted mansion-like dwellings like kudzu. Our Morris Brown College president's cottage sat on Diamond Hill next door to the Herndon Mansion, where Perry's successor and America's most successful black contractor,

Walter H. "Chief" Aiken, built it in about 1940.[6] "No other city boasted black achievements in housing as great as Atlanta," calculated real estate scholar Andrew Wiese, who rather blithely describes this explosive West Side expansion as "Ozzie and Harriet enclaves." As well, Wiese's "Ph.D. Row" encapsulated the special residential significance of the four-college complex of Clark, Morehouse, Morris Brown, and Spelman encircling Atlanta University.

Out along Simpson Road, lined with conspicuous-consumption pools and tennis courts, which sociologist E. Franklin Frazier lampooned in his soon-to-be translated *La bourgeoisie noire,* Alice Urnestine's dear friend Lucy Rucker Aiken welcomed the Lewises. Lucy's husband, Walter Aiken, came in 1921 to Atlanta, where a house construction partnership with First Church's Reverend William Faulkner introduced him to Lucy Rucker, daughter of Internal Revenue Inspector Henry Rucker, one of the last Progressive Era black presidential appointees. Lucy's bloodlines were of an aristocratic purple. Her mother was the daughter of Jefferson Franklin Long, Georgia's lone representative to the 1870 Reconstruction Congress. Tall, commanding Aiken practiced what most of his business associates considered a respectful collaborationism with Atlanta's white "power structure." Exceptional for his time and race, he familiarized himself fully with both the regulations and the officers of the Federal Housing Administration.

In 1952, the Metropolitan Planning Commission, with the muted complicity of the black business community's West Side Mutual Development Committee, conceived a master plan for "proper areas in which Negroes may build and live without racial or economic conflict." Chief Aiken's response to the MPC master plan—"that Negro housing not far from white residential areas would help white owners find servants and help"—was vintage Atlanta "power structure" reasoning, insists civil rights historian Tomiko Brown-Nagin. In fact, that very term *power structure* came from a North Carolina sociologist's Atlanta scholarship that found it necessary to run "a separate study in the Negro community. There is a power structure there," Floyd Nelson House discovered, "that cannot be overlooked."[7] As hundreds of homes for the black elite rose near Hunter Road (today's Martin Luther King Boulevard) and thousands of mass-produced "economy houses" filled agreed-upon city pockets, Chief Aiken helped reshape Atlanta's racial residential map on horseback. Much of the capital for these sprawling black neighborhoods flowed from Auburn Avenue ("Sweet Auburn"), where Norris Herndon's Atlanta Life Insurance Company, Lorimer Milton's Citizens Trust Bank, and Jesse Blayton's Atlanta Mutual Federal Savings & Loan Association thrived within the nation's Jim Crow economics.[8]

PRESIDENT LEWIS DEFERRED HIS INAUGURATION UNTIL THE RESULTS OF Morris Brown's stress test were finished. We, his family, took the ninety-thousand-dollar endowment contribution from the self-liquidating GEB as an unexpected vote of confidence. His new faculty committee was charged to make a granular analysis of present strengths and weaknesses. "A revision of curricular offerings in the light of accepted educational standards was run." Library holdings were said to be considerably augmented. The faculty was strengthened by recent PhD holders. Boston University's first African American philosophy PhD, Frank Cunningham, arrived with the new president. The psychology department's new head, Robert Williams, was a young GI Bill PhD greatly admired by students. Albert Nathaniel Whiting, Father's choice for dean of the college, was a 1938 Amherst alum and an American University sociology PhD. Dean Whiting, more in the Talented Tenth mold, proved a better representative of Morris Brown's mature interests in the Atlanta University consortium.[9] Nor did the administration neglect its paying clients. Food service was modernized and student government encouraged with improved office space.

The Lewis administration's second year gained Morris Brown provisional approval of stress test results by the Southern Association of Colleges and Schools (SACS). Full accreditation membership stipulated that adequate student housing neglected by the previous regime required urgent remedy. To solve that costly absence, President Lewis obtained construction funds from the decade-old United Negro College Fund, canceled the few apartment leases, and turned the Morris Brown Apartments into the Sara Allen Quadrangle for junior and single women.[10] The structure's U shape was squared by a large lounge and director's living space. Additional male living space in a Bauhaus-like concrete building rose near the campus perimeter. When Morris Brown College's eighth president was formally installed on April 9, 1953, full accreditation seemed a steady certainty. "Representatives of seventy colleges, universities, and learned societies attended," cheered the college historians, "and several others sent greetings."[11] Francis C. Stifler, Father's Yale Divinity classmate and secretary of the American Bible Society, delivered the inaugural address. Mother wrote to me that the whole show was truly memorable.

I read about that day as a sixteen-year-old undergoing my own inauguration as a sophomore in Fisk University's experimental Basic College Program. I'd spent much of the second semester treading water in a pool of Mensa competitors. Charles S. Johnson's recent ascent as Fisk's first black president had followed a storied role as impresario of the Harlem Renaissance and director of Fisk's famous Race Relations Institute. As President Johnson was a scholar more adroit than Du Bois at foundation politics, his reputation and unique Rosenwald Fund trusteeship made his school the ideal crucible for racial experimentation. The first Phi Beta Kappa chapter at an HBCU had been installed two years previously. Thirty-five African American high school exceptions, almost evenly divided by sex, had won full four-year Fisk scholarships funded by the Ford Foundation. The racial inequities in secondary education—especially in the segregated South—had engendered an educational consensus that black high school students' societal contributions could be optimized by accelerated collegiate entry.[12] Charles Johnson's educational philosophy, as its beneficiaries soon realized, was premised upon success within *Plessy* not as separate but equal but as separate and superior.

I recall an intelligence test and special consideration enabling a leap from ninth directly to eleventh grade at Booker T. Washington High

School in 1951. In the fall of 1952, I entered the class of 1956 as a paying Basic College student without graduating from high school. My score on the College Board test was merely respectable, but my parents decided that I should proceed after consulting with the Fisk University registrar. The four-year Fisk experience combined the benefits of a superior boarding school with the independence of the University of Chicago system inspired by Robert Maynard Hutchins: headmasters/mistresses assigned to dormitories separate from the conventional student population; small classes taught by outstanding teachers and renowned professors; flexible matriculation speeds geared to individual test results; comprehensive humanities/science curriculum respectively personified by Robert Hayden, Lee Lorch, and a quixotic August Meier. Similar HBCU early entrance options were tried somewhat later at Morehouse, as I recall.

The Basic College demographic drew from the urban South, East, and Midwest, with a broad swath of high school students from South Carolina to Texas. Its junior-year exchange program reciprocated Fisk men and women with Oberlin, Pomona, Whittier, Wooster, and Denison juniors for one semester of residency. I mostly kept pace with a future published political theorist; a Stuyvesant High School future Peace Corps negotiator; two future women college presidents; a musical genius whose lyrics would sweep the country (briefly); a premedical genius whom Johns Hopkins declined but Sweden's Uppsala turned into a leading neuroradiological authority; a Virginia cousin by marriage who left his imprint on the Kerner Commission; Enid Johns, who deceived the Basic College prediction that she would marry Morehouse's Maynard Jackson; and Estella Redmond, who married an African prince, I was told years later. Preston King and I matched the Oxford University Debating Team in the International Student Center, where Martin Luther King Jr. would speak to us a month after his Montgomery bus boycott victory.

DWIGHT DAVID EISENHOWER'S INAUGURATION AS THE THIRTY-FOURTH U.S. president preceded John Henry Lewis's by three months. Despite President Truman's symbolic and substantial civil rights credits—NAACP

Address, Civil Rights Committee, desegregation of the armed services, opposition to restrictive covenants—Morris Brown's president voted the party of Lincoln. When the Eisenhower administration appointed Mother's cousin and Chicago alderman Archibald Carey Jr. as the alternate U.S. delegate to the United Nations, a portion of the black electorate nodded approval. A telephone call on behalf of the White House soon thereafter sent a frisson through our house at 601 University Place. Special White House Assistant E. Frederic Morrow, uncle of a Basic College classmate, was assembling a dossier on prospective federal appointments. Father asked Mother straight-facedly if Monrovia or Port-au-Prince appealed.[13]

What mattered, though, was a feeling of positive movement in Washington. Eisenhower's executive decision desegregating Washington, DC, a national capital whose residential restrictions matched apartheid Johannesburg's and subjected dark-skinned embassy personnel to harassments that "embarrassed the nation." The public scandal of elite Sidwell Friends' 1947 rejection of Ralph Bunche's daughter and the school's continued refusal to admit African Americans rankled middle-class blacks. More than a decade later, when Sidwell Friends persisted in its racial waffle and integration stalled, it made me proud to learn that my half brother John Jr. refused IBM's recommendation to relocate to Washington with his family. But in the summer of 1953, equipped with a driver's license, I partnered with Dad to drive us to the desegregated capital, good Morehouse pal Leroy Henderson on board as copilot.

I remember the trip as being an enjoyable family conceit—a big new Buick on a round-trip circuit to DC, Manhattan, New Haven, Nashville, Atlanta. New Haven was meant to be nostalgic for my father and a law school prospect for me. Broadway theater for Mother. After a stroll on the Mall and photos of ourselves framed by history, the Buick was surrendered to the Washington Statler valet. Our check-in and dinner reservations confirmed, we descended two hours later as racial role models and dined bounteously (a glass of wine for Mother). Awaiting our car the next morning, all of us remembered my father's takeaway: "My Lord, desegre-

Mom, middle-aged, c. 1955

gation is plenty expensive. What will integration cost?" Neither my father nor President Eisenhower could have answered what appeared to be such an unlikely question in the summer of 1953.

AS IT HAPPENED AND REMAINED LARGELY UNKNOWN TO BLACK AND WHITE readers alike, *An American Dilemma* only occurred because the Carnegie Corporation encountered its own American dilemma in the last years of the New Deal. If American ideals had intrinsic meaning in the close-run battle between democracy and totalitarianism, then the surging anti-imperialisms in Asia and Africa, and the new African American assertiveness, demanded much more than recycled pieties.[14] At the time, the Carnegie Corporation's priority was, as social scientist Maribel Morey states, "the making of a White World Order." For innovative Carnegie Corporation president Frank Keppel in 1937, the problem was W. E. B. Du Bois. Although Keppel had "scrimped" money to finance publication of *Black Reconstruction in America*, his trustees recoiled at the prospect of damage wrought to Eurocentric social science by a Burghardt Du Bois armed with a quarter million dollars of research money. Keppel promptly discovered and persuaded the Swedish economist and parliamentarian Gunnar Myrdal to become the American Negro's Tocqueville.[15]

In Gunnar Myrdal's eloquent formulation of the "American Creed," his *An American Dilemma: The Negro Problem and Modern Democracy* made patently clear why and how Americans must solve their great problem: "Although the Negro problem is a moral issue both to Negroes and to whites, we shall in this book have to give *primary* attention to what goes on in the minds of white Americans. . . . It is thus the white majority group that naturally determines the Negro's 'place.'" The author of a monumental investigation that includes "economics, social, and political race relations," Sweden's noted economist and prominent Social Democrat banished, therefore, economics and politics to his appendices because the quintessential takeaway for readers was Myrdal's postulate: "The Negro problem is primarily a 'white man's problem [*to solve*].'"

As Myrdal biographer Walter Jackson stresses, "[Myrdal] put aside his Social Democratic goals . . . and adapted his economic analysis to the realm of the possible in American politics."[16] The economics of white people's morals Myrdal left to be inferred, making his American dilemma very different from the projected Du Bois Marxian interpretation. Jackson Davis, now himself a senior official at the GEB, was delegated to break the Myrdal news to a surprised Du Bois at Atlanta University in November 1938. Burghardt Du Bois had believed that *What the Negro Wants* channeled a Myrdalian liberalism that would be found wanting in the long run to racial adjustment. The contrarian who had spoiled the 1948 Boule convention at Wilberforce wanted his privileged disciples to understand that "equality of opportunity" was meaningful only to those already able to buy it.

To us, amused by John Lewis's wry question as we left the Statler Hotel, Du Bois's economic egalitarianism was discounted as intellectually quarrelsome. Moreover, in the spring of 1954 my well-connected parents were part of the great majority of educated colored people ("representative Negroes") who believed that racial "integration" was politically and juridically improbable and, for that good reason, illusory to such a degree as to distract thoughtful people from extracting their unconscionably denied Fourteenth Amendment rights from *Plessy v. Ferguson.*

Only three years earlier, Dartmouth College alumnus and new National Urban League president Lester Granger had asked in *The Crisis*, "Does the Negro Want Integration?" Granger, who bore a striking resemblance to Eisenhower, had seemed to answer the question with an observation: "If we are perfectly honest with ourselves . . . there are literally millions of Negroes [unready and unwilling] to undergo desegregation." In her prizewinning monograph *Courage to Dissent*, civil rights historian Tomiko Brown-Nagin found that for many black Atlantans, "separate" but actually "equal" solutions were preferable to integration's chimera.[17]

So had argued Thurgood Marshall in *Morris v. Williams*, the Little Rock case in which he, his client, and my father would have regarded the award of salary parity a victory. Then, a decade later, leading a squad of Legal Defense Fund attorneys representing five civil rights cases cobbled together as *Brown v. Board of Education of Topeka, Kansas*, Marshall finally abandoned the legal incrementalism that would have sustained *Plessy* indefinitely. His success was to sway nine Supreme Court justices with the civil rights axiom that segregation, as South Carolina judge J. Waties Waring insisted in *Briggs v. Elliott*, was "per se inequality."[18]

After Chief Justice Earl Warren delivered his unanimous decision that May, William Burghardt Du Bois, although disheartened by the McCarthyite conformity abroad in the land, exclaimed, "I have seen the impossible happen. It did happen on May 17, 1954." *The Chicago Defender* assured its huge readership, "This means the beginning of the end of the dual society in American life and the system . . . of segregation which supports it."[19] There were to be a conundrum of reasons—jurisprudential, presidential, political, economic, cultural, and bewilderingly contingent—why Du Bois, the *Defender*, and the Lewis family were to be soon disappointed and ultimately deceived by the real-world outcomes of *Brown I* and *Brown II*. For thousands of unsettled Americans, the Warren court's

1955 enforcement decree of "all deliberate speed" was, as Du Bois spluttered, "an oxymoron." "We assumed that *Brown* was self-executing," historian James Patterson notes of many citizens of all social ranks. "When
the Supreme Court speaks that's the law," Governor James "Big Jim" Fol-
som of Alabama announced.[20]

Thurgood Marshall had to have known that *Brown II* was the judicial
price of Earl Warren's unanimous *Brown I*, and he reacted with "What
the hell!" The more he thought about it, "it was a damned good decision."
"Segregation," said he, would be nonexistent in "under five years." To
much of Atlanta's black leadership, however, the *Brown II* decision was
calibrated as just about right for the self-serving reason of being, as influential John Wesley Dobbs decided, "a very wise one" that had "a tendency
to forestall the extremists and hotheads on both sides of the controversy."[21] Colonel Austin Thomas Walden, perennial head of the black
Gate City Bar Association, was the pragmatic personification of Atlanta's
top-down biracial comity. My few weeks as a University of Michigan Law
School student would owe something to Walden's pathbreaking record in
Ann Arbor. A half century later, I recognized the colonel's perfect professional profile in *Courage to Dissent*: "A top-down leadership; an awareness
that multiple layers of racial equality pervaded society; and a skepticism
that courts and legalism could alone, or could effectively, bring about
positive racial change."[22]

A meld of hope cautioned by history's disappointments would explain the poll cited a year and a half after *Brown I* showing that "only 53
percent of blacks living in the South approved of the Court's historic ruling." The court's definitive scholar Richard Kluger had already noticed
the same quietus in the summer of 1954. "The reaction within the black
community was muted. There was no dancing on the tables in Harlem,"
he heard. Among my studious Fisk classmates, both before and after the
sunny prescription of "all deliberate speed," a speculative unease prevailed.[23] At times like these my mother wondered what Cousin Walter
would have said about race relations. I had met "Fuzzy" White and white
wife Poppy Cannon in the summer of 1951 when they stopped briefly

after the Atlanta NAACP Convention to meet and reminisce at 601 University Place with the parents. On the evening of May 17, 1954, the civil rights showman who led the NAACP for twenty-six indefatigable years was tape-recorded at a small celebratory gathering, warning, "Right now the rest of the world is looking at us in America with very great skepticism."[24] A fatal coronary just before the second *Brown* announcement silenced "Mr. NAACP" under a cloud of intermarriage reproach.

That White's caution was misunderstood by the same Howard Odum who had fretted with William Couch over *What the Negro Wants* already spoke to the largely unsuspected biases of Dwight David Eisenhower, whose opposition to Truman's military desegregation order had been rock-solid. An optimistic Odum, the South's foremost social scientist, predicted, "The South is likely to surprise itself and the nation and do an excellent job of readjustment."[25] Eisenhower believed Earl Warren fully understood that no surprises from the court were required. To repeated questions from the press about his opinion of *Brown v. Board of Education*, the jovial thirty-fourth president variously answered, "I think it makes no difference whether or not I endorse it," or, "the Supreme Court has spoken and I am sworn to uphold the constitutional processes in this country."

To be sure, historians and legal scholars were to debate a plethora of inadequacies and errors in their constitutional autopsies of both *Browns*: (a) the ruling's failure to require district courts to mandate that school districts formulate desegregation plans within a set time frame; (b) the opinion's flawed eleventh footnote, citing Myrdal's American creed and Kenneth Clark's ambiguous dolls; (c) the court's delay in refuting South Carolina's constitutional evasion that *Brown* "merely forbids the use of governmental power to enforce segregation"; (d) the failure to nullify outright *Plessy* by recourse to Justice Harlan's famous "color-blind" dissent that the "Constitution . . . neither knows nor tolerates classes among citizens. In respect of civil rights, all citizens are equal before the laws." Marshall's oral arguments before the nine justices uttered their marching orders to the nation were, as reported by Harvard professor Charles

Ogletree, hardly utopian: "That if an unyielding Supreme Court issued a stern decree, and if the executive branch supported it, the American people would follow, and desegregation would occur without major social upheaval." Had the president ever considered stating that segregation was "morally wrong," Eisenhower's biographer Stephen Ambrose believed that Marshall's prediction could have been achieved.[26]

Jim Hagerty, the president's press secretary, recorded the Kansan's fears that the South would cancel all public education "and harm the poor whites and the black," that overturning *Plessy v. Ferguson* was folly because "it's all very well to talk about school integration—if you remember that you may also be talking about social disintegration." Of his chief justice—his "biggest damn fool appointment"—it was said that the president had tried coaxing some common sense into Warren after a White House stag dinner party: "These are not bad people. All they are concerned about is to see that their sweet little girls are not required to sit in school alongside some big overgrown Negroes."[27] Courtly Virginia Senator Harry Byrd and the Dixiecrat paladin Strom Thurmond of South Carolina (anonymous father of a sweet little black girl) trumpeted "Massive Resistance"—a Southern Manifesto clarion call (edited by Arkansas's J. William Fulbright) that was subscribed to by ninety-nine Democrats and two Republicans from the former Confederate states by March 1956. Lest it be said that only the Deep South protected little white girls from Ike's "overgrown Negroes," the little Delaware town of Milford, 17 percent black, descended into prolonged rioting after an outsider frightened the timid school board.[28]

As he followed the Central High School debacle, Father finally decided that President Eisenhower had inflicted what should have been an entirely manageable crisis upon himself as well as the country at large. Dad found the educational damage caused by Governor Orval Faubus infuriatingly personal. Several of the nine students chosen to enter Central High School by the NAACP in collaboration with Daisy and L. C. Bates attended Dunbar or, like small, wily Jefferson Thomas and sturdy Ernest Green, had parents who taught there.[29] His academically superior Dunbar became a spurious "magnet school," shuttered for a year after a school board meeting that left no recorded deliberations.[30] Instead, a brand-new and segregated Horace Mann High School of woefully mediocre design replaced Sue Morris's historic building. She must have been present, though, when the faculty and Father's successor, forthright LeRoy Christophe, heard their first principal deliver Dunbar's last commencement address on May 27, 1955.[31]

AFTER THE TERRIBLE 1955 SUMMER, IN WHICH THE BLOATED BODY OF Emmett Till traveled on display through inner cities, the black people of Montgomery, Alabama, discovered at the end of the year a twenty-six-year-old Boston University–trained Baptist preacher capable of shaping their pent-up anger over the municipal bus system's racialized abuse. From December 1955 to December 1956 Reverend Michael King—helped by Professor Jo Ann Robinson's Women's Political Council, Joe Azbell's *Montgomery Advertiser*, anonymous carpool drivers, a loan from Lloyd's of London, and donations from NAACP chapters—emerged world-famous from his bookended success. His face disfigured on the cover of *Time*, a cascade of honorary doctorates bestowed, awarded the NAACP's Spingarn Medal at age twenty-eight, the rhetoric that would soon spellbind the nation uttered at the May 1957 Prayer Pilgrimage for Freedom in the nation's capital, Michael King's impending civil rights significance would be captured by popular historian Lerone Bennett. "It looks simpler now than it did then," believed the author of *Before the Mayflower*. "We can see clearly that events were foreclosing the possibilities of the dominant Negro leadership styles. The grain of history was moving in King's direction."[32]

Yet Michael King's upper-middle-class Atlanta—black and white—was not the most welcoming receptacle for historical grains. Georgia's elegant Governor Ernest Vandiver made known the displeasure of the city's vaunted power structure with its black counterpart. News had spread that Reverend King's relocation from Montgomery to Atlanta was imminent. Black Atlanta's counterpart, as expressed in the Republican Scott family's *Daily World,* editorialized proudly of Dr. King's Montgomery results but implied that mass disruption was not the Atlanta way. "Atlanta was the fount of black wealth and, *ergo*, black wisdom in the deep South," as I wrote in my biography of King. The sum of its wisdom was—as Howard Zinn learned as a Spelman College historian—to wait. In the summer of 1958, the embryonic organization that would become the Southern Christian Leadership Conference (SCLC) established its headquarters in Atlanta under the capable superintendence of Ms. Ella Baker, a former field secretary for the NAACP.[33] The first historical grains had come.

In June 1958, his name altered, Martin Luther King Jr.'s political stature earned a place beside Roy Wilkins, Asa Randolph, and Lester Granger in an Oval Office meeting granted by Eisenhower. These leaders came to plead for the issuance of a proclamation squarely endorsing the morality of *Brown*. "Reverend," protested the president, "there are so many problems . . . Lebanon . . . Algeria. . . ." As Eisenhower had publicly finessed inclusion of local jury trials for voting rights violations in the first congressional civil rights legislation since 1875, the president would have thought his obligations to his party's black constituency more than fulfilled after Little Rock.[34]

Weak as was the Civil Rights Act of 1957, tough-minded Attorney General Herbert Brownell did establish the Justice Department's Civil Rights Section, which opened this author's twenty-first-century eyes to the truth of his first cousin John Levering Jr.'s fatal beating by police at the Lincoln Golf Club on Simpson Road in the winter of 1948. Alexandra Wood's July 2021 emails from Northeastern University's Civil Rights and Restorative Justice Project introduced herself by asking what I knew of my cousin's demise. I recalled my mother's distress at the time but was certain that she did little more than condole her brother from Wilberforce, as Levering's burial had been executed rapidly. From the files of the Civil Rights Act of 1957 came several more documents and a full report from Atlanta's *Daily World,* the nation's only black daily, mailed from

Northeastern University: Five county police officers, responding to noise from a club, secured the premises and arrested and proceeded to beat the three young men. Levering was in his fourth year at Clark College as a twenty-one-year-old senior. Five packs of cigarettes, eighteen dollars, and a chisel and hammer were recovered. My cousin was released on a thousand-dollar bond to his parents, John Levering and Emma Davis Bell, only to die later at Grady Hospital.

Tall, graceful Little Jack, whose image from an afternoon's Atlanta sojourn I still conjure, was arrested in the company of two others on the night of February 12, 1948. Arresting officer Ralph Holland's photocopied document from the Justice Department's Civil Rights Division states: "Jack L. Bell, Jr., victim. Allegedly beaten to death by subjects after his arrest on 2-12-48. On charge of burglary." Omitted is Levering's parental confidence that Lieutenant Holland struck him full force across the cranium, snarling, "One of them curly-headed niggers." The *Daily World* filled in the young naïf's last hours: REPORT BELL BEATEN BY POLICE UPON ARREST AT COUNTRY CLUB. YOUTH DIES AT GRADY HOSPITAL AFTER HEMORRHAGE. This large February 19 article stated that "his father indicated that no autopsy would be held on the body and discounted the idea that Bell's death might be due to injury received at the hands of county police."

My response to Ms. Wood encapsulated all the racial vulnerability my life had managed to avoid: "I am still stunned by my uncle's autopsy decision." I might have said "disgusted." "It's plain to see that the *Atlanta Daily World* wanted to make much more of my cousin's butchery."[35] Yet, no thanks to John Levering Bell Sr., his son's death may still have been useful to the campaign for black policemen. "Get your ten thousand colored voters," Mayor William Hartsfield had challenged the black power structure. An *Atlanta Journal-Constitution* news reporter captured future Atlanta mayor Maynard Jackson's grandfather's shout: "Great God almighty! Look at those black boys in those uniforms!" Eight were appointed for the first time to patrol duty in the Auburn Avenue district that summer.[36]

IN SUCH DIRE TIMES, MY PARENTS' CONCERN BECAME OBSESSIVE THAT A double major in history and philosophy might lead to the workhouse, as Dad said. Nevertheless, the promise of the class of '56 ought have been reassuring. Three of us entered the Rhodes Scholarship competition from New York and Georgia, the first contenders of color since the epicene Alain Locke in 1907: Richard Paul Thornell from New York and Preston Theodore King and me, both from Georgia. My committee of Falstaffian Atlanta gentlemen drawled a fine old greeting to my father before selecting another worthy candidate. The Rhodes interval resulted in kinder, gentler family discussions of realistic professional options.

My parents accepted my articulate agnosticism as a bar to my benefiting from the Yale Divinity School legacy. I offered law school as a welcome option, a profession likely to earn retainers ample enough to support a future family. Johnnie Lee, Father's amazing secretary, who typed my Fisk senior history thesis and whose advice Mother prized, opined that I was bound for success in anything I tried. A Morris Brown graduate who deferred NYU Business School to save Morris Brown's president from a secretarial pool incompetent, Ms. Johnnie Lee Clark soon married, raised children, became Georgia's first black female certified public accountant, and would manage the Atlanta subway system decades later.

Fisk's president showed ego-bolstering confidence in two of his Basic College seniors, me and Richard Thornell. He selected us during the graduation summer of 1956 as rapporteurs for a Rosenwald foundation conceit that assembled some twenty scientists, philosophers, lawyers, belletrists, university administrators of extraordinary culture and renown, all housed at the Jewish Theological Seminary of America in Manhattan. Among these luminaries whom both of us would especially remember was accessible Columbia University philosopher Charles Frankel, twenty years later inaugural president of the National Humanities Center at North Carolina's Triangle Research Park. Richard and I would walk together with the utterly brilliant physicist Richard Feynman (future 1965 Nobel laureate) to express our gratitude to the departing Charles John-

son. I know that Richard, who was on his way to Princeton's Woodrow
Wilson School of Public and International Affairs, anticipated, as did I,
a well-connected future with well-connected professionals. News that
President Johnson, a master-of-the-universe leader, had died of a coronary on the train to Nashville was devastating.

To satisfy the parents' career obsessions about my future, as well as
deflect my uncle Doc's childless wish fulfillment ("medical school without
a care"), I submitted LSATs to several law schools and succeeded in gain-
ing admission to Vanderbilt (the first known African American to do so)
and Michigan, choosing Ann Arbor over the totally familiar Nashville.
As I'd given not much thought to law school tuition, I found my father's
solution to the problem questionably pragmatic. Faulkner's economically
deranged South, still adamant about ignoring *Brown,* would rather finance
out-of-state tuition than admit me to the law school at Athens. A brilliant, determined Georgia army veteran, Horace T. Ward, represented by
the NAACP's Constance Baker Motley and our family friend and attorney Donald Hollowell, had been denied the Athens law school on spurious grounds of bad faith the year before.[37]

A morning at city hall, forms requested by Father, details provided by
me with my signature, made me a party to a disgraceful charade. Moreover, Colonel A. T. Walden might have been heartbroken to learn that
after handily surviving a single law school semester and a good moot
court paired with a sharp Nicholas Longo, I would leave on a Greyhound
for New York City and Columbia University. Mother wrote that John
Henry was too busy with Morris Brown matters to be angry over my decision. She worried over long-distance calls about his heart. His brother,
S.M., told her his brother had to reduce and rest to live a few more years.

It was the tired, familiar struggle to run an AME college or university without the divided polls of accountability between presidents and
bishops. My father was determined that his next round of accreditation
review would merit full and firm accreditation. The accreditation sine
qua non, however, imposed the physical removal from campus of the office of the presiding bishop. As for my uncle's coronary caveats, my father's commitment to the United Negro College Fund campaign to raise

millions for HBCU salaries and endowments precluded more and more of a reduced regimen. CITY TO GET CLOSEUP OF 31 NEGRO COLLEGE PREXIES announced the *Cleveland Call and Post* for the arrival of so many presidents on March 7, 1956.

The full-page photo of Father with these hard-pressed college presidents evoked mixed emotions of group pride upon finding this imposing lineup from a determined era. The UNCF speeches given at Saint Paul, Minnesota, or Buffalo, New York, and several more campaign whistle-stops resonated with the same "cash value" determination carried over from a public statement in May 1954: "Integration means competition with the best. No 'business as usual' attitude will suffice. In spite of our blunted weapons, we can win, if we begin now, wherever we are, use whatever we can now, and redouble our determination." It was vintage Lewis.

I know my father would have regretted my irresponsibility had my Manhattan academic caper been transferred entirely to him. By and

John Henry Lewis Sr., third from left,
with Atlanta University presidents, 1954

large, my half siblings stood on steady family legs: Milton as head of an Ohio Urban League branch; John Jr. and his new wife Long Island success stories.[38] Today, James Walker's erratic married life might have benefited from a PTSD diagnosis. My parents had mortgaged a large tenement building on Chicago's South Lawndale Avenue with the idea that rental income would support my half sister Anita and her husband. Instead, landlords Anita and Willy McClinton were increasingly loath to collect rent from their Dunbar High migrants. South Lawndale Avenue was sold in the mid-1950s. Mr. and Mrs. William McClinton and two children moved with the shared proceeds to the Maywood suburbs. I managed Columbia without an appeal to Atlanta.

Today, the success my self-confidence yielded certainly could not happen. Columbia's Faculty of Arts and Sciences dean was one of America's most famous intellectual historians. Jacques Barzun's surprised secretary returned almost immediately to say that Dean Barzun, author of

First Phi Beta Kappa inductees at a black institution,
Fisk University—the author, standing, center—1956

Darwin, Marx, Wagner, would see me. I explained that I came without family or other support to pursue U.S. history after a single law school semester at Ann Arbor. I said I was a history-philosophy double major at Fisk University and entirely confident of holding my own at Columbia. Jacques Barzun must have suppressed some mirth before accepting my challenge to meet Columbia graduate school standards. There was a master's degree scholarship available, said he. Should I obtain the history MA in record time, the cost of the scholarship would be forgiven.

A Pomona College exchange acquaintance in his first year at Columbia Presbyterian passed along a convenient residential possibility near Teachers College. Stephen and Ethel Dunn, both impaired by cerebral palsy, required live-in mobility assistance in their faculty apartment on West 123rd. Somehow, devoid of references and all nursing experience, I survived a grilling by Stephen's renowned father (of Dunn and Dobzhansky, *Heredity, Race and Society*). Ethel and Steve wrote significant poems and their good-size apartment was a fulcrum of like-minded outliers. Pushing Stephen's wheelchair to campus many mornings from January to June 1957, I paralleled his obligations with my classes from Dumas Malone on Jefferson, Henry Graff on historiography, Garrett Mattingly on imperial Spain, Fritz Stern on the Third Reich, and John Hine Mundy on medieval Toulouse, and my thesis adviser's lively building-blocks American history seminar.

John Hope Franklin's appointment as chair of Brooklyn College's history department inspired an unannounced morning office visit. Franklin had been our favorite Fisk professor's student. On February 15, 1956, a *New York Times* front-page story ballyhooed HOWARD UNIVERSITY PROFESSOR WILL BE FIRST OF RACE TO HOLD THAT RANK HERE. From Princeton and Morningside Heights, Richard Thornell and I brought reinforcing news of our own achievements. I came back to Columbia in the fall with the body of research completed for a thesis on Harvard librarian and elephantine public intellectual John Fiske — "A Transitional Figure in American Social Darwinism," I finally called it. A professor's spouse across the hall from the Dunns professionally typed the finished work for submission to Richard B. Morris, the distinguished Gouverneur Morris Professor of History. Earned at Columbia in 1958, the degree, as it were, paid for itself. The thesis language examination in French was passed in June or so, after some smart lessons conducted by Mother.

MY PARENTS ALLOWED ME TO FEEL MY ACADEMIC OATS THAT SUMMER. Father found time to know how I planned to adjust to the tutorial structure he assumed was on offer at the London School of Economics and Political Science. I was surprised to hear that one of the Rhodes examiners had called Father to say how near to selecting me some of his committee had been. I had put on a good show downtown, which made him proud. Looking back at this era of good feelings about graduate study abroad, it may seem odd—given the civil rights turbulence and organizational disaggregation only months in the future—how few seniors questioned the timing of this temporary expatriation. One vocal naysayer had recently left us, however. Uncle Doc, who had issued medical caveats about the parents' restorative California, had died of a heart attack in his Auburn Avenue office shortly before Alice and John returned from vacation.

My parents seemed to understand my intellectual wanderlust as more than personal ambition. From the principled altitude from which they scoped the civil rights stasis of the Eisenhower decade, a terrible regret for time lost to the nation's progress was almost palpable in their affect. So much of what Father and Mother wished they would be alive to enjoy and contribute to was to be found in the racial inclusiveness and economic justice beyond their century. An extended foreign sabbatical in cultural zones where one's historical identity was—if of much significance at all—an optional curiosity was an existential drawing card. To be sure, to exit the New South's Atlanta in the late 1950s seemed to many advantaged contemporaries a display of deplorable timing.

When *Fortune* magazine extolled Atlanta's black economy in 1956, John Wesley Dobbs and Austin T. Walden must have recalled *Forbes* magazine's discovery of miraculous Standard Life in 1924. In the generation from *Forbes* to *Fortune*, the first fabulously scripted by Eric Walrond, the second smartly written with meaningful statistics, editor Emmet John Hughes celebrated "The Negro's New Economic Life" as a black way out of no way out that was "truly a new deal." "No less remarkable will be the way all this may come to pass," Hughes revealed, "for it will be, in great measure, the product, not of national conscience, nor of preachment, nor of lawmaking, but of that most earth-bound of miracles, the American economy."[39] Atlanta's civil rights will come by way of "unsegregated dollars," Hughes promised after seeing Auburn Avenue and strolling Hunter Road.

By July 1958, after three years of all deliberate speed in the *Fortune* magazine version of Atlanta, my parents agreed with me that the promise of *Brown* awaited a seismic shift that spoke to the truly disadvantaged as well as the privileged alienated. To make the point, Mother showed me the unexpected greeting sent from Father to Burghardt Du Bois on his ninetieth birthday in 1958. Years later, I would find the letter in Herbert Aptheker's third volume of *The Correspondence of W. E. B. Du Bois*.[40] Its third paragraph had Mother's distinct input, I thought: "As we look back over the past five decades, we realize that the fight for the American Negro for civil rights, which culminated in the Supreme Court Decision of May 1954, had its beginning when *The Crisis* was founded. We realize, further, that you had much to do with the recognition of common cause and brotherhood which now binds the darker races of the world. . . . We wish for you more useful and happy years."

In that same year, when Father brought me along to drive to his birthplace in Schley County, Georgia, for the naming of the eponymous John H. Lewis High School, we experienced with a sad, polite restraint another example of the white South's bait-and-switch response to the Warren court's admonitions: the building in his name whose fifty-year-late construction cheated its black taxpayers and mocked integration. Schley County drew the suppressed past from Father on the return drive to 601 University Place on Diamond Hill. I learned about John Lewis during those four July hours that he had lived deliberately with as much speed as possible.

SHORTLY THEREAFTER, I WAS ON THE BOAT TO LONDON FOR MY DOC-toral studies at the London School of Economics. Only a few weeks later, I learned my father had passed. Mother's October telegram to me in London repeated his last words to me before our goodbye handshake: "Wait until you can be useful." The family history epilogue remained to be written, as did their American story.

ACKNOWLEDGMENTS

This book owes its life to a morning phone call that came just as I was leaving for London ten years ago to assuage the loss of my wife of thirty years. I thought better of answering. The caller, Henry Holt's John Macrae, was the editor of two successful books of mine. Conversations with Jack were notable for length or significance, neither of which in my present mental state was I inclined to indulge. The London getaway meant two compatible weeks in a family time-share: random strolls, music aplenty, Cambridge, museums and movies, free-range conversation. Haphazardly packed and anxious to leave, I risked the landline. He had heard that I had a new book in mind. "Tell me in just a few words about it," Jack insisted. In fact, as I said hurriedly, whatever I had in mind was then too inchoate to formulate. "One word," he insisted. "The Lewis family history told as the American story," I laughed. "Back in two weeks," I said to end our exchange. Before I cradled the phone, the voice guaranteed I would hear from it again in two weeks. John Macrae swore me to silence until then.

A decade after that London fortnight, followed by a Triangle Building meeting with Holt panjandrums excited about an imagined family book, such a book finally appears from Penguin Random House. *The Stained Glass Window* follows this author's ill-timed *The Improbable Wendell Willkie.* John Macrae III, retired and promised the family history told as the American story, is a cherished memory along with my unforgettable spouse Ruth Ann Stewart. Twelve books in a career is a respectable enough number to sign off with a much overdue dedication to my deceased parents, John Henry and Alice Urnestine Lewis. To my indispensable Dolores, above all, whose surname is the Root of my resilient life, I also dedicate this book.

Some I already knew, but there are ancestors met through my grandmother Alice's memorial window whose surprising materiality was conjured by more than a score of dedicated archivists. To chief archivist Elaine DeNiro of the Research Library and Archives of the Roswell Historical Society, Roswell, Georgia, without whose interest and efficient generosity the stained glass window would have remained opaque, and this family history impossible. To Ellie Loudermilk, director of the Perry Area Historical Museum and Society, Perry, Georgia, who provided indispensable knowledge of the Houston County Belvins, their plantation house, Minerva Academy, and the Belvin AME Church. Her assistant Wayne Chapman was a worthy neighborhood guide. At Macon, Georgia, an assistant librarian in the Washington Memorial Library's Genealogical & Historical Room linked me to Lavoris Gail Alexander-Maiden, whose past and present records of Houston County black families (*We Came in Chains: "lost Links" History and Lineage of African-American Families from Houston County, Georgia*) are unique.

Hope Henderson, manager of Lake Blackshear Regional Library, Americus, Georgia, assembled city directories in advance along with descriptions of family papers her library held of local white Lewises and other antebellum business successes. As for the postbellum struggles of Macon County's black Lewises, a long day spent in Deeds and Records at Oglethorpe's Superior Court House revealed a valiant economy of gradual impoverishment. Yet not all was *plus ça change* in Oglethorpe in the summer of 2021: we encountered reluctant white subordinates until Superior Court clerk Juanita Laidler warmly greeted Clarence White, Dolores, and me.

At Andersonville National Historic Site near Americus, Georgia, Evan Kutzler and associates at Georgia Southwestern State University have rediscovered a major African American cultural and political presence that significantly complicates much Reconstruction knowledge. Federal funding of *In Plain Sight: African Americans at Andersonville National Historic Site, A Special History Study* portends ongoing research of front-rank significance to black family studies centered at such Atlanta institutions as Administrator Victor Simmons's Auburn Avenue Research Library on African American Culture and History (AARL) with its full First Congregational Church archive. A most revelatory record of Deep South color, marriage, class, and money from which *The Stained Glass Window* greatly benefited is Clark Atlanta University's Robert W. Woodruff Library, whose manifold collections are distinguished by its invaluable Chautauqua Circle Archive.

Morris Brown College emeritus faculty and retired officials who returned one morning at President Stanley Pritchett's entreaty to abide my questions may well think this book to be a poor compensation of my debt after a decade of waiting.

To Aaisha N. Haykal, manager of archival services, Avery Research Center for African American History and Culture, College of Charleston, much appreciation for the extraordinary access arrangements during the center's late summer of 2019 closure. A special gratitude to Marianne Cawley, South Carolina History Room, Charleston County Public Library, whose follow-up Bell family correspondence was essential. To the South Carolina Historical Society, College of Charleston, where staff facilitated scrutiny of tax capitation records and city directories by race and profession, my obligation is truly profound.

For time devoted and information provided, Bernard Powers, director emeritus of the study of slavery at the College of Charleston, the author's gratitude rivals his regret that we never met in person. A similar casualty of research options available in a short sojourn tugs at my conscience: not to have broken bread with my Fisk contemporary and prominent Charleston physician and his spouse, the Leonard Davises. What Dolores and I might have discovered had we followed through on an impulse to extend our stay—even to have rented a month of space in the city—we thought we had merely temporarily forfeited. COVID-19 would prevent little more than a day's exploration of Goose Creek.

The various professional and geographical migrations of my parents from Atlanta to Little Rock, Arkansas, to Atlanta were noted by the omnicompetent John D. Rockefeller General Education Board (GEB) at Sleepy Hollow, New York, where responsive archivist Monica Blank enabled the author's optimal recovery of a rather complicated history. Felicitous fortune also at Yale University and the University of Chicago, where Yale's registrar, Lisabeth Huck, and Beinecke's Michael Morand provided context for John Henry Lewis's divinity school tenure; as did Chicago's assistant registrar, Gail Middleton, of analogous material. At Daniel Payne Theological Seminary, Wilberforce, Ohio, archivist Lynn Ayers has lived her institution's history so deeply that research requests can divulge superabundant responses.

Eight colleagues who remain my friends accepted invitations to read discrete chapters. Each found mistakes of judgment or, worse, factual errors. My debt to all of them is large because I know that the surviving mistakes of judgment and fact might have been even greater. Matthew Guterl of Brown University and Kendra Field of Tufts were early readers who encouraged me to write more. David Nicholson, once assistant editor of *The Washington Post Book World*, listened and encouraged. Adele Alexander, professor emerita of George Washington University, commented on matters of concubinage and class. Chapel Hill's Kenneth Janken offered advice similar to Columbia's Ira Katznelson about uncurated generalizations. Dolores Root of University of Massachusetts Amherst mapped inspired anthropological expertise over the historical insights of the complete manuscript. Joni Cherbo read two chapters in her Florida exile and asked for more. Lauret Savoy of Mount Holyoke College unraveled a key family puzzle.

My list of so many persons who indulged the author's labors as occasional researchers, incidental readers, conscripted listeners, and participants providing unique expertise begins with my friend Clarence White. His lived experience of the Deep South and peerless investigative prowess surely optimized whatever success befalls this family history. Genealogist Shannon Christmas's Through The Trees wizardry follows, for it irreversibly complicates this author's knowledge of himself. To Carol Preece, friend of many decades, the author owes his geneticist consultation decision. Mary Helen Thompson not only recommended the successful Through The Trees experiment, but her nimble configuration of family lineages made possible this book's author's sprawling family tree. My cousin Bettye Lovejoy Scott has shared the life of this book. David Mayers and Elizabeth Jones of Newton, Massachusetts, offered their healing London time-share ten years ago and shared a gratifying Savannah escapade together with Dolores not so many months ago.

In grateful alphabetical order, I thank: Michael Henry Adams of Manhattan; Reverend Dwight Andrews of Atlanta; Ms. Clara Axam of Atlanta; Ms. Johnnie Lee Clark of Atlanta; Professor Irvin Frederick Gellmann of Philadelphia; Francis Gipe of Shelburne Falls, Massachusetts; Ms. Sandra Guterl of Providence; Winifried Hemphill of Atlanta; Professor Alexa B. Henderson of Atlanta; Professor John A. Kirk of Little Rock; Ms. Lolinda Lewis of Houston; Ms. Pamela Lewis of Stamford, Connecticut; Stephen Loring of the Smithsonian; Herman "Skip" Mason Jr. of Atlanta; Dr. Sandra Masur of Manhattan; Professor David Nasaw and Dinitia Smith of Manhattan; Dr. Jesse Porter of Little Rock; Mrs. Oren Root of Bedford, New York; Dr. Victor Schuster of Manhattan; Josiah Simpson of Albany; Michael Singer of Vermont; Caroline Sydney of Penguin; Tashell Thompson of Atlanta; Richard P. and Carolyn Thornell of the District of Columbia; Dr. Kenneth Wheeler (deceased); Ms. Jayme Coleman Williams of Atlanta (deceased).

Andrew Wylie's reputation as the literary world's unrivaled literary agent makes for felicitous editorial results. Penguin's Virginia Smith is an author's nirvana. Patient, intuitive, a forgiving blue pencil in hand,

"Ginny's" Yankee schooling and southern sensibility admirably suited our southern collaboration shaped by the past yet inspired by the future. And, again, to my beloved, deceased Dolores, who improved everything.

David Levering Lewis,
Manhattan's Upper West Side and
Shelburne Falls, Massachusetts, May 1, 2024

NOTES

PROLOGUE

1. "150th Anniversary Celebration: Building on Purpose," First Church, United Church of Christ, Atlanta, October 1, 2017; "Ruth Ann Stewart" (obituary), *New York Times*, June 8, 2014, available on legacy.com; "Ruth Ann Stewart Celebration of Life," Riverside Church, New York, September 13, 2014; Ruth Ann Stewart, Joni Maya Cherbo, and Margaret Jane Wyszomirski, eds., *Understanding the Arts and Creative Sector in the United States*, Rutgers series: The Public Life of the Arts (New Brunswick, NJ: Rutgers University Press, 2013); David Levering Lewis, "Wendell Willkie," in *Profiles in Leadership: Historians on the Elusive Quality of Greatness*, ed. Walter Isaacson (New York: W. W. Norton, 2013).

2. E.g., William Julius Wilson, *The Truly Disadvantaged: The Inner City, the Under-class, and Public Policy* (Chicago: University of Chicago Press, 1987); Charles Murray, *The Bell Curve: Intelligence and Class Structure in American Life* (New York: Simon & Schuster, 1994); *Losing Ground: America's Social Policy, 1950–1980* (New York: Basic Books, 1984); Allen J. Matusow, *The Unraveling of America: A History of Liberalism in the 1960s* (New York: Harper & Row, 1984).

3. Ta-Nehisi Coates, "The Case for Reparations," *Atlantic*, June 2014.

4. D. L. Henderson, *South-View: An African American City of the Dead* (Dunwoody, GA: Carrelspin Press, 2018), 222.

5. "Historical Sketch of First 100 Years," First Congregational Church Collection, UCC, Atlanta, Georgia, box 1, folder 12, Robert W. Woodruff Library, Atlanta University Center; Joe M. Richardson, *Christian Reconstruction: The American Missionary Association and Southern Blacks, 1861–1890* (Athens: University of

Georgia Press, 1986); Clarence A. Bacote, *The Story of Atlanta University: A Century of Service, 1865–1965* (Atlanta: Atlanta University Press, 1969), esp. 59–60.

6. Augustus Field Beard, *A Crusade of Brotherhood: A History of the American Missionary Association* (1909; repr., New York: Pilgrim Press, 1972), 159–60.

7. Bacote, *Story of Atlanta University,* 9 and 12; Richardson, *Christian Reconstruction,* 37.

8. First Congregational Church, "Historical Sketch," box 1, folders 1 and 12; "Historical Time Line of First Congregational Church, UCC, Atlanta, from 1893 to 2012," Robert W. Woodruff Library, Atlanta University Center; David Fort Godshalk, *Veiled Visions: The 1906 Atlanta Race Riot and the Reshaping of American Race Relations* (Chapel Hill: University of North Carolina Press, 2005), 189–90.

9. Author's personal memory of church interior and visitors; "Historical Time Line of First Congregational Church."

10. First Congregational Church, "Historical Sketch," box 1, folder 7; First Congregational Church, United Church of Christ Atlanta; cf. "A Look at the Early History of First Church through Our Hand-Painted Stained Glass Windows," n.d.; Board of Christian Education, Mary Alice Bestle, director, "Our Stained Glass Windows Come to Life: A Dramatic Interpretation of the Historic Stained Glass Windows at First Congregational Church, UCC" (presentation, March 23, 2012).

11. David Levering Lewis, Doctor of Humane Letters, Honoris Causa, Emory University, May 27, 2003.

12. Kathleen Adams, taped interview, November 12, 1987; recorded interviews of Du Bois biography research in David Levering Lewis Papers, Du Bois Library, UMass Amherst; David Levering Lewis, *W. E. B. Du Bois: Biography of a Race: 1868–1919* (New York: Henry Holt, 1993), 628.

13. Malcolm Bell Jr., *Major Butler's Legacy: Five Generations of a Slaveholding Family* (Athens: University of Georgia Press, 1987), esp. 159–69.

14. Cf. Erskine Clarke, *Dwelling Place: A Plantation Epic* (New Haven, CT: Yale University Press, 2005), 190–91; Tammy Harden Galloway, ed., *Dear Old Roswell: The Civil War Letters of the King Family of Roswell, Georgia* (Macon, GA: Mercer University Press, 2003); Roswell Georgia Convention & Visitors Bureau, "A Southern Trilogy: The Historic Homes of Roswell," n.d.

15. Galloway, *Dear Old Roswell,* 6–9; Joe McTyre and Rebecca Nash Paden, *Historic Roswell Georgia* (Mount Pleasant, SC: Arcadia, 2001); Clarke, *Dwelling Place,* 191.

16. Elaine DeNiro, email to David Lewis, April 16, 2015; David Lewis, email to Elaine DeNiro, April 16, 2015.

17. Clarke, *Dwelling Place*; Robert Manson Myers, ed., *The Children of Pride: A True Story of Georgia and the Civil War,* 3 vols. (New York: Popular Library, 1972); Annette Gordon-Reed, *Thomas Jefferson and Sally Hemings: An American Controversy* (Charlottesville: University of Virginia Press, 1997).

18. Joseph J. Ellis, *American Sphinx: The Character of Thomas Jefferson* (New York: Vintage Books, 1998); Harriet Bey Mesic, *Cobb's Legion Cavalry: A History and Roster of the Ninth Georgia Volunteers in the Civil War* (Jefferson, NC: McFarland,

2009); Erskine Clarke, *Wrestlin' Jacob: A Portrait of Religion in Antebellum Georgia and the Carolina Low Country* (1976; repr., Tuscaloosa: University of Alabama Press, 2000), 5–6.

19. Galloway, *Dear Old Roswell*, 8–9.
20. Cf. David Levering Lewis, "Historians of Color Are Revolutionizing the Narrative of American Exceptionalism," *The Nation*, September 1, 2015.

1. SETTING UP SLAVERY: ST. SIMONS ISLAND TO ROSWELL

1. Elaine DeNiro, email to David Lewis, May 21, 2015; Elaine DeNiro, email to David Lewis, May 23, 2015.
2. Ronald Smothers, "Roswell Journal; the Darker Side of a Beloved Founder" (account of Malcolm Bell's book talk at the Roswell Historical Society), *New York Times*, February 10, 1988; David Lewis, email to Charles Grogan, May 27, 2015.
3. David Lewis, email to Elaine DeNiro, June 15, 2015; David Levering Lewis, *Prisoners of Honor: The Dreyfus Affair* (New York: William Morrow, 1973); David Levering Lewis, *When Harlem Was in Vogue* (New York: Knopf, 1981); David Levering Lewis, *W. E. B. Du Bois: The Fight for Equality and the American Century: 1919–1963* (New York: Henry Holt, 2000); David Levering Lewis, *The Improbable Wendell Willkie: The Businessman Who Saved the Republican Party and His Country, and Conceived a New World Order* (New York: Liveright/Norton, 2018); Elaine DeNiro, email to David Lewis, May 21, 2015 ("Do you know if Alice King Bell's mother was Clarissa King?"); Elaine DeNiro, email to David Lewis, May 23, 2015 ("I do believe that Clarissa King is the mother of Alice. Clarissa is the child of Elsie").
4. Bill of sale, January 20, 1822 ("Unto Barrington King . . . all those negro and mulatto slaves named Nancy March Yorick Hester Elsie Candis and William"); "Negroes Owned by B. King, 1 January 1849," in Barrington King's ledgers, 1835–1864 (listing William, 28, Elsie, 29, Clarissa, 13, Louisa, 9, John, 5, Jemima, 3½, and Thomas, 1).
5. "Negro Property, Sept. 1852 – Clarissa, Kitty, & child 1425.00," in Barrington King's ledgers, 1835–1864; David Lewis, email to Elaine DeNiro, May 27, 2015 ("I wish I knew the answer to your question"); Elaine DeNiro, email to David Lewis, June 4, 2015 ("Clarissa is listed living next to/or in the household of J. W. Belvin in the 1870 census. . . . I am not sure that we can presume that he was the one who bought her, but it is possible").
6. Elaine DeNiro, email to David Lewis, June 16, 2015 ("There is no male associated with Clarissa as a 'husband' in either of the census records. . . . The children are listed as M [mulatto] in the census and not B [black]").
7. *The Private Mary Chesnut: The Unpublished Civil War Diaries,* C. Vann Woodward and Elisabeth Muhlenfeld, eds. (Oxford University Press, 1984), 42 (Chesnut quote); Henry Wiencek, *The Hairstons: An American Family in Black and White* (New York: St. Martin's Press, 1999); Adele Logan Alexander, *Ambiguous Lives:*

Free Women of Color in Rural Georgia, 1789–1879 (Fayetteville: University of Arkansas Press, 1998); Joel Williamson, *New People: Miscegenation and Mulattoes in the United States* (New York: Free Press, 1980); Charles W. Chesnutt, *The House behind the Cedars* (New York: Houghton Mifflin, 1909).

8. Cf. Marie Jenkins Schwartz, *Ties That Bound: Founding First Ladies and Slaves* (Chicago: University of Chicago Press, 2017), esp. chap. 2; Bettye Kearse, *The Other Madisons: The Lost History of a President's Black Family* (Boston: Houghton Mifflin Harcourt, 2020), esp. chap. 3.

9. Of interest are Captain Thomas Edward King, 1829–1863, and Captain James Roswell King, 1827–1897; cf. Frances Anne (Fanny) Kemble's displeasure at Roswell King Jr.'s multiple mulatto offspring: Malcolm Bell Jr., *Major Butler's Legacy: Five Generations of a Slaveholding Family* (Athens: University of Georgia Press, 1987), 280–81; Erskine Clarke, *Dwelling Place: A Plantation Epic* (New Haven, CT: Yale University Press, 2005), 70–72.

10. Bell, *Major Butler's Legacy*, xx–xxi, 19–24.

11. Bell, 27.

12. Bell, xx; Butler and Pinckney at Philadelphia convention: Max Farrand, ed., *The Records of the Federal Convention of 1787*, vol. 3 (New Haven, CT: Yale University Press, 1911, 1966), "Supplementary Records of the Proceedings in Convention," Appendix A, esp. 102–3, 253–54, 301–6.

13. Bell, *Major Butler's Legacy*, 40, 78–81; Gloria J. Browne-Marshall, *The U.S. Constitution, An African-American Context*, 2nd ed. (New York: Law and Policy Group, 2010), esp. 19; cf. Fergus M. Bordewich, *America's Great Debate: Henry Clay, Stephen A. Douglas, and the Compromise That Preserved the Union* (New York: Simon & Schuster, 2012).

14. Cf. Joseph E. Inikori and Stanley J. Engerman, eds., *The Atlantic Slave Trade: Effects on Economies, Societies, and Peoples in Africa, the Americas, and Europe* (Durham, NC: Duke University Press, 1992); Lorenzo Greene, *The Negro in Colonial New England, 1620–1776* (New York: Columbia University Press, 1942), 206, 222; Ronald Bailey, "The Slave(ry) Trade and the Development of Capitalism in the United States: The Textile Industry in New England," in Inikori and Engerman, *Atlantic Slave Trade*, 212.

15. Bailey, "Slave(ry) Trade and the Development of Capitalism," 229; Leon Litwack, *North of Slavery: The Negro in the Free States, 1790–1860* (Chicago: University of Chicago Press, 1965), 3.

16. Henry Wiencek, *Master of the Mountain: Thomas Jefferson and His Slaves* (New York: Farrar, Straus and Giroux, 2012), 7–8, 96–97.

17. Bell, *Major Butler's Legacy*, 164.

18. Bell, 132.

19. Samuel Momodu, "Igbo Landing Mass Suicide (1803)," *Black Past*, October 25, 2016, blackpast.org/american-history/igbo, 1–8; Bell, *Major Butler's Legacy*, 132; Orlando Patterson, *Slavery and Social Death: A Comparative Study* (Cambridge, MA: Harvard University Press, 1982).

20. Lewis, *W. E. B. Du Bois*, vol. 1, 157–58.

21. Johnhenry Gonzalez, *Maroon Nation: A History of Revolutionary Haiti* (New Haven, CT: Yale University Press, 2019), 80–83; Edward E. Baptist, *The Half Has Never Been Told: Slavery and the Making of American Capitalism* (New York: Basic Books, 2014), 48–49 (Alexander Hamilton quote); Gordon S. Wood, *Empire of Liberty: A History of the Early Republic, 1789–1815* (New York: Oxford University Press, 2009), 367–68.

22. Ulrich Bonnell Phillips, *American Negro Slavery: A Survey of the Supply, Employment and Control of Negro Labor as Determined by the Plantation Regime* (1918; repr., Baton Rouge: Louisiana State University Press, 1966), 165; Sven Beckert, *Empire of Cotton: A Global History*, 106–7; Gordon S. Wood, *Empire of Liberty*, 369–70; Baptist, *Half Has Never Been Told*, 30.

23. Walter Johnson, *River of Dark Dreams: Slavery and Empire in the Cotton Kingdom* (Cambridge, MA: Harvard University Press, 2019), 3; Beckert, *Empire of Cotton*, 107.

24. Wiencek, *Master of the Mountain*, 90; Manisha Sinha, *The Slave's Cause: A History of Abolition* (New Haven, CT: Yale University Press, 2016), 89–90; Baptist, *Half Has Never Been Told*, xxiii, 18; Ira Berlin and Philip D. Morgan, eds., *The Slaves' Economy: Independent Production by Slaves in the Americas* (UK: Frank Cass, 1991), 136.

25. Baptist, *Half Has Never Been Told*, 113–20; Inikori and Engerman, *Atlantic Slave Trade*, 220–21; Beckert, *Empire of Cotton*, 109–10.

26. Johnson, *River of Dark Dreams*, 5; Sven Beckert and Seth Rockman, *Slavery's Capitalism: A New History of Economic Development* (Philadelphia: University of Pennsylvania Press, 2016), 15.

27. Inikori and Engerman, *Atlantic Slave Trade*, 221; Baptist, *Half Has Never Been Told*, 128.

28. Beckert and Rockman, *Slavery's Capitalism*, 181; Bailey, "Slave(ry) Trade and the Development of Capitalism," 67–88; Johnson, *River of Dark Dreams*, 1.

2. CLARISSA'S BARGAIN: THE BELVINS OF HOUSTON COUNTY

1. "A bit blurry, but legible," Elaine DeNiro to David Levering Lewis, September 1, 2015.

2. Gary M. Pomerantz, *Where Peachtree Meets Sweet Auburn: A Saga of Race and Family* (New York: Scribner, 1996), 123; August Meier and David L. Lewis, "History of the Negro Upper Class in Atlanta, Georgia, 1890–1958," *Journal of Negro Education* 28, no. 2 (Spring 1959): 128–39, esp. 131.

3. Harriet Cornelia Cooper, *James Oglethorpe: The Founder of Georgia* (New York: D. Appleton, 1904); Ned and Constance Sublette, *The American Slave Coast: A History of the Slave-Breeding Industry* (Chicago: Lawrence Hill, 2016), 177, 237–39.

4. Cooper, *James Oglethorpe*, 47–48, 117.

5. Manisha Sinha, *The Slave's Cause: A History of Abolition* (New Haven, CT: Yale University Press, 2016), 17–18; Malcolm Bell Jr., *Major Butler's Legacy: Five Generations of a Slaveholding Family* (Athens: University of Georgia Press, 1987),

98–99; Augustus Field Beard, *A Crusade for Brotherhood: A History of the American Missionary Association* (1909; repr., New York: Pilgrim Press, 1972), 5; A. Leon Higginbotham Jr., *In the Matter of Color: Race & the American Legal Process; The Colonial Period* (New York: Oxford University Press, 1978), 242–45.

6. Erskine Clarke, *Wrestlin' Jacob: A Portrait of Religion in Antebellum Georgia and the Carolina Low Country* (Tuscaloosa: University of Alabama Press, 2000), 5.

7. Clarke, 7; Charles Beard, *An Economic Interpretation of the Constitution of the United States* (1913; repr., New York: Free Press, 1941), 30, 192.

8. Bell, *Major Butler's Legacy*, 28; Erskine Clarke, *Dwelling Place: A Plantation Epic* (New Haven, CT: Yale University Press, 2005), 41.

9. Robert Manson Myers, ed., "Prologue," in *The Children of Pride* (New York: Popular Library, 1972), vol. 1.

10. Joel Williamson, *New People: Miscegenation and Mulattoes in the United States* (New York: Free Press), 28.

11. Reginald Horsman, "United States Indian Policies, 1776–1815," in *History of Indian-White Relations,* vol. 4, ed. Wilcomb E. Washburn (Washington, DC: Smithsonian Institution, 1988), 32.

12. Gordon S. Wood, *Empire of Liberty: A History of the Early Republic, 1789–1815* (New York: Oxford University Press, 2009), 126–27.

13. Walter Johnson, *River of Dark Dreams: Slavery and Empire in the Cotton Kingdom* (Cambridge, MA: Harvard University Press, 2013), 19–20.

14. Stuart Banner, *How the Indians Lost Their Land: Law and Power on the Frontier* (Cambridge, MA: Harvard University Press, 2000); Edward Baptist, *The Half Has Never Been Told: Slavery and the Making of American Capitalism* (New York: Basic Books, 2014), 33.

15. Peter Cozzens, *Tecumseh and the Prophet: The Shawnee Brothers Who Defied a Nation* (New York: Knopf, 2020), 202.

16. Cozzens, 144, 202.

17. Cozzens, xii.

18. Cozzens, 262–65.

19. Gregory Evans Dowd, "The American Revolution to the Mid-nineteenth Century," in *Southeast,* vol. 14, ed. Raymond D. Fogelson (Washington, DC: Smithsonian Institution, 2004), 148–49; Richard J. Hryniewicki, "The Creek Treaty of Washington, 1826," *Georgia Historical Quarterly* 48, no. 4 (1964): 425–41, http://www.jstor.org/stable/40578419.

20. Pete Belvin, "The Story of James Wiley Belvin, His Ancestors and Descendants" (unpublished manuscript, 1970), electronically reproduced for the author by Ellie Loudermilk, Perry Area Historical Society.

21. Joseph Reidy, *From Slavery to Agrarian Capitalism in the Cotton Plantation South, Central Georgia, 1800–1880* (Chapel Hill: University of North Carolina Press, 1992), 15–21.

22. Sublette, *American Slave Coast*, 43; Sven Beckert and Seth Rockman, *Slavery's Capitalism: A New History of Economic Development* (Philadelphia: University of Pennsylvania Press, 2016), 17; Belvin, "Story of James Wiley Belvin," 90.

23. Walter Johnson, *Soul by Soul: Life Inside the Antebellum Slave Market* (Cambridge, MA: Harvard University Press, 1999), 90.

24. Belvin, "Story of James Wiley Belvin"; Thomas Sully, portraits of John Wiley Belvin and Eliza Judith Belvin, done at the home of Allen Little in 1845.

25. Reidy, *From Slavery to Agrarian Capitalism*, 25.

26. Sven Beckert, *Empire of Cotton: A Global History* (New York: Knopf, 2014), 110.

27. Reidy, *From Slavery to Agrarian Capitalism*, 85; Edward Baptist, "Toward a Political Economy of Slave Labor," in *A New History of American Economic Development*, ed. Sven Beckert and Seth Rockman (Philadelphia: University of Pennsylvania Press, 2016), 42–43.

28. Solomon Northup, *Twelve Years a Slave* (1853; repr., Compass Circle, 2019), 47, 84.

29. Erskine Clarke, *Wrestlin' Jacob*, i–xviii; Ira Berlin, *Many Thousands Gone: The First Two Centuries of Slavery in North America* (Cambridge, MA: Harvard University Press, 1998), 2; Ophelia Settle Egypt, J. Masuoka, Charles S. Johnson, eds., *The American Slave: A Composite Autobiography,* vol. 18 (1941; repr., New York: Greenwood, 1972), ii; Richard S. Dunn, *A Tale of Two Plantations: Slave Life and Labor in Jamaica and Virginia* (Cambridge, MA: Harvard University Press, 2014), esp. 43, 272.

30. Northup, *Twelve Years a Slave*, 47; Pete Belvin, "Family History."

31. Mathew Karp, *This Vast Southern Empire: Slaveholders at the Helm of American Foreign Policy* (Cambridge, MA: Harvard University Press, 2016), 99–100; Reidy, *From Slavery to Agrarian Capitalism,* 86–88; Fergus Bordewich, *America's Great Debate: Henry Clay, Stephen A. Douglass, and the Compromise That Preserved the Union* (New York: Simon & Schuster, 2012).

32. Lavoris Gail Alexander-Maiden, *We Came in Chains: History and Lineage of African-American Families from Houston County, Georgia* (Charlotte, NC: Conquering Books, 2003), 42.

33. Elaine DeNiro, email to David Lewis, January 9, 2017.

34. Daina Ramey Berry and Leslie M. Harris, eds., *Sexuality & Slavery: Reclaiming Intimate Histories in the Americas* (Athens: University of Georgia Press, 2018), 164.

35. Kent Anderson Leslie, *Woman of Color, Daughter of Privilege: Amanda America Dickson, 1849–1893* (Athens: University of Georgia Press, 1995), 4; Berry and Harris, *Sexuality & Slavery*, chap. 9; Brenda E. Stevenson, "What's Love Got to Do with It? Concubinage and Enslaved Women and Girls in the Antebellum South," *Journal of African American History* 98, no. 1 (Winter 2013); Jean Fagan Yellen, *Harriet Jacobs: A Life; The Remarkable Adventures of the Woman Who Wrote Incidents in the Life of a Slave Girl* (New York: Basic Books, 2004); Deborah Gray White, *Ar'n't I a Woman? Female Slaves in the Plantation South* (1885; repr., rev. ed., New York: W. W. Norton, 1999); Amrita Chakrabarti Myers, *Forging Freedom: Black Women & the Pursuit of Liberty in Antebellum Charleston* (Chapel Hill: University of North Carolina Press, 2011); Adele Logan Alexander, *Ambiguous Lives: Free Women of Color in Rural Georgia, 1789–1879* (Fayetteville: University of Arkansas Press, 1991), 185–89.

36. *Harriet Jacobs, Incidents in the Life of a Slave Girl, Written by Herself,* ed. Jennifer Fleischner (New York: Bedford/St. Martin's, 2010); Sublette, *American Slave Coast,* 21.

37. Cf. Catherine Clinton, ed., *Fanny Kemble's Journals* (Cambridge, MA: Harvard University Press, 2000), 156–57.

38. Belvin, "Story of James Wiley Belvin," 14.

39. Belvin, 31.

40. Belvin, 31.

41. *Georgia Journal and Messenger,* April 14, 1858; Belvin, 12–13.

42. Berry and Harris, *Sexuality and Slavery,* 1.

43. Belvin, 15–18.

44. Belvin, 16–18; Edwin C. Bearss, *Fields of Honor: Pivotal Battles of the Civil War* (Washington, DC: National Geographic, 2006), esp. 97, 116.

45. Macon County Historical Society, Facebook, February 17, 2013; Belvin, "Story of James Wiley Belvin," 16.

46. "Sam Belvin, One Family's Hero," *Valdosta Times,* March 4, 2001.

47. John Hope Franklin, *Reconstruction after the Civil War* (Chicago: University of Chicago Press, 1961), 42; Reidy, *From Slavery to Agrarian Capitalism,* 140.

48. David Levering Lewis, "Introduction," in W. E. B. Du Bois, *Black Reconstruction in America, 1860–1880* (1935; repr., Oxford University Press, 2007), 238; C. Mildred Thompson, "Chronology," in *Reconstruction in Georgia* (1915; repr., Macon, GA: Mercer University Press, 2017).

49. Belvin, "Story of James Wiley Belvin," 13.

50. Belvin, 92; Edmund L. Drago, *Black Politicians and Reconstruction in Georgia: A Splendid Failure* (Baton Rouge: Louisiana State University Press, 1982), 23–25; Stephen Ward Angell, *Bishop Henry McNeal Turner and African American Religion in the South* (Knoxville: University of Tennessee Press, 1992), 3, 63.

51. A. B. Caldwell, ed., *History of the American Negro: North Carolina Edition* (Atlanta, GA: A.B. Caldwell Publishing Co., 1921), 89–90.

52. Charles S. Johnson, *Shadow of the Plantation* (1934; repr., Chicago: University of Chicago Press, 1941), 27; Franklin, *Reconstruction after the Civil War,* 220; Drago, *Black Politicians and Reconstruction,* 103–11.

53. Belvin, "Story of James Wiley Belvin," 17.

54. Alexander-Maiden, *We Came in Chains,* 52; Du Bois, *Black Reconstruction,* 35.

55. Reidy, *From Slavery to Agrarian Capitalism,* 12.

56. 1870 U.S. Census, Houston County, Georgia, December 5, 1874 ("James Milton Belvin, son of Cap. J. P. Belvin of this county, aged eight years, died in Milledgeville on Saturday last of yellow fever").

57. Leslie, *Woman of Color,* 9.

58. 1880 U.S. Census, Atlanta (Elsie Givens, 55; household members: Charles, James, Alice, 8; on Wheat Street).

59. Drago, *Black Politicians and Reconstruction,* 133 ("By 1870 Georgia had produced the largest cotton crop to date"); Beckert, *Empire of Cotton,* 291; Belvin, "Story of James Wiley Belvin," 20.

60. Belvin, 21.

61. W. C. McKinley, "The Late Capt. J. P. Belvin," *Valdosta Times*, April 18, 1917; Albert Pendleton, "Sam Belvin, One Family's Hero," *Valdosta Times*, March 7, 2001.

62. J. W. Belvin, "The Last Will of James W. Belvin," Marshallville, Georgia, November 29, 1886; J. W. Belvin, "Codicil to the Will," Macon County, Georgia, July 4, 1887.

63. Belvin, "Story of James Wiley Belvin," 20.

64. Belvin, 20.

65. Mary Helen Thompson, email to David Levering Lewis, August 17, 2020; David Levering Lewis, email to Shannon Christmas, August 28, 2020; Shannon Christmas, email to David Levering Lewis, August 30, 2020; Shannon Christmas to David Levering Lewis, "Alice King's Paternity," Through The Trees, October 9, 2020, https://throughthetreesblog.tumblr.com/consulting.

66. Through The Trees, October 9, 2020, to the author.

67. Clarence White, email to David Levering Lewis, March 10, 2020; deed of sale, Old Wheat Street, New Wheat Street, September 19, 1879, Fulton County Superior Court; Leonard Dinnerstein, *The Leo Frank Case* (Athens: University of Georgia Press, 1987); David Levering Lewis, "Parallels and Divergencies: Assimilationist Strategies of Afro-American and Jewish Elites from 1910 to the Early 1930s," in *Bridges and Boundaries: African Americans and American Jews*, ed. J. Salzman (New York: Braziller/Jewish Museum, 1992); Gary M. Pomerantz, *Where Peachtree Meets Sweet Auburn: A Saga of Race and Family* (New York: Scribner, 1996).

68. 1880 U.S. Census, Atlanta (Elsie Givens, 55; household members: Charles, James, Alice, 8; James is a tailor; Charles is a carpenter; they are at 276 Wheat Street in 1887).

69. Indenture, recorded October 6, 1881, by C. H. Strong CSC, Fulton County Superior Court (transcribed and typed by Elaine DeNiro); Elaine DeNiro, email to David Levering Lewis, July 7, 2016.

70. The Court of Ordinary, Glynn County, December 1, 1927.

71. *Atlanta City Directory* (Atlanta: Polk & Co., 1890), 798–99.

3. AN IDENTITY OF THEIR OWN: THE BELLS OF GOOSE CREEK AND AUBURN AVENUE

1. Clarence A. Bacote, *The Story of Atlanta University: A Century of Service, 1865–1965* (Atlanta: Atlanta University Press, 1969), esp. 29–30.

2. Cf. Robert Olwell, "Becoming Free: Manumission and the Genesis of a Free Black Community in South Carolina, 1740–90," *Slavery and Abolition* 17, no. 1 (June 2008): 1–19, esp. 5–6; Michael J. Heitzler, *Goose Creek: A Definitive History*, vol. 1, *Planters, Politicians and Patriots* (Charleston, SC: History Press, 2005), esp. 121, 123; 1790 U.S. Census, South Carolina; Margaret Peckham Mote, *Free Blacks and Mulattoes in South Carolina 1850 Census* (Baltimore: Clearfield Publishing Company, 2000), 14.

3. Ira Berlin, *Slaves without Masters: The Free Negro in the Antebellum South* (New York: Pantheon, 1974), xiv, 251; Marina Wikramanayake, *A World in Shadow: The Free Black in Antebellum South Carolina* (Columbia: University of South Carolina Press, 1973); Larry Koger, *Black Slaveowners: Free Black Slave Masters in South Carolina, 1790–1860* (Jefferson, NC: McFarland, 1985).

4. Koger, *Black Slaveowners*, 80–81; cf. Carter G. Woodson, ed., *Free Negro Owners of Slaves in the United States in 1830: Together with Absentee Ownership of Slaves in the United States in 1830* (Washington, DC: Association for the Study of Negro Life and History, 1924), v, vi.

5. Joel Williamson, *New People: Miscegenation and Mulattoes in the United States* (New York: Free Press, 1980), 19, 24; Wikramanayake, *World in Shadow*, 14–15.

6. Koger, *Black Slaveowners*, 12.

7. Peter H. Wood, *Black Majority: Negroes in Colonial South Carolina from 1670 through the Stono Rebellion* (New York: W. W. Norton, 1975), xiv; David Levering Lewis, *W. E. B. DuBois: Biography of a Race, 1868–1919* (New York: Henry Holt, 1993), 158.

8. Brown Fellowship Society, box 1 (microfilm); cf., Robert L. Harris Jr., "Charleston's Free Afro-American Elite: The Brown Fellowship Society and the Humane Brotherhood," *South Carolina Historical Magazine* 82, no. 4 (October 1981): 289–310; also, esp., Thomas Bonneau in Daniel Alexander Payne, *Recollections of Seventy Years* (1888; repr., New York: Arno Press and *New York Times*, 1968), 52–53.

9. Payne, *Recollections*, 19–25, 39–40; James T. Campbell, *Songs of Zion: The African American Methodist Episcopal Church in the United States and South Africa* (New York: Oxford University Press, 1995).

10. Joel Williamson, *New People: Miscegenation and Mulattoes in the United States* (New York: Free Press, 1980), chap. 1; Robert L. Harris Jr., "Charleston's Free Afro-American Elite," 289–310, esp. 304–5.

11. Michael P. Johnson and James L. Roark, *Black Masters: A Free Family of Color in the Old South* (New York: W. W. Norton, 1984), xiii; Thomas Holt, *Black over White: Negro Political Leadership in South Carolina during Reconstruction* (Champaign: University of Illinois Press, 1977), 17–21.

12. Bernard E. Powers, *Black Charlestonians: A Social History, 1822–1885* (Fayetteville: University of Arkansas Press, 1994), 57–59; Williamson, *New People*, 23; A. B. Wilkinson, *Blurring the Lines of Race & Freedom: Mulattoes & Mixed Bloods in English Colonial America* (Columbia: University of South Carolina Press, 2005); Koger, *Black Slaveowners*, 177–78; 1790 U.S. Census, Fairfield County.

13. Scott L. Malcomson, *One Drop of Blood: The American Misadventure of Race* (New York: Farrar, Straus and Giroux, 2000), 47–49; Michael J. Heitzler, *Goose Creek: A Definitive History*, vol. 1 (Charleston, SC: History Press, 2006), chap. 2.

14. Olwell, "Becoming Free"; Wood, *Black Majority*, xvii, 113, 310–19; Charles Joyner, *Down by the Riverside: A South Carolina Slave Community* (Champaign: University of Illinois Press, 1985), 13–14; Anne C. Bailey, *The Weeping Time: A Memory of the Largest Slave Auction in American History* (New York: Cambridge University Press, 2017), 62.

15. Wood, *Black Majority*; Joseph E. Holloway, *A History of Slave Resistance in the United Sates* (Porter Ranch, CA: New World African Press, 2016).

16. John K. Thornton, "African Dimensions," in Mark D. Smith, ed., *Stono: Documenting and Interpreting a Southern Slave Revolt* (Columbia: University of South Carolina Press, 2005), 82.

17. South Carolina, State Agricultural Society, *The Negro Law of South Carolina*, comp. John Belton O'Neall, Columbia, printed by J. G. Bowman, 1848, https://www.loc.gov/item/10034474/; Ira Berlin and Philip D. Morgan, eds., *The Slaves' Economy, Independent Production by Slaves in the Americas* (London: Frank Cass, 1991), 144; Joseph Reidy, *From Slavery to Agrarian Capitalism in the Cotton Plantation South, Central Georgia, 1800–1880* (Chapel Hill: University of North Carolina Press, 1992), esp. 29–32.

18. Olwell, "Becoming Free," 2.

19. Cf. John Hope Franklin, *From Slavery to Freedom: A History of African Americans* (New York: McGraw Hill, 2021).

20. Olwell, "Becoming Free," 4–6.

21. Heitzler, *Goose Creek*, vol. 1, 121, 149; reprint of 1790 U.S. Census, 122–23.

22. "Inventory of the Bell Family Papers, circa 1926–1972," Avery Research Center for African American History and Culture, Charleston, SC.

23. Heitzler, *Goose Creek*, vol. 2, 23, 25; Edward Ball, *Slaves in the Family* (New York: Farrar, Straus and Giroux, 1998), 139.

24. Leon Litwack, *North of Slavery: The Negro in the Free States, 1790–1860* (Chicago: University of Chicago Press, 1961), 40–45; Berlin, *Slaves without Masters*, 104.

25. Wikramanayake, *World in Shadow*, esp. 13; David W. Dangerfield, "Turning the Earth: Free Black Yeomanry in the Antebellum South Carolina Low Country," *Agricultural History* 89, no. 2 (Spring 2015): 201; Frank L. Owsley, *Plain Folk of the Old South* (Nashville: Vanderbilt University Press, 1949).

26. Koger, *Black Slaveowners*, 104; Dangerfield, "Turning the Earth," 200–222, esp. 212–13.

27. 1820 U.S. Census, South Carolina.

28. Joyner, *Down by the Riverside*, esp. 12.

29. MyHeritage Family Trees, June 14, 2021.

30. Joyner, *Down by the Riverside*, 42.

31. Daniel Rasmussen, *American Uprising: The Untold Story of America's Largest Slave Revolt* (New York: Harper Perennial, 2012), esp. 128; Berlin, *Slaves without Masters*, 85–86; Joseph E. Holloway, *A History of Slave Resistance in the United States* (Porter Ranch, CA: New World African Press, 2016), 169.

32. Dennis C. Dickerson, *The African Methodist Episcopal Church: A History* (New York: Cambridge University Press, 2020), 48; Koger, *Black Slaveowners*, 172–74; Holloway, *History of Slave Resistance*, 175–76; Campbell, *Songs of Zion*, 35.

33. Howard D. Gregg, *History of the A.M.E. Church* (Nashville, TN: AMEC, 1980), 12; Gayraud S. Wilmore, *Black Religion and Black Radicalism: An Interpretation of the Religious History of African Americans* (Ossining, NY: Orbis Books, 1998), 82–83; Dickerson, *African Methodist Episcopal Church*, 25–31.

34. Wilmore, *Black Religion and Black Radicalism*, 85.

35. Holloway, *History of Slave Resistance*, 176–78; Koger, *Black Slaveowners,* 174–75; Dickerson, *African Methodist Episcopal Church*, 48.

36. Johnson and Roark, *Black Masters*, 40, 41–43.

37. Koger, *Black Slaveowners*, 176–81.

38. Dickerson, *African Methodist Episcopal Church*, 47–48; Wikramanayake, *World in Shadow*, 176.

39. Heitzler, *Goose Creek*, vol. 2, esp. 36–39; Sven Beckert and Seth Rockman, eds., *Slavery's Capitalism: A New History of American Economic Development* (Philadelphia: University of Pennsylvania Press, 2016), 3; Robert W. Remini, *The Life of Andrew Jackson* (Harper & Row, 1984), chap. 19.

40. Manisha Sinha, *The Slave's Cause: A History of Abolition* (New Haven, CT: Yale University Press, 2016), esp. 197, 206; Scott L. Malcomson, *One Drop of Blood*, 195; Heitzler, *Goose Creek*, vol. 1, 38–39.

41. Johnson and Roark, *Black Masters*, 46.

42. Harris, "Charleston's Free Afro-American Elite," esp. 305.

43. Wikramanayake, *World in Shadow*, 77, 176–77.

44. Frederick L. Olmsted, *The Cotton Kingdom: A Traveller's Observations on Cotton and Slavery in the American Slave States, 1853–1861* (1861; repr., Mason Bros., 2017), 225.

45. Harris, "Charleston's Free Afro-American Elite," 308–9; Powers, *Black Charlestonians*, esp. 43, 50–55.

46. Michael P. Johnson and James L. Roark, eds., *No Chariot Let Down: Charleston's Free People of Color on the Eve of the Civil War* (Chapel Hill: University of North Carolina Press, 1984), 6.

47. Powers, *Black Charlestonians*, 45–47, 64.

48. Johnson and Roark, *Black Masters*, xi; Harris, "Charleston's Free Afro-American Elite," 298.

49. Johnson and Roark, *No Chariot Let Down*, 7.

50. Johnson and Roark, *Black Masters*, 269.

51. Johnson and Roark, *No Chariot Let Down*, esp. 9, 85; Johnson and Roark, *Black Masters*, 274.

52. 1840 U.S. Census, Goose Creek, South Carolina; 1850 U.S. Census, Goose Creek, South Carolina; myheritage.com; Shannon Christmas, email to David L. Lewis, June 29, 2021; Through The Trees, Isaac Bradwell Family (1784–1868); Heitzler, *Goose Creek*, vol. 2, 49.

53. Marianne Cawley (librarian, South Carolina Room, Charleston County Public Library), email to David Lewis, April 13, 2021; Dangerfield, "Turning the Earth," 218; Jeremiah L. Bell: "S.C., U.S. Wills and Probate Records, 1670–1980, 1857," ancestry.com.

54. Dangerfield, "Turning the Earth," 217; Ariela J. Gross, *What Blood Won't Tell: A History of Race on Trial in America* (Cambridge, MA: Harvard University Press, 2008), 30–45.

55. Powers, *Black Charlestonians*, 65–66; Holt, *Black over White*, 6.

56. Powers, 80–85.

4. UP FROM SLAVERY: THE BLACK BELT LEWISES

1. "The History of the Sim and Hattie Lewis Family," by Susie B. Jenkins, was completed in October 1956. She died on January 5, 1957. Several copies of this document remained with various family members for many years. The author is especially indebted to his niece Pamela Lewis for a photocopied reproduction.

2. Cf., *Ellaville and Schley County: An Historical Sketch* (Ellaville, GA: 1976), 132.

3. Jenkins, "History of the Sim and Hattie Lewis Family," 2.

4. *Americus City Directory, 1908*, Lake Blackshear Regional Library, Special Collections, Americus, Georgia.

5. Jenkins, "History of the Sim and Hattie Lewis Family," 5.

6. *Ellaville and Schley County*, 124.

7. Edmund L. Drago, *Black Politicians and Reconstruction in Georgia: A Splendid Failure* (Baton Rouge: Louisiana State University Press, 1982), 98; George Goodwin, "Schley County Justly Proud of Its Modern White Schools; Setup for Negroes Suffers from Over-all Lack of Funds," *Atlanta Journal*, June 18, 1949.

8. Goodwin, "Schley County Justly Proud."

9. Legal Defense Fund, "The Southern Manifesto and 'Massive Resistance' to Brown," n.d., naacpldf.org/brown-vs-board/southern-manifesto-massive-resistance-brown /#:~:text=On%20February%2025%2C%201956%2C%20Senator,forestall% 20and%20prevent%20school%20integration; David R. Goldfield, *Black, White, and Southern: Race Relations and Southern Culture 1940 to the Present* (Baton Rouge: Louisiana State University Press, 1990), 75.

10. Clarence White, email to David Lewis, February 28, 2022.

11. *Ellaville and Schley County*, 123–24; Clarence White, email to David Lewis, January 31, 2022.

12. Drago, *Black Politicians and Reconstruction in Georgia*; Thomas Holt, *Black over White: Negro Political Leadership in South Carolina during Reconstruction* (Champaign: University of Illinois Press, 1977); Eric Foner, *Reconstruction: America's Unfinished Revolution, 1863–1877* (New York: Harper & Row, 1988), 604; Joseph P. Reidy, *Illusions of Emancipation: The Pursuit of Freedom and Equality in the Twilight of Slavery* (Chapel Hill: University of North Carolina Press, 2019); W. E. B. Du Bois, *Black Reconstruction in America, 1860–1880* (1935).

13. Foner, *Reconstruction*, 59; Gerald David Jaynes, *Branches without Roots: Genesis of the Black Working Class in the American South, 1862–1882* (New York: Oxford University Press, 1986), 103; Leon F. Litwack, *Trouble in Mind: Black Southerners in the Age of Jim Crow* (New York: Knopf, 1998), 121–22.

14. See Stephen Ward Angell, *Bishop Henry McNeal Turner and African-American Religion in the South* (Knoxville: University of Tennessee Press, 1992), 64.

15. Roger L. Ransom and Richard Sutch, *One Kind of Freedom: The Economic Conse-*

quences of Emancipation (New York: Cambridge University Press, 1977), 35; C. Mildred Thompson, *Reconstruction in Georgia: Economic, Social, Political, 1865–1872* (1915; repr., Macon, GA: Mercer University Press, 2017), 297.

16. Angell, *Bishop Henry McNeal Turner*, 63; Dorothy Sterling, ed., *The Trouble They Seen: The Story of Reconstruction in the Words of African Americans* (Cambridge, MA: DaCapo Press, 1976), vii; David W. Blight, *Frederick Douglass, Prophet of Freedom* (New York: Simon & Schuster, 2018), 560; Foner, *Reconstruction*, 105.

17. Russell Duncan, *Freedom's Shore: Tunis Campbell and the Georgia Freedmen* (Athens: University of Georgia Press, 1986) 19; Foner, *Reconstruction*, 70, 71–72.

18. Foner, 179.

19. Reidy, *Illusions of Emancipation*, 78; Foner, *Reconstruction*, 60, 159; Bruce Levine, *Thaddeus Stevens: Civil War Revolutionary, Fighter for Racial Justice* (New York: Simon & Schuster, 2021), 226–31; Wesley Gaines, *African Methodism in the South: Twenty-five Years of Freedom* (Atlanta: Franklin, 1890), 12.

20. Drago, *Black Politicians and Reconstruction in Georgia*, 29; W. E. B. Du Bois, "Reconstruction and Its Benefits," in *W. E. B. Du Bois: A Reader*, ed. David Levering Lewis (New York: Henry Holt, 1993), 180.

21. Franklin, *Reconstruction after the Civil War*, 65–67; Reidy, *Illusions of Emancipation*, 339–40.

22. Foner, *Reconstruction*, 31; Franklin, *Reconstruction after the Civil War*, 55, 73; Thompson, "Chronology," in *Reconstruction in Georgia*.

23. James T. Campbell, *Songs of Zion: The African Methodist Episcopal Church* (Chapel Hill: University of North Carolina Press, 1998), 82–83; Drago, *Black Politicians and Reconstruction in Georgia*, 29; Franklin, *Reconstruction after the Civil War*, 23, 42.

24. Evan Kutzler et al., *In Plain Sight: African Americans at Andersonville National Historic Site, A Special History Study* (Andersonville, GA: National Park Service, 2020), esp. 125.

25. W. E. B. Du Bois, *The Souls of Black Folk*, centennial ed. (New York: Modern Library, 2003), 126; Kutzler et al., *In Plain Sight*, xi; Lewis, *W. E. B. Du Bois*, 177.

26. Kutzler et al., *In Plain Sight*, xii.

27. Kutzler et al., 35.

28. Kutzler et al., "The Sumter School, 1866–1874," in *In Plain Sight*, 29; Du Bois, *Black Reconstruction*, 645. I am obliged to Mr. Clarence D. White's unpublished essay "Reverend Jessie Dinkins, African American Politician and Methodist Minister from Schley County, Georgia."

29. Thompson, *Reconstruction in Georgia*, lx–lxix.

30. Drago, *Black Politicians and Reconstruction in Georgia*, 25–26, 40; Angell, *Bishop Henry McNeal Turner*, 86–87.

31. Cf. Russell Duncan, *Freedom's Shore: Tunis Campbell and the Georgia Freedmen* (Athens: University of Georgia Press, 1986), 48.

32. Thompson, *Reconstruction in Georgia*, 298; Drago, *Black Politicians and Reconstruction in Georgia*, 44.

33. "Records of the Assistant Commissioner for Georgia, Bureau of Refugees, Freed-

men and Abandoned Lands, 1865–1869," microfilm M798n, roll 32, National Archives.

34. Kutzler et al., *In Plain Sight*, 75.

35. Angell, *Bishop Henry McNeal Turner*, 91; James T. Campbell, *Songs of Zion: The African Methodist Episcopal Church in the United States and South Africa* (Chapel Hill: University of North Carolina Press, 1998), 78–83.

36. Kutzler et al., *In Plain Sight*, 71.

37. Kutzler et al., 75; H. W. Pierson, "A Letter to Hon. Charles Sumner, with 'Statements' of Outrages upon Freedmen in Georgia and an Account of my Expulsion from Andersonville, Ga., by the Ku-Klux Klan" (Washington, DC: Chronicle Print, 1870), 88.

38. I am indebted to Clarence D. White. His unpublished "A Reign of Terror: Bloody Outrages and Voter Suppression in Reconstruction Schley County, Georgia" superbly assimilates material from Kutzler et al., *In Plain Sight*, and Pierson, "A Letter to Hon. Charles Sumner."

39. W. Calvin Smith, "The Reconstruction 'Triumph' of Rufus B. Bullock," *Georgia Historical Quarterly* 52, no. 4 (December 1968): 414–25.

40. Pierson, "Letter to Hon. Charles Sumner," 5, 12.

41. Alexander Keyssar, *The Right to Vote: The Contested History of Democracy in the United States* (New York: Basic Books, 2008), 95–96; Foner, *Reconstruction*, 446.

42. Pierson, "Letter to Hon. Charles Sumner," 18.

43. Thompson, *Reconstruction in Georgia*, 297; Joseph Reidy, *From Slavery to Agrarian Capitalism in the Cotton Plantation South, Central Georgia, 1800–1880* (Chapel Hill: University of North Carolina Press, 1992), 208–9.

44. Pierson, "Letter to Hon. Charles Sumner," 4.

45. Pierson, 3–12; Kutzler et al., *In Plain Sight*, 36; Ron Chernow, *Grant* (New York: Penguin Press, 2017), 701–7.

46. Drago, *Black Politicians and Reconstruction in Georgia*, 98; Russell Duncan, "Rufus Bullock, 1834–1907," *New Georgia Encyclopedia*, June 2007, georgiaencyclopedia .org/articles/government-politics/rufus-bullock-1834-1907/.

47. John B. Lewis, 1860 U.S. Census, Slave Census, Macon County, Georgia.

48. Leon F. Litwack, *Trouble in Mind: Black Southerners in the Age of Jim Crow* (New York: Knopf, 1998), 122.

49. Litwack, 87.

50. General Index to Deeds & Mortgages, Macon County, books P and S, 1899–1910.

51. "S. M. Lewis" entry in Arthur Bunyan Caldwell, *History of the American Negro, Georgia Edition, 1920* (Atlanta: A. B. Caldwell, 1920), 253–55.

52. Caldwell, *History of the American Negro*, 255.

53. George A. Sewell and Cornelius V. Troup, *Morris Brown College: The First Hundred Years, 1881–1981* (Atlanta: Morris Brown College, 1981).

54. Sewell and Troup, 39.

55. Dennis C. Dickerson, *The African Methodist Episcopal Church: A History* (New York: Cambridge University Press, 2020), 13, 176; Campbell, *Songs of Zion*, viii; Litwack, *Trouble in Mind*, 392; Thomas C. Holt, *Children of Fire: A History of*

African Americans (New York: Hill & Wang, 2010), 224–25; Stephen Ward Angell, *Bishop Henry McNeal Turner and African American Religion in the South* (Knoxville: University of Tennessee Press, 1992), 238; Andrew E. Johnson, *The Forgotten Prophet: Bishop Henry McNeal Turner and the African-American Prophetic Tradition* (UK: Lexington Books, 2012), 90.

5. THE ARC OF WHITE SUPREMACY: THE OPTIMISTIC ATLANTA BELLS, 1865–1894

1. C. Vann Woodward, *Origins of the New South, 1877–1913* (Baton Rouge: Louisiana State University Press, 1951), 107.
2. Augustus Field Beard, *A Crusade of Brotherhood: A History of the American Missionary Association* (1909; repr., Cleveland, OH: Pilgrim Press, 1972), 159.
3. Beard, 168; Edmund L. Drago, *Initiative & Race Relations: Charleston's Avery Normal Institute* (Athens: University of Georgia Press, 1990), esp. 2–5; Adele Logan Alexander, *Ambiguous Lives: Free Women of Color in Rural Georgia, 1789–1879* (Fayetteville: University of Arkansas Press, 1991), esp. 173–74.
4. Ira Berlin, *Slaves without Masters: The Free Negro in the Antebellum South* (New York: Pantheon, 1974); Marina Wikramanayake, *A World in Shadow: The Free Black in Antebellum South Carolina* (Columbia: University of South Carolina Press, 1973); Robert L. Harris Jr., "The Brown Fellowship Society and the Humane Brotherhood," *South Carolina Historical Magazine* 82, no. 4 (October 1981): 289310.
5. Charleston Public Library email correspondence.
6. Cf. Find a Grave Index, 1600s–Current; Isaac Bradwell, 1784–1868, Springhill United Methodist Church Cemetery; Bradwell memories shared by Urnestine A. Bell.
7. My great-grandmother's South-View Cemetery granite tombstone reads "In Loving Memory of Our Dead Mother. Adalaide Bell, Born 1821. Died 1911."
8. John W. Bell, 1850 and 1870 U.S. Censuses, South Carolina and Georgia; Dennis Dickerson, *African American Preachers and Politics: The Careys of Chicago* (Jackson: University Press of Mississippi, 2010).
9. C. Mildred Thompson, *Reconstruction in Georgia: Economic, Social, Political, 1865–1872* (1915; repr., Macon, GA: Mercer University Press, 2017).
10. Eric Foner, *Reconstruction: America's Unfinished Revolution, 1863–1877* (New York: Harper & Row, 1988), 582.
11. Joe M. Richardson, *Christian Reconstruction: The American Missionary Association and Southern Blacks, 1861–1890* (Athens: University of Georgia Press, 1986), 37; Clarence A. Bacote, *The Story of Atlanta University: A Century of Service, 1865–1965* (Atlanta: Atlanta University Press, 1969); John Hope Franklin, *From Slavery to Freedom: A History of African Americans* (New York: McGraw Hill, 2021).
12. First Congregational Church, UCC, Atlanta, GA, Collection, box 1, Robert W. Woodruff Library, Atlanta University Center, Atlanta; Bacote, *Story of Atlanta University*, 11–14.

13. First Congregational Church, UCC, Atlanta, GA, Collection, Robert W. Woodruff Library, Atlanta University Center, Atlanta.

14. 1880 U.S. Census, Fulton County, Georgia; J. M. Beall, cf., Fulton and Campbell counties, Georgia, cemetery records, 1857–1933, Atlanta census index 1890: No. 331, Bell, John.

15. Ariela J. Gross, *What Blood Won't Tell: A History of Race on Trial in America* (Cambridge, MA: Harvard University Press, 2008), esp. chaps. 6, 7; Scott L. Malcomson, *One Drop of Blood: The American Misadventure of Race* (New York: Farrar, Straus and Giroux, 2000).

16. Bacote, *Story of Atlanta University*, esp. 4, 27–28.

17. Bacote, 272.

18. Bacote, 29–30, 147; Atlanta University, *Catalogue of the Officers & Students of Atlanta University, Atlanta, Georgia, with a Statement of Courses of Study, Expenses, Etc., 1889 – '90* (Atlanta: Mutual Printing, 1890).

19. Bacote, *Story of Atlanta University*, 32–33.

20. Bacote, 29–30, 44; David Levering Lewis, *When Harlem Was in Vogue* (1981; repr., New York: Penguin, 1997), 144; Adele Logan Alexander, *Princess of the Hither Isles: A Black Suffragist's Story from the Jim Crow South* (New Haven, CT: Yale University Press, 2019).

21. Devin Leonard, *Neither Snow nor Rain: A History of the United States Postal Service* (New York: Grove, 2016), 71–72.

22. Walter White, *A Man Called White: The Autobiography of Walter White* (New York: Viking, 1948), 136.

23. Robert L. Dorman, "The Creation and Destruction of the 1890 Federal Census," *The American Archivist* 71, no. 2 (Fall–Winter 2008): 350–83.

24. "Bell, John H," in *Atlanta City Directory*, 1892, 403; Clarence White, email to David Lewis.

25. *Atlanta City Directory*, 1890, 798.

26. Edward A. Hatfield, "Auburn Avenue," *New Georgia Encyclopedia*, June 2, 2006, georgiaencyclopedia.org/articles/counties-cities-neighborhoods/auburn -avenue-sweet-auburn/.

27. Richard Kluger, *Simple Justice: The History of Brown v. Board of Education, the Epochal Supreme Court Decision That Outlawed Segregation and of Black America's Century-Long Struggle for Equality under Law* (New York: Vintage Books, 1975), 75; Peter S. Canellos, *The Great Dissenter: The Story of John Marshall Harlan, America's Judicial Hero* (New York: Simon & Schuster, 2021), 21–25.

28. George Sinkler, "Benjamin Harrison and the Matter of Race," *Indiana Magazine of History* 65, no. 3 (1969): 197–213, http://www.jstor.org/stable/27789595; Kluger, *Simple Justice*, 50–65; Philip Dray, *At the Hands of Persons Unknown: The Lynching of Black America* (New York: Random House, 2002), chap. 4.

29. David A. Bateman, Ira Katznelson, and John S. Lapinski, *Southern Nation: Congress and White Supremacy after Reconstruction* (Princeton, NJ: Princeton University Press, 2018), esp. 140–57; Rayford W. Logan, *The Negro in American Life and Thought: The Nadir, 1877–1901* (New York: Dial Press, 1954), esp. 60–63.

30. Bateman, Katznelson, and Lapinski, *Southern Nation*, 143.
31. Bateman, Katznelson, and Lapinski, 143.
32. Jenkins and Peck, "Blair Education Bill," *Southern Nation*, 149.
33. Bateman, Katznelson, and Lapinski, *Southern Nation*, 185–87.
34. James T. Campbell, *Songs of Zion: The African Methodist Episcopal Church in the United States and South Africa* (New York: Oxford University Press, 1995), 78, 79; cf. Kendra T. Field, *Growing Up with the Country: Family, Race, and Nation after the Civil War* (New Haven, CT: Yale University Press, 2020).

6. IN THE FOLD OF WHITE SUPREMACY: THE DECEIVED BELLS, 1895–1906

1. Henry Hugh Proctor, *Between Black and White: Autobiographical Sketches* (Boston: Pilgrim Press, 1925), 7.
2. Proctor, 29.
3. Proctor includes "A New Ethnic Contribution to Christianity" in *Between Black and White*, chap. 5.
4. Louis R. Harlan, *Booker T. Washington: The Making of a Black Leader, 1856–1901*, vol. 1 (New York: Oxford University Press, 1972), esp. 206–7.
5. Historical marker for Booker T. Washington in Piedmont Park.jpg; Harlan, *Booker T. Washington*, vol. 1, 204–5; Thomas Holt, *Children of Fire: A History of African Americans* (New York: Hill & Wang, 2010), esp. 193–200.
6. Harlan, *Booker T. Washington*, 213–16.
7. Family lore told to me by A. U. Bell; Proctor, *Between Black and White*, 100; David Levering Lewis, *W. E. B. Du Bois: Biography of a Race, 1868–1919* (New York: Henry Holt, 1993), 174–75.
8. Proctor, *Between Black and White*, 45; cf. Robert W. Rydell, *World of Fairs: The Century-of-Progress Expositions* (Chicago: University of Chicago Press, 1993); "Address by Booker T. Washington, Principal, Tuskegee Normal and Industrial Institute, Tuskegee, Alabama, at Opening of Atlanta Exposition, Sept. 18, 1895."
9. "Address by Booker T. Washington."
10. Harlan, *Booker T. Washington*, 220.
11. Harlan, 225; Proctor, *Between Black and White*, 101–2; Lewis, *W. E. B. Du Bois*, 175.
12. Lewis, 119–20.
13. Phillip Dray, *At the Hands of Persons Unknown: The Lynching of Black America* (New York: Random House, 2002), 112.
14. Dray, 119; David Levering Lewis, "An American Pastime," *New York Review of Books*, November 21, 2002.
15. Mark Elliott, *Color-Blind Justice: Albion Tourgée and the Quest for Racial Equality, from the Civil War to Plessy v. Ferguson* (New York: Oxford University Press, 2006), chap. 9, esp. 280–90; Peter S. Canellos, *The Great Dissenter: The Story of John Marshall Harlan, America's Judicial Hero* (New York: Simon & Schuster, 2021),

esp. 346–51; David A. Bateman, Ira Katznelson, and John S. Lapinski, *Southern Nation: Congress and White Supremacy after Reconstruction* (Princeton, NJ: Princeton University Press, 2018), 226.

16. Cf. Canellos, *Great Dissenter,* 343; Elliott, *Color-Blind Justice,* 274–77.

17. Elliott, 284–85.

18. Elliott, 342; Canellos, *Great Dissenter,* 5.

19. Canellos, 346.

20. Richard Kluger, *Simple Justice: The History of Brown v. Board of Education, the Epochal Supreme Court Decision That Outlawed Segregation and of Black America's Century-Long Struggle for Equality under Law* (New York: Vintage Books, 1975), 80.

21. Holt, *Children of Fire,* 219.

22. Cf. Ridgely Torrence, *The Story of John Hope* (New York: Macmillan, 1948), 114–15.

23. Holt, *Children of Fire,* 204.

24. David W. Blight, *Frederick Douglass: Prophet of Freedom* (New York: Simon & Schuster, 2018), 474–75; W. E. B. Du Bois, *Black Reconstruction in America: 1860–1880* (1935; repr., New York: Free Press, 1992), esp. 231, 241; cf. C. Vann Woodward, *Origins of the New South, 1877–1913* (Baton Rouge: Louisiana State University Press, 1951).

25. Cf. Dray, *At the Hands of Persons Unknown,* 116–19.

26. Dray, 118; Bernard C. Nalty, *Strength for the Fight: A History of Black Americans in the Military* (New York: Free Press, 1986), 64.

27. Nalty, 64.

28. Nalty, 66–69.

29. Howard Zinn, *A People's History of the United States* (New York: HarperCollins, 1999), 309.

30. Cf. Zinn, 313; cf. Ivan Musicant, *Empire by Default: The Spanish-American War and the Dawn of the American Century* (New York: Henry Holt, 1998), 246.

31. W. E. B. Du Bois, "Strivings of the Negro People," *Atlantic Monthly*, August 1897. Du Bois revised the article as "Of Our Spiritual Strivings" in *The Souls of Black Folk* (1903); cf. Lewis, *W. E. B. Du Bois,* vol. 1, 198–201.

32. Lewis, *W. E. B. Du Bois,* vol. 1, 256.

33. Lewis, *W. E. B. Du Bois,* vol. 1, 220.

34. W. E. B. Du Bois, "Of the Passing of the First Born," in *The Souls of Black Folk* (1903; repr., New York: Modern Library, 2003), 215.

35. George A. Sewell and Cornelius V. Troup, *Morris Brown College: The First Hundred Years, 1881–1981* (Atlanta: Morris Brown College, 1981), 269–72; Clarence A. Bacote, *The Story of Atlanta University: A Century of Service, 1865–1965* (Atlanta: Atlanta University Press, 1969), 95–99.

36. Cf. David Zucchino, *Wilmington's Lie: The Murderous Coup of 1898 and the Rise of White Supremacy* (New York: Atlantic Monthly Press, 2020).

37. Mark Bauerlein, *Negrophobia: A Race Riot in Atlanta, 1906* (New York: Encounter Books, 2001), 62.

38. Woodward, *Origins of the New South*, 360–61; W. E. B. Du Bois, *The Philadelphia Negro* (Philadelphia: University of Pennsylvania Press, 1899).

39. Du Bois, "The Talented Tenth," in *The Negro Problem*, ed. B. T. Washington (New York: James Pott & Co., 1903).

40. W. E. B. Du Bois, "Of Mr. Booker T. Washington and Others," in *The Souls of Black Folk*.

41. Lewis, *W. E. B. Du Bois*, vol. 1, 322.

42. Lewis, *W. E. B. Du Bois*, vol. 1, 330.

43. Andree E. Johnson, *No Future in This Country: The Prophetic Pessimism of Bishop Henry McNeal Turner* (Jackson: University Press of Mississippi, 2020), 160–62; Stephen Ward Angell, *Bishop Henry McNeal Turner and African-American Religion in the South* (Knoxville: University of Tennessee Press, 1992), 244; David Fort Godshalk, *Veiled Visions: The 1906 Atlanta Race Riot and the Reshaping of American Race Relations* (Chapel Hill: University of North Carolina Press, 2005), 70.

44. Bauerlein, *Negrophobia*, 34; Godshalk, *Veiled Visions*, 70–73.

45. Cf. C. Vann Woodward, *Tom Watson: Agrarian Rebel* (1938; repr., New York: Oxford University Press, 1976), 378–79; Charles Crowe, "Racial Violence and Social Reform—Origins of the Atlanta Riot of 1906," *Journal of Negro History* 53 (July 1968): 234–56.

46. Godshalk, *Veiled Visions*, 90; Lewis, *W. E. B. Du Bois*, vol. 1, 335.

47. Godshalk, 93.

48. Godshalk, 132.

49. Bauerlein, *Negrophobia*, 184; cf. Godshalk, *Veiled Visions*; Janken, *Man Called White*; A. J. Baime, *White Lies: The Double Life of Walter F. White and America's Darkest Secret* (Boston: Mariner Books, 2022), 8–9; Gary M. Pomerantz, *Where Peachtree Meets Sweet Auburn: The Saga of Two Families and the Making of Atlanta* (New York: Scribner, 1996), 76; Terrell mansion: the author's memory of his mother's and uncle's testimony.

50. Godshalk, *Veiled Visions*, 197.

51. Godshalk, 138–39; Bauerlein, *Negrophobia*, 211–12.

52. Godshalk, *Veiled Visions*, 117–18.

53. Bauerlein, *Negrophobia*, 218.

54. Godshalk, *Veiled Visions*, 141.

55. Walter White, *A Man Called White: The Autobiography of Walter White* (Athens: University of Georgia), 10–11.

7. SEPARATE AND UNEQUAL: BELLS AND LEWISES, 1906–1930

1. Cf. Louis R. Harlan, *Booker T. Washington, 1901–1915* (New York: Oxford University Press, 1983), 39–40.

2. Joel Williamson, *A Rage for Order: Black-White Relations in the American South since Emancipation* (New York: Oxford University Press, 1986), esp. 150–51.

3. David Fort Godshalk, *Veiled Visions: The 1906 Atlanta Race Riot and the Reshaping of American Race Relations* (Chapel Hill: University of North Carolina Press, 2005), 124–25.

4. Godshalk, 126; cf. David Zucchino, *Wilmington's Lie: The Murderous Coup of 1898 and the Rise of White Supremacy* (New York: Atlantic Monthly Press, 2020).

5. Godshalk, *Veiled Visions,* 127–28.

6. David Levering Lewis, *W. E. B. Du Bois: Biography of a Race, 1868–1919* (New York: Henry Holt, 1993), 336–37.

7. Lewis, 129.

8. Cf. Harlan, *Booker T. Washington*, 39–40; Mark Bauerlein, *Negrophobia: A Race Riot in Atlanta, 1906* (New York: Encounter Books, 2001), 218–19.

9. Thomas Holt, *Children of Fire: A History of African Americans* (New York: Hill & Wang, 2010), 208; Douglas A. Blackmon, *Slavery by Another Name: The Re-enslavement of Black Americans from the Civil War to World War II* (New York: Anchor Books, 2008), 56; C. Vann Woodward, *Origins of the New South, 1877–1913* (Baton Rouge: Louisiana State University Press, 1951), 398.

10. David Levering Lewis, *When Harlem Was in Vogue* (New York: Knopf, 1981; repr., New York: Penguin, 1997), 170–71.

11. Bauerlein, *Negrophobia*, 205; Lewis, *W. E. B. Du Bois: Biography of a Race*, 223.

12. Godshalk, *Veiled Visions*, 138; cf. Harlan, *Booker T. Washington*, 302.

13. Godshalk, *Veiled Visions*, 141–42.

14. Godshalk, 160.

15. Lewis, *W. E. B. Du Bois: Biography of a Race*, 216–17.

16. Cf. Harlan, *Booker T. Washington,* chap. 1; cf. Lewis, *W. E. B. Du Bois: Biography of a Race*, 330–31; cf. Blackmon, *Slavery by Another Name*, 156–57.

17. Lewis, *W. E. B. Du Bois: Biography of a Race*, 331–32; Bernard C. Nalty, *Strength for the Fight: A History of Black Americans in the Military* (New York: Free Press, 1986), esp. 91–93.

18. Harlan, *Booker T. Washington*.

19. Lewis, *W. E. B. Du Bois: Biography of a Race*, 330–33; cf. Florette Henri, *Black Migration: Movement North, 1900–1920, the Road from Myth to Man* (New York: Anchor Books, 1976), 52, 242.

20. Godshalk, *Veiled Visions*, 190.

21. Archives of First Congregational Church, Auburn Avenue History Research Center, Atlanta.

22. Proctor, *Between Black and White*, 99, 101–2.

23. Godshalk, *Veiled Visions*, 213.

24. Proctor, *Between Black and White*, 100–101; cf. Treasurers Record Books, First Congregational Church Boxes, 1908–9, Auburn Avenue History Research Center, Atlanta.

25. Archives of First Congregational Church, box 1, pages 15–16, Robert W. Woodruff Library, Atlanta University Center, Atlanta.

26. Proctor, *Between Black and White*, 109.

27. Godshalk, *Veiled Visions*, 211.

28. Gary M. Pomerantz, *Where Peachtree Meets Sweet Auburn: The Saga of Two Families and the Making of Atlanta* (New York: Scribner, 1996), 77; Lewis, *W. E. B. Du Bois: Biography of a Race*, 364–65.

29. Clarence A. Bacote, *The Story of Atlanta University: A Century of Service, 1865–1965* (Atlanta: Atlanta University Press, 1969), 144.

30. Cf. George A. Sewell and Cornelius V. Troup, *Morris Brown College: The First Hundred Years, 1881–1981* (Atlanta: Morris Brown College, 1981), esp. 58; Susie B. Jenkins, "The History of the Sim and Hattie Lewis Family" (unpublished manuscript, October 1956); Clarence D. White, "Rev. Dr. John H. Lewis 1884–1958: Eminent African American Educator and Methodist Minister from Schley County, Georgia," files.usgwarchives.net/ga/schley/bios/lewis.txt.

31. Cf. August Meier, *Negro Thought in America, 1880–1915* (Ann Arbor: University of Michigan Press, 1963); David Levering Lewis, *King: A Biography* (Champaign: University of Illinois Press, 2011), esp. 86–87; Tony Martin, *Race First: The Ideological and Organizational Struggles of Marcus Garvey and the Universal Negro Improvement Association* (Dover, MA: The Majority Press, 1976).

32. John Henry Lewis to Edward Lewis Curtis, December 28, 1908; Edward Lewis Curtis to John Henry Lewis, January 12, 1909. (All correspondence between John Henry Lewis Sr. and Yale Divinity School provided by Michael Moran, Yale University.)

33. John Henry Lewis to Edward Lewis Curtis, February 23, 1909.

34. John Henry Lewis to Edward Lewis Curtis, July 27, 1910; Edward Lewis Curtis to John Henry Lewis, May 7, 1910.

35. John Henry Lewis, junior year, middle year, senior year, 1911–13: Yale Divinity School, Yale University (New Haven, CT: Tuttle, Morehouse & Taylor Press, 1913).

36. Charles H. Wesley, *The History of Alpha Phi Alpha: A Development in College Life* (Baltimore, MD: Alpha Phi Alpha Foundation, 1929; repr., 1950), xiii, 87.

37. Cf. August Meier and Elliott Rudwick, *Black History and the Historical Profession, 1915–1980* (Champaign: University of Illinois Press, 1986), 77–78.

38. *Encyclopedia of Alabama*, s.v. "George Williamson Crawford," n.d., encyclopediaofalabama.org/article/george-williamson-crawford/.

39. John Henry Lewis, Transcript of Academic Record, University of Chicago, August 20, 2019; cf. Robert E. Park and Booker T. Washington, *The Man Farthest Down: A Record of Observation and Study in Europe* (New York: Doubleday, 1912).

40. Lewis, *When Harlem Was in Vogue*, esp. 20–21.

41. Lewis, 21; Barbara W. Tuchman, *The Guns of August* (New York: Macmillan, 1962), chap. 6.

42. Pomerantz, *Where Peachtree Meets Sweet Auburn*, 77.

43. Sewell and Troup, *Morris Brown College*, 57–60.

44. Sewell and Troup, 57–62.

45. Lewis, *W. E. B. Du Bois: Biography of a Race*, 501–2.

46. Lewis, 518–22.

47. "John Henry Lewis," in *Who's Who in America* (1950), 1619; Clarence White, "Rev. Dr. John H. Lewis (1884–1953)," usgwarchives.org/ga/gafiles; Jenkins, "The History of the Sim and Hattie Lewis Family," 6.

48. Nell Irvin Painter, *Exodusters: Black Migration to Kansas after Reconstruction* (New York: W. W. Norton, 1992).

49. Cf. David M. Oshinsky, *"Worse Than Slavery": Parchman Farm and the Ordeal of Jim Crow Justice* (New York: Free Press, 1996), 94–96.

50. Meier and Rudwick, *Black History and the Historical Profession*; cf. Kenneth R. Janken, *Rayford Logan and the Dilemma of the African American Intellectual* (Amherst: University of Massachusetts Press, 1997); Lewis, *W. E. B. Du Bois: The Fight for Equality and the American Century, 1919–1963* (New York: Henry Holt, 2000), chap. 10.

51. Lewis, 353.

52. Cf. Jay Winston Driskell Jr., *Schooling Jim Crow: The Fight for Atlanta's Booker T. Washington High School and the Roots of Black Protest Politics* (Charlottesville: University of Virginia Press, 2014), 143–44; Godshalk, *Veiled Visions*, 247–48.

53. Jane Fraser, *Walter White, Civil Rights Leader* (New York: Chelsea House, 1991), 31–32; cf. A. J. Baime, *White Lies: The Double Life of Walter F. White and America's Darkest Secret* (Boston: Mariner Books, 2022), 17. For a much less contrarian version, see Driskell, *Schooling Jim Crow*, 167.

54. Lewis, *When Harlem Was in Vogue*, 144–45.

55. Driskell, *Schooling Jim Crow*, 159–60.

56. *The Encyclopaedia of the African Methodist Episcopal Church*, comp. Richard R. Wright, 2nd ed. (Philadelphia: A. M. E. Book Concern, 1947), s.v. "Lewis, Rev. John H.," 183.

57. John Bell, Lot 99, Section 1, South-View Cemetery, March, 1906; cf., Alice King, Atlanta, Georgia, Oakland Cemetery Records, 1773–1999.

58. Pauli Murray, *Proud Shoes: The Story of an American Family* (Boston: Beacon Press, 1956), xiii.

59. Mother's memory, related to the author.

60. Ginger Rutland, email to David Levering Lewis, September 22, 2019.

61. Alexa Benson Henderson, "Heman E. Perry and Black Enterprise in Atlanta, 1908–1925," *Business History Review* 61, no. 2 (Summer 1987): 216–42; Alexa Benson Henderson, *Atlanta Life Insurance Company: Guardian of Black Economic Dignity* (Tuscaloosa: University of Alabama Press, 1990), esp. 57–59.

62. Henderson, "Heman E. Perry and Black Enterprise," 223.

63. Henderson, *Atlanta Life Insurance Company*, 59 (photo on page 57).

64. Henderson, "Heman E. Perry and Black Enterprise," 245.

65. Cf. Arthur Bunyan Caldwell, *History of the American Negro and His Institutions*, Georgia Edition (Atlanta, GA: Caldwell, 1920), 253.

66. Charles Wesley, *Negro Labor in the United States: 1850 to 1925* (UK: Russell & Russell, 1927), 283; Henderson, *Atlanta Life Insurance Company*, 72–74.

67. Godshalk, *Veiled Visions*, 223–24; Henderson, *Atlanta Life Insurance Company*,

72–75; cf. Chad L. Williams, *The Wounded World: W. E. B. Du Bois and the First World War* (New York: Farrar, Straus and Giroux, 2023).

68. A. Urnestine Bell, senior class, Normal School, in *Atlanta University Bulletin* 2, no. 3 (1911).

69. Treasurer's Record Books, 1922, 1924, First Congregational Church Boxes, box 2, Auburn Avenue Research Center, Atlanta, Georgia.

70. Lewis, *W. E. B. Du Bois: Biography of a Race*, 214.

71. David Levering Lewis, "Introduction," in W. E. B. Du Bois, *The Souls of Black Folk* (New York: Modern Library, 2003), xvi.

72. Walter White, *A Man Called White: The Autobiography of Walter White* (1948; repr., Athens: University of Georgia Press, 1995), 12.

73. Cf. Godshalk, *Veiled Visions*, 227–29; Driskell, *Schooling Jim Crow*, 117–19.

74. Driskell, 162; Mother's memory, related to the author.

75. Driskell, *Schooling Jim Crow*, 159; cf. Godshalk, *Veiled Visions*, 237.

76. Driskell, *Schooling Jim Crow*, 151.

77. Pomerantz, *Where Peachtree Meets Sweet Auburn*, 84–85; Eugene Moore, "Atlanta's Great Fire 50 Years Ago," *Atlanta Constitution*.

78. Driskell, *Schooling Jim Crow*, 16.

79. Cf. 1918 *Atlanta City Directory*; Clarence White, email to David Levering Lewis, July 4, 2021.

80. Driskell, *Schooling Jim Crow*, 198–99.

81. Driskell, 198.

82. Godshalk, *Veiled Visions*, 248.

83. Driskell, *Schooling Jim Crow*, 202.

84. Driskell, 216–17.

85. White, *Man Called White;* Driskell, *Schooling Jim Crow*, 216.

86. Driskell, 218.

87. Driskell, 227.

88. Driskell, 225.

89. Godshalk, *Veiled Visions*, 250; Driskell, *Schooling Jim Crow*, 231.

90. Henderson, "Heman E. Perry and Black Enterprise," 228.

91. The Reference Staff, Harvard University Archives, October 15, 2019: summer school examination, 1923.

92. *Atlanta Independent,* October 22, 1925.

93. James Davis, *Eric Walrond: A Life in the Harlem Renaissance* (New York: Columbia University Press, 2015), esp. chap. 4.

94. Eric D. Walrond, "The Largest Negro Commercial Enterprise in the World," *Forbes,* February 2, 1924, 503–33.

95. Walrond, 504.

96. Henderson, "Heman Perry and Black Enterprise," 220.

97. Henderson, 231–32.

98. Cf. Henderson, *Atlanta Life Insurance Company*, 101–2.

99. Henderson, 102, 106.

100. Henderson, 103.

101. Robert J. Alexander, "Negro Business in Atlanta," *Southern Economic Journal* 17, no. 4 (April 1951): 455.

102. "Bell (Colored)," *Atlanta Constitution*, January 1, 1926; John H. Bell, Death Certificate, Bureau of Vital Statistics, December 29, 1925.

8. NEGOTIATING FAMILY AND WHITE SUPREMACY: THE LEWISES

1. W. E. B. Du Bois, "The Souls of White Folk," *The Independent* 69 (August 18, 1910): 339–42; Herbert Aptheker, ed., *W. E. B. Du Bois: Writings in Periodical Literature, 1910–1934*, vol. 2 (Kraus-Thomson, 1982), 25–29.

2. W. E. B. Du Bois, *Darkwater* (New York: Atria, 2004), 24; cf. Chad Williams, *The Wounded World: W. E. B. Du Bois and the First World War* (New York: Farrar, Straus and Giroux, 2023), 189–90; Cameron McWhirter, *Red Summer: The Summer of 1919 and the Awakening of Black America* (New York: Henry Holt, 2011), chap. 2; David Levering Lewis, *When Harlem Was in Vogue* (1979; repr., New York: Penguin, 1997), 18–21.

3. David Levering Lewis, *W. E. B. Du Bois: Biography of a Race, 1868–1919* (New York: Henry Holt, 1993), 578–79; McWhirter, *Red Summer*, 15.

4. Du Bois, *Darkwater*, 26, 36.

5. Chautauqua Circle Archives of Atlanta, Georgia, Robert W. Woodruff Library, Atlanta University Center, Atlanta; cf. David Levering Lewis, *W. E. B. Du Bois: The Fight for Equality and the American Century, 1919–1963* (New York: Henry Holt, 2000), 22.

6. Cf. Jacquline A. Rouse, *Lugenia Burns Hope, Black Southern Reformer* (Athens: University of Georgia Press, 1989), 79; Jay Winston Driskell Jr., *Schooling Jim Crow: The Fight for Atlanta's Booker T. Washington High School and the Roots of Black Protest Politics* (Charlottesville: University of Virginia Press, 2014), 233–34.

7. Lewis, *W. E. B. Du Bois: The Fight for Equality*, 21.

8. Cf. Paul Schor, *Counting Americans, How the Census Classified the Nation* (New York: Oxford University Press, 2017), esp. 157; Ridgely Torrence, *The Story of John Hope* (New York: Macmillan, 1948), 105; cf. August Meier and David L. Lewis, "History of the Negro Upper Class in Atlanta, Georgia, 1890–1950," *Journal of Negro Education* (Spring 1959): 128–39. Both Meier and Lewis heard stories of "passing" from their many interviews.

9. Cf. "Honoring Black History in Pasadena," January 31, 2024, https://www.visit pasadena.com/blog/honoring-black-history-in-pasadena/.

10. J. H. Lewis to C. R. Brown, July 6, 1920.

11. George A. Sewell and Cornelius V. Troup, *Morris Brown College, The First Hundred Years, 1881–1981* (Atlanta, GA: Morris Brown College, 1981), 60–61.

12. Cf. John Hope Franklin and Evelyn Brooks Higginbotham, *From Slavery to Freedom: A History of African Americans* (New York: McGraw Hill, 2009), 410; Sewell and Troup, *Morris Brown College*, 67.

13. College File, Morris Brown University, September 14, 1925: General Education Board Records. Morris Brown College, 1921–1930, box 37, Georgia reel 29.

14. Cf. Sewell and Troup, *Morris Brown College,* 50 ("Even before the public controversy . . . of Booker T. Washington and W. E. B. Du Bois developed, Morris Brown College recognized the need to provide alternative educational opportunities for Blacks").

15. James D. Anderson, *The Education of Blacks in the South, 1860–1935* (Chapel Hill: University of North Carolina Press, 1988), 247.

16. Cf. GEB: Gerald Jonas, *The Circuit Rider: Rockefeller Money and the Rise of Modern Science* (New York: W. W. Norton, 1989), 22–25; Raymond B. Fosdick, *Adventure in Giving: The Story of the General Education Board, a Foundation Established by John D. Rockefeller* (New York: Harper & Row, 1962), 8–14.

17. Anderson, *Education of Blacks in the South,* 252, 249 (college data).

18. Anderson, *Education of Blacks in the South,* esp. 256–59; Lewis, *W. E. B. Du Bois: Biography of a Race,* 548–51.

19. Lewis, *W. E. B. Du Bois: Biography of a Race,* 549–51.

20. Thomas Jesse Jones, ed., *Negro Education: A Study of the Private and Higher Schools for Colored People in the United States* (1917; repr., New York: Arno Press and *New York Times,* 1969); cf. John H. Stanfield, *Philanthropy and Jim Crow in American Social Science* (Westport, CT: Greenwood, 1985); Robert A. Margo, *Race and Schooling in the South, 1880–1950: An Economic History* (Chicago: University of Chicago Press, 1990), 18–24.

21. Lewis, *W. E. B. Du Bois: Biography of a Race,* esp. 548–49.

22. Anderson, *Education of Blacks in the South,* 253.

23. W. E. B. Du Bois, "Negro Education," *The Crisis* 15 (February 1918): 173–78; cf. Lewis, *W. E. B. Du Bois: Biography of a Race,* esp. 547–51.

24. Lewis, *W. E. B. Du Bois: The Fight for Equality,* 417.

25. Atticus Haygood, "Building a Christian College," appendix B, in Sewell and Troup, *Morris Brown College,* 270.

26. "Memorandum re: Morris Brown University, Atlanta, Georgia," March 28, 1921, General Education Board Records.

27. Jackson Davis to Eban Sage, "Morris Brown College," September 14, 1925, page 2, General Education Board Records.

28. Eban C. Sage to John H. Lewis, March 29, 1921, General Education Board Records; Eban C. Sage to John H. Lewis, June 7, 1921, General Education Board Records; "Morris Brown College," page 2, General Education Board Records.

29. Eban Sage to Jackson Davis, June 29, 1921, General Education Board Records; teachers: cf. Anderson, *Education of Blacks in the South,* 245.

30. John H. Lewis to Dr. E. C. Sage, October 3, 1921, General Education Board Records; E. C. Sage to Jackson Davis, October 10, 1921, General Education Board Records.

31. John H. Lewis to Trevor Arnett, September 22, 1923, General Education Board Records; cf. "Morris Brown College," page 1, General Education Board Records.

32. W. E. B. Du Bois, "The Negro Church," in *W. E. B. Du Bois: A Reader,* ed. David Levering Lewis (New York: Henry Holt, 1995), 259.

33. Sewell and Troup, *Morris Brown College,* 64.

34. Sewell and Troup, 65–66.

35. Sewell and Troup, esp. 179–81, 184.

36. Cleveland G. Allen, "Morris Brown Plans Million Dollar Drive," *Pittsburgh Courier,* May 1, 1926.

37. Cf. Anderson, *Education of Blacks in the South,* 268.

38. Raymond Wolters, *The New Negro on Campus: Black College Rebellions of the 1920s* (Princeton, NJ: Princeton University Press, 1975); cf. Anderson, *Education of Blacks in the South,* 268–69; Lewis, *W. E. B. Du Bois: The Fight for Equality,* 134–35.

39. Anderson, *Education of Blacks in the South,* 266.

40. Sewell and Troup, *Morris Brown College,* 72.

41. Will W. Alexander to John H. Lewis, January 4, 1927, General Education Board Records; cf. Harvard Sitkoff, *A New Deal for Blacks: The Emergence of Civil Rights as a National Issue in the Depression Decade* (New York: Oxford University Press, 1978), esp. 73–74.

42. AME Church historian Professor Dennis Dickerson explains that California's presiding bishop (Henry Parks) held Lewis in high regard. Dennis Dickerson, email to David Levering Lewis, July 25, 2023.

43. Sewell and Troup, *Morris Brown College.*

44. Cf. Steve Ammidown, "Eva Rutland (1917–2012)," April 5, 2022, romancehistory .com; "Eva Rutland Obituary," *Sacramento Bee,* March 17–19, 2012; Eva Rutland, *When We Were Colored: A Mother's Story,* produced by Sacramento Repertory, 2016; Lena Horne: cf. Herman "Skip" Mason Jr., *Black Atlanta in the Roaring Twenties* (Mount Pleasant, SC: Arcadia, 1997), 58; author's multiple recollections of Eva Neal Rutland.

45. Tashell Thompson, email to David Levering Lewis, November 7, 2019; David Levering Lewis, email to Tashell Thompson, December 1, 2019; cf. *Aurora* 1, no. 1 (July 1928).

46. Details drawn from *Aurora,* esp. 11–14.

47. Chautauqua Circle of Atlanta, box 1, folders 12 and 18, box 2, folders 1 and 46, Robert W. Woodruff Library, Atlanta University Center, Atlanta.

48. Cf. G. William Domhoff, "Power Structure Research and the Hope for Democracy," April 2005, whorulesamerica.net; Floyd Hunter, *Community Power Structure: A Study of Decision Makers* (Chapel Hill: University of North Carolina Press, 1959); Tomiko Brown-Nagin, *Courage to Dissent: Atlanta and the Long History of the Civil Rights Movement* (New York: Oxford University Press, 2011).

49. Clarence A. Bacote, *The Story of Atlanta University: A Century of Service, 1865–1965* (Atlanta: Atlanta University Press, 1969), esp. 258–61.

50. Anderson, *Education of Blacks in the South,* 205–6.

51. Cf. Driskell, *Schooling Jim Crow,* 233; Anderson, *Education of Blacks in the South,* 210–11.

52. Anderson, 206.

53. Anderson, 206, 210.

54. R. C. Hall to Dr. Frank T. Bachman, June 22, 1928, P. L. Dunbar School, General Education Board Archive.

55. John H. Lewis to the editor of *The Crisis*, September 20, 1930, W. E. B. Du Bois Papers, University of Massachusetts Amherst.

56. Anderson, *Education of Blacks in the South*, 222.

57. Cf. John Kirk, "Paul Laurence Dunbar High School," *Encyclopedia of Arkansas*.

58. Anderson, *Education of Blacks in the South*, 208; Jackson Davis to F. P. Bauman, General Education Board, October 29, 1928, P. L. Dunbar School, General Education Board Archive.

59. John H. Lewis to W. E. B. Du Bois, March 31, 1930; W. E. B. Du Bois to J. H. Lewis, April 3, 1930; W. E. B. Du Bois to John H. Lewis, April 10, 1930; Du Bois Papers, University of Massachusetts Amherst. Author has not confirmed that John Hope spoke at Dunbar High School, as advertised in the "Along the Color Line" section of *The Crisis*. John A. Kirk, *Redefining the Color Line: Black Activism in Little Rock, Arkansas, 1940–1970* (Gainesville: University Press of Florida, 2002), 13.

60. Death certificate, Eva Walker Lewis, July 12, 1930, Arkansas State Board of Health; transcript, John Lewis, University of Chicago, August 20, 2019; marriage license, Alice Urnestine Bell and John H. Lewis, Fulton County, Georgia, August 29, 1931.

61. Cf. Grif Stockley, *Blood in Their Eyes: The Elaine Massacre of 1919* (Fayetteville: University of Arkansas Press, 2008); Grif Stockley, *Daisy Bates: Civil Rights Crusader from Arkansas* (Jackson: University Press of Mississippi, 2005), 33.

62. Cf. Kirk, *Redefining the Color Line*, 22.

63. Stockley, *Daisy Bates*, 33.

64. Cf. John A. Kirk, "Black Activism in Arkansas, 1940–1970" (PhD diss., Department of History, University of Newcastle upon Tyne, April 1997), 23–24.

65. Cf. Andrew Buni, *Robert L. Vann of the Pittsburgh Courier: Politics and Black Journalism* (Pittsburgh: University of Pittsburgh Press, 1974).

66. John H. Lewis to Dr. G. W. S. Ish, October 31, 1955, box 2, folder 9, David Levering Lewis Papers, University of Massachusetts Amherst.

67. Cf. Kirk, "Black Activism in Arkansas," 18.

68. Author's memory, based on frequent family recollection of these two events.

69. Daisy Bates, *The Long Shadow of Little Rock: A Memoir* (1962; repr., Fayetteville: University of Arkansas Press, 1986), 35.

70. Stockley, *Daisy Bates*, 38–39.

71. Kirk, "Black Activism in Arkansas," 32–34.

72. Kirk, *Redefining the Color Line*, 39.

73. Scipio Jones with Thurgood Marshall, May 1942, Teachers' Salaries Cases, Part II: The Campaign for Educational Equality, 1913–1950, Series B: Legal Department and Central Office Records, 1940–1950, reel 5, NAACP Papers, Library of Congress.

74. Mark V. Tushnet, *The NAACP Strategy against Segregated Education, 1925–1950* (Chapel Hill: University of North Carolina Press, 1987), 90.

75. John Kirk, "Separate and Unequal: Sue Cowan Morris Won the Battle to Equalize Pay of Black and White Teachers. It Cost Her Her Job," *Arkansas Times*, June 11, 2015, 1–8.
76. Cf. Michael G. Long, ed., *Marshalling Justice: The Early Civil Rights Letters of Thurgood Marshall* (New York: HarperCollins, 2011), 114–15.
77. Kirk, *Redefining the Color Line*, 41–42.
78. Kirk, "Separate and Unequal," 5.
79. Thurgood Marshall to Walter White, September 30, 1943, Teachers' Salaries Cases, Part II: The Campaign for Educational Equality, 1913–1950, Series B: Legal Department and Central Office Records, 1940–1950, reel 5, NAACP Papers, Library of Congress.
80. Thurgood Marshall to John H. Lewis, July 16, 1943, Teachers' Salaries Cases, Part II: The Campaign for Educational Equality, 1913–1950, Series B: Legal Department and Central Office Records, 1940–1950, reel 5, NAACP Papers, Library of Congress.
81. John H. Lewis to Thurgood Marshall, July 1943, Teachers' Salaries Cases, Part II: The Campaign for Educational Equality, 1913–1950, Series B: Legal Department and Central Office Records, 1940–1950, reel 5, NAACP Papers, Library of Congress.
82. Tushnet, *NAACP Strategy against Segregated Education*, 92.

9. STRIVING FOR EXCELLENCE: THE WILBERFORCE YEARS

1. Rayford Whittingham Logan, ed., *What the Negro Wants* (1944; repr., Chapel Hill: University of North Carolina Press, 1969), xix, xx, xxii.
2. Cf. John Edgerton, *Speak Now against the Day: The Generation before the Civil Rights Movement in the South* (New York: Knopf, 1994), 272; cf. William Shands Meacham, "The Negro's Future in America," *New York Times Book Review*, November 5, 1944; E. Franklin Frazier, "Wanted Equality," *Nation*, December 23, 1944; J. Saunders Redding, "Fourteen Negro Voices," *New Republic*, November 20, 1944.
3. "Documents of the History of Payne's Leadership," Archives of Payne Theological Seminary, Wilberforce University, Wilberforce, OH.
4. Daniel A. Payne, *Recollections of Seventy Years* (1888; repr., New York: Arno Press and *New York Times*, 1968), 221–24, 254; James T. Campbell, *Songs of Zion: The African Methodist Episcopal Church in the United States and South Africa* (New York: Oxford University Press, 1995), 40–41.
5. Edgerton, *Speak Now against the Day*, 273; Howard Odum, *Race and Rumors of Race: The American South in the Early Forties* (Chapel Hill: University of North Carolina Press, 1943), 31.
6. Logan, *What the Negro Wants*, 71–77, esp. 71.
7. Campbell, *Songs of Zion*, 262–63; David Levering Lewis, *W. E. B. Du Bois: Biography of a Race, 1868–1919* (New York: Henry Holt, 1993), chap. 7.
8. Today historical markers on access roads narrate the history of Wilberforce

University's evolution from Tawawa Springs. See Payne, *Recollections of Seventy Years*, 150, 170, 225; *The Encyclopaedia of the African Methodist Episcopal Church*, comp. Richard R. Wright, 2nd ed. (Philadelphia: Book Concern of the AME Church, 1947), s.v. "Lewis, Rev. John H.," 183.

9. "Documents of the History of Payne's Leadership."

10. Payne, *Recollections of Seventy Years*, 221–24, 254; Campbell, *Songs of Zion*, 40–41.

11. Cf. "Annual Report[s] of John H. Lewis, Dean, to the Board of Directors of Payne Theological Seminary," June 11, 1947, page 2, Archives of Payne Theological Seminary, Wilberforce University, Wilberforce, OH; cf. Dennis C. Dickerson, *The African Methodist Episcopal Church: A History* (New York: Cambridge University Press, 2020), 359–60; Annetta L. Gomez-Jefferson, *The Sage of Tawawa: Reverdy Cassius Ransom, 1861–1959* (Kent, OH: Kent State University Press, 2002), chap. 10.

12. Dickerson, *African Methodist Episcopal Church*, 361.

13. "Documents of the History of Payne's Leadership," 13–14.

14. "Documents of the History of Payne's Leadership," 13–14.

15. *Payne Theological Seminary Alumni Journal* 1, no. 1 (February 1947): 2, Archives of Payne Theological Seminary, Wilberforce University, Wilberforce, OH; Pittsburgh Annual Conference of the 3rd Episcopal District, St. James AME Church, September 18–22, 1946, 34.

16. Dickerson, *African Methodist Episcopal Church,* 357–59.

17. Payne Theological Seminary Archives, Wilberforce, Ohio.

18. Author's memory of Dean Charles R. Brown's overnight Wilberforce stay and inaugural Daniel Payne Lecture, April 1946.

19. John H. Lewis, "The Achievements of 50 Years at Payne Theological Seminary: A Justification of Our $300,000 Building" (pamphlet), Archives of Payne Theological Seminary, Wilberforce University, Wilberforce, OH.

20. Lewis, "Achievements of 50 Years."

21. "Ground Breaking Ceremony at Payne Theological Seminary, Wilberforce, Ohio" (unsigned typescript), Archives of Payne Theological Seminary, Wilberforce University, Wilberforce, OH.

22. "Annual Report of John H. Lewis, Dean, to the Board of Directors of Payne Theological Seminary," June 11, 1947, Archives Payne Theological Seminary, Wilberforce University, Wilberforce, OH.

23. Dickerson, *African Methodist Episcopal Church*, esp. 352–59; cf. Gomez-Jefferson, *Sage of Tawawa*, chap. 10.

24. Howard D. Gregg, *History of the A.M.E. Church* (Nashville, TN: AMEC, 1980), 289.

25. See David Nicolson, *The Garretts of Columbia* (Columbia: University of South Carolina Press, 2024).

26. Charles Leander Hill, "Report of Wilberforce University to the Thirty-third Quadrennial Session of the General Conference of the AME Church," *Wilberforce University Bulletin* 32 (May 1948): 3; "The Truth about Wilberforce: A Statement Issued Jointly by the Board of Trustees, College of Education and

Industrial Arts and the National Alumni Association of Wilberforce University," June 26, 1947; Gomez-Jefferson, *Sage of Tawawa*, chap. 10.

27. Dickerson, *African Methodist Episcopal Church,* 360–61; "Truth about Wilberforce," 5.

28. Cf. State Relations at Wilberforce University, Committee Study of State Relations at Wilberforce, ca. 1947.

29. "'Will Stand on Record,' Dr. Wesley Tells Bishop," *Xenia Newspaper,* 1947; Gomez-
Jefferson, *Sage of Tawawa*, 229.

30. *Cleveland Call and Post,* n.d.

31. Gomez-Jefferson, *Sage of Tawawa,* 244–46; David Levering Lewis, recorded interview with Dr. Jayme Coleman Williams, November 19, 2019, Atlanta; "Jayme
Coleman Williams," n.d., *The History Makers,* thehistorymakers.org/biography
/jamye-coleman-williams-39.

32. "Truth about Wilberforce," *Chicago World,* 5; Hill, "Report of Wilberforce University."

33. Hill, 3–4.

34. "Thomas Jefferson and Sally Hemings, a Brief Account," Monticello and the University of Virginia in Charlottesville, monticello.org/thomas-jefferson/jefferson
-slavery/thomas-jefferson-and-sally-hemings-a-brief-account/.

35. *Joan of Arc,* directed by Walter Wanger, RKO, 1948.

36. Ira Katznelson, *When Affirmative Action Was White: An Untold History of Inequal-
ity in Twentieth-Century America* (New York: W. W. Norton, 2002); cf. John H.
Lewis, DD. '13, "Consolidation Sheet—Alumni Information," Office of University
Development, Yale University.

37. Dickerson, *African Methodist Episcopal Church,* 361–62; Hill, "Report of Wilberforce University," 14.

38. "Annual Report of John H. Lewis, Dean, to the Board of Directors of Payne
Theological Seminary," June 9, 1948, Archives of Payne Theological Seminary,
Wilberforce University, Wilberforce, OH; David McCullough, *Truman* (New
York: Simon & Schuster, 1992); Alonzo Hamby, *Man of the People: A Life of Harry
S. Truman* (New York: Oxford University Press, 1995), 433–35.

39. "Annual Report of John H. Lewis," June 9, 1948.

40. "Annual Report of John H. Lewis, Dean, to the Board of Directors of Payne Theological Seminary," June 8, 1949, Archives of Payne Theological Seminary, Wilberforce University, Wilberforce, OH; John Alexander Gregg, 1877–1953, Kansas
Historical Society, April 2009.

41. David Levering Lewis, *W. E. B. Du Bois: Biography of a Race, 1868–1919* (New
York: Henry Holt, 1993), xi, chap. 7.

42. David Levering Lewis, *W. E. B. Du Bois: The Fight for Equality and the American
Century, 1919–1963* (New York: Henry Holt, 2000), 337–38.

43. Cf., Peter S. Canellos, *The Great Dissenter: The Story of John Marshall Harlan,
America's Judicial Hero* (New York: Simon & Schuster, 2021), 340–47.

44. Author's recollections; cf. Richard Gergel, *Unexampled Courage: The Blinding of*

Sgt. Isaac Woodard and the Awakening of President Harry S. Truman and Judge J. Waties Waring (New York: Farrar, Straus & Giroux, 2019), chap. 9; Robert L. Zangrando and Ronald L. Lewis, *Walter F. White: The NAACP's Ambassador for Racial Justice* (Morgantown: West Virginia University Press, 2019), 207, 230.

45. "Annual Report of John H. Lewis, Dean, to the Board of Directors of Payne Theological Seminary," June 7, 1950, Archives of Payne Theological Seminary, Wilberforce University, Wilberforce, OH.

46. "Annual Report of John H. Lewis, Dean, to the Board of Directors of Payne Theological Seminary," June 13, 1951, Archives of Payne Theological Seminary, Wilberforce University, Wilberforce, OH.

47. Author's recollection; cf. *Encyclopedia of Cleveland History*, s.v. "Dunbar Life," case.edu/ech/articles/d/dunbar-life.

48. Cf. "Payne Seminary's 62-Year Dream Near Reality," *Columbus Citizen*, March 11, 1956, 4B.

49. I am aware that the Supreme Court declared segregated interstate dining cars unnecessary in May 1950. However, I do not doubt the accuracy of this memory.

10. WITH ALL DELIBERATE SPEED: THE LEWISES

1. *The African Methodist Episcopal Church: A History* (Cambridge, UK: Cambridge University Press, 2020); cf. Jack Salzman, David Lionel Smith, and Cornel West, eds., *Encyclopedia of African-American Culture and History*, vol. 5 (New York: Macmillan, 1996).

2. George A. Sewell and Cornelius V. Troup, *Morris Brown College: The First Hundred Years, 1881–1981* (Atlanta: Morris Brown College, 1981), 80–82, 83–84.

3. Sewell and Troup, 84.

4. Chautauqua Circle of Atlanta, Georgia, box 4, folder 4, Robert W. Woodruff Library, Atlanta University Center, Atlanta.

5. Cf. Andrew Wiese, *Places of Their Own: African American Suburbanization in the Twentieth Century* (Chicago: University of Chicago Press, 2004), 167–69; John Levering Bell and Mrs. J. H. Lewis, indenture no. 901365, and Dr. H. E Welton, Fulton County, Georgia, May 1942; Alexa Benson Henderson, "Heman E. Perry and Black Enterprise in Atlanta, 1908–1925," *Business History Review* 61, no. 2 (Summer 1987): 216–42.

6. Wiese, *Places of Their Own*, 174; author's recollection of Hunter Road development.

7. Wiese, *Places of Their Own*, 165, 168–69, 174; Tomiko Brown-Nagin, *Courage to Dissent: Atlanta and the Long History of the Civil Rights Movement* (New York: Oxford University Press, 2012), 70; also Gary M. Pomerantz, *Where Peachtree Meets Sweet Auburn: The Saga of Two Families and the Making of Atlanta* (New York: Scribner, 1996), 180–81.

8. Clarence A. Bacote, *The Story of Atlanta University: A Century of Service, 1865–1965* (Atlanta: Atlanta University Press, 1969), 285; Emmet John Hughes, "The Negro's New Economic Life," *Forbes*, September 1956, 248–50; Pomerantz, *Where Peachtree Meets Sweet Auburn*, 281–82.

9. Sewell and Troup, *Morris Brown College*, 91; "In Memoriam: Albert Nathaniel Whiting, 1917–2020," *Journal of Blacks in Higher Education,* June 15, 2020; "Robert E. Williams, 61, Dies," *Washington Post,* October 10, 1981.

10. Sewell and Troup, *Morris Brown College*, 91.

11. Sewell and Troup, 90–91.

12. Cf. Marybeth Gasman, "Nurturing African American Scholars and Leaders: An Explanation of Fisk University's Basic College Program (1951–1956)," ERIC report no. ED431056, 1999.

13. Archibald Carey and phone call from author's memory; E. Frederic Morrow, *Black Man in the White House* (New York: Coward-McCann, 1963); Dennis C. Dickerson, *African American Preachers and Politics: The Careys of Chicago* (Jackson: University Press of Mississippi, 2011).

14. Walter A. Jackson, *Gunnar Myrdal and America's Conscience* (Chapel Hill: University of North Carolina Press, 1990), 116; David Levering Lewis, *W. E. B. Du Bois: The Fight for Equality and the American Century, 1919–1963* (New York: Henry Holt, 2000), 448.

15. Cf. Maribel Morey, *White Philanthropy: Carnegie Corporation's An American Dilemma and the Making of a White World Order* (Chapel Hill: University of North Carolina Press, 2021), esp. 1; Lewis, *W. E. B. Du Bois: The Fight for Equality*, 448.

16. Gunnar Myrdal, *An American Dilemma: The Negro Problem and Modern Democracy* (1944; repr., New York: McGraw-Hill, 1964), 669; cf. Jackson, *Gunnar Myrdal and America's Conscience*, 115–16. Four decades later, John Lewis's son's search of assorted Du Bois correspondence at Fisk University would unearth the manipulated fate of *The Encyclopedia of the Negro*: "Ed, somebody tells me that Keppel has rented the forty-sixth floor of the Chrysler Building and turned it over to a Swede. . . . What's it all about?" asked University of Chicago president Robert Maynard Hutchins of Rosenwald Fund president Edwin Embree. "Bob," clarified Embree, "not Negro education, but the whole realm of the negro [*sic*] in American civilization [to] take the place of the proposed Negro Encyclopedia the Phelps Stokes Fund has been greatly interested." Robert Maynard Hutchins to Edwin Embree, September 27, 1939, Julius Rosenwald Fund Archives, Fisk University, Nashville; Edwin Embree to Robert Maynard Hutchins, September 29, 1939, Julius Rosenwald Fund Archives, Fisk University, Nashville.

17. Brown-Nagin, *Courage to Dissent*, esp. 87, 102; cf. James T. Patterson, *Brown v. Board of Education: A Civil Rights Milestone and Its Troubled Legacy* (New York: Oxford University Press, 2001), 8.

18. Richard Kluger, *Simple Justice: The History of Brown v. Board of Education and Black America's Struggle for Equality* (New York: Vintage, 1977), 366; cf. Richard Gergel, *Unexampled Courage: The Blinding of Sgt. Isaac Woodard and the Awakening of President Harry S. Truman and Judge J. Waties Waring* (New York: Farrar, Straus and Giroux, 2019), 214–15. Incrementalism: cf. Robert L. Zangrando and Ronald L. Lewis, *Walter F. White: The NAACP's Ambassador for Racial Justice* (Morgantown: West Virginia University Press, 2019), 372–73.

19. Patterson, *Brown v. Board*, xiv; Lewis, *W. E. B. Du Bois: The Fight for Equality*, 557.

20. Patterson, *Brown v. Board*, 70–72.

21. Patterson, 80.

22. Brown-Nagin, *Courage to Dissent*, 22; David Levering Lewis, a semester at University of Michigan Law School, 1956.

23. Patterson, *Brown v. Board*, xxvi; Kluger, *Simple Justice*, 710; White/Cannon photo: Kenneth Janken, email to David Levering Lewis, November 15, 2023; David Levering Lewis, email to Kenneth Janken, November 14, 2023.

24. A. J. Baime, *White Lies: The Double Life of Walter F. White and America's Darkest Secret* (Boston: Mariner Books, 2022), 315.

25. Kluger, *Simple Justice*, 711; Gergel, *Unexampled Courage*, 163.

26. Charles J. Ogletree Jr., *All Deliberate Speed: Reflections on the First Half-Century of Brown v. Board of Education* (New York: W. W. Norton, 2004), 126; Stephen E. Ambrose, *Eisenhower: Soldier and President* (New York: Simon & Schuster, 1990), 368.

27. Ambrose, *Eisenhower*, 367–68; Patterson, *Brown v. Board*, 82; Kluger, *Simple Justice*, 753.

28. Patterson, *Brown v. Board*, 73.

29. John A. Kirk, *Redefining the Color Line: Black Activism in Little Rock, Arkansas, 1940–1970* (Gainesville: University Press of Florida, 2002), 43.

30. National Park Service, "Little Rock Central High School: Crisis Timeline," n.d., nps.gov/chsc/learn/historyculture/timeline.htm.

31. "Final Dunbar High School Graduation—May 27, 1955," Little Rock Culture Vulture, May 27, 2019; David Lewis to John A. Kirk, March 13, 2024; John A. Kirk to David Lewis, March 14, 2024; Dr. Jess Porter to David Lewis, March 19, 2024.

32. David Levering Lewis, *King: A Biography* (1970; repr., Champaign: University of Illinois Press, 2013), 112; cf. Civil Rights Act: Ambrose, *Eisenhower*, 444–45.

33. Lewis, *King*, 108, 112.

34. Lewis, 94; cf. Ambrose, *Eisenhower*, 445; cf. Robert Caro, *The Years of Lyndon Johnson: Master of the Senate* (New York: Knopf, 2002), 992.

35. Alexandra Wood, email to David Lewis, July 22, 2021; David Lewis, email to Alexandra Wood, July 22, 2021; "Report Bell Beaten by Police upon Arrest at Country Club," *Atlanta Daily World*, February 19, 1948, 1.

36. Pomerantz, *Where Peachtree Meets Sweet Auburn*, 163–64.

37. Maurice C. Daniels, *Saving the Soul of Georgia: Donald L. Hollowell and the Struggle for Civil Rights* (Athens: University of Georgia Press, 2013) 50–51.

38. "Lewis Leaves Urban League," *The Canton Depository*, November 3, 1960; John H. Lewis & the Roslyn School Board," *Scope*, May 9, 1966.

39. Emmet John Hughes, "The Negro's New Economic Life," *Forbes*, September 1956, 248.

40. Herbert Aptheker, ed., *The Correspondence of W. E. B. Du Bois*, vol. 3, *1944–1963* (Amherst: University of Massachusetts Press, 1978), 428.

INDEX

Page numbers in *italics* refer to photographs.